WITHDRAWN

MODERN KOREA

THE INSTITUTE OF PACIFIC RELATIONS

The Institute of Pacific Relations is an unofficial and non-political organization, founded in 1925 to facilitate the scientific study of the peoples of the Pacific area. It is composed of autonomous National Councils in the principal countries having important interests in the Pacific area, together with an International Secretariat. It is privately financed by contributions from National Councils, corporations and foundations. The Institute, as such, does not advocate policies or doctrines and is precluded from expressing opinions on national or international affairs. It is governed by a Pacific Council composed of members appointed by each of the National Councils.

In addition to the independent activities of its National Councils, the Institute organizes private international conferences every two or three years. Such conferences have been held at Honolulu (1925 and 1927), Kyoto (1929), Shanghai (1931), Banff, Canada (1933), Yosemite Park, California (1936), Virginia Beach, Virginia (1939), Mont Tremblant, Quebec (1942). It conducts an extensive program of research on the political, economic and social problems of the Pacific area and the Far East. It also publishes the proceedings of its conferences under the title Problems of the Pacific, a quarterly journal Pacific Affairs, and a large number of scholarly books and pamphlets embodying the results of its studies.

NATIONAL COUNCILS

Australian Institute of International Affairs
Canadian Institute of International Affairs
China Institute of Pacific Relations
Netherlands-Netherlands Indies Council, Institute of Pacific Relations
New Zealand Institute of International Affairs
Philippine Institute of International Affairs
Royal Institute of International Affairs
U.S.S.R. Council, Institute of Pacific Relations
American Council, Institute of Pacific Relations

International Secretariat and Publications Office
1 East 54th Street, New York

MODERN KOREA

By
ANDREW J. GRAJDANZEV
Research Associate
Institute of Pacific Relations

INTERNATIONAL SECRETARIAT
INSTITUTE OF PACIFIC RELATIONS
Publications Office, 1 East 54th Street, New York
Distributed by
THE JOHN DAY COMPANY
New York
1944

This Book is Manufactured under Wartime Conditions in Conformity with All Government Regulations Controlling the Use of Paper and Other Materials.

COPYRIGHT, 1944, BY INTERNATIONAL SECRETARIAT, INSTITUTE
OF PACIFIC RELATIONS
PRINTED IN THE UNITED STATES OF AMERICA BY THE HADDON CRAFTSMEN, INC.

AUTHOR'S PREFACE

This book was begun when there was still complete silence about Korea on the international scene. It has been completed at a time when Korea has come into the news. The heads of the American, British and Chinese Governments at their meeting in Cairo in November 1943 expressed their determination that "in due course" Korea would become free and independent. The day that happens this book, written about contemporary Korea, will become a book about her past; I will be the first to rejoice at this change.

In the meantime, however, the Japanese militarists are still supreme in Korea and some acquaintance with their deeds and methods there may be helpful to those who are taking an active part in the Pacific war and may have responsibilities in Japan's present colonies after her defeat.

I do not expect that all readers will agree with my conclusions at every point. In particular those who are easily impressed with the outward manifestations of "material progress" in Korea may feel that I have been too unsympathetic with Japan's achievements. Others who under the influence of wartime emotions, see the Japanese as sub-human monsters, may not appreciate the record of such development as has occurred in Korea under Japanese rule. I have tried to present the conclusions as they seem to me to emerge from the record of Japanese reports and statistics and the impressions of foreign observers in Korea. But in any case I have presented the facts; others who would draw different conclusions will have to take these facts into account.

I must express my sincere gratitude to J. M. Bernstein, Professor R. Haig, Mr. W. L. Holland, Mr. Bruno Lasker, Dr. G. McCune, Dr. S. McCune, Professor N. Peffer, Professor Russell Smith, Miss Frances Friedman and Miss Clara Spidell for their advice and help in many respects. Though the study has been made as part of the international research program of the Institute of Pacific Relations, I am solely responsible for the statement of facts, opinions and interpretations as given in the book.

A. J. GRAJDANZEV

New York,
December 15, 1943

CONTENTS

	Page
AUTHOR'S PREFACE...................................	v
I. INTRODUCTION.................................	3
II. KOREA'S GEOGRAPHICAL SETTING...............	8
Area and Elevation..........................	8
Inland Waters..............................	9
Climate....................................	14
III. HISTORY......................................	23
The Protectorate...........................	39
Political Movements after 1919..............	64
IV. POPULATION...................................	72
Distribution	74
Japanese in Korea..........................	75
Urbanization...............................	80
Emigration.................................	81
V. AGRICULTURE IN KOREA.........................	84
Introduction...............................	84
The Structure of Korean Agriculture.........	86
Agricultural Policy.........................	92
Increase of Area under Cultivation...........	94
Kaden	95
Irrigation..................................	95
Annual Frequency of Utilization.............	99
Improvements in Seed Material..............	100
Fertilizers.................................	100
Agricultural Machinery and Implements......	102
Livestock	103
The Social Stratification of the Korean Village.	105
Japanese Seizure of Korean Agricultural Land..	105
Ownership and Tenancy....................	107

		Page
VI.	FORESTRY AND FISHING	123
	Forestry	123
	Fishing	127
VII.	POWER AND MINERAL RESOURCES	131
	Power Resources of Korea and Their Exploitation	131
	Water Power and Generation of Electricity	133
	Mining	139
	Other Minerals	144
VIII.	INDUSTRIAL DEVELOPMENT	148
	Size, Character, and Distribution of Industry	148
	Modern Industry	152
	Metal Industry	156
	Ceramics	158
	Chemical Industry	159
	Lumber Industry	166
	Printing	166
	Food and Beverages	166
	Alcoholic Beverages	168
	Gas and Electricity	170
	The Problem of Nationality in Industry	171
	Labor Conditions	177
	Nationality of Workers	178
	Women and Children in Industry	182
	Hours of Work	184
IX.	TRANSPORT AND COMMUNICATIONS	185
	Description of Railways	188
	Private Railways	190
	Roads	191
	Ports and Communications	193
	Air Lines	197
	Post, Telegraph, Telephone, Radio	198
X.	MONEY AND BANKING	201
	Money and Prices	202
	Banks in Korea	204
	Interest Rates	207

CONTENTS

		Page
XI.	Public Finance	210
XII.	The External Trade of Korea	226
XIII.	The Government of Korea	238
	The Government General	238
	Departments and Bureaus	239
	Civil Service	243
	The Central Council	243
	The Army in Control	245
	Provincial Administration	246
	Provincial Councils	246
	City (*fu*), County (*gun*) and Island (*shima*) Organization	248
	Towns and Townships (*Yu* and *Men*)	248
XIV.	Courts, Prisons, Police	250
	Courts	250
	Crime	253
	Police System	254
XV.	Health, Education and Religion	259
	Health	259
	Education	261
	Libraries	270
	Theaters, Cinemas, Playgrounds	271
	Newspapers and Magazines	272
	Religion	273
XVI.	Problems of Korean Independence	276
	Material and Human Prerequisites	276
	Proofs of Organizing Experience	278
	Korean Nationalists	279
	The Nub of the Case	280
	Form of Government	281
	The Danger of Class Government	282
	Form of Social Organization	284
	Nationalization of Japanese Enterprises in Korea	286
	A Cooperative Commonwealth	286

APPENDICES

	Page
I. Agricultural Statistics of Korea	291
II. Reliability of Korean Agricultural Statistics	296
III. Some Industrial Statistics	300
IV. External Trade of Korea	305
V. List of Equivalents of Geographical Names in Korea in Japanese and Korean Languages	310
Bibliography	317

MAPS

Korea	2
Physiographic Diagram of Tyosen	11
Geomorphic Provinces	12
The Seasonal Distribution of Precipitation in Korea	17
Korea's Climatic Regions	20
The Limit Lines of Important Crops	91

MODERN KOREA

HARBIN
HSINKING
KIRIN
MUTANKIANG
FENGTIEN
CHINCHOW
CHINHSIEN
ANTUNG
TUNGHUA
CHIENTAO
YENKI
DAIREN
RYOJUN
Korea Bay
Chinnampo
Heijo
Pegi Shan
Kanko
Higashichosen Bay
Gensan
Seishin
Rashin
Kaishu
KEIJO
Jinsen
Kunsan
Taikyu
Masan
Fusan
PUSAN
Urusan
Keishu
Utsuryo I.
Saishu I.
Kyomon I.
Chosen Str.
Tsushima Str.
Tsushima Is
SHIMONOSEKI
Oki I.
J A P A N
MATSUE
KANAZAWA
NAGASAKI
Sasebo
Goto Is
MATSUYAMA
KOBE
OSAKA
KYOTO
KAGOSHIMA
MIYAZAKI
Nobeoka
C.Sada
C.Muroto
Yingkow
Panshan
Shanhaikwan
Weihaiwei
C.Shantung
Liaoyuan
Ssupingkai
Kaiyuan
Tiehling
Fushun
Liaoyang
Haicheng
Chosen
YELLOW SEA

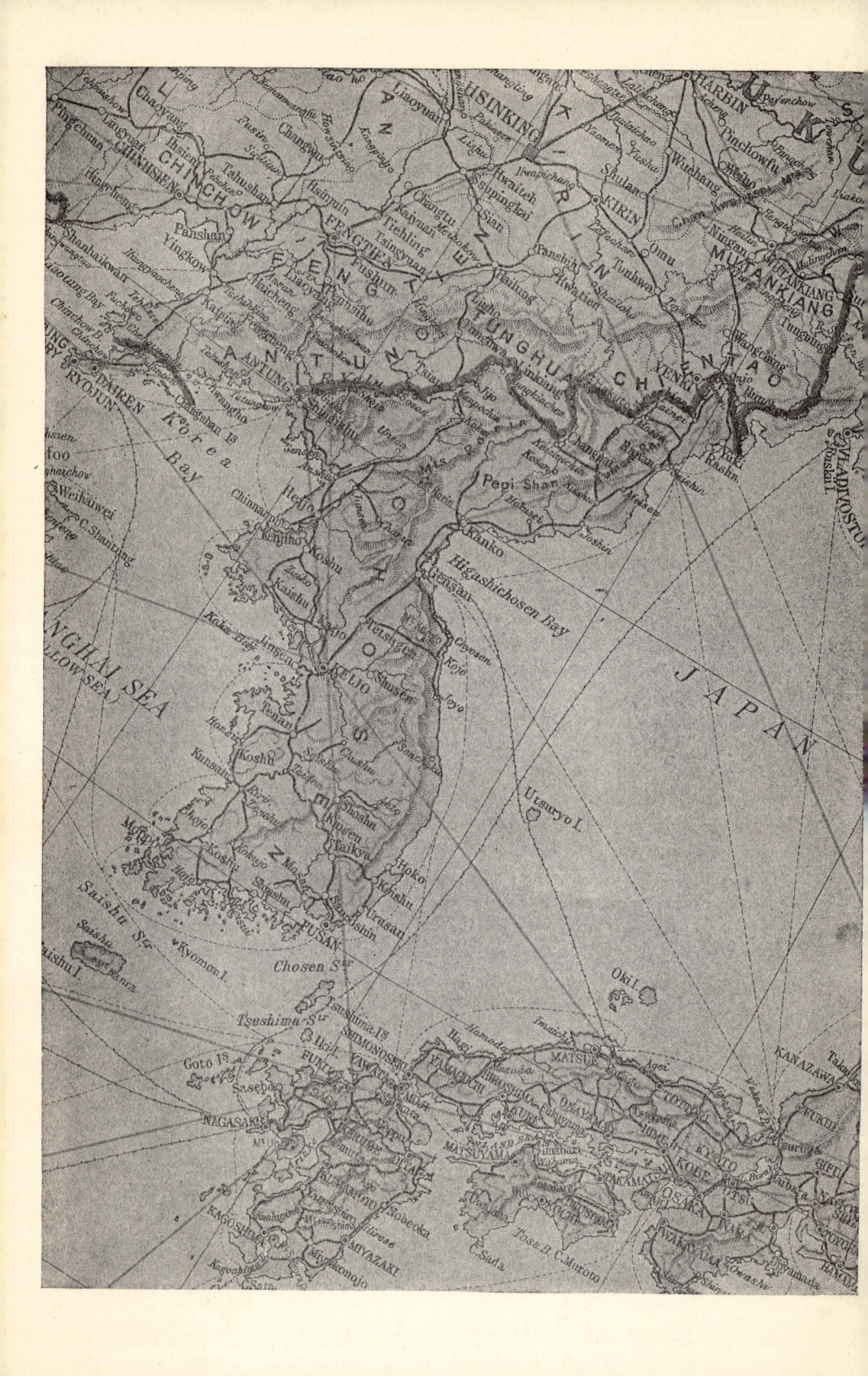

CHAPTER I

INTRODUCTION

Anyone interested in Korea knows that relatively few books, other than official Japanese accounts, have been written about that country since it became a part of the Japanese Empire in 1910. There is probably no other country in the world with so large a population and so strategic a position that has received so little attention in Western literature. In 1919-21, during and immediately after the movement in Korea for the restoration of independence, a few books were published on the subject, chiefly in the English language. But this interest soon died, and almost all the books that have appeared since 1921 may be included under one of two categories: they are either published by the Japanese government or "inspired" by it; or they represent "glimpses" of Korea caught by travelers who had neither the time nor the inclination to study Korean problems seriously. The publications of the Japanese government in the English language have a special purpose. The facts which they present are for the most part correct, but they are carefully selected and their interpretation is often biased.

It is not difficult to explain the lack of objective studies of Korea. Under the conditions existing just before the present war, Japanese scholars were not able to present to the outside world a truthful picture of the Korean situation; any scholar in Japan who tried to preserve even a semblance of independent thinking was persecuted by the Government or by chauvinist organizations. Foreign scholars, except those who were missionaries in Korea, had no access to the country; and the missionaries generally kept silent so as not to complicate the already difficult position of their churches.

But there are several reasons why Korea should be better known. First of all, it is a nation with a population of twenty-four million. Moreover, it is a country with a long and brilliant history—a country which at one time was in the forefront of human civilization. Secondly, for thirty-seven (counting from the date of formal annexation, thirty-two) years Korea has been a Japanese colony, and is therefore of interest as an example of Japanese colonial administration. Speaking of Formosa, W. H. Chamberlain notes: "However justly it may be criticized on these and similar counts, Japanese imperialism in Formosa has not been of a decadent parasitic type. It has been efficient and hardworking. It has brought incidental benefits in the shape of railways, roads, schools, hospitals, and assured safety of life and property."[1] In Korea, too, Japanese imperialism has built many railways and roads, quite a number of schools, and some hospitals; and, in certain ways, it has "assured safety of life and property" in Korea, as it has in Formosa. The very exercise of domination over a colony demands railways, roads, some schools, and some hospitals. The Japanese authorities have constantly stressed this side of their activities in Korea in their foreign propaganda. The annual reports of the Government-General of Korea abound in pictures of roads, post offices, hospitals, and improved types of sheep. But the purpose and the effects of these achievements should be carefully examined before they are recognized as unqualified "benefits."

It may be argued that it is difficult to find a criterion for an objective appraisal of Japan's colonial regime in Korea. However, a suitable criterion is supplied by the Japanese themselves. In the rescript of the last Korean Emperor, by which he ceded sovereignty to the Japanese Emperor, he wrote (under the dictation of his Japanese advisers): "We have ceded all rights of sovereignty over Korea to His Majesty the Emperor of Japan in whom we have placed implicit confidence . . . in order to consolidate the peace of the Extreme East and ensure the welfare of Our people." The Japanese Emperor, in his rescript on the annexation of Korea, declared: "All Koreans, being under our direct sway, will enjoy growing prosperity and welfare, and with assured repose and security will come a marked expansion in industry and trade. We confidently believe that the new order of things now inaugurated will serve as a fresh guarantee of enduring peace in the Orient."[2]

Did the Korean people enjoy a growing measure of prosperity and welfare between 1910 and 1942? Did the annexation of

[1] W. H. Chamberlain, *Japan Over Asia*, New York, 1937, p. 172. Unfortunately, in this book on Japan's imperial policy, Chamberlain devoted only two lines to Korea.

[2] Quoted from the *Annual Report on the Administration of Chosen*, 1933-34, pp. 198-199.

INTRODUCTION

Korea contribute to enduring peace in the Orient? These questions can be answered with reasonable accuracy. As a yardstick for measuring the prosperity and welfare of the Korean people under Japanese rule, comparable data for the Japanese people in Japan will be used in this book. It was not to be expected that the Japanese would raise the level of prosperity and welfare of the Korean people above that of the Japanese. But in view of the pledges given by successive Japanese administrators, there was reason to expect that Korean welfare would approach the level enjoyed by the Japanese people. The Korean people are called the "junior brother of the Japanese people."; Japan and Korea are declared to form one body (*naisen ittai*). Thus we have some basis for comparison and a yardstick for measuring the prosperity and welfare of the Korean people so solemnly promised by the Emperor of Japan.

It should also be noted that the climate of Korea is not very different from Japan's and that, for the last thirty-two years, Japan and Korea have been for all practical purposes part of the same economic units, with free movement of capital between them, the same monetary unit, the same tariff wall, and the same official language. Only 120 miles separate Fusan (southeastern port of Korea) from Shimonoseki in Japan. Writing in 1907 Professor F. H. King noted:

"Coming from China into Korea, and from there into Japan, it appeared very clearly that in agricultural methods and appliances the Koreans and Japanese are more closely similar than the Chinese and Koreans, and the more we came to see of the Japanese method the more strongly the impression became fixed that the Japanese had derived their methods either from the Koreans or the Koreans had taken theirs more largely from Japan than from China."[3]

Such similarities are to be found in many other respects and these increase the value of comparisons between conditions in the two countries.

The war in the Pacific provides a third reason for the study of Korea at this time, inasmuch as Japan's economic capacity to conduct war is to a considerable degree dependent upon the Korean economy. Korea is now supplying Japan with rice, fish, cotton, iron, coal, gold, fertilizers, and many other products of great importance to the Japanese war effort. No serious study of the Japanese war economy is possible without an apprecia-

[3] F. H. King, *Farmers of Forty Centuries*, p. 374.

tion of the role and importance of the Korean economy for Japan. The countries of southeastern Asia that have fallen into Japanese hands may be potentially richer than Korea, but Korean resources have already been pressed into service. Large investments have been made, lines of communication have been established, and a considerable labor force has been trained. The entire economy of Korea has long been adjusted to the needs of Japan's war machine, while in southeastern Asia such adjustments are still a matter of the future. Moreover, the route to southeastern Asia is long: from Singapore to Kobe is about 2,800 miles, as compared with only 120 miles from Shimonoseki to Fusan; and as long as China is not conquered, the southern route is exposed to enemy attacks, while the route to Korea passes through the closely guarded Chosen and Tsushina Straits. All this makes Korea especially important to the Japanese war effort.

A fourth reason relates to the problems of peace. When the United Nations will have achieved victory, the problem of Korea will inevitably occupy a prominent place in the peace settlement of the Western Pacific. A free Korea will be the best guarantee against new attempts on the part of Japan's rulers to build a new empire. A Formosa restored to China and a free Korea (now promised in the Cairo declaration of December 1, 1943) will be barriers to new outbursts of imperialistic expansion on the part of Japan. But, it may be asked, has Korea all the prerequisites for an independent existence in the modern world? True, she has had a long and brilliant history and was a civilized country at a time when Imperial Rome started on its road to conquest. But in the final decades before annexation, her king—and later emperor—was one of the worst examples of an Oriental despot, and for the last thirty-two years the country has been a Japanese colony. How soon will she again be able to stand on her own feet? Are there enough Koreans of education and experience to guide the country? Has Korea sufficient economic resources to be really independent? In short, is there any real basis for confidence with respect to her future as an independent country? The form of government itself and the type of economic organization may be decided for Korea at the peace conference; and those who will be responsible for the decisions should be in a position to know the most important facts about Korea as it has developed during the long period of Japanese administration.

The present investigation, then, is an attempt to throw light on some of these problems. Unfortunately, reliable information about Korea is scanty. The Japanese Government-General has made every effort to hide parts of the truth from the world. Many reports are not made public even in Japanese. Other reports recently published in Japanese were not permitted to leave the country.[4] Moreover, after Pearl Harbor all American and British connections with Japan and her dependencies were severed, and current information is meager. However, the absence of recent works on Korea and the urgency of the problems which confront us in connection with the war justify the attempt to supply such significant information on Korea as may be gleaned from those official sources which are available.

[4] The author received the invariable answer from Japanese publishing houses to requests for such publications that these were "not available"; efforts to obtain such publications through the good offices of Japanese educational and cultural organizations likewise failed.

CHAPTER II

KOREA'S GEOGRAPHICAL SETTING

Area and Elevation

Geographically, Korea consists of the Korean peninsula projecting from the mainland of Asia, and of 3,479 islands—most of them mere rocks. It is separated from Manchuria by the Yalu River, the Paitoushan, or White Head Mountains (Hakutosan in Japanese), and by the Tumen River. Near its mouth this river separates Korea from the Maritime Province of the Soviet Union. On the east the peninsula is washed by the Sea of Japan and on the west by the Yellow Sea. The Straits of Chosen (Korea) and Tsushima separate the peninsula from Honshu, the main island of Japan, and from Kyushu.

The geographic coordinates of Korea are as follows: its easternmost point is 130° 57′ longitude (i.e., almost the same as Yakutsk in the north and Port Darwin in Australia); its westernmost point, 124° 11′; its northernmost point 43° 1′ northern latitude (about the same as Portsmouth, New Hampshire); and its southernmost point 33° 7′ northern latitude (about the same as Charleston, South Carolina). Placed over the western Mediterranean, Korea would occupy an area from northern Spain to central Morocco.

The area of Korea is 220,741 sq. km. or 85,228 sq. miles,[1] i.e., slightly larger than that of Minnesota, Utah, or Great Britain (with Scotland, but without Northern Ireland). The longest distance in the peninsula from north to south is 463 miles; and the broadest distance from west to east is 170 miles.[2] The coast line of the peninsula is about 5,400 miles and that of the islands around it about 6,000 miles.[3] The east coast has relatively few good harbors, while the western and southern coasts abound in

---

[1] This figure is given in *Annual Reports on the Administration of Chosen*; *The Financial and Economic Annual of Japan* gives 220,769 sq. km., and *Chosen Nenkan* 220,788 sq. km.

[2] H. K. Lee, *Land Utilization and Rural Economy in Korea*, New York and Shanghai, 1936, p. 7.

[3] This does not mean that the islands are big; only one of them, Saishu (or Quelpart) is more than 700 square miles.

them. But on the west coast the difference between high and low tide reaches as much as thirty-three feet at Jinsen. On the east coast near Gensan the difference is only three feet.

The general character of the country is mountainous.

> "There is no spot in the country in which a mountain does not form a part of the landscape. Only a scant fourth of the land has an altitude of less than 100 metres (330 feet). In the north only fourteen per cent of the area is as low and level as that. More than half of the northern part, but only one-fifth of the rest of Korea is 500 metres (1641 feet) or more above sea level."[4]

The principal mountain range runs from the Paitoushan on the Manchurian frontier southward toward the east coast, with lateral branches and spurs extending in a southwesterly direction. The slopes to the east are steep and those to the west gentle. This feature of the mountains has permitted the construction of tunnels through them and the diversion of waters from west to east so as to exploit the great difference in the fall for the generation of electricity. The elevation of the mountains (from sea level) may be seen from the following table:[5]

Number of Peaks	Elevation
1	Above 9,000 feet (Paitoushan)
6	8,001-9,000 feet
29	7,001-8,000 feet
26	6,001-7,000 feet
4	5,001-6,000 feet
5	4,001-5,000 feet

The mountain range slopes down toward the south, thus making the southeastern part of the country fairly level and the northern part mountainous or hilly. Because of this, the southeastern region is Korea's granary and most of its population is concentrated in that area.[6]

Inland Waters

The direction of the mountains and their lateral spurs, as well as the relative narrowness of the peninsula, makes most of the streams short and swift. This, combined with the concentration of rainfall in the summer months, causes many disastrous floods. The length of the most important rivers (those flowing more

---
[4] E. De Schweinitz Brunner, *Rural Korea*, New York, 1928, p. 109.
[5] *Chosen Nenkan*, 1941, p. 46.
[6] For detailed data, see below, p. 72 et seq.

than one hundred miles) and their basins may be seen from the following table:[7]

River	Length (in miles)	Basin (in square miles)	Notes
Yalu	491	24,185	Frontier river, only about one-half of its basin in Korea
Tumen Kan	324	15,185	Frontier river, also between Manchuria and Russia, only about one-third in Korea
Kan (Han)[8]	292	12,871	Flows near Keijo (Seoul)
Rakuto (Naktong)	326	9,251	Near Fusan, southeastern Korea
Daido (Taidong)	247	7,485	Heijo (Pyengyang) and Tsinnanpo are on this river
Kin	149	3,817	Kunsan is at its mouth
Seisen	123	3,655	In the northwest; Shinanshu is on this river
Senshin	132	1,891	In the south, on the boundary line between Zenro and Keisho
Reisei	108	1,563	
Hudson River, U.S.A.	306		
Seine River, France	475		

This table shows that Korean rivers are short. Most of them are shallow or have sand-banks or rapids. The Yalu is navigable for about 420 miles by motor boats and by native junks. Timber is floated in rafts down the Yalu from the upper reaches of the river. On the Daido, steamships of up to two thousand tons can sail upstream for 39 miles, and junks for 152 miles from its mouth. Sailing and motor boats can navigate the Tumen for 53 miles, the Kan for 186 miles, the Rakuto for 214 miles, and the Kin for 81 miles. There are no large lakes in the peninsula; the largest one, Yokyo, has a surface of only 2,044 acres.

Geomorphologically, A. H. Robinson and S. McCune divide Korea into eleven provinces.[9] The first one, the *Northern Interior,* almost coincides with their climatic region I (see below), minus only the Tumen River valley. It is a relatively high mountainous region with a northward and westward slope.

[7] *Chosen Nenkan,* 1941, p. 47.

[8] Names in brackets here and elsewhere in this book represent Korean pronunciation of the characters.

[9] See their article which is followed here, *Notes on a Physiographic Diagram of Tyosen (Korea),* in the *Geographical Review,* Vol. XXXI, No. 4, Oct. 1941, pp. 653-658.

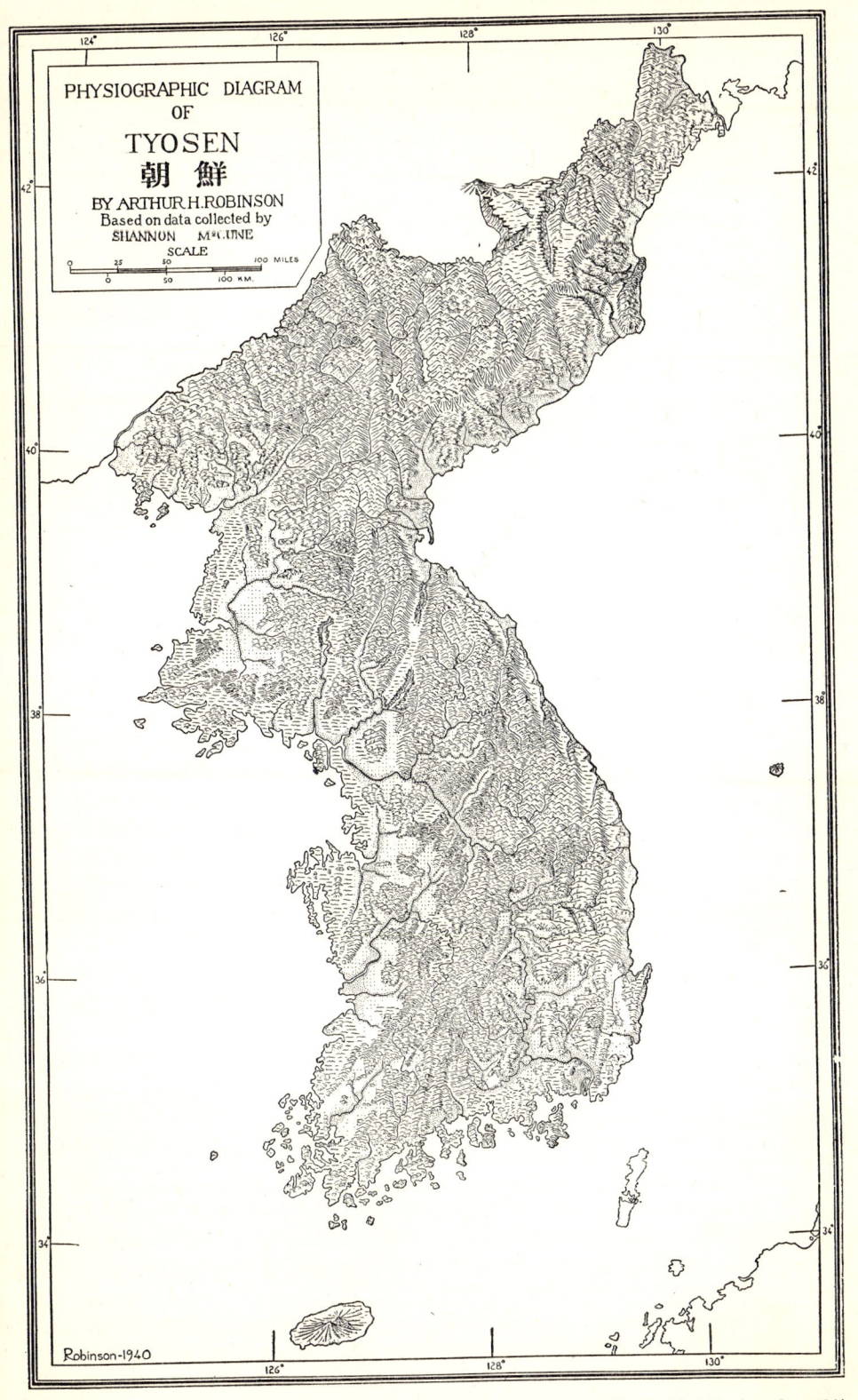

Reprinted by courtesy of *The Geographical Review*, Oct. 1941

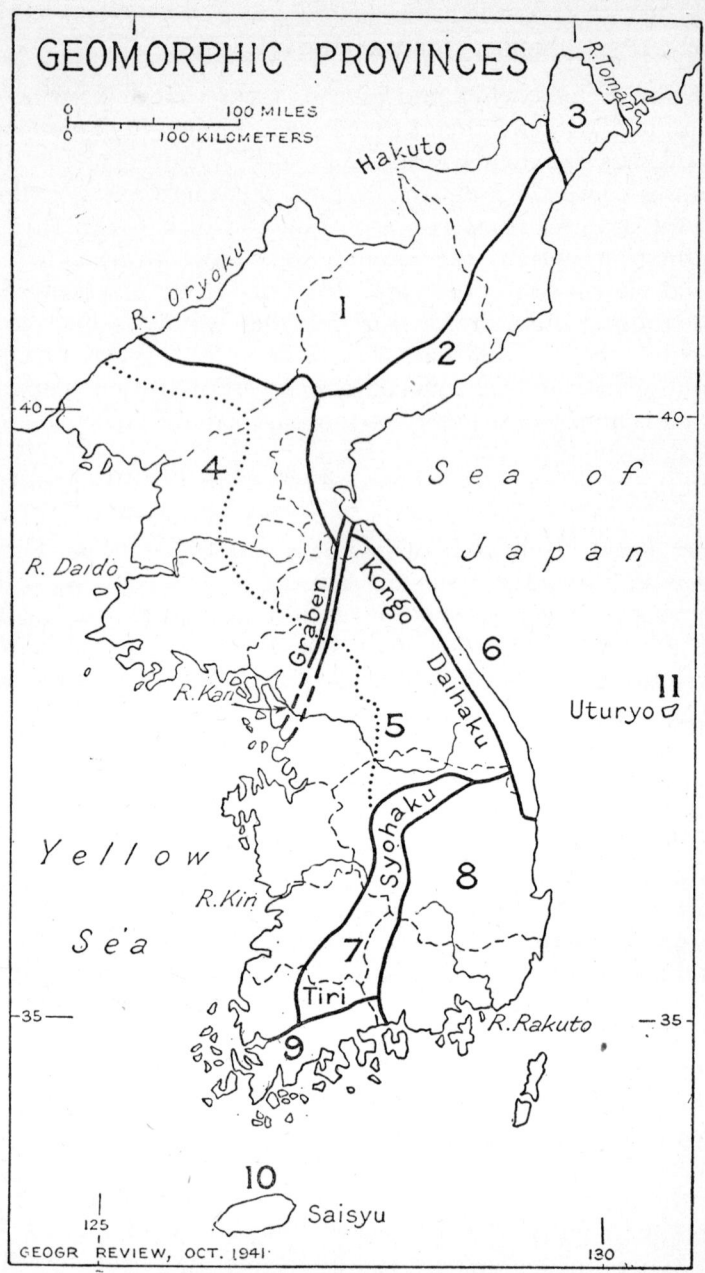

Geomorphic provinces of Tyosen (Korea). The dashed lines denote the political provincial boundaries; the solid lines, the geomorphic provincial boundaries; the dotted lines, the subdivisions. Key: 1, Northern Interior; 2, Northeastern Coastal Hills and Valleys; 3, Toman River Basin; 4, Northwestern Tyosen; 5, Central Tyosen; 6, Southeastern Littoral; 7, Southern Mountains and Valleys; 8, Rakuto River Basin; 9, Southern Littoral; 10, Saisyu Island; 11, Uturyo Island.

Archean, metamorphic, and igneous rocks were leveled before the middle Miocene, then lifted by volcanism. The Tumen and Yalu Rivers and their tributaries are deeply entrenched in their winding courses. Level land is rare, but there are rich forest and water-power resources; a portion of which is exploited by building tunnels in the mountainous range overlooking the coastal (Japan Sea) valley and diverting rivers east instead of west, causing them to flow through these tunnels. The second province, the *Northeastern Coastal Hills and Valleys,* consists of old granite and metamorphic rock with many small streams falling from the escarpment to the sea, forming their own flood and delta plains.

In the valleys one finds irrigated rice fields and fishing villages are located all along the coast. The third province, the *Tumen River Valley,* is an area of low hills and valleys. The Tumen valley and several convenient harbors on the coast make this province an important link between Manchuria and Japan. The fourth province, *Northwestern Korea,* was a geosyncline with later crustal disturbances including intrusion, overturned folding and thrust faulting. The western part of this province has extensive plains along the shallow Yellow Sea. The eastern part is a complex land of high relief. The western part of the province is good for agriculture, though chiefly for dry crops. There are also considerable mineral resources, especially coal.

Northern Korea is divided from southern Korea by a graben, the lava field of which is sterile. The fifth province, *Central Korea,* is an upraised crustal block. During the Miocene the block was faulted in the east and tilted to the west. Along the lower courses of the Kan River and its tributaries there are extensive plains and rounded hills. Plains are fertile and produce much rice under irrigation. Many hillsides are eroded although some erosion has been checked by afforestation. Farther east are the Kongo Zan, or Diamond Mountains, remarkable for the beauty of their forms resulting from unequal weathering of rocks. The sixth province, the *Southeastern Littoral,* is a series of short valleys and rocky headlands. The mountains to the west isolate this region and even the valleys have no convenient connections. The seventh province, the *Southern Mountains and Valleys,* divides the Rakuto basin from the Kan and Kin Rivers. The major mountain range, the Shohaku Zan, breaks into parallel ridges in the south, the highest of which is Chiri Zan. A pass in the Shohaku Zan is used by the main railway of Korea. The eighth province, the *Rakuto River Basin,* occupying southeastern Korea, is a hilly country. The structural basins, some with diluvial deposits, and the flood plains of the rivers are broad. The ninth province, the *Southern Littoral,* is formed by thousands of islands, peninsulas, hills, and very small plains. The low extensions of the Shohaku Zan reach the coast here. The last two provinces are formed by volcanic islands: *Saishu* (Quelpart) and *Uturyo* (Dagelet). The principal volcano of Saishu was last active in 1007 A. D.

Climate

Korea is predominantly an agricultural country, and climate is one of the most important factors in agriculture. That of Korea is a monsoon climate but, being further from the ocean, Korea is a transitional area, half-way between the continental climate of China and the marine climate of Japan.

COMPARISON OF AVERAGE ANNUAL TEMPERATURES

	Latitude	Average annual temperature (Fahrenheit)
Moppo, south Korea	34°47'	55.6
Osaka, Japan	34°39'	59.0
Atlanta, U.S.A.	33°45'	61.2
Keijo, central Korea	37°34'	51.6
Niigata, Japan	37°56'	54.9
Richmond, U.S.A.	37°32'	57.9
Heijo, northwest Korea	39°2'	48.6
Mizusawa, Japan	39°8'	49.6
Baltimore, U.S.A.	39°18'	55.4

Source: For Korea and Japan—Hishimoto, *Chosenbei no kenkyu,* Tokyo, 1938; for U. S. A.—*Statistical Abstract of the United States,* Washington, 1941.

The average annual temperatures in Korea are seen to be lower than in points of corresponding latitude in Japan and in the United States, the difference being smaller in the case of Japan. However, the difference is not striking: 1 to 4 degrees lower than in Japan and 6 degrees lower than in the United States.

This table shows that while maximum temperatures in Korea are slightly higher than in Japan, minimum temperatures are considerably lower, and the further to the north, the more

KOREA'S GEOGRAPHICAL SETTING

MAXIMUM AND MINIMUM TEMPERATURES

	Latitude	Average Maximum	Average Minimum
Zenshu, southern Korea	35°35'	87.3	21.0
Tokyo, Japan	35°39'	85.8	29.5
Keijo, central Korea	37°34'	86.4	14.9
Niigata, Japan	37°56'	86.0	29.5
Heijo, northwest Korea		86.4	8.6
Yamagata, Japan		85.8	21.7

Source: *Hishimoto, Chosenbei no kenkyu.*

striking the difference becomes. In short, the climate of Korea is nearer to the continental type than that of Japan. But this table also shows that the difference is felt chiefly in winter and especially in northern Korea, temperatures of southern Korea being in many respects like those of central Japan. We may go further and compare the average temperatures for the four summer months (June to September), which are the most important for agriculture:

COMPARISONS OF SUMMER TEMPERATURES IN KOREA, JAPAN AND THE UNITED STATES
(averages given)

	June	July	August	Sept.	Average of 4 months
Moppo, southern Korea	69.1	76.3	79.0	71.1	73.9
Osaka, Japan	71.3	79.0	81.2	74.2	76.4
Atlanta, U.S.A.	76.0	78.1	77.0	72.4	75.9
Zenshu, southern Korea	70.5	78.1	78.6	68.7	74.0
Tokyo, Japan	68.9	75.8	78.1	68.0	72.7
Asheville, U.S.A.	68.7	71.7	70.5	65.0	69.0
Keijo, central Korea	70.2	76.5	77.9	68.0	73.2
Niigata, Japan	67.1	74.8	78.3	70.5	72.7
Richmond, U.S.A.	74.1	78.5	76.5	70.5	74.9
Heijo, northwest Korea	68.9	75.2	75.8	65.9	71.5
Mizusawa, Japan	63.7	71.6	74.1	65.5	68.7
Baltimore, U.S.A.	72.7	77.2	75.5	68.5	73.5

Hishimoto, *op. cit.*; *Statistical Abstract of the United States.*

This table shows that summer temperatures for the same latitudes are higher in Korea than in Japan, but somewhat lower than in the United States. This means that in spite of cold winters Korea receives enough warmth in summer for its latitude.

AVERAGE HOURS OF SUNSHINE AND PERCENTAGE OF POSSIBLE SUNSHINE

	June	*July*	*Aug.*	*Sept.*	Total for 4 months	Per cent of Total Possible Sunshine
Moppo	205h	193h	241h	208h	848h	53
Tokyo	148h	190h	209h	143h	689h	43
Atlanta	68%	61%	61%	64%		60
Keijo	236h	182h	210h	213h	841h	56
Yamagata	178h	176h	196h	131h	681h	37
Richmond	66%	66%	62%	64%		60
Heijo	263h	212h	218h	273h	929h	62
Mizusawa	154h	138h	153h	115h	561h	37
Baltimore	64%	65%	63%	64%		59

Source: Hishimoto, *op. cit.*; *Statistical Abstract of the United States*.

In the matter of sunshine, too, Korea is favored. The annual percentage there is considerably higher than it is in Japan and, while slightly below American figures, it is above them in the north. During the four summer months Korean fields receive much more sunshine than Japan's—from 850 to 930 hours.

The distribution of precipitation is more varied than that of temperature, so a larger number of localities are given in the following table.

AMOUNT OF PRECIPITATION IN KOREA, JAPAN, AND THE UNITED STATES

Korea	Annual amount of precipitation	*April*	*May*	*June*	*July*	*Aug.*	*Sept.*	*Oct.*	Total for 7 months	% of annual total
Moppo	42.5	3.7	3.6	5.6	8.6	6.5	4.6	2.0	34.6	81
Zenshu (WSW)	49.7	3.3	3.2	5.3	13.2	10.2	4.5	2.1	41.8	84
Taikyu (ESE)	39.0	3.0	2.9	5.2	9.1	6.7	5.4	1.5	33.8	86
Keijo (Center)	49.7	3.0	3.5	5.0	15.0	10.5	4.6	1.6	43.2	87
Heijo (WNW)	37.0	1.8	2.8	2.9	9.9	8.7	4.7	1.8	32.6	88
Shingishu (NW)	42.0	1.7	4.7	5.3	10.0	12.6	3.5	1.6	39.4	93
Genzan (NE)	53.5	2.8	3.5	4.8	11.2	12.4	7.1	3.1	44.9	84
Japan										
Nagasaki	79.0	7.6	6.1	14.2	10.4	6.6	11.4	4.3	60.6	77
Hiroshima	59.6	6.5	5.8	9.5	8.7	4.1	7.5	4.3	46.4	78
Osaka	53.1	5.4	5.0	7.7	6.1	4.0	7.1	5.2	40.5	76
Nagoya	65.2	6.2	6.3	8.3	7.5	6.5	9.7	6.0	50.5	77
Tokyo	61.2	5.2	6.1	6.3	5.2	6.0	9.4	7.9	46.1	75
Yamagata	47.9	2.9	3.2	3.2	5.5	5.4	5.7	3.8	30.4	63
Hakodate	46.8	2.8	3.3	3.5	5.3	5.4	6.8	4.8	31.9	68
United States										
Atlanta	48.3	3.6	3.5	3.7	4.7	4.5	3.0	2.6	25.6	53
Asheville	40.3	3.0	3.4	3.9	4.3	4.2	3.0	2.8	24.6	61
Richmond	42.0	3.5	3.8	3.9	4.7	4.4	3.6	2.9	26.8	64
Baltimore	42.6	3.3	3.5	3.9	4.6	4.4	3.4	2.9	26.0	61

Source: As in preceding tables.

KOREA'S GEOGRAPHICAL SETTING 17

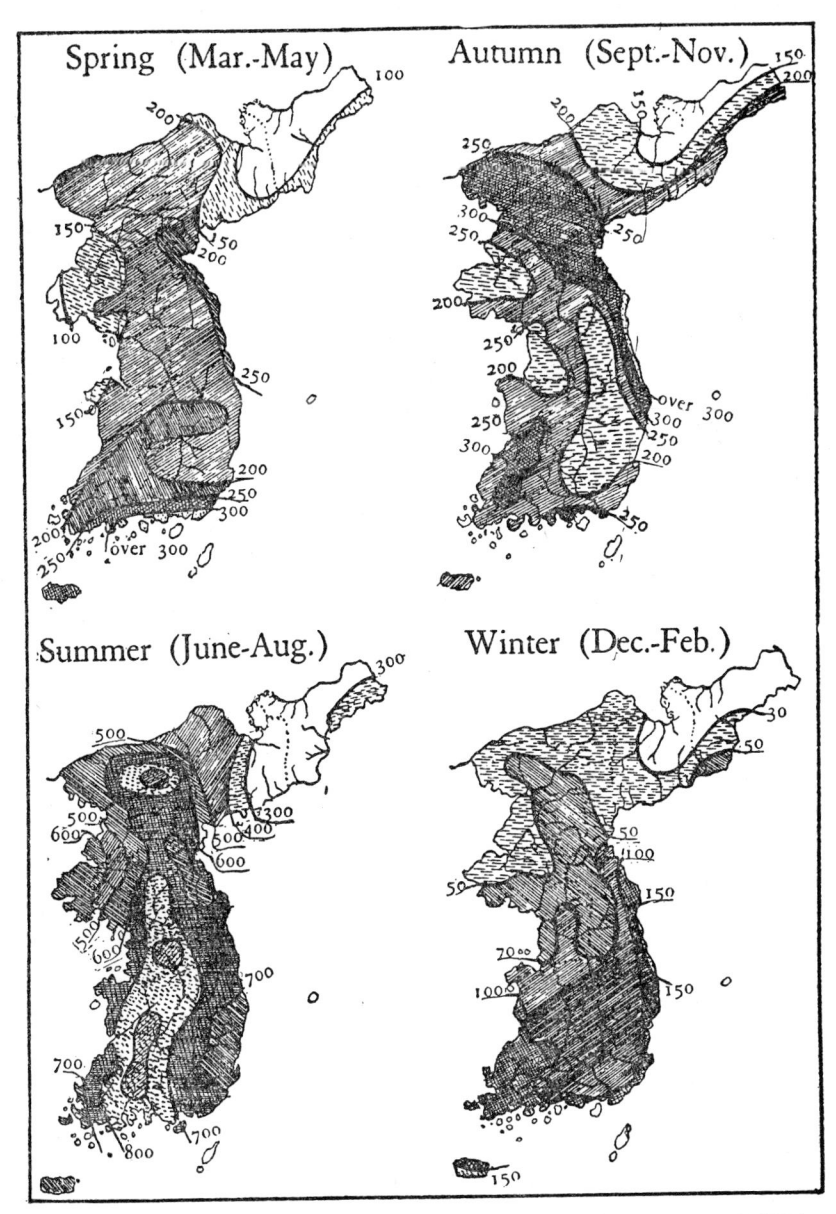

THE SEASONAL DISTRIBUTION OF PRECIPITATION IN KOREA
(IN M.M.)
Based on the Report Made by the Meteorological Observatory of Chosen, 1925.

This table indicates that the annual amount of precipitation in Korea is not very large. It varies from 53.5 inches in Genzan to 37 inches in Heijo; this is considerably less than in Japan and more nearly comparable with data for the corresponding places on or near the Atlantic seaboard of the United States. But the figures for the seven months most important for plant growth (April to October) show a different picture. If precipitation were distributed equally through the year, the precipitation during these months would constitute about 58 per cent of the total. Points in the United States come very near to this figure, varying from 53 to 64 per cent. Points in Japan receive a much larger share of precipitation in these months—from 75 to 78 per cent, only in the north and in Hokkaido is the percentage as low as 63 and 68 per cent respectively. But in Korea in these seven months there is from 81 to as much as 93 per cent of the annual amount of precipitation. Because of this, the soil in Korea receives much more water during these critical months than in the United States, and almost as much as in Japan—in some places more. This would normally be regarded as a favorable circumstance for Korean agriculture. However, two circumstances militate against its beneficial effect: first, in some years a tremendous amount of water falls in too short a period—in one day or a few hours—causing destructive floods; second, there are great fluctuations in the amount of precipitation from year to year, so that in some years disastrous crop failures occur. There is a saying in Korea that of every three harvests one is good, one fair, and one very poor. The following examples show the seriousness of floods as a source of crop failure.

EXAMPLES OF EXCESSIVE RAINFALL

Place	Month and day	Amount of precipitation in inches	This day's rainfall as percentage of the average annual rainfall
Moppo	July 15	7.8	18
Zenshu	July 20	7.8	16
Taikyu	July 18	5.6	14
Keijo	August 2	14.1	28
Heijo	August 1	8.3	22
Shingishu	August 25	7.2	17
Genzan	September 3	9.5	18

Source for columns two and three: Hishimoto, *Chosenbei no kenkyu.*

In the course of a few hours, and sometimes even minutes, from 14 to 28 per cent of the annual precipitation may fall on the fields. At Keijo more water fell in a single day than at Stalingrad, Russia in a whole year. These floods, as may be seen from the dates, occur at a time when in most cases the crop is still standing.

PRECIPITATION IN KOREA IN 1939 AS PERCENTAGE OF MANY YEARS' ANNUAL PRECIPITATION

	April	May	June	July	August	September
Moppo	62	59	62	24	126	82
Zenshu	57	61	47	22	43	125
Keijo	88	117	86	23	18	38
Shingishu	137	44	66	54	80	383
Genzan	95	117	86	23	171	141

Source: Calculated from data in *Chosen Nenkan*, 1941.

In June and July 1939, the country received from one quarter to one half of the rainfall it used to get during those months in previous years. August in Keijo was even worse—only 18 per cent of the usual rainfall was received; but floods came to Shingishu in September and to Genzan in August. The year 1939, about which more will be said later, emphasized two unsolved tasks for Korea: the necessity of drought prevention and irrigation on the one hand, and that of drainage on the other.

The number of frostless days in Korea is about 145 in the north, about 175 in the center, and about 220 in the south,[10] thus permitting two crops in one year in southern Korea. As to the typhoons which are so devastating in the Philippines, Taiwan (Formosa), and Japan, they are rare in Korea and not as destructive; the strongest winds occur early in the spring in Heijo, Taikyu and Zenshu, and in December in Shingishu. Only in Genzan and Moppo were violent storms (with a speed of 85 and 113 feet per second respectively) registered in July,[11] while in Japan they are frequent in August and September, when the crop is still standing.

This short survey of Korea's climate shows that there are significant climatic differences between various regions. S. McCune who has published a special study of climatic condi-

[10] H. K. Lee, *op. cit.*, p. 12.
[11] Hishimoto, *op. cit.*, p. 35.

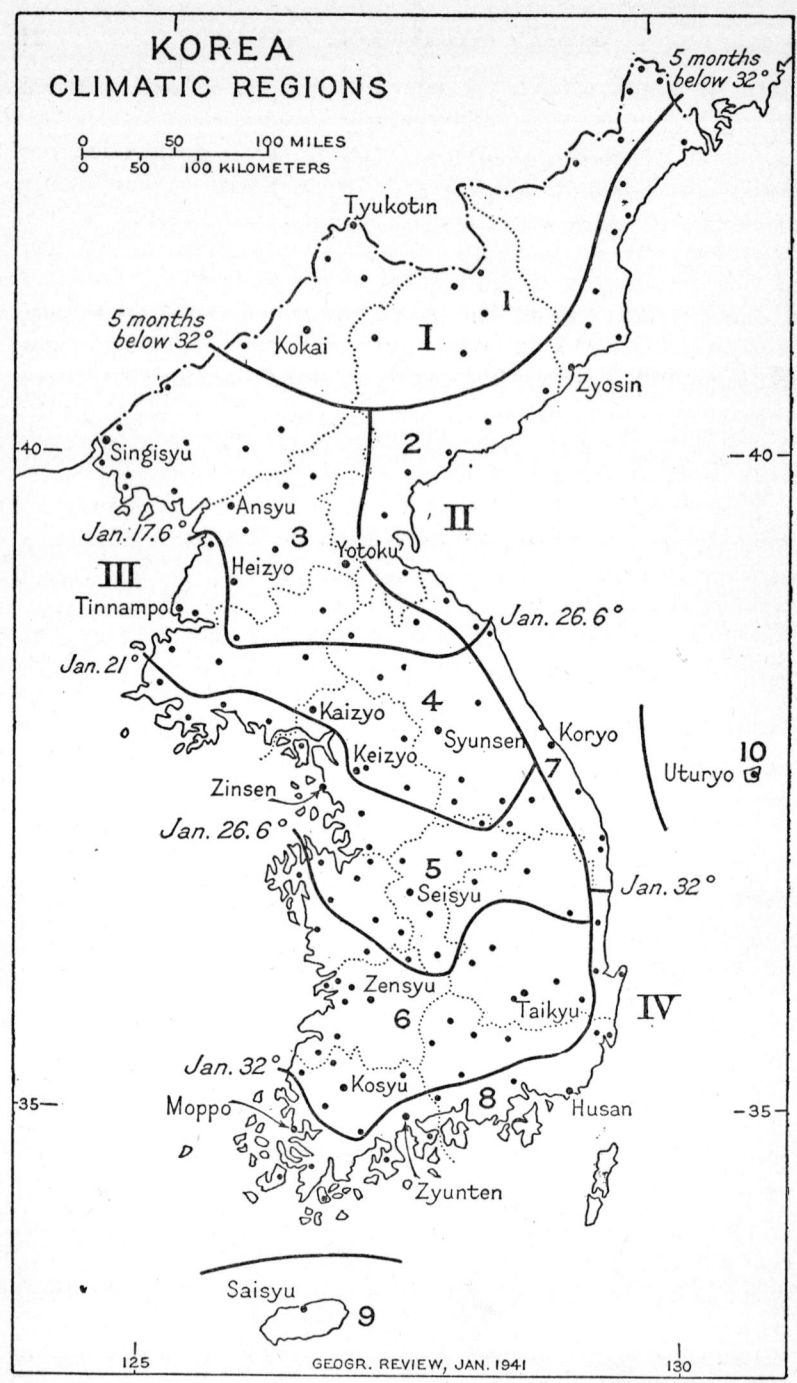

Climatic regions of Korea. The roman numerals refer to climatic provinces, the arabic numerals to the regions. I-1, Northern Interior; II-2, Northeastern Littoral; III-3, Northwest; III-4, Central-west; III-5, Southwest; IV-6, South; IV-7, Southeastern Littoral; IV-8, Southern Littoral; IV-9, Quelpart Island; IV-10, Dagelet Island. The dots show location of meteorological stations. Scale approximately 1 : 7,500,000.

tions in Korea divides the country into ten climatic regions taking isotherms as boundary lines.[12]

The first region, *Northern Interior*, has a long, cold, dry winter with five months below 32° F. and with a short, warm summer. It is a region of spruce, fir, larch, pine forests, of firefields (see chapter on Agriculture), potatoes, oats, millet, and of rice grown only at the bottom of the valleys.

The second region, the *Northeastern Littoral*, has three months below 32° F., a warm summer, with precipitation ranging from 28.5 inches in the center to almost double that in the south. Fogs are prevalent along the coast. Dry crops (millet, barley, oats, potatoes) are more important than rice; fishing is likewise of importance.

The third region, *North West,* has a cold, dry winter and a mean January temperature below 17.6° F. The precipitation is high on the mountains, but low on the coast. Abundant summer rains permit cultivation of rice (single crop) and of dry crops.

The fourth region, *West Central*, has a mean January temperature between 17.6° and 21°; and some double cropping is possible with wheat and barley as winter crops. The mountainous interior has larger precipitation and grows more rice; the northern littoral relies on dry crops. Apples and native cotton are grown in the north, and ginseng in the south.

The fifth region, *West Southern,* has a mean January temperature of 21° to 26.6° and the mean precipitation is from 34 to 54 inches. In the plains rice is raised, with winter barley as a second crop where a second crop is possible. On the hill slopes millet and American cotton are raised.

The sixth region, *South*, has a mean January temperature of 26.6°-32°, and an annual precipitation of from 35.2 to 59.3 inches with occasional droughts. Precipitation increases from east to west. The region is a rice and double-cropping region par excellence, with American cotton and soy beans as important crops. The population is very dense and poor, and frequent crop failures cause large emigration.

The seventh region, the *Southeastern Littoral,* is a narrow, coastal belt separated from the rest by the Daihaku mountains. It has a mild winter (26.6°-32° average January temperature)

[12] Description of regions given here follow his article, *Climatic Regions of Korea and Their Economy*, published in *The Geographical Review*, January 1941, pp. 95-99.

and heavy summer precipitation; double cropping is practiced and fishing is important.

The eighth region, the *Southern Littoral,* has a mild winter (an average January temperature above 32°). Bamboo thickets are frequent and barley is the usual second crop. American cotton is of importance.

The ninth and tenth regions are formed by the *Saishu* (Quelpart) and *Uturyo* (Dagelet) islands. Saishu has a mean January temperature of 40.1° and the precipitation on the north coast of 55.6. Uturyo, unlike the rest of Korea, has a heavy winter precipitation. The mean January temperature is 34.7° and the mean annual precipitation 59 inches.

CHAPTER III[1]

HISTORY

Korea is inhabited by a Mongoloid people, many of whom are tall and robust and have a lighter complexion and more regular features than other peoples of the Mongol family. The Koreans have a language of their own, differing from Japanese or Chinese as much as the French language differs from German or Russian. For many centuries, however, Korea was under the cultural influence of China and borrowed from it the ideographic script, written language, Confucianism, and much of its art. Because of this, there are many words of Chinese origin in the Korean language, although these are pronounced in a way unintelligible to the Chinese. The legends of Korean history go back to before 2,000 B. C., and Chinese appeared in the country about 1,100 B. C. For many centuries Korea was divided among small kingdoms often at war with each other. Toward the end of the seventh century A. D. the whole country was united under the native dynasty of Silla, although it recognized the suzerainty of China.

Koryo, a later dynasty from which the name Korea is derived, was established in 918 A. D. as a result of the rebellion of Wang Kien. In the thirteenth century, while this dynasty was still in power, Korea was invaded by the armies of Genghis Khan. In 1392 another rebellion brought forth a new dynasty, that of Yi, which held the Korean throne until 1910. It was under this dynasty that the name Chosen (in Japanese pronunciation), or Morning Calm, was adopted for the kingdom.

Under the Silla dynasty the influence of Buddhism was paramount, but in later years adherents of this religion were persecuted and Confucianism became the official religion. The people, however, continued to embrace a primitive animism combined with some elements of Buddhism and Confucianism.

Before the seventeenth century Korea was in the forefront of

[1] This chapter does not pretend to give a full history of Korea. Its purpose is to survey Korean-Japanese relations since 1875, the period of the protectorate and annexation, and of the country's development under Japanese rule.

human civilization and many important innovations and inventions may be credited to her people. The earliest astronomical tower, the early use of moving metal type for printing (in 1403), a phonetic alphabet (in the fifteenth century), the use of the compass (in 1525), the use of cannon, shells, and iron-clad warships (in the war of 1592)[2]—these and other original contributions as well as the works of her artists show that the Koreans are not merely able imitators but creators as well.[3] It was through or from Korea that the Japanese received Buddhism, learned the cultivation of the silkworm, mastered their advanced architecture, the painting of pictures, the making of beautiful porcelain ware and other arts and crafts.[4] Unfortunately, this flourishing period of Korean history was brought to an end by the Japanese invasion of 1592.

In 1586 the Japanese general, Toyotomi Hideyoshi, rose to the position of Dajo-Daijin ["Prime Minister"], and after many reforms at home he turned his attention abroad to Korea and China,

"his fertile imagination going so far as to make him plan the establishment of a great Oriental Empire centered in the Japanese Sovereign. With the ultimate aim of conquering China, Hideyoshi dispatched the expeditionary force to Chosen in 1592."[5]

Although Korea, then a vassal of China, received help from the Chinese Emperor, the country was overrun by the Japanese, pillaged and burned. When, after six years of devastating war, the Japanese were compelled to retreat to their islands, they left the country in ruins. Untold treasures and thousands of

[2] "The first half of the fifteenth century was characterized by a series of marvelous advances in every sphere of life in Korea . . . A Commission was appointed which . . . evolved an alphabet which, for simplicity of construction and phonetic power, has not its superior in the world . . . About the same time the King ordered the casting of metal printing-types. These were the first movable metal printing-types ever made, and anticipated their manufacture in Europe by fifty years . . . He [Admiral Yi Sun-sin] had invented a curious iron-clad in the shape of a tortoise . . . With his boat he met and engaged a Japanese fleet . . . and soon threw the whole fleet in confusion . . ." H. Hulbert, *The Passing of Korea*, New York, 1906, pp. 92-98.

[3] The following curious definition of the "Korean" is given in Webster's *New International Dictionary*, p. 1197: "A member of the native race of Korea . . . of an adept imitative rather than profound intelligence."

[4] This is written not in order to show actual superiority of Koreans over Japanese, but simply to reveal that the Koreans had a highly developed culture, and are gifted with original creative powers.

[5] Kenzo Akiyama, *The History of Japan*, Tokyo, 1941, p. 193.

Korea's best artisans and artists were taken by the invaders to Japan. The country never recovered from this blow. It closed its frontiers to all nations except China whose suzerainty it recognized. For three hundred years Korea was a hermit nation, striving to keep out her powerful neighbors. Official relations with Japan consisted of the dispatch of a congratulatory mission each time a new *shogun* was appointed in that country. The last of these missions was received in 1811 on the island of Tsushima. Only forty Japanese junks a year were permitted to visit Fusan for purposes of trade, but each year a Korean emissary was sent to Peking to pay tribute to the Chinese Emperor. In 1860 Korea acquired a third powerful neighbor, Russia, when the latter obtained the Maritime Province from China.

After 1860 many powers showed a great interest in the Hermit Kingdom, and a number of incidents arose because the Koreans were determined to keep out all foreigners. In 1875 a Japanese gunboat was engaged in surveying the mouth of the Korean river Han, which it had no right to do. The ship was fired upon by Koreans, and this was regarded as an "incident" justifying the dispatch of Japanese gunboats and military transports into Korean waters to enforce certain demands. The result was a Korean-Japanese treaty of commerce, signed on February 26, 1876. The first clause of this treaty recognized Korea as

"an independent state enjoying the same sovereign rights as does Japan."[6]

Some historians refer to this treaty and to Japan's conduct after its conclusion as evidence that Japan had no desire to bring Korea under her control.[7] But the following quotation from a Japanese source gives a different interpretation of Japan's attitude:

"Upon his return [that of Soyejima Taneomi, the Foreign Minister] in July [1873, from China], therefore, he proposed the conquest of Korea. The issue reached a crisis in October, and the debate divided the [Japanese] Council of State for ten days, October 14-23. It was in the course of that memorable debate that Okubo [the famous Japanese statesman, 1830-1878] rose to the fearless height of a prophet and pointed out that Japan was still in a transition stage and financially too weak for such an adventure."[8]

[6] *Treaties and Conventions between Corea and Other Powers*, compiled by Hunry Chung, New York, 1919, p. 205.
[7] See Payson J. Treat, *The Far East*, New York and London, 1928, pp. 293-294; and P. H. Clyde, *A History of the Modern and Contemporary Far East*, New York, 1937, p. 266.
[8] R. H. Akagi, *Japan's Foreign Relations*, Tokyo, 1936, p. 116.

This and other statements in Japanese works[9] indicate that Japanese statesmen were fully agreed as to the *necessity* of conquering Korea; but that the most capable among them believed that Japan was not yet ready to undertake the task.

The treaty of 1876 was important in still another respect. Less than twenty years before, Japan had signed "unequal treaties" with foreign powers, and all during the intervening years she had bitterly complained of the injustice done to her. But now she entered into a treaty with an Asiatic power; and her first demand, which she succeeded in obtaining, was for extraterritorial privileges in Korea. This was an omen of sinister portent, but few foreigners saw the danger in it at that time or later.

The treaty with Japan was followed by treaties with other powers;[10] Korea was soon opened to foreign trade,[11] and the country became a fertile field for international intrigue. On April 18, 1885, Hirobumi Ito, [author of the Japanese Constitution and on several occasions Prime Minister of Japan, 1841-1909] as the representative of Japan, and Li Hung-chang [Viceroy of Chihli and famous Chinese statesman, 1823-1901] as the representative of China, concluded a convention at Tientsin. By this convention

"the forces under the Chinese resident, as well as the Japanese legation guards were to be completely withdrawn from the Kingdom. The Korean king was to be invited to organize a Korean army, in the formation of which neither Chinese nor Japanese were to be employed. In case any serious disturbance in Korea made it necessary for either China or Japan to send troops into the peninsula the country sending the troops must notify the other, previously and in writing, of the intention to do so, and the troops should be withdrawn when the matter had been settled."[12]

In 1894 a rebellion of the Tong Hak, a religious group, took place, and on June 2 the Korean Court asked the Chinese Government for assistance. The Chinese Government notified the

[9] See, for example, Kijiro Watanabe, *History of Sino-Japanese and Russo-Japanese Wars* (in Japanese), Tokyo, 1937, chapter on "Discussion of Conquest of Korea."

[10] It is said that Li Hung-chang, the famous Chinese statesman, in charge of China's relations with Korea, her vassal, privately advised the Koreans in 1879 to conclude treaties with as many powers as possible. G. Nye Steiger, *A History of the Far East*, Boston, 1936, p. 622.

[11] Maritime customs were the most reliable source of income of the Korean king; after 1882 they fell under the control of the British.

[12] Steiger, *op. cit.*, p. 623.

Japanese Government of its decision to send troops to Korea and dispatched a small force. Japan was not asked by the Korean Government to send any troops, but the Japanese Government sent six times as many soldiers as the Chinese. It turned out that the help was not needed, because the Korean Government suppressed the rebellion before the arrival of foreign troops. Nevertheless, the Japanese Government offered to cooperate with China in the introduction of reforms in the administration of Korea. The reply of the Chinese Government was that

"Even China, whose vassal Korea has always been, would not interfere in the internal administration of the Kingdom; Japan, having from the beginning recognized Korea as an independent state, cannot claim any right to interfere."[13]

This did not stop Japan from proceeding with the proposed reforms. On July 23, 1894, the Japanese troops in the Korean capital attacked the palace, seized the King, and a few days later started their war with China.[14] With the Korean King a prisoner of Japan, a new "Korean" Government was organized, and on July 24, this Government issued a decree denouncing the treaties with China and asking Japanese help in driving the Chinese from Korea. In August a treaty of alliance was signed with Japan[15] which provided that Korea would give every facility for the movement of Japanese troops and the supply of provisions, while the Japanese Government promised "to maintain the independence of Korea on a firm footing."[16]

[13] Quoted by Steiger, *op. cit.*, p. 625.
[14] As is usual with the Japanese Government, its warships torpedoed Chinese vessels a few days before the break in diplomatic relations and the declaration of war. The sinking of the *Kowhsing* in 1894 with more than a thousand soldiers on board, the attack on Port Arthur in 1904, the attack on Mukden in 1931, the attack at the Marco Polo Bridge in 1937 and Pearl Harbor in December 1941 are examples of a continuous pattern of behavior. According to Prof. Treat: "The surprise attack on Port Arthur, which preceded the formal declaration of war, while much criticized at the time, was later found to be in keeping with precedent." *Op. cit.*, p. 374.
[15] The text of the treaty is given in McKenzie, *The Tragedy of Korea*, London, 1908, p. 46.
[16] H. Chung *op. cit.*, p. 339. Chung dates this treaty July 14, 1894, but this is certainly erroneous because as late as July 22 the Korean Government, answering the Japanese note, replied that "the Chinese troops came to Seoul at its request and would not leave unless similarly requested" (Treat, *op. cit.*, p. 298). *After that* the Japanese attacked the Palace, and, as Professor Treat puts it, "secured possession of the King's person." It is important to note that it was not only anxiety over Korean independence that worried the Japanese. According

The war ended in a quick defeat of China, and by the treaty of Shimonoseki, signed on April 20, 1895, China recognized "the full and complete independence and autonomy of Korea."

It might have seemed at that time that a happy period would follow for Korea since both Japan and China had recognized her full independence. But Japan already had advisers in Korea who were busy "reforming" Korean life. Viscount Miura, Japanese Minister at Seoul, treated "independent" Korea as a conquered region. This aroused energetic opposition on the part of the Koreans under the direction of the strong-willed Queen. Japanese troops, at the command of Miura, together with some Japanese and Korean civilians, attacked the royal palace on October 8, 1895, murdered the Queen and others and again "secured possession of the King's person."[17] For four months the Japanese ruled the country. But then the unexpected happened: on February 11, 1896, the King, carrying with him his seal of state, fled with his ministers to the Russian Legation in Seoul and resumed his rule over the country from that Legation.

The Imperial Government of Russia had been "interested" in Korea since 1880, twenty years after the acquisition of the Ussuri region bordering on Korea. In 1884 Russian officers were invited to help in the reorganization of the Korean army; a year later the Russian Government attempted to secure the use of a Korean port by the Russian Navy, and this interest in Korea was steadily intensified. Under these conditions the flight of the King to their Legation was viewed by the Russians as a heaven-sent opportunity. The King remained at the Legation for more than a year. He dismissed the Japanese officials and

---

to McKenzie (*Korea's Fight for Freedom*, London, 1920, pp. 45-50), the Japanese also demanded from the King wholesale concessions, railway rights, and a monopoly of gold mining in Korea; and when "the King and his ministers implored Mr. Otari [the Japanese Minister at Seoul] to withdraw his soldiers from the royal presence, Mr. Otari agreed to do so, at a price, which was the royal consent to a number of concessions that would give Japan almost a monopoly of industry in Korea. The Japanese Government presented further demands to the King that would have meant the entire trade of Korea being monopolized by their countrymen. These demands went so far that the foreign representatives protested."

[17] McKenzie, *op. cit.*, pp. 262-268 quotes in full the findings of the Japanese Court of Preliminary Inquiries, concerning Miura and his associates in this affair. These findings indicate clearly the guilt of Miura and others, yet "notwithstanding these facts, there is no sufficient evidence to prove that any of the accused committed the crime originally meditated by them."

employed some Russians. Russian adventurers connected with the Imperial Court received mining concessions along the Tumen and forest concessions on the Yalu. Russian military instructors were engaged to train the Korean Army. An attempt was also made by Russia to get control of the Korean customs.[18] This situation strained relations between Japan and Russia, and successive steps were taken by both sides to reach an agreement on Korea in the Waeber-Komura memorandum of May 14, 1896, the Yamagata-Lobanov Protocol of June 9, 1896, and, finally, the Nishi-Rosen Protocol, signed on April 25, 1898, by which both countries recognized "the sovereignty and entire independence of Korea" and agreed "to refrain from all direct interference in the internal affairs of that country,"[19] although Russia recognized Japan's interest in the "development of the commercial and industrial relationship between Japan and Korea." It should be pointed out that in all these negotiations the question of Korea was only one of the problems under consideration between these two countries, and that Korea became a pawn in the larger game of Russo-Japanese rivalry in northeastern Asia.[20]

However, it soon became apparent that the two parties interpreted the Nishi-Rosen agreement differently. The Japanese Government thought that the agreement had placed Korea at its disposal, but when it became obvious that the Russian Government did not intend to leave Korea completely to Japan, the Japanese Government began to strengthen its army and navy. At the same time it strengthened its political defenses by the Anglo-Japanese Alliance, the formal negotiations for which started in August 1901 and were concluded on January 30, 1902. In the negotiations with Russia which two years later led to war with that country, Japan insisted upon her right to send troops to Korea and to advise and assist the Korean Government, at the same time confirming once again "the independence and

[18] The British Customs Commissioner refused to surrender control and was backed by the British Government. Several years later the Japanese made a similar attempt and this time British protests went unheeded.
[19] F. A. McKenzie, *The Tragedy of Korea, op. cit.*, p. 302.
[20] Marquis Ito, mentioned before, has often been represented as a champion of Korean independence and a friend of the Korean people. However, it should be noted that it was he who during these negotiations offered the Russian Government complete freedom of action in Manchuria in exchange for Japan's freedom of action in Korea. Akagi, *op. cit.*, p. 174.

territorial integrity of the Korean Empire."[21] However, the Russian Government refused to grant Japan freedom of action in Korea in exchange for a free hand in Manchuria, and war followed.

On January 21, 1904 the Korean Government proclaimed Korea's neutrality in case of war between Japan and Russia; but this did not prevent Japan from landing troops in Korea. Soon Korea was overrun, and on February 23, 1904, after two weeks of resistance, the Korean Emperor was compelled to sign a treaty of alliance with Japan. By this treaty the Emperor permitted the use of Korean territory as a base for military operations against Russia, while in return the Japanese Government "definitely guaranteed the independence and territorial integrity of the Korean Empire."[22] In the treaty itself the Korean Emperor expressed his desire to "place full confidence in the Imperial Government of Japan" and undertook to "institute reforms in internal affairs."

In March 1904, Marquis Ito paid a visit to Korea and, as a result, the Japanese Government in May 1904 reached the following decisions: "(1) Korea should be made a Japanese protectorate at the proper time; (2) until the arrival of such an opportunity, Japan should strive to obtain practical results in giving political, diplomatic, and military protection and in developing Japan's interests in Korea. Both [the Prime Minister] Count Katsura [1847-1913] and [the Minister of Foreign Affairs] Baron Komura [1855-1911] feared the objection of the Powers should Japan announce these decisions at once, espe-

[21] King Yi Hyeung of Korea in October 1897 assumed the title of Emperor of Korea in the hope that this would give Korea an equal status with the three powerful Empires, neighbors of Korea.

Professor P. J. Treat notes that "The Japanese proposal [to the Russian Government] as a basis of understanding [between Japan and Russia] was very simple and might easily have been accepted by Russia in its entirety . . . if Russia had accepted these terms she would have had a free hand in Manchuria . . . while Japan . . . would have covenanted not to impair Korean sovereignty or the open-door policy in Korea." Treat, *op. cit.*, p. 369.

In view of the repeated Japanese promises to respect the independence of Korea and their actual record there, it is not clear what Professor Treat understands by "sovereignty" in this case.

[22] Akagi, (*op. cit.*, pp. 240 and 266) and H. Chung (*Treaties and Conventions* . . .) assert that it was a protocol; Professor H. M. Vinacke (*A History of the Far East in Modern Times*, New York, 1928, p. 168) and Professor G. Nye Steiger (*op. cit.*, p. 730), speak of a treaty of alliance.

cially in the face of the declared purpose of war against Russia, and so adopted a plan of a more gradual procedure."[23]

These discussions and decisions are important for the evaluation of the events that followed. They show that Marquis Ito, who has been described by some scholars and missionaries as the great friend of the Korean people, planned the annexation of Korea a few days after the conclusion of the alliance and the recognition of "Korean independence and territorial integrity." Some writers of that period (see below) explained to the American and British public the necessity of Korea's annexation by Japan by references to the obstinate refusal of the Koreans to be "reformed" and improved. But it appears from the above quotation that this subsequent refusal of the Koreans to be "reformed" had little to do with the annexation, which had already been decided upon as early as March 1904. Indeed, as has been pointed out, Japanese statesmen sought to conquer Korea as early as 1873, but the more prudent among them saw at that time that Japan was too weak for such an enterprise. Now, in 1904, the moment was ripe; but it was important to proceed carefully in order to mislead the world.

Though the Russo-Japanese War was not yet over, Japan went ahead with her plans. In July 1904 she forced the Korean Government "to accept a Japanese financial adviser and to consult the Japanese Government on all matters affecting foreign affairs."[24] This demand was granted, and under a second agreement signed on August 22, 1904, Mr. [later Baron] Megata, a financial expert of the Japanese Finance Ministry, was appointed to the post of Financial Adviser and D. W. Stevens, an American in the service of the Japanese Foreign Office, became Diplomatic Adviser.[25] These advisers were followed by Japanese advisers on police, judicial, and military matters. "Japan's minister at Seoul, Mr. [later Viscount] Gonsuke Hayashi, was authorized to exchange views with the Korean Government and *to supervise the entire Korean administration*,[26] as well as all special Japanese advisers."[27] In April 1905, by another agree-

[23] Akagi, *op. cit.*, pp. 266-267.
[24] Steiger, *op. cit.*, p. 730.
[25] Mr. D. W. Stevens paid with his life for his activities. He was killed by a Korean in San Francisco in March, 1908, while proceeding to Washington on furlough.
[26] My italics. A. G.
[27] Seiji Hishida, *Japan Among the Great Powers*, London, 1940, p. 120.

ment, the Korean postal, telegraph, and telephone services were taken over by Japan. Thus the ground was prepared for negotiations with the Great Powers.

On July 29, 1905, the Japanese Premier, Count Katsura, and William Howard Taft, then Secretary of War of the United States in Theodore Roosevelt's administration, had a recorded conversation. Count Katsura declared that "Japan does not harbor any aggressive designs whatever against the Philippines." Taft expressed his belief that the President [Theodore Roosevelt] would agree that "the establishment by Japanese troops of suzerainty over Korea to the extent of requiring that Korea enter into no foreign treaties without the consent of Japan was the logical result of the present war and would directly *contribute to permanent peace*[28] in the East."[29] Later "President Roosevelt, through his personal representative, had given the Tokyo Foreign Office an assurance that the reorganization of Korea by the Japanese would meet no opposition from the United States."[30]

On August 12, 1905, the British Government, on signing the treaty for the renewal of the Anglo-Japanese Alliance, stated that:

"Japan possessing paramount political, military, and economic interests in Korea, Great Britain recognizes the right of Japan to take such measures of guidance, control, and protection in Korea, as she may deem proper and necessary to safeguard and advance these interests."[31]

On September 5, 1905, defeated Russia signed the Portsmouth Treaty under the terms of which she recognized Japan's "paramount political, military, and economic interests" in Korea. The way was now clear for Japan's advance.

In November 1905, Marquis Ito arrived at the Korean capital on a special mission—to put relations between Japan and Korea on a new basis. On November 15 he presented to the Korean Emperor demands which amounted to the establishment of a Japanese protectorate over Korea. Japan was to handle Korean foreign affairs, and be represented at the Korean capital by a Resident-General with Residents in smaller towns, etc. In return, Japan was to guarantee "to maintain the security and

[28] My italics. A. G.
[29] Quoted in Akagi, *op. cit.*, p. 272.
[30] Steiger, *op. cit.*, p. 730.
[31] Akagi, *op. cit.*, p. 270.

respect the dignity of the Korean Imperial House." The treaty was to be effective "until the moment arrives when it is recognized that Korea has attained national strength"—a new promise which Japanese statesmen never showed any intention of fulfilling.

The Korean Emperor and ministers at first refused to sign the new treaty, but when Japanese soldiers were placed around the palace with machine guns, and when the Korean Prime Minister Han Kew-sul was dragged out of the conference hall by Japanese officers,[32] the ministers signed the treaty. Several high officials, including Min Yong-whan, former Minister of War, committed suicide.

The Emperor then sent a secret mission to the President of the United States, asking for help and pointing out that the treaty was obtained "at the point of the sword and under duress." In the treaty between Korea and the United States, ratified by the United States on February 13, 1883, there was the following clause:

"If other Powers deal unjustly or oppressively with either Government, the other will exert their good offices, on being informed of the case, to bring about an amicable arrangement, thus showing their friendly feelings."[33]

But President Theodore Roosevelt, as the Japanese put it, "completely ignored the appeal." According to Professor P. H. Clyde, "Roosevelt himself had no respect for the Koreans for, as he said, 'they could not strike one blow in their own defense.' "[34] This last statement, as will be shown later, was not supported by subsequent events.

Korea thus became a protectorate of Japan, and Marquis Ito assumed the post of first Resident-General at Seoul in February 1906. Most Europeans and Americans, especially the missionaries who were on the spot, generally welcomed the Japanese victory[35] and the change in Korea.

[32] Chung, *op. cit.*, p. 55.
[33] *Ibid.*, p. 329.
[34] Clyde, *op. cit.*, p. 436.
[35] In the opinion of Paul S. Reinsch (*Outlook*, September 16, 1905) Japan in 1904-5 "has fought our [the United States'] battle as well as her own"; the peace of Portsmouth he calls "an unfortunate peace" because Japan was robbed of the fruits of her victory. Professor Reinsch later became American Minister to China and the champion of "American rights and, in particular, those of American bankers" (Clyde, *op. cit.*, p. 499). Professor Ernest W. Clement in the

"When the Japanese landed in Korea in 1904, the missionaries welcomed them. They knew the tyranny and abuses of the old government and believed that the Japanese would help to better things. The ill-treatment of helpless Koreans by Japanese soldiers and coolies caused a considerable reaction of feeling. When, however, Prince Ito became Resident-General, the prevailing sentiment was that it would be better for the people to submit and to make the best of existing conditions, in the hope that the harshness and injustice of Japanese rule would pass."[36]

Another witness, George Kennan [1845-1924], a well-known American writer and an old friend of Theodore Roosevelt, whose views on Korea influenced the President, visited Korea in 1905 and described his impressions in several articles published in the *Outlook*, a very influential magazine of the period. These articles begin with a description of the Korean Government:

"The Government. Under this head are comprised (a) the Emperor's Cabinet, consisting of nine ministers; (b) the sorcerers, soothsayers, fortune-tellers, and mudangs or spirit mediums, who influence and often control legislation; (c) the governors of the thirteen provinces; and (d) the magistrates or prefects of the 344 prefectures into which the provinces are divided. All the official positions in classes (c) and (d) are nominally filled by Imperial appointment, but the selection of appointees is subject to court influence, 'pull,' or intrigue, and, as a rule, the offices are sold to the highest bidder. Provincial governors pay from ten thousand to forty thousand Korean dollars for their places, and then not only recoup themselves but amass fortunes by robbing the defenseless people whom they are sent to govern. As there are no independent law courts, and as every governor or prefect is a judge as well as an administrator, a Korean who is robbed must seek redress from the robber . . .

"The methods of robbery in the provinces and prefectures are illegal and excessive taxation, 'squeezes' on all official business . . . seizure of property without warrant or excuse of any kind, and barefaced extortion on pretexts that are often so fantastic and preposterous as to be almost incredible . . .

"The Korean people have been accustomed to 'squeezes' and illegal exactions for centuries and . . . they protest or resist only when robbery passed the extreme limit of endurance . . . The natural and inevitable result of such a state of affairs is impoverishment and demoralization . . .

"The activities and operations of the existing Korean Government may briefly be summarized as follows: it takes from the people, directly and

---

sixth edition of his *Handbook of Modern Japan*, Chicago, 1905, (on p. 311) quotes in support of this point of view the following words of Captain Brinkley: "She [Japan] is fighting the battle of free and equal opportunities for all without encroachment upon the sovereign rights or territorial integrity of China or Korea."

[36] McKenzie, *op. cit.*, p. 210.

indirectly, everything that they earn over and above a bare subsistence, and gives them in return practically nothing. It affords no adequate protection to life or property; it provides no educational facilities that deserve notice; it builds no roads; it does not improve its harbors; it does not light its coasts; it pays no attention whatever to street-cleaning or sanitation; it takes no measures to prevent or check epidemics; it does not attempt to foster national trade or industry; it encourages the lowest forms of primitive superstition; and it corrupts and demoralizes its subjects by setting them examples of untruthfulness, dishonesty, treachery, cruelty, and a cynical brutality in dealing with human rights that is almost without parallel in modern times."[37]

But what about the Korean people? In his second article Kennan wrote the following:

"The first impression that the Korean people make upon an impartial and unprejudiced newcomer is strongly and decidedly unfavorable. In the fantastic and unbecoming dress of the Ming Dynasty, which they all wear, they look so much like clowns in a circus, or minor characters in a comic opera, that it is difficult to take them seriously.[38] The domestic environment and personal habits of the lower classes are filthy and repulsive in the extreme; the moony expressionless faces of the petty officials and gentlemen of leisure who saunter through the streets fanning themselves or smoking long-stemmed pipes show no signs of character or traces of experience; and the unemployed workingmen in dirty white cotton jackets and baggy trousers, who lie here and there asleep on the ground with flies crawling over their closed eyelids, do not compare at all favorably with the neat, alert, industrious laborers of Japan. Generally speaking, the whole Korean population seems to be lacking in dignity, intelligence, and force.

"As one's field of observation widens, so as to take in country as well as town, and to include moral as well as physical and intellectual characteristics, one's first impressions harden and one's bad opinion of the people settles into a conviction. They are not only unattractive and unsympathetic to a Westerner who feels no spiritual or religious interest in them, but they appear more to be lazy, dirty, unscrupulous, dishonest, incredibly ignorant, and wholly lacking in the self-respect that comes from a consciousness of individual power and worth . . . They are the rotten product of a decayed Oriental civilization."[39]

Such was Korea as Kennan saw it in 1905 and as many for-

[37] *Outlook*, October 7, 1905, p. 310 *et seq.*, *Korea: a degenerate state*, by G. Kennan.
[38] However, Ellasue Wagner (*Korea: the Old and the New*, New York, 1931 p. 65) writes: "Nowhere on earth can one find a costume more dignified, more majestic, than that of the Korean gentleman." The present writer during his visits to Korea likewise failed to notice that the Koreans look like "minor characters in a comic opera" or "like clowns in a circus."
[39] *Outlook*, 1905, p. 409, *et. seq.*

eigners, unfortunately, saw it at the time. Let us now see how Kennan viewed the Japanese activities in Korea.

"The first mistake, perhaps, that the Japanese Government made in its dealings with Korea was in attempting to reconcile Korean independence with effective Japanese control. The Japan-Korean convention of 1904 definitely '*guaranteed the independence* of the Korean Empire' and the 'safety and repose of the Imperial Korean House' but at the same time it stipulated that the Korean Government should '*adopt the advice* of the Japanese Government *with regard to improvement* in administration' . . .

"If the two sets of rulers had been equal [i.e. the Korean officials and the Japanese advisers] in mental equipment and experience, and if their aims and purposes had been the same, they might, perhaps, have worked harmoniously and effectively together;[40] but when they had absolutely nothing in common except a mutual feeling of dislike and distrust, there was no possibility of successful cooperation . . . The whole scheme was practically unworkable, from the beginning; and it would have been much better, I think, if, instead of trying to keep up the pretense of Korean independence, Japan had frankly assumed temporary control of Korean administration for the purpose of bringing about necessary reforms."

Kennan considers that the attempt to realize Nagamori's scheme (appropriation of Korean unimproved lands, see below) was premature, and that the first task to be accomplished was administrative reform, after which "they might have put through even the Nagamori land scheme." Then he suggests what should be done, namely the appointment of a man like Yun Chi-ho as minister of Home Affairs.[41] In Kennan's words:

"Suppose that they had brought over from Japan a hundred intelligent samurai policemen and twelve or fifteen police inspectors" [to listen to complaints and to check them] "then there would have been a very considerable improvement in Korean administration and a very desirable change for the better in the feeling and attitude of the Korean people toward the Japanese . . .

"[The] third mistake [consisted] in allowing their own countrymen to swarm into Korea by tens of thousands before they had provided any legal machinery for the adjudication and settlement of disputes between the immigrants and the natives . . . The immigrants not only cheated the natives when they had opportunity, but, relying upon the absence of legal control, often ill-treated them personally and deprived them of their property by force . . ."[42]

[40] It seems to us that here Kennan misses one point: if the two sets of rulers had been equal in mental equipment and experience and if their aims and purposes had been the same, then what would have been the need for Japanese advisers?

[41] Later on we shall see what kind of appointment the Japanese administration found for Baron Yun Chi-ho.

[42] *Op. cit.*, p. 609 *et seq.*

Next, Kennan turns to the real achievements of the Japanese. He outlines the reforms which the Japanese Government planned for Korea.

"[But] it found itself opposed at the outset by the most obstinate, corrupt, and incapable bureaucracy in the world, backed by the influence and power of an absolutely impossible Emperor . . . In the first place, by a great sacrifice of men and money, she [Japan] has relieved Korea from all fear of Russian domination, and that alone, from my point of view, is not only a great work, but a work which should entitle her to the gratitude of the whole Korean people. Japanese rule, at first, may be blundering, exacting, and irritating, but it will make ultimately for education, progress, and freedom, while Russian domination at best would never raise the country above the low economic and educational level of eastern Siberia and the Caucasus. In the second place, Japan has built a railroad through the country from one end to the other, and has thus increased the value of an immense area of productive land and given to the Korean farmers freer and cheaper access to the world's markets . . . In the third place, Japan has lent the Korean Government three million yen, and has laid the foundation of a financial reform . . . Finally, Japan has made an encouraging attempt, at least, to prepare text-books and get teachers for schools, to improve the sanitation of the principal towns; to increase shipping facilities at sea-ports; to limit unnecessary and wasteful expenditures; to reorganize the army; and to discourage demoralizing and degrading superstitions . . .

"Every honest and dispassionate opinion has some value, and I do not hesitate, therefore, to say that, in my best judgment, Japan, first of all, should abandon the pretense of treating Korea as if she were really a sovereign and independent state . . .

"In the second place, Japan should pay more attention to the rights of the Korean people . . . If she allows things to drift, as they are drifting now, the anti-Japanese feeling in the peninsula will become so strong that years of good government will hardly overcome it . . ."[43]

These were the views of a man who was very influential in his day. They show that Kennan shared the hatred of Russia which prevailed in certain groups at that time, a hatred so great that even such a talented writer was unable to see the contradictory character of the assertion that Japan relieved Korea of the *fear* of Russian domination[44] by bringing her under actual Japanese domination. Kennan's comments also reveal the naive belief,

[43] *Ibid.*, p. 669 *et seq.*

[44] This fear was not as evident in Korea as in Kennan's mind, because, according to Japanese sources, on the eve of the war of 1904-5 "the Emperor was dominated by Yi Yong-ik . . . whose foreign affiliations were wholly Russian, and the palace coterie was almost entirely pro-Russian. Consequently Japan's difficult task was being traitorously blocked in the very heart of the country which she was trying to save." (Akagi, *op. cit.*, p. 265.)

prevalent even today, that ports, railways, and lighthouses in themselves represent welfaré. Almost every book on Korea repeats those Japanese "achievements" without any attempt to analyze them.[45] It is true that the old Korean government did not light its coasts. But it did not like the idea of foreign trade, because it was afraid that with it would come foreign domination. Again, there is no question that the Korean government was corrupt and inefficient. But the horrors of life under such a government are grossly exaggerated, because even if there were no written laws, there was unwritten custom. Squeeze was prevalent, but the needs of the officials were not too great. The situation definitely deteriorated under the Japanese, partly through no fault of their own, for new conditions bring new crimes; partly as a result of their conscious efforts, as in the case of the licensed houses of prostitution and opium smoking, which were prohibited in Korea while she was independent[46] and permitted by the Japanese not only as a means of breaking the morale of the Korean people, but also as a means of accumulating capital.

The most serious fault in Kennan's appraisal, however, is that he utterly ignores the fact that new forces were arising within the country which would eventually have brought about its liberation from a corrupt despotism as was the case in Russia, Turkey, and Mexico. Sweeping generalizations with respect to the Korean people, stamping them as filthy, dirty, lazy, lacking in dignity, intelligence and force are completely unjustified. The transformation of the Asiatic despotism that had existed in Korea for centuries into a modern form of society was in itself a difficult task, complicated by the rivalries of three powerful neighbors. It could not have been a painless and rapid process. But at the beginning of the twentieth century, young Koreans were demanding freedom and participation in government; hundreds of young men were imprisoned, killed, or escaped

[45] H. M. Vinacke writes (op. cit., pp. 365-6); "It is clear that the material condition of the country has been greatly improved. As in Formosa, roads have been improved and railroads built; harbors have been improved; electric lighting, introduced into Seoul, has been extended to other cities; lands have been reclaimed and the agricultural system has been improved; better sanitary methods have been introduced; a modern banking system has been instituted; industry has been promoted; and the export and import trade has expanded."
Writes P. J. Treat: "No region in the whole Far East showed such material progress." (Op. cit., p. 392).
[46] McKenzie, op. cit., p. 81.

abroad. This struggle against the oppressive and corrupt government would certainly have continued, and, after the Russian and Chinese Revolutions, better government would undoubtedly have come to Korea, and it would have been a *native* government. Western writers who are horrified when they see that an Oriental people's copper currency is unstable and its sanitation and plumbing deficient sometimes fail to understand why such a people should prefer to live under a bad native government rather than under a good foreign one, and this failure leads them, as it did Mr. Kennan, to adopt the standards of "law and order" and "natural progress" as their sole criteria for judging a colonial regime.

The Protectorate

The Japanese Protectorate over Korea lasted from 1905 to 1910. Many historians present Prince Ito (promoted from Marquis), the first Resident-General, and the man who prepared the annexation of Korea, as a very kindly statesman whose only preoccupation was the freedom and welfare of Korea, but whose laudable efforts were obstructed by the Korean administration so that, disappointed, he finally left the post. Ungrateful Koreans killed him at Harbin in 1909 and then annexation followed. According to this interpretation, the Japanese did not really desire annexation, but were forced to take this step because of Korean opposition to the reforms instituted by Japan.[47]

[47] That this is not an exaggeration may be seen from the following excerpts from the work of three historians.
Paul H. Clyde writes:
"While there were so many prominent Japanese who believed that annexation was the only solution of the Korean problem, Ito was not one of them. Early in 1906, his first act . . . was to propose . . . a comprehensive program of reform . . . Some progress was made, but the program was blocked at many points by the inefficiency of the Korean ministers and their natural resentment . . . This state of affairs dragged on into 1907 . . . This [abdication of the Emperor] was followed by an agreement . . . Under its terms all matters of internal administration as well as foreign affairs were placed under Japanese control. This new formula . . . produced results which from Japan's point of view were equally disappointing . . . By July 1909, he [Ito] was finally convinced that neither could an efficient government be formed, nor could Japan's interests be preserved by any system short of annexation . . . During July, the government determined on annexation . . . On October 26, he was assassinated by a Korean fanatic. His death . . . evoked popular demands for immediate annexation . . ." (*op. cit.*, pp. 436-437).
Writes Herbert H. Gowen, historian and clergyman:
"The first years of the protectorate were full of difficulty, though the Resident, Prince Ito, did his utmost in the way of conciliation . . . Meanwhile, an

This interpretation of events closely resembles the official Japanese version. At the time of annexation the Tokyo Foreign Office published the following announcement:

"In its solicitude to put an end to disturbing conditions the Japanese Government made an arrangement in 1905 for establishing a protectorate over Korea, and they have ever since been assiduously engaged in works of reform, looking forward to the consummation of the desired end. But they have failed to find in the regime of a protectorate a sufficient hope for a realization of the object which they had in view, and a condition of unrest and disquietude still prevails throughout the entire peninsula. In these circumstances, the necessity of introducing fundamental changes in the system of government in Korea has become entirely manifest, and an earnest and careful examination of the Korean problem has convinced the Japanese Government that the regime of a protectorate cannot be made to adapt itself to the actual condition of affairs in Korea, and that the responsibilities devolving upon Japan for the due administration of the country cannot be justly fulfilled without the complete annexation of Korea to the Empire."[48]

This explanation of the reasons for the annexation, however, ignores the fact that the Katsura Cabinet, with the participation

---

enormous amount of reform was accomplished in the direction of the establishment of banks, post offices, telegraph lines, schools and so on. In some instances these reforms were carried out untactfully and without sympathy, but the sullen resistance of the Koreans made the situation extraordinarily difficult. One insurrection cost the lives of some 21,000 persons. In 1909 Ito retired, discouraged, from his thankless task. Four months later he was murdered at Harbin." (*Asia. A Short History*, Boston, 1938, p. 239).

It should be mentioned that post offices and telegraph lines were not in need of any reform because they were already in Japanese hands and functioned effectively; establishment of banks did not and could not in view of their nature encounter "the sullen resistance of the Koreans."

Writes Payson J. Treat:

"He [Ito] believed that through advice Korea could be brought in time to a position of strength and independence. He was opposed to annexation . . . All these measures of reform [worked out by Ito] were carefully investigated and some advance was made, but Ito and his staff of Japanese experts soon ran into difficulties . . . The Koreans . . . blocked the reform measures. Within two years the protectorate had proven a failure in practise . . . The agreement of July 24, 1907, placed the Resident-General in a position of real authority . . . but his powers were, after all, negative rather than positive. He could give advice . . . but he could not carry out his measures in the face of sullen opposition. He had consistently opposed annexation, but by July 1909, he had come to the conclusion that a complete control of the administration could alone guarantee consistent progress. He therefore retired . . . Steps were now being taken to prepare for annexation in the very near future. In October . . . the great Japanese statesman and the real friend of Korea was shot down by a Korean fanatic . . ." (*op. cit.*, pp. 390-391).

[48] As quoted in Steiger, *op. cit.*, p. 732.

of Marquis Ito, had already decided as early as May 1904 that Korea should be absorbed. But fearing objections from the Powers and the unfavorable impression which might be produced in the world, the Japanese Government was compelled to advance step by step. Ito knew, of course, about the plan and was instrumental in bringing about its fruition. It is therefore completely erroneous to present the process of annexation as having taken place against the wishes of Japanese statesmen and as having been caused only by the stupidity and obstinacy of the Koreans.

It is true that there was opposition on the part of the Korean bureaucracy and the Korean people to the introduction of the Japanese-controlled regime, but this opposition was not directed against any genuine reforms. There was no opposition to prison reforms; there was no opposition to the construction of port facilities, etc. There was, however, opposition to many other alleged "reforms" because behind them the Koreans correctly saw a policy of destroying their national freedom. It has already been mentioned that opium smoking was permitted under the new administration. Another measure which aroused great popular excitement and indignation was Nagamori's land scheme. Nagamori was a Japanese financier who sought to obtain a monopoly of the "undeveloped" lands of Korea and thus acquire gratis no less than a quarter of the total area of the country. Mr. Nagamori was no ordinary adventurer, he was a financial genius. He asked for a fifty year concession to reclaim waste and fallow lands in Korea and to cultivate and use them for the exclusive benefit of his corporation. The concession was to be free of charge and exempted even from ordinary taxation for a period of five years. It was estimated at the time that his concession would cover one-fifth to one-third of Korea. The Japanese administration favored this concession and was surprised and disconcerted by the hostile reaction of the Korean public. The scheme was dropped for the time being but one can easily imagine the impression it left on the Koreans.[49] During this period, however, hundreds of thousands of acres were acquired by the Japanese "at a nominal price, less than one-twentieth of the real value."[50]

[49] Kennan believed that *after* the administrative reform the Japanese "might have put through even the Nagamori land scheme."
[50] McKenzie, *op. cit.*, p. 81 *et seq.*

But there remained one obstacle to complete Japanese domination—a Korean Army, the last vestige of Korean independence. The Japanese used the first pretext at hand to destroy this "reorganized" army. In June 1907 the Korean Emperor secretly sent a delegation, headed by Yi Sung-sol and accompanied by an American, H. B. Hulbert, to the Second International Conference at The Hague in order to appeal to the Powers. The delegation protested against the failure of the Conference to notify the Korean Government of its convening, pointing out that Korea was an independent country since the agreement of 1905 had been signed under duress and was, therefore, invalid. The Powers paid no attention to this delegation, but the Japanese Resident-General did. The Emperor was compelled to abdicate in favor of his weak son, and a new "agreement" was reached whereby "all matters of internal administration were brought under the complete control of the Japanese Resident-General in Seoul."[51] Each department of the Korean Government received a Japanese vice-minister who became the actual head of the department. Police, courts, and prisons were taken over completely by the Japanese, and on August 1, 1907, the Korean Army was disbanded.

In March 1909 Prince Ito, a member of the Genro and acting Resident-General in Korea, came to Tokyo; and on April 10, a meeting of Ito, Prime Minister Katsura, and Foreign Minister Komura took place. The three statesmen agreed that only annexation would "solve" the Korean question. On July 6, the Japanese Cabinet Council approved the decision to annex "and immediately obtained the Emperor's sanction. The decision was kept in strict secrecy, and Viscount Sone, successor to Prince Ito, was expected to put it into effect when a proper opportunity should present itself."[52] The death of Prince Ito in Harbin in October, 1909, at the hand of a Korean did not cause or accelerate the annexation of Korea by Japan. In fact, it was postponed for one year, because the Japanese Government sought to avoid the impression that the annexation was an act of revenge.

[51] Tatsuji Takeuchi, *War and Diplomacy in the Japanese Empire*, Garden City, N. Y., 1935, p. 163. Among the new powers of the Resident General was the exclusive right to appoint or dismiss officials.
[52] M. Komatsu, *Chosen Hiegono Rimen*, pp. 15-17, as quoted by Hishida, *op. cit.*, p. 175.

On May 30, 1910, General Terauchi, War Minister since 1902 and a leading militarist, was appointed Governor-General of Korea, retaining at the same time his post of War Minister.

"On June 14, a sweeping change was made in high governmental posts, followed by a dispatch of 600 gendarmes to Korea on June 17. The following day, Prime Minister Katsura announced the intended annexation of Korea to the press. A few days later, a bureau of colonial affairs was established under the direct supervision of the prime minister himself. Accordingly, by the end of the month, the entire kingdom [of Korea] was under strict control of the gendarmerie, in preparation for the final step . . . General Terauchi left Tokyo on July 15 and arrived at Seoul on July 23 under heavy guard. All organs of public opinion in Korea were suspended or ruthlessly suppressed."[53]

On August 22, the treaty of annexation was signed, and Korea became a Government-General in the Japanese Empire.[54]

In this connection it is interesting to note that, according to Seiji Hashida, "The Il-chin Hai Reform Society, organized by one million Koreans and headed by Ye Yong-koo, petitioned both the Korean Emperor and Resident-General Sone for amalgamation of the two countries."[55] Il-chin Hai (*isshinkai*, in Japanese) was an organization improvised by the Japanese and, according to official figures, its membership in 1910 was only 140,715.[56] Furthermore, it is doubtful whether the organization as such (and not some Japanese-appointed dignitaries) petitioned the Resident-General, because on the eve of annexation it was dissolved, together with eleven other organizations, including the Education Association, the Literati Association, the Progressive Party, and the like.

This destruction of Korean independence between 1905 and 1910 was not accomplished without popular protest and struggle. Despite President Theodore Roosevelt's scornful dismissal of

[53] These details are taken from Takeuchi, *op. cit.*, p. 165.

[54] According to Treat "the relinquishment of sovereignty by the Emperor of Korea was not much different from the relinquishment of sovereignty over the Filipino people by the King of Spain." (*op. cit.*, p. 392) However, there was a difference. The King of Spain relinquished sovereignty as a result of war and defeat; the Emperor of Korea was an ally of Japan; and the integrity and independence of Korea, as shown above, had been guaranteed by the Japanese Government time and again. No American Government had guaranteed the independence of the Philippines before 1900 or the "safety and repose" of the Spanish Crown.

[55] *Op. cit.*, p. 175. The Government-General's reports call Il-chin Hai "a great political party."

[56] Government-General of Korea, *Annual Report*, 1910-1911, p. 86.

the Korean people as being unwilling to strike one blow in their own defense there were many popular insurrections in Korea and their motives were well known to the Japanese Government. One of the official reports notes:

"The chief motive of insurrection is undoubtedly to combat the new regime undertaken by the Korean Government under the Japanese protectorate."[57]

The first insurrection broke out in May 1906 at Hong-Ju in South Chyung-Chyong [in Japanese-Chusei] province. Its leader, Ming Chong-silk, commander of the Eui-pyong, or Righteous Army, declared that his purpose was the emancipation of his countrymen from Japanese intervention.

"He especially denounced the treaty stipulation which gives Japan the control of Korea's foreign affairs. The insurgents captured the city of Hong-Ju . . ."

A detachment of the Japanese Army defeated them and eighty rebels were killed, one hundred and fifty captured.

"The next insurrection was instigated by Choi Ik-Ryon, a literati [scholar] of the old school . . . He sent out to all parts of the country seditious documents denouncing the convention which had been concluded in November 1905, regarding the establishment of the Resident-General, and inciting scholars and young men in the provinces to the point of insurrection."

Eventually he combined forces with Yim Pyong-chan, a leader of insurgents in North Chyulla [in Japanese-Zenra] province, but in July 1906 he was compelled to surrender.

"Riots occurred in Seoul in the summer of 1907 caused by the abdication of the Ex-Emperor. This measure and the dismantling of the Korean Army in the summer of 1907 were followed by disturbances and mutiny in the capital . . . They were soon put down by the Japanese Army and police. But the news of the abdication and of these riots subsequently provoked insurrection in the country districts . . . Thus the insurrection became almost general throughout the country except in two or three provinces."

From July 1907 to the end of 1908, according to Japanese statistics, 14,566 insurgents were killed, and 8,728 surrendered.[58]

[57] *Report of the Resident-General of Korea 1908-1909*, p. 77. The following information of insurrections is taken from the *Reports* for 1908-1909 to 1915-1916. The Japanese authorities recognized the purely political character of these insurrections; but for the American theologian and philosopher George Trumbull Ladd (1842-1921), the insurgents were only "brigands and assassins."

[58] The population of Korea at that time was estimated at 12-13 million.

An estimate of the number wounded is not given, but it must have been large. The insurgents were defeated first of all because of their primitive arms. In thirteen months the Japanese administration confiscated 4,800 rifles, pistols, and cannons, 133,000 cartridges, and 88,000 spears and swords. It was a war largely of medieval spears and swords against the machine guns of the twentieth century. In 1909, 3,000 insurgents were killed, and 2,844 captured, while 2,091 surrendered. Between September 1910 and August 1911 there were fifty-two encounters; in 1911-12 only thirteen and in 1912 only five. In July 1915, Chai Ung-on, Kim Chong-chol and Kim Chong-kun, leaders of the insurgents, surrendered to the Japanese Army, but the struggle continued in the mountainous northern districts. Many rebels moved to Manchuria and made forays across the frontier. But the country on the whole was pacified, through ruthless measures adopted by the Japanese Army and gendarmerie. The Koreans could and did strike blows in their own defense, but they were practically unarmed and faced an enemy who would stop at nothing to attain his goal.

The annexation itself was combined with attempts to appease the Korean aristocracy and conservative elements. The Korean Emperor became the Prince of the Shotoku Palace, and the Crown Prince—Prince Heir. The title of "Imperial Highness" was bestowed on them and their wives, and an annual grant of 1,500,000 yen was made to the Court from the budget of the Government-General.[59] Members of the imperial family were treated with the same consideration; and two relatives of the Emperor received a grant of 840,000 yen "for the maintenance of their households." Ex-ministers of State who had served in the Korean Government were made peers. Altogether six marquises, three counts, twenty-two viscounts and forty-five barons were created and each of them received a grant. These grants were made to 3,645 persons in all and amounted to 6,790,000 yen. The following groups received a much smaller per capita grant: 2,809 persons over 60 years of age, some *literati* and 7,002 old *yangbans* (gentry) each received twenty-four yen; also 1,768 "dutiful sons and daughters" (out of several million) were found and each was rewarded with ten yen; and

[59] *The Report* for 1911-1912 (p. 1) notes: "Their Highnesses Prince Li Junior and Prince Li Senior, being set free from political responsibilities or troubles, are now enjoying a happier and safer life."

out of three to four million wives 1,441 were selected as "virtuous wives" and received ten yen each for their virtues; widows and orphans, numbering 70,902, had to be satisfied with grants of three yen each.

The new regime established in Korea was relatively simple.[60] At the head of the Administration was a Governor-General, a military man, responsible to the Japanese Emperor who appointed him. He was the chief executive, the commander-in-chief, and had the right to issue decrees and appoint judges. Of the thirteen posts of provincial governors seven were given to Japanese. Even the posts of district magistrate and village head were in many places taken from Koreans, though from time immemorial every city had had its elected mayor and every village its elected village head, and even a "corrupt" Korean Government "never interfered with this privilege of local self-government."[61] All school principals and almost all judges appointed were Japanese.

There was also created an advisory body for the Governor-General, called Chusuin or Central Council (September 1910), the members of which were "exclusively chosen from among native Koreans of ability and reputation to give advice whenever the Governor-General chooses to consult it upon administrative measure." Its members, who should be persons "of high character and good reputation," were appointed "upon the recommendation of the Governor-General for Imperial approval." During the thirty odd years of its existence the Central Council has been consulted upon the following measures:

1. "Revision of regulations governing burial grounds and crematories" (1919).
2. "Regulation for inheritance and family relations" (1921).
3. "Opinions on 'the conditions of the people'" (1929).
4. "Conditions prevailing in country districts" (1930).
5. "Measures needed for making the living of the masses secure in view of the prevailing local conditions" (1931).
6. "Measures to be enforced . . . on the guidance of thought . . . in view of the prevailing local conditions" (1932).
7. "A new measure . . . of Envigorating Agricultural and Fishing villages. Regulations for simplifying matters pertaining to ceremonies and observances" (1933).

[60] For details see the chapter on Administration. There have been very few changes since the annexation.
[61] Henry Chung, *op. cit.*, p. 62.

8. Answers—either verbally or in writing—to the question: "What are the concrete plans for envigorating the popular mind in the cities? Also an investigation of the old customs and institutions and the changes of manners practised in the past and being practised at the present" (1934).
9. "Subjects for revival of Native Beliefs, promotion and guidance of existing religions" (1935).[62]

This enumeration shows that the Central Council was consulted mainly on matters of customs and beliefs, and no measures of importance were referred to it.

The staff of the Korean Government-General (including affiliated offices) was at first composed of fifteen thousand persons, but by 1916 it had increased to 42,312 (of whom 4,146 were "maintained through other funds"). Of this number 23,483 were Japanese, with Koreans occupying only minor positions. Gendarmes and police were more numerous than all the teachers, physicians, priests, geomancers, and sorcerers taken together. They had not only the right to enter any residence at any time and to take part in court procedures; to serve as prosecutors in district courts, and to arrest without warrant; but also the right to pass "summary judgment" on those arrested. The punishment which policemen applied in such cases was usually flogging—thirty strokes. Out of eight thousand or more cases handled directly by the police each year, only thirty to fifty persons were able "to prove their innocence," about one thousand were "pardoned," and the rest were either fined or flogged. Flogging was never used to punish Japanese nationals, but only Koreans, because it was allegedly an old Korean custom. Political prisoners were invariably flogged. The number of Koreans flogged between 1910 and 1920 was more than 200,000.

The conditions of public life during this period may be judged from the official reports. It was mentioned above that on the eve of the annexation all *political* organizations were dissolved. Other organizations soon shared a similar fate.

"An association having Confucianism as its object existed in Koshu district, Kokai province, and, showing itself inimical to the public peace by teaching so-called 'natural law or doctrine,' was advised by the authorities concerned to dissolve which it did in April 1911. Another association, organized by followers of Confucius in Mosan district, was advised in October 1911 to

[62] This enumeration of subjects is taken from the *Annual Report on Administration of Tyosen* 1936-37, pp. 42-43.

dissolve on the same ground. The so-called Communal Association . . . reported its dissolution to the police in April 1911, on having been given advice to that effect. In July a branch office of the Business Association in Zenshu district was ordered to dissolve as its condition was prejudicial to the public peace. The holding of public meetings or the gathering of crowds out of doors was also prohibited, except for religious gatherings or school excursions, permission for which might be obtained from the police authorities. Several open-air gatherings, held by school boys against teachers, tenants, against landowners, and an agitation against the purchase of land for railways took place during the year 1911. All these, however, were amicably dispersed."[63]

As time went on, cases of dissolution disappeared from the reports for the simple reason that there were almost no organizations left to be dissolved.

Before proceeding to the history of Korea after these "reforms" were instituted, let us see how they were reported to the Western public. As a typical example, we may take the article by G. Trumbull Ladd, a well-known theologian, philosopher, and teacher,[64] published in the *Yale Review* of July 1912 on "The Annexation of Korea; an essay in 'benevolent assimilation.'" In this, the author first described the problems which Japan faced in Korea:

"The most stupendous attempt at economic and educational uplift of a vast and heterogeneous population ever made by a foreign nation, is undoubtedly that of the British government in India . . . For vastness and intrinsic difficulties the attempt at so-called benevolent assimilation which Japan has taken upon itself in the annexation of Korea, is, of course, not comparable to the attempt of the British government in India. It has, however, some peculiar features, both of difficulty and of hopefulness, as well as of world wide interest." (p. 639)

What are the difficulties to which Dr. Ladd refers? First, the character of the Korean people, their dissatisfaction:

"It was not so much that Korea lost its independence and ceased to exist as a nation among the nations of the earth, as that in losing all this, living Koreans did not 'save their face.' Some did indeed attempt this saving of

[63] *Annual Report*, 1911-12, p. 54.
[64] He was also the author of a book, *In Korea with Marquis Ito*, mentioned in a previous note. In this book he wrote among other things: "Of the sincere desire of Japan for peace with the whole world, no one who knows the nation can have the slightest honest doubt" (p. 459), and "There is no essential reason why Japanese and Koreans should not become one nation in Korea. Whether this nation be called Korea or Japan, time alone can tell. That it will be a happier, more prosperous, more moral, and truly religious people than the present Korean people, there is sufficient reason to predict . . ." (p. 462).

the face by suicide, and some by turning brigands and assassins; but the nation did not respond in any large way to the call to die as patriots." (p. 643) "Further difficulties are those arising from the poverty of Korea, the undeveloped condition of its resources, the pressing need of all kind of modern improvements, and the inexpediency and even impossibility of providing funds for any considerable proportion of all this, by taxing the Koreans themselves." (p. 645)

Later on it will be shown that what was "inexpedient" and "impossible" was, nevertheless, done by the new administration. A third difficulty was that "of finding even the smallest number of honest, intelligent and brave men among the Koreans themselves." (p. 644)

But where does the hopefulness lie?

"If we may add to all this the determination of the government of Japan not to stop short, with patience, wisdom, and goodwill, in the effort to accomplish a genuine and truly benevolent assimilation, we may surely take a somewhat unusually hopeful estimate of the prospect of a final success." (p. 624)

And again:

"Is Japan still striving to pay the price and do the work of bringing about a social and spiritual oneness of Chosen with the rest of the Japanese Empire? I believe that this question may be answered with a hopeful affirmative. And if this affirmative answer becomes historically true, Japan will have taught a fine and much needed lesson to the entire Christian world." (p. 646)

It should be said in justice to Dr. Ladd that he adduced a number of facts on which he based these hopes. They were (1) remittance of "many taxes in arrears and fines for misappropriated stores"; (2) "more than five per cent reduction of the land tax for the autumn";[65] (3) the rewards to "filial sons" and "faithful wives," mentioned above; and (4) the words of General Terauchi himself:

"If judicious guidance and direction be steadily used, it will not necessarily be very difficult to attain the goal of complete harmony and assimilation . . . The essential point lies in . . . eradication of distinction between Japanese and Koreans, by which the weal of the greater nation will be promoted and the foundation of the state ever more modified." (p. 656)

It may be noted, however, that while according to Ladd, Japan was teaching a lesson to the Christian world and was striving for spiritual oneness with Korea and the educational

[65] The process of "alleviation" of the tax burden is further described in some detail.

uplift of the later,[66] the Japanese themselves call the policy applied in this period of Korean history (1910-1919) *budanteki tojisaku*, or that of "control by military force."[67]

The achievements of the Japanese administration in the economic sphere during this period received widespread praise from western observers. Even a critic of this administration, F. A. McKenzie, gives us the following picture of Korean progress in the ten years under consideration:

"Between the annexation in 1910 and the uprisings of the people in 1919, much material progress was made. The old effete administration was cleared away, sound currency maintained, railways were greatly extended, roads improved, afforestation pushed forward on a great scale, agriculture developed, sanitation improved and fresh industries begun."[68]

Though McKenzie considers this period as "ranking among the greatest failures of history,"[69] it is on grounds other than those of material progress. Almost all Western writers who wrote about Korea between 1910-1920 admired the sound currency, the improved roads and the afforestation, but on closer scrutiny we find that these Japanese achievements meant little in terms of greater welfare for the Korean people as a whole.

At the time of annexation more than eighty per cent of the population of Korea were farmers, who had, properly speaking, a natural, and not a monetary economy. "Sound" currency did not mean much to them. Admittedly, the old monetary system was bad, consisting of copper, silver, and nickel coins which had no fixed ratio of exchange among themselves. But the so-called "sound" Korean currency introduced by Baron Megata has never kept prices stable. Between 1907 and 1914 prices in Korea on the average doubled; if we take the level of prices in December 1914 as 100, we find that it stood at 369 in March 1920, i.e. in six years the value of the currency had depreciated by more than three and a half times; by 1925 it had fallen to 210, or almost by half; by 1931 the price level

[66] I do not know whether the Governor-General influenced Ladd's description or vice versa, but the *Annual Report* for 1911-12 on p. 12 contains the following statement: "Especially since the annexation have Koreans come to regard the Japanese as seniors and the latter to regard the former as juniors, and so their brotherhood is being cemented by mutual respect."

[67] *Chosen Keizai Nempo*, 1939, p. 80: the translation of the term is made according to the definition given in the *Kanwa taijiten* by Koyanagi.

[68] McKenzie, *op. cit.*, p. 183.

[69] *Ibid.*, p. 183.

was about 110, only one third of the level of 1920; by 1933 it rose to 150; by 1938 to 240; by 1940 to 360. The value of currency under the old inefficient, corrupt regime did not fluctuate as violently as did the "sound," "stable," currency introduced by Baron Megata.

Let us take the second achievement, "railways greatly extended and roads improved." We may recall Kennan's words, quoted above, concerning the increase in land values that was to follow this construction program. The reader will have noted also that meetings of Koreans for "agitation against the purchase of land for railways" were "amicably dispersed." In 1916, Dr. Yashino, professor of the Imperial University of Tokyo, described (in *Chuokoron*) after a trip to Korea, his impressions of road construction in the country in the following terms:

"Without consideration and mercilessly they [the Administration] have resorted to laws for the expropriation of land, the Koreans concerned being compelled to part with their family property for nothing. On many occasions they have also been forced to work in the construction of roads without receiving any wages. To make matters worse, they must work for nothing only on the days which are convenient to the officials, however inconvenient these days may be to the unpaid workers."[70]

How were these roads used? Here is a description by an American traveller in 1920:

"So perfect a road made the empty plateau look more desolate than ever. The dwellers in these squalid huts would never have built it; neither would the people of the valleys who used it only occasionally when they bartered with the people in the valleys beyond. The crooked trail that we could half make out in the rough grass at the side of the big road would do very well for such meager trade as the faraway town on the other side of the pass demanded. Just what, then, did the road mean? Korea's commerce did not necessitate it. This highway could be but one thing—a military road to fortify a conqueror's power."[71]

The good roads were there, but the poor inhabitants had nothing to carry on them.

"Afforestation pushed on a large scale," said F. A. McKenzie in 1920. "Reforestation of denuded countryside was undertaken in 1911, and by 1925, millions of seedlings had been planted," said P. H. Clyde in 1937; "Afforestation was pushed forward on a truly astounding scale, no less than half a bil-

[70] Quoted in H. Chung, *The Case of Korea*, pp. 110-111.
[71] Alice Tisdale, *A Korean Highroad*, as quoted in H. Chung, *op. cit.*, p. 109.

lion young trees set out by the Japanese forestry service on the bare, brown hillsides," wrote H. H. Gowen in 1938.

But these "billions" mean very little unless they are related to the number of trees annually cut down. Actually, the reforestation in Korea proceeded more slowly than the destruction of the standing forests (for details see Chapter VI).

These few examples of the "material progress" in Korea have been given in order to show how careful an investigator must be in reading Japanese official reports, and how often increased economic activity under colonial conditions is not accompanied by any improvement in the lot of the natives.

It is true that from 1910 to 1920 a certain growth of industry did take place in Korea. But this increase was very modest because the Administration did not wish to develop industries in Korea and permitted only such growth as was necessitated by the influx of the Japanese and the needs of Japanese commerce and transportation (repair shops, production of bricks, some foodstuffs produced locally, etc.). Immediately after the annexation, laws were published concerning the formation, control, and supervision of corporations—law so strict that it was practically impossible to establish new businesses. The Korean Government-General explained these restrictions as follows:

"Indeed, a much stricter control and supervision [of corporations] than that exercised in Japan over business conducted by corporations was really necessary in the peninsula, partly to guard Koreans lacking in business knowledge and experience against irresponsible schemers, and partly to guard Japanese or foreign capitalists, not sufficiently well-acquainted with the real state of things existing in the new territory, from unwarily investing in obscure enterprises, so that a healthy development of business activity might thereby be promoted.

"These regulations, however, were much criticized by certain business circles in Japan, if not altogether denounced, on the ground that such restrictions would discourage business enterprises."[72]

K. Takahashi quotes the chief of *Shokusankyoku* (Department of Industry), Hozumi, to the effect that corporations

[72] *Annual Report, 1915-16*, p. 113. The report also adds how much General Terauchi regretted such a state of affairs: "It is regrettable that, following the enforcement of the corporation regulations, reputable firms or capitalists in Japan have not as yet tried Korea as a field for the investment of their organized capital, especially in mining undertakings, although the Governor-General has personally exercised his efforts in inviting such sound capitalists." *Ibid.*, pp. 113-14.

which desired to establish branches in Korea could do this only with "extraordinary difficulties" during the Terauchi period, and adds that "after the annexation of Korea its industrial development was consciously checked."[73]

There remains the question of the Government-General's attempt to stamp out foreign influence. After the annexation, there was only one institution left in Korea that had foreign connections and that institution was the Christian Church (or, better, Churches). In the autumn of 1911 one hundred and thirty-five of the most influential Korean Christians were arrested on the charge that they had conspired to assassinate the Governor-General. Among those arrested was Baron Yun Chi-ho, a former member of the Korean Cabinet, President of the Southern Methodist College at Songdo, and Vice-President of the Korean Y.M.C.A.[74] Three of the accused persons died in prison, possibly as a result of tortures; nine were banished without trial; and out of one hundred twenty-three, one hundred and six were sentenced to imprisonment for from five to ten years.

However, this act aroused Christian circles in the United States where the case received much publicity. Appeals were made to the Japanese. Dr. W. W. Pinson, of the Southern Methodist Episcopal Church, made a special trip to Korea to investigate the case and describes the accused in the following way:

"One of the striking things about this body of prisoners is its personnel. If one is here looking for weak and cringing cowards or brazen desperadoes he will be disappointed. Instead, he will see men erect, manly, self-respecting and intelligent. There are many faces that bear the marks of unusual strength and nobility of character. As a whole they are a body of men of far better quality than one would expect to see in the same number of men anywhere in this country. On closer investigation it is made clear that the gendarmes have thrust their sickle in among the tallest wheat. These men do not belong to the criminal or irresponsible class of society. Most of them are Presbyterians, trained after the strictest sect of the Shorter Catechism. These are not the type of men to be guilty of such a plot as that with which they are charged. They are too intelligent. They might be capable of a desperate venture for a great cause, but they could not possibly undertake anything idiotic."[75]

[73] *Gendai Chosen Keizairon*, pp. 349-350.
[74] This was the same Yun Chi-ho who in Kennan's scheme was to save Korea with the help of Japanese policemen.
[75] *New York Herald*, September 29, 1912, where the full report was published. See also *The Korean Conspiracy Trial. Full Report of the Proceedings*, by the Special Correspondent of the *Japan Chronicle*, 1912, pp. 136.

The protests in the United States brought a revision of the case in the Court of Appeals which was instructed by the Governor-General to use "conciliatory methods."[76] The Court absolved ninety-nine and reduced the sentences of others, including Baron Yun Chi-ho. On the accusations abroad concerning tortures applied to the accused, the official report has the following to say:

"How then could anyone imagine that it is possible for officials under him [i.e., the Governor-General] to act in any other way than in accordance with the provisions of the law!"[77]

In other words, if tortures are not mentioned in Japanese laws, they do not exist.[78]

In October 1916, Count Masakata Terauchi resigned from the post of Governor-General to become the Prime Minister of Japan (for twenty-three months), and was succeeded by Count Hasegawa, former Commander of the Japanese troops in Korea. During Hasegawa's governorship the land survey, begun in 1910, was finished in 1918 at a cost of thirty million yen. This survey led to a revision of the land tax, encouraged the purchase of land because the rights of the owner became more certain, and brought to light lands which had not been taxed before. Only since that year have Korean agricultural statistics been on a sound basis. And yet it may be questioned whether this was the best way of spending thirty million yen, at a time when the Government-General was annually spending only 300,000 yen on schools and 400,000 yen on hospitals, and when the total annual budget of all the local governments was only a few million yen.

As far as public life was concerned, the regime of oppression bequeathed by Terauchi continued unabated under Hasegawa. But by 1918 a new spirit of nationalism was making itself felt in all colonial countries. President Wilson's "Fourteen Points" were being universally discussed, and news of them reached the Korean people, who had not forgotten their independence in the ten years that had passed since the annexation. They responded to the ideal of national self-deter-

[76] *Annual Report,* 1911-12.
[77] H. Chung, *op. cit.,* p. 163.
[78] This case shows that the pressure of public opinion in foreign countries was able to produce positive results for Korea. Unfortunately, too many believed that Japan should not be criticized lest the position of the Koreans be worsened.

mination and sought to achieve this self-determination for themselves. Their leaders were well aware that an armed rebellion was impossible—they had no arms. But even without an army, the Koreans were strong enough to demonstrate to the whole world that they were worthy of freedom.

After the funeral of the old Korean Emperor, who died on January 20, 1919, thirty-three distinguished Koreans, representatives of the entire country, prepared and signed a "Proclamation of Korean Independence." On March 1, this proclamation was read before throngs of people; speeches were made, Korean flags waved and there were shouts of *Mansei*. At least half a million Koreans took part in the demonstrations which spread from Seoul all over the country.[79] The Japanese Administration was taken by surprise, although the spy system was probably better developed in Korea than anywhere in the world, and the Administration knew that something was in the offing. Despite this, so well organized were the demonstrations, so profound was the devotion of the Koreans to their national cause, that the police were kept in the dark concerning the nature, purposes, and dimensions of the movement—and this increased the fury of the police and army chiefs. The Japanese Administration suppressed the movement in a most ferocious way in two months.[80] [81]

According to the Japanese Administration, 553 Korean "agitators" were killed, 1,409 wounded and 19,054 (of whom 471 were women) imprisoned during the suppression.[82] It is not clear whether the 10,592 demonstrators who were flogged were included in the above figures or not. 11,831 Koreans remained in prisons for nearly two years after their arrest, awaiting their

[79] According to the official *Annual Report* for 1918-21, pp. 158-9, "the aggregate number of rioters approximated half a million," and there is no doubt that this official estimate is an under-estimate. The total number of adult Korean men was between four and five million that year.

[80] James Dale Van Buskirk, in his book *Korea, Land of the Dawn* (New York, 1931), states: "This independence movement was put down by military measures that were not free from atrocities similar to those reported from other lands where militarism has enforced its will."

[81] Representatives of the Koreans abroad affirmed at the time that suppression of the movement took much longer, and the official reports indirectly confirm this by the following statement (*Annual Report*, 1922, p. 196): "Though there are still some rebellious Koreans secretly trying to mislead the people by scattering wild rumors or seditious writings, their efforts are foredoomed to failure."

[82] *Annual Report*, 1918-1921, pp. 158-9. It is interesting, by the way, to note that for three years after the rebellion the *Annual Report* did not appear.

trial.[83] Korean writers give the number of those killed and executed at over 7,000.[84] But even from the official figures it is clear that this was a genuine national movement.[85]

The Japanese Administration had great difficulties in explaining the movement, the more so because in each *Annual Report* prior to the rebellion it had emphasized the love and loyalty of Korea for its older brother, Japan. It blamed German influence, and the Koreans' belief that a speedy German victory was near [in March 1919!]; in the same breath it blamed Bolshevik influence and, not least of all, President Wilson's doctrine of self-determination for small nations, "the full meaning of which they [the Koreans] were apparently unable to grasp" . . .[86]

The movement had important repercussions abroad, especially in the United States, and even in Japan, where for the first time the population heard that something was wrong in their "thriving" colony. General Hasegawa was recalled and in August 1919 Admiral Makoto Saito (Baron and later Viscount) was appointed as the new Governor-General. On his assumption of office he announced the adoption of a new Japanese policy and stated that a liberal and righteous administration would be established in the peninsula.

[83] H. Chung, *op. cit.*, p. 316.

[84] *Ibid.* In this book there is an excellent description of the movement and its suppression.

[85] P. H. Clyde asserts that "casualties among both Koreans and Japanese were numerous" (*op. cit.*, p. 441). This statement is misleading and claims more than the Japanese do. Here is a table of casualties on both sides according to the official statistics.

	Killed	Wounded
Officials	8	158
Civilians	1	28
Agitators	553	1,409

Source: *Annual Report*, 1918-1921, pp. 158-159.

Now, among the officials and civilians there was a certain number of Koreans; among the agitators there were no Japanese. The cause of the disparity is clear: the demonstrators were unarmed and their intentions were peaceable; when the army and police attacked them, burning their homes and entire villages, they responded in some places with stones. But even the Japanese do not speak of "numerous casualties." The official report states: "In the course of time, however, their [the rebels'] attitude took a dangerous turn, mobs began to attack and destroy official buildings, many police officers and local officials were roughly handled and some even killed" (*ibid.*, p. 194).

[86] *Annual Report*, 1936-37, p. 176.

"The principles upon which the reforms were based were: stabilization of peace and order, deference to public opinion, abatement of officialism, reform in administration, improvement of general living, and advancement of popular culture and welfare. And to accomplish these essential points definite plans were drawn up regarding the following:
1. The post of the Governor-General to be opened not only for military; but also for civilians;
2. Non-discrimination between Japanese and Koreans;
3. Simplification of laws and regulations;
4. Promptness in conducting state business;
5. Decentralization of power;
6. Revision of local organization;
7. Respect for native culture and customs;
8. Freedom of speech, meeting, and press;
9. Spread of education and development of industry;
10. Reorganization of the police force;
11. Expansion of medical and sanitary organizations;
12. Guidance of popular thought;
13. Opportunity for men of talent;
14. Friendly feeling between Japanese and Koreans."[87]

This program of reforms evoked a burst of enthusiasm in certain groups abroad. We have seen how some writers admired Marquis Ito and Count Terauchi and quoted their promises. Now it was Admiral Makoto Saito's turn. According to Professor Clyde,

he "was recognized as a great administrator and a man of generous and humane character . . . His appointment symbolized a new and better day for Korea . . . The results of this changed policy were soon evident."[88]

Also;

"This marked improvement in Korean political affairs after 1919 may be traced to a number of excellent reforms and to the spirit and manner of their execution."[89]

A few lines further on, Saito's Administration is called "humane and tolerant," and whatever difficulties existed were explained as due to the Koreans' refusal to cooperate.

"Their minds remaining fixed on the ideal of national independence, they withheld both interest and participation in any reform program introduced by any Japanese administration."

[87] *Annual Report*, 1936-37, pp. 7-8.
[88] Clyde, *op. cit.*, p. 441.
[89] *Ibid.*, pp. 442-443.

Alleyne Ireland writes:

"During the past year [1925 or 1926] the news from Korea justifies the hope that a trend in this direction [cooperation of Koreans with the Japanese] has already set in. To whatever extent it exists, the credit is due chiefly to the humane and conciliatory attitude of Governor-General Saito toward the Korean people, and to the wise measures which, for more than six years, have been the fruit of an unstinting employment of his unusual energy and of his still more unusual administrative talents."[90]

The demonstrations that took place in the spring of 1919 opened the eyes of the Japanese to one important fact. The official report expressed it this way:

"Generally speaking . . . the Koreans of the upper and middle classes, including those in government employ and men of local influence, were far too prudent to take part in the disturbance, while many of them openly expressed their views against the independence movement."[91]

The Japanese acted promptly to capitalize on this situation. At the time of the annexation in 1910 they had tried—more or less successfully—to bribe the Korean nobility. Now they attempted to bribe the upper and middle classes. Unfortunately for the Japanese, the possibilities in that direction were much more restricted in 1919 than they had been in 1910 because, first, Japan herself was not a country enjoying political freedom, and, of course, a Japanese colony could not be given more freedom than existed in Japan. Secondly, whatever the concessions, there would always remain a small group even among the upper and middle classes which would demand nothing less than full independence and would use any freedom given them to that end, so that too much freedom could not be given without endangering the whole system. In 1910 the problem was to bribe a small number of the nobility; in 1919—to bribe a larger number of members of the upper and middle classes which are not hereditary and are constantly acquiring new

[90] *The New Korea,* New York, 1926, p. 61. Here we may add a panegyric from a German source—that of Dr. Richard Goldschmidt: "He [Saito] has understood how to win the confidence of the peaceful and kind people through justice and a high ethical conception of his duty, and how to take the first steps toward real reconciliation." (*Neu Japan,* Berlin, 1927, p. 288; translated from the German by the author). Also: "From an economic point of view, Japanese domination is, undoubtedly, a blessing for the population which, of course, is much better off under a strong and orderly rule than in the corrupt old state." (*ibid.,* p. 289).

[91] *Annual Report,* 1921-22, p. 193.

recruits from below—and losing some members. Thirdly, by that time vested colonial interests had arisen which would not countenance any change in their status—or any new competition.

Before examining the course and character of the "reforms," one fact about Saito's administration may be noted, which is not mentioned elsewhere in Western literature. Admiral Saito was appointed Governor-General in August 1919 and immediately was confronted with a difficult situation: the country experienced a drought, "the severest for fifty years."[92] In the official report it is stated that the new government undertook the following measures in connection with the crop failure: it appropriated 1,700,000 yen for road building; 400,000 yen for subsidies for private enterprises; four million yen for loans at a low rate of interest; and, finally, one million yen for the purchase of food for famine sufferers. As a result of these measures, "practically not a single person died from starvation."

Official statistics show a crop failure in 1919, as compared with normal years, of about 16-18 per cent, which does not fit in with the description of the drought as the "severest for fifty years." However, even if the official figures are correct, it is evident that the shortage was acute. If we assume that half of the indirect appropriations and all of the one million yen directly appropriated went to the relief of starving farmers, this would amount to about four million yen, a sum sufficient at that period to buy only about 200,000 *koku* of cereals, or only one-fifteenth of the total deficit. How under these conditions "practically not a single person died from starvation" is not clear; but what is clear is that Saito's new administration can hardly be called very humane under the circumstances, particularly since the annual revenue of the Government-General at that time was about 150 million yen.

Among the new measures introduced into Korea by the Saito administration was one opening the post of Governor-General to Japanese civilians, and almost every writer has referred to this "important" fact.[93] However, this promise has never been realized. After Admiral Saito came General Ugaki, General

[92] *The New Administration of Chosen,* published by the Korean Government-General, 1921, p. 50.

[93] F. G. Carpenter, *Japan and Korea,* p. 260: "But since the present policy of the Japanese toward greater liberalism in the administration of Korea, the post is now open to a civilian."

Yamanashi, Admiral Saito again, General Ugaki, General Minami, and most recently General Koiso.

As to non-discrimination between Japanese and Koreans, and opportunity for men of talent—these innovations remained in the realm of promises. In fact, after 1919, the situation gradually grew worse in this respect. At the time of annexation some Koreans remained as governors of provinces, though their actual position was scarcely more than that of figureheads. However, by 1940, twelve out of thirteen provincial governors were Japanese. In the list of more than one thousand high officials in Korea given in *Chosen Nenkan*, 1941, it is difficult to find more than a dozen Koreans. And this does not represent something new, a sharp break with the liberal policy of Admiral Saito, but rather a gradual strengthening of the policy that started in 1905 under the "liberal" Ito and continued under the "militarist" Terauchi who declared that through "judicious guidance and direction . . . the goal of complete harmony and assimilation" in Korea would not be difficult to attain, and that the "essential point lies in eradication of distinctions between Japan and Korea"—almost the same words as those used by the "liberal" Saito. But the government apparatus was becoming more and more Japanese, with Koreans relegated to the position of clerks and janitors.

KOREANS AND JAPANESE IN HIGH POSITIONS IN THE KOREAN GOVERNMENT[94]

	Koreans	Japanese
1909, (December) total	650	337
1920, in Korean Government-General	13	152
1920, officials attached to Government-General	318	693
1920, total	331	845

As for the "simplification of laws and regulations" and "promptness in conducting state business," these reforms were limited in practice to abolition of uniforms and swords worn by all officials, including teachers; fewer periodical reports to the Government-General, and permission to the provincial governors to appoint or dismiss some subordinate officials (below a certain rank) without first asking the approval of the Governor-General.

[94] Data for 1909 from the official *Material Progress of Korea for the Last Five Years, 1910*. Data for 1920 from the official *New Administration in Chosen, 1920*. No later figures are available. As was mentioned, the list of *Chosen Nenkan*, 1941, shows that by now only a dozen Koreans are left in such positions.

The examples given by K. Takahashi show that there was little change in the methods of the Government-General. When a plan for increased rice exports to Japan was worked out, the local authorities were "advised" to form *suiri kumiai* (Irrigation Associations). The people were compelled to form these *kumiai* even in North Korea where no paddy fields existed.

Similarly, when the Government-General decided to encourage sericulture in Korea, it planned how many mulberry trees were necessary for this, arbitrarily assigned numbers to provinces, districts, and villages, and distributed the saplings, paying no attention to the difference in conditions, or to whether there was suitable land available.[95]

The next reform—decentralization of power—consisted in placing police and sanitary officers, who formerly were independent of local authorities, under the Governors of provinces. Actually this was rationalization rather than decentralization since it was found that the former situation, under which the Governors had to ask the Governor-General for the use of police, was cumbersome and in some cases dangerous because it delayed the use of the police force and made the Governors less disposed to use it.

"Revision of local organization" was an attempt on the part of the Japanese to induce rich Koreans to cooperate with them. Municipal and village councils were made elected bodies, but with important limitations on the franchise which lessened the significance of the change. Thus, in 1920, the Japanese, who made up only 25 per cent of the municipal population, elected 203 members of the municipal councils out of 268.[96]

With regard to "respect for native culture and customs," unfortunately, for Korea, the Government here took a backward rather than a forward step. The customs and culture which it undertook to respect were the most primitive and repellent—permission to have graves in one's own yard and to kill animals in the manner of old Korea. This was no liberalization of policy but an attempt to secure the loyalty of the most backward and reactionary Korean groups.

As to freedom of speech, assembly and press, anyone who is acquainted with the Korean situation knows that under Japa-

[95] K. Takahashi, *op. cit.*, pp. 79-80.
[96] See also Chapter XIII.

nese domination such freedoms are non-existent in Korea. The official description of the situation is as follows:

"Under the old regime the issue of newspapers was limited to those few already in existence, and it was practically impossible for any one to start a new journal, but such restrictions being thought unnecessarily severe and too great a prevention to a full expression of public opinion, permission was given from December 1919 onward for the publication of several new daily papers by natives or Japanese. Restrictions on public meetings were also much mitigated; and even political meetings, the holding of which was formerly absolutely forbidden, were permitted in certain circumstances. Freedom of meeting being thus generally recognized so far as it was not inimical to the public peace, associations of every description have since sprung up and number at present three thousand, some of which are of a purely political nature. Meetings are held by them everywhere and almost every day, and comparatively few of them are reported as having been ordered suspended or dispersed by the authorities."[97]

Actually, in 1920 three newspapers were permitted to be published in Keijo (Seoul) and "some few papers in the provinces."[98] However, almost all of them were published by the Japanese Administration (directly or indirectly), while independent Korean publishers spent most of their time paying fines and going to prison. No improvement has occurred since that time.[99]

As for organizations, those mentioned in the official report were business, religious, and sports organizations, none of which was political in nature unless it had been organized by the Government-General, with Japanese in commanding positions. In this respect, again, there has been no change whatever since the regime of Terauchi and Hasegawa. The Korean Government-General, however, does not publish statistics of societies or public meetings authorized by the police, or of arrests of persons convicted of anti-government activities, of "dangerous thoughts" or similar crimes. For fourteen years (1921-1935) the official reports had a chapter on the *Police* containing the same sentence to the effect that "since 1919 the people have been aware of the futility of any movement of insurrection"; and some foreign writers have taken this statement at its face value. Only the report for 1934-35 and the year following mentioned the events of 1923: wholesale arrests, nationalist struggle, socialist and communist activities, and the like.

[97] *Annual Report* 1918-21, p. 8.
[98] *Annual Report* 1918-21, pp. 7-8.
[99] See chapter on *Culture*.

Prior to the reforms of the Saito Administration, the Korean police force consisted of "police" and "gendarmerie" (military police). According to the official report,

"the policy of using gendarmerie [in Korea] as the principal police force, except in war time, was much criticized at home and abroad, but it may be said that, had it not been for this half-military, half-police system, peace and order could never have been preserved during the time of strain. However, it was clear that indefinite continuation of the system adopted as a temporary expedient would be unjustifiable and undesirable, and the Government itself desired to discard it. The police system then [1919] underwent a sweeping change. They [the gendarmes] were dispensed with . . . this was completed four months after the reform."[100]

What actually happened, however, was that the gendarmes were now called policemen, and some new ones were brought from Japan:

"To fill the shortage caused by the adoption of a truly civil police system, about 1,500 former gendarmes and about 1,500 police officers and men from Japan were taken into service, in addition to which more than three thousand men were recruited in Japan and a number of auxiliary Korean gendarmes engaged as policemen."[101]

The results are interesting. Before the reform, the combined force of gendarmes and police was 14,358[102] but in 1922 the total force was 20,771, an increase of 45 per cent; before the reform, Japanese constituted 42 per cent of the total force, in 1922—58.6 per cent. Before the reform the Japanese officers constituted 58.7 per cent of the gendarmerie and police officers, and Koreans—41.3 per cent; after the reform the corresponding figures were 73.3 per cent and 26.7 per cent.

Such were the remarkable results of the police reform. Concerning education, industrial development, and health services, more will be said later. Here it may be mentioned that the creation of "friendly feeling between Japanese and Koreans" consisted of showing Japanese films in Korea and of organizing excursions of Korean teachers and businessmen to Japan.

In addition to these reforms during Admiral Saito's Administration one significant fact deserves mention. In the first year of his administration, the sown area under poppy cultivation (for opium) in Korea was 90 hectares; while in the last year it was 738 hectares.

[100] *Annual Report,* 1923-24, p. 141.
[101] *The New Administration in Chosen* (official publication) p. 57.
[102] *Ibid.*

Political Movements after 1919.

The independence movement was cruelly and ruthlessly suppressed in 1919, but its after-effects were felt in Korea for many years.

"Rumor has raised its head anew each year as March 1, the day of the 'rising' or August 29, the anniversary of the annexation, drew near, that something would occur, and the atmosphere has appeared threatening . . ."[103]

Immediately after the repressions there was organized in Keijo the Chosen Labor Mutual Help Society, the forerunner of the proletarian movement.[104]

"Innumerable Young Men's Associations were formed in Korea in the summer of 1920, and they united into a League of Korean Young Men's Associations, which, however, was rapidly dispersed by the Government. In 1922, a Union of Proletarian Comrades (*Musan Doshikai*) with clearly socialist principles was organized under the slogan 'Proletarians, defend your living rights'."[105]

According to the *Annual Reports*, the Korean nationalists cooperated with the socialists for the common cause of political emancipation and "availed themselves of every opportunity to arouse a national spirit among Koreans."[106] In 1924 a General Union of Chosen Workers and Farmers was organized, but its meetings were immediately forbidden, and "the new organs existed only in name." But these organizations, though "existing only in name," started building units throughout Korea. Soon after, the Korean Communist Party and the Korean Communist Young Men's Association made their appearance.[107] In November 1925, "the greater part of their associates" were arrested at Shingishu. Others succeeded them and restored the organization but were also arrested in June 1926, together with conspirators who sought to use the state funeral of Prince Yi

---

[103] *Annual Report*, 1923-24, p. 145. Takahashi (*op. cit.*, p. 113) asserts that for many years the independence movement worried the Japanese Government. "It was a cancer for the consecutive administrations . . ."

[104] *Sekai Nenkan*, 1939, p. 164.

[105] *Ibid.*

[106] *Annual Report*, 1934-35, p. 177.

[107] It is important to note that communism and other "dangerous thoughts" came to Korea from Japan. "What greatly concerns me are the Korean students and laborers crossing to Japan proper who are apt to introduce various radical thoughts into Chosen after being infected in Japan Proper." (from a speech of Governor-General Ugaki, made in 1933).

Wang for a demonstration. New members, braving prosecution, arrest, torture and execution, again restored the organization but were arrested in Keijo in 1929. At the same time, according to the *Annual Reports*, wholesale arrests of communists were made in Shingishu and Heijo. But the members of the Communist Party, "in spite of repeated arrests," continued their propaganda and organizational work. We know from the authorities that during these years the nationalist, socialist, and communist movements "led the thoughts of young men into more dangerous ways, and many disgraceful occurrences took place," but we are left in the dark as to the nature of these disgraceful occurrences.

In the winter of 1929-30, a new incident flared up. A Japanese student in Koshu (Kwangju, the capital of South Zenra Province) publicly made an insulting offer to a Korean school girl. The Korean students demanded an apology which was denied. Thereupon, they went on strike, paraded the streets and sang national songs. There were also clashes between the Japanese and Korean students. The authorities held a large number of the Korean students for trial, but none of the Japanese. Rumors spread through the country that several Korean students had been killed during these clashes and that others had died in prison after torture. As a result, Korean students throughout the country went on strike, staged demonstrations, and demanded that the students arrested in Koshu be released. The police arrested hundreds of the demonstrators, but the population joined in the demonstrations. Prisons were filled with arrested Koreans, and the methods used in dealing with the demonstrators were the same as in 1919, although at that time the Governor-General was not General Hasegawa, but Admiral Saito.

As mentioned above, centers of rebellion continued to function in the northern part of the country after the repression of the insurrections of 1907-1912. Soon a new haven for Korean refugees was found. Expropriation of the land compelled many Koreans to emigrate, chiefly to Manchuria and Siberia. Large numbers of Koreans settled in the Chientao region, across the Tumen River, where in some places the Koreans formed a majority of the population. From that time onward, the *Annual Reports* invariably contained one sentence: "However, bands of Koreans living across the Yalu did at times succeed in crossing the border and wantonly committed murder, arson, and pillage in the districts invaded by them."[108] But the Koreans lived in Chinese territory and the Japanese were powerless to control them, though they made many attempts to do so. The bands which crossed the frontier were by no means ordinary criminals, as may be seen from the following statement:

"Moreover, they have frequently sent secret emissaries for the assassination of Government and public officials, and in some cases have even managed to accomplish their wicked designs."[109]

In 1920, according to the Japanese version,

"Korean outlaws formed themselves into a band, four hundred strong, and, aided by Chinese bandits and Russian Bolsheviks, attacked Hunchun [a town on Chinese soil] in September and October, 1920, during which months they set fire to and destroyed the Japanese consulate and some Japanese houses, looted valuable articles, and killed many Japanese, Koreans, and Chinese, including women and children. At the same time, refractory Koreans in North Chientao began to move, menacing the safety of Japanese and law-abiding Koreans living there. Under these circumstances, the Government dispatched a military expedition . . . After a campaign of a few weeks the expedition succeeded in suppressing the Korean outlaws. About five thousand of them surrendered . . ."[110]

However, Korean sources reveal a different story. They say that the Japanese, having been defeated by a band of Koreans and unable to punish them, "wreaked their vengeance upon wholly peaceful people in the Kando [Chientao] region. They slaughtered four thousand Koreans and burned their bodies in the center of the principal town."[111] The behavior of the Imperial Japanese Army in the Russian Far East in 1918-1922 and in China in the present war lends credence to the Korean version. This punishment of the Koreans on *Chinese* territory took place under Admiral Saito's Administration. When the Japanese occupied Manchuria in 1931-32, they immediately undertook the "pacification" of Chientao:

"Since the establishment of Manchukuo it became possible to clear radically Chientao region, the base of operation of anti-Japanese plotters."[112]

[108] See, for example, the *Annual Report* for 1926-27, p. 158.
[109] *The New Administration in Chosen*, p. 73.
[110] *The New Administration in Chosen*, p. 73.
[111] *Korea Must Be Free,* prepared by the Korean Commission to America and Europe, 1930, p. 26.
[112] K. Takahashi, *op. cit.*, p. 26.

But this did not diminish Korean resistance. The last available official Japanese report states that "though the bandits, centering around the Korean Revolutionary Army" in Manchuria, fighting together with nationalist and communist detachments against the Japanese "have been greatly weakened by the extension of the police force coupled with scarcity of food and materials," they still "have been making attempts to enter Tyosen (new transcription for Chosen) through frontier districts. Several police guards have fallen victims of their attacks."[113] Their numbers were estimated by the Japanese at sixteen thousand.

Elsewhere, too, Korean terrorists were active. In 1932 they made an unsuccessful attack on the life of the Japanese Emperor in Tokyo (the case of Sakuradamo) and an attempt on the life of General Shirakawa. Underground activities were widespread, especially in North and South Kankyo provinces, and even wholesale arrests in 1936 could not stop them. Koreans in China issued a call to Koreans to go to China to obtain military training there. Nine Korean revolutionary organizations united and formed the *Tyosen Minzoku Kakumeito* (Korean National Revolutionary Party), and the Korean Provisional Government, first organized in Shanghai after the suppression of the rebellion of 1919, then moved to Hangchow, now is functioning in Chungking, has an army fighting against the Japanese and claims to be the oldest Government-in-Exile in the world.

This information, meager as it may be, clearly shows that the masses of the Korean population were not reconciled to Japanese domination and were not inclined to follow the advice of those moderate Koreans who wished "to develop the inner resources of the Korean nation and to wait for a more favorable opportunity in the future."[114] The Korean students

[113] *Annual Report,* 1936-37, pp. 178-79.
[114] The *Annual Report,* 1934-35, p. 177. This advice coincides with that of Herbert Welch, former Methodist Bishop to Korea and Japan, as given in the *Korean Student Bulletin,* May 1929. He said that the strategic need for Korea was courage, hard work, and initiative. He thought that with Korean capital and Korean trained skill it would be possible to develop the natural resources of Korea. He believed that with natural and human resources and conditions of law and order there was no reason why the progress of Korea should not be steady and gratifying. The Japanese and Japanese rule were not mentioned in his advice to the students.

in the United States, coming naturally from the upper income groups in Korea, took the same "moderate" position.

"Commonly speaking, to die for his or her country is a patriotism, and of course it is true, but it cannot be the right kind of patriotism for our young people . . . A true patriotism of Korean young men and women of today is not the dead penalty, but the living service. By dying you accomplish nothing . . . Let us study what Korea needs most today. The political independence? Yes, it is true, but there are also many other things just as important, and needed, if not more, as the political independence. And they are social reformation, a strong religious foundation, and above all the development of industries, by which the people and the whole nation may gain the economic independence. Unless we gain our economic independence we will not be able to gain our political independence . . ."[115]

But just how this economic independence could be won under existing conditions was not made clear. In this respect a letter to the same journal provides a remarkable refutation. It is quoted here almost in full because it describes real conditions in Korea in 1928, conditions which in many respects had changed only for the worse up to the present war:

"Some time ago a vernacular newspaper reported that there were practically one thousand applicants for twenty secretarial positions needed in a local government office. Furthermore, every position of possible income here is occupied by the Japanese. Even the running of a street car is done mostly by the Japanese . . . In turn, masses of the able Koreans are out of work. Even many of the well-educated Koreans just returned from abroad are lingering around, simply because there is no place to work, nor a possibility to do anything in this tightened environment. I never have imagined such an antagonism between the theory and the practice. All this economic and political pressure has led the people to a state of unrest and anarchy . . . Education means nothing here. The young people are going to school because they have nothing else to do in the village or the city . . . The graduation from a school in itself brings them nothing . . ."[116]

And this situation was not only characteristic of educated youth. The position of the Korean farmers was described by Governor-General Ugaki in 1933 as follows:[117]

"The result [of former oppressions] was shortage of food . . . In the poverty season of spring[118] from lack of food they would dig out and eat

[115] Editorial in the *Korean Student Bulletin*, official organ of the Korean Student Federation of North America, March 1926.
[116] By C. C. Hahn, *Korean Student Bulletin*, December 1928.
[117] *Thriving Chosen*, 1935, p. 82.
[118] Called so in Korea because by that season no grain is left for the farmer and his family.

the roots of trees on the mountains and fields or would beg from every door to keep themselves alive. In short, there are very few Korean peasants who could hope to succeed brilliantly in the future on account of their poverty in the past and of their suffering in the present. Generally speaking, the reason why we could not remedy these bad conditions and easily save the farmers from poverty, since the time of annexation, has been the lack of self-confidence among the Korean farmers."[119]

This description of the plight of the Korean farmers coming from so authoritative a source as the Governor-General himself epitomizes Japanese achievements in the peninsula in the quarter of a century since the annexation.

The situation was scarcely any better in industry. Living conditions of the working population will be dealt with in the chapter on industry. Here we wish only to show how difficult it was for anyone to become an entrepreneur. It is true that in 1920 the early corporation law was repealed, but, according to Takahashi,[120] the new official policy was to encourage only small-scale industries working on local raw materials—and even this only after careful investigation by the authorities. Among the "desirable" industries enumerated were firecrackers, mats, lacquer ware, bamboo ware, willow ware, straw ware, etc. The decisive change in Japanese industrial policy in Korea came only after the establishment of "Manchukuo." By this time the militarists had already made plans for the coming campaign in Asia, and Korea was slated to play an important part in the Japanese war economy. A rapid development of Korean industry did occur after 1931, but it would be a mistake to think that this development meant a fundamental change for the Koreans. The huge new plants built or planned were Japanese enterprises in which Koreans could hope only to be employed as workers.

At the same time, war brought to Korea a further deterioration of living conditions, greater control over all kinds of activities, compulsory savings to be invested in Japanese bonds, compulsory participation in the "spiritual" mobilization of patriotic anti-communist organizations, which now have three

[119] In the same publication (p. 33) there are given budgets of three "representative Korean farmers," each one of which shows (1) a deficit (income below expenditures by 10-20 yen) and (2) "shortage of foodstuffs." Such has been the lot of the "representative" farmers who make up 75 to 80 per cent of the population, as given in the official publication ironically entitled *Thriving Chosen*.

[120] *Op. cit.*, pp. 349-350.

million "members," permission to volunteer for the war against the Chinese, "enthusiastically welcomed" by the population; and huge meetings at which the oath *Naisen Ittai* ("Japan and Korea as one body") is sworn in Japanese. These developments stand out against a background of a failure of crops in 1939, when the rice crop was only 58 per cent of that in the preceding year.

The war brought new sufferings to the Korean people, but it may be assumed that it has also brought new hopes for their eventual liberation. In 1935, Hozumi, head of the Production Department of the Korean Government-General, declared at a conference in Tokyo that after the occupation of Manchuria and the rebuff to the League of Nations and the Great Powers the Japanese could now expect greater cooperation from the Koreans who had formerly believed that the Japanese Government was weak.[121] If this reasoning is correct, we may assume that the reverse is also true, and that every item of news (or rumor) about failures or defeats of the Japanese Army is bound to intensify Korean opposition to the Japanese regime.

In connection with recent Korean history two questions are worthy of consideration. The first is: why have so many Western writers shown partiality to the Japanese on the Korean question? It would appear that this represents a conscious or unconscious acceptance of the theory that some peoples are incapable of ruling themselves, and that other peoples are endowed with special ability to rule such peoples, i.e., a fascist or Nazi theory, though sometimes carefully masked by high-sounding phrases.

H. B. Drake was quite outspoken in this respect when in 1931 he wrote:

"The fact remains that Japan found Korea in a state of apathetic exhaustion due partly at least . . . to misrule of the native Korean court, and from this apathetic exhaustion Japan is striving, with all her resources of ingenuity and power, to lift the country to the level of a modern nation . . . But all the Korean sees is that, whereas water was free, he must now pay three yen a year, and that he may only chop such wood for his house and his fire as the authorities permit . . . Well, what can you do with such a people? One can sympathize with the Japanese irritation; indeed, one wonders why they do not retire and leave the Koreans to themselves. The obvious answer to that is that Korea is strategically necessary and commercially profitable. But there is another, more fundamental one, the

[121] Takahashi, *op. cit.*, pp. 69-70.

answer which Japan, sincerely or not, prefers to make, the answer, indeed, which the British make when questioned concerning India. Left to themselves the Koreans would rot, which would affect not Korea alone but the whole world. Not that Korea is very vast or very vital. To allow India to rot, for instance, would be a much more serious proposition. But the principle is the same. No nation, however insignificant, can be allowed to fall into neglect and decay. And this is an essential justification of the Japanese rule in Korea . . . The Koreans . . . show not the least aptitude for organized control. If a people continues to be badly governed it is because they have it in them to be badly governed. Actively or passively they must be held responsible, and not weakly pitied as innocent victims of an evil beyond their power, and the Koreans are such a people. One is tempted to couple them with the Chinese, possibly the Russians, and to form a theory that certain races, like certain individuals, are lacking simply in the qualities necessary for industry. And in either case such a lack can be made good from outside. Brains for organization can be imported like coal or steel. And not merely brains for organization, but that peculiar gift for judicial rectitude and political honesty which is the portion in some measure of all western nations, but in the East of the Japanese alone."[122]

This "theory" illustrates the underlying idea. Japan is now attempting to spread the blessings of her "gift for judicial rectitude and political honesty" over China and Southeast Asia, just as Germany has attempted to spread hers over Soviet Russia and the conquered nations of Europe.

The second question is the influence of the colonial regimes in Korea, Formosa—and, later, in Manchuria—on Japan itself. There is not yet enough material available to show this influence. However, it is clear that the enslavement of the Koreans and Chinese had much to do with the strangulation of the weak shoots of Japanese liberalism. It was in Formosa, Korea, and Manchuria that the Japanese army built its organization uncontrolled by the Diet or any civilian authority; it was there that the taste to rule over alien peoples deprived of civil rights was acquired; and it was there that fascist ideology and plans of further conquests appeared and ripened.

[122] Drake, *Korea of the Japanese*, New York, 1931, pp. 146-149.

CHAPTER IV

POPULATION

There are two sets of figures for the Korean population—current statistical estimates for every year since the Japanese annexation and the censuses of population, taken once in five years beginning with 1925. Usually there is a difference between these two sets of figures in all countries.

POPULATION OF KOREA
(in thousands)

	Census Statistics (on October 1)	Current Estimates	Difference
1925	19,523	19,014	509
1930	21,058	20,257	801
1935	22,899	21,891	1,008
1940	24,326	23,000[a](approx.)	1,300 (approx.)

Source: *Takumu Tokei*, and *Chosen Nenkan*.

[a] The figure for 1940 is not yet available; however, the figure for 1939 and the amount of natural increase for the same year is available, so our estimate cannot be more than 100,000 above or below the official figure.

This table shows that the census figures consistently exceed the figures of current statistical estimates, and that the difference has been increasing with the years. It is substantial: 4.6 per cent in 1935 and probably as high as 5.7 in 1940, and it is interesting to note that it is larger in the case of men than of women. The first question which arises is, which set of figures is more accurate? The comparison of the data of current estimates with that of the censuses shows that current estimates rise immediately after the census (censuses are taken on October 1, current statistics as of December 31); and that these rises are so large (4-5 per cent in one year) that they can be explained only in one way: the authorities adjust their current statistical figures to those of the census, though they still lag behind. This would indicate that the authorities consider the census figures more accurate. Later we shall touch upon the question of the possible cause of the discrepancy. Here it is sufficient to note that (1) the annual statistics are rough estimates which are adjusted by the authorities as much as 5 per cent and even 6 per cent in one year and are therefore not suitable for calculations where greater accuracy is necessary; (2) they are persistently below the census figures by 3-4 per cent, and the difference is increasing.

Let us compare the figures of the population for the first years after annexation.

POPULATION OF KOREA 1909-1917
(in thousands)

	Population according to current estimates	Difference as compared with preceding year Absolute	Per Cent
1909	13,091		
1910	13,313	222	1.70
1911	14,056	743	5.58
1912	14,827	771	5.20
1913	15,459	632	4.26
1914	15,930	471	3.05
1915	16,278	348	2.19
1916	16,648	370	2.27
1917	16,669	21	0.13

Again we see that population increases in one year reach as high a figure as 5.58 per cent—a most unlikely figure. The net immigration of Japanese in any of these years was never more than 25,000, i.e. it could not cause such increases, and since there was no other large-scale immigration into Korea which would account for them, the conclusion may be drawn that the population of Korea in 1910 was underestimated by at least two million. This is important because it shows that the population statistics given out in the first few years after annexation were gross underestimates, though so many authors used them as if they were census figures. After annexation, the population of Korea increased from about 15 million to 24.3 million in 1940—an increase of about 60-65 per cent in thirty years, or of 1.8-1.9 per cent a year (a geometric average)—a high increase, though not exceptionally high; Costa Rica, Guatemala, Salvador, and Palestine have a higher rate of increase, and Egypt, Argentina, and Bulgaria have had about the same rate. The present population of Korea is double that of Argentina or Canada and is almost equal to that of Spain. This means that, given a corresponding development of her economy, an independent Korea may occupy an important place in the comity of nations.

Distribution

The following table shows how this population is distributed among Korea's thirteen provinces.[1]

DISTRIBUTION OF KOREA'S POPULATION BY PROVINCES
(December 31, 1939)

Province Paddy region[a]	Area in sq. km.	Area in sq. mi.	Per cent of total	Population	Per cent of total	Density per sq. mi.
Keiki	12,821	4,950	5.8	2,590	11.3	524
South Chusei	8,106	3,130	3.6	1,525	6.7	487
North Keisho	18,989	7,332	8.6	2,432	10.7	332
South Keisho	12,305	4,751	5.6	2,209	9.7	465
North Zenra	8,553	3,302	3.9	1,543	6.8	467
South Zenra	13,887	5,362	6.3	2,491	10.9	465
sub-total	74,661	28,827	33.8	12,790	56.1	443
Mixed region[a]						
Kokai	16,745	6,465	7.6	1,722	7.6	266
Kogen	26,263	10,140	11.9	1,592	7.0	157
North Chusei	7,418	2,864	3.3	900	3.9	314
sub-total	50,426	19,469	22.8	4,214	18.5	216
Dry field region[a]						
South Heian	14,939	5,768	6.8	1,656	7.3	287
North Heian	28,441	10,981	12.9	1,538	6.7	140
South Kankyo	31,978	12,347	14.5	1,661	7.3	135
North Kankyo	20,347	7,856	9.2	935	4.1	119
sub-total	95,705	36,952	43.4	5,800	25.4	157
Grand Total	220,792	85,248	100.0	22,804	100.0	268

[a] Paddy region—those provinces where paddy fields occupy from 50 to 100 per cent of the arable area.
Mixed region—those provinces where paddy fields occupy from 20 to 50 per cent of the arable area.
Dry field region—those provinces where paddy fields occupy from 0 to 20 per cent of the arable area.
This division is taken from the work of Sadanao Shirushi, *Chosen no nogyo chitai*.

On October 1, 1940, according to the census, Japan's population was 73,114,308 and Korea's 24,326,327, or almost exactly one third of Japan's; the density of population in Japan was 495 persons per square mile and that in Korea only 285 per-

[1] The population given here is not the census population, so it is an underestimate by about 5-6 per cent; however, since here we are interested more in relationships, this is not so important unless the degree of underestimation is not the same for each province.

sons.[2] However, it should be taken into consideration that (1) Japan includes a considerable portion of territory which is more to the south than Korea; (2) Japan is an industrial country, while Korea is agricultural. Let us take a few Japanese provinces corresponding to Korea's by their geographic position and by the nature of their occupations:

(in 1940)

Density of Yamagata	464
Tottori	536
Ishikawa	398
Aomori	269
Hokkaido[3]	142

Comparison of these figures with those given in the preceding table shows that the density of population in these Japanese provinces is equal to or below that in the Korean provinces;[4] yet we have heard much about over-populated Japan and little about a population problem in Korea.

Japanese in Korea.

In 1898 there were only 15,000 Japanese in Korea; by 1910 their number had risen to 171,500. The influx was caused chiefly by expectations of rapid enrichment. Indeed, the new immigrants were so unprincipled and rapacious that the authorities were compelled to send many of them back to Japan. Most of the Japanese in Korea at that period were poor: they owned only 5,600 houses, which were valued at 26 million yen; 3,400 owned land, valued at 8,900,000 yen; and 600 owned forests, valued at 900,000 yen. There were also 750 Japanese corporations with a total capital of 9,700,000 yen; thus the average capital per corporation was only thirteen thousand yen and only four corporations had a capital of more than 300,000 yen each.[5] The total Japanese investments at that period were only 45,500,000 yen, or an average of 26.5 yen (about thirteen American dollars) per person. This shows that it was not capitalists, looking for investments, who came to Korea, but chiefly

[2] For the sake of comparison, the density of population in the United States in 1940 was, nationally, 442; North Carolina 727; Virginia 671; Pennsylvania 219.8; New York 281.2; Connecticut 348.9.

[3] The greater part of Hokkaido is in more northern latitudes than Korea.

[4] One should also bear in mind that Korean figures relate to the year 1939 and that, as was shown above, they are underestimates.

[5] *Chosen Keizai Nempo*, 1939, pp. 38-39.

adventurers, seeking government positions. The growth of the Japanese population in Korea may be seen from the following table:

JAPANESE POPULATION IN KOREA

	Number (in 1,000)	Per cent of increase as compared with preceding period	Japanese population as per cent of total population of Korea
1910	171.5	—	1.3
1915	303.7	77	1.9
1920	347.9	15	2.0
1925	424.7	22	2.2
1930	501.9	18	2.5
1935	583.4	16	2.7
1939	650.1	11 [a]	2.9

[a] Four-year growth, while the other figures represent five-year growth.
Source: *Chosen Keizai Nempo*.

This table shows that the Japanese population in Korea increased in 29 years from 172,000 to 650,000; in 1910 it formed 1.3 per cent of the population (probably less, because the Korean population was underestimated); in 1939 this percentage was 2.9. But even now Korea is peopled predominantly by Koreans who constitute about 96.6 per cent of the total.[6]

This increase of the Japanese in the total population, slow as it is, is chiefly due to immigration. Between 1930 and 1935 only about 29 per cent of the absolute increase was due to the natural growth of the Japanese colony. If on the average the same proportion has existed throughout the period, then the average net immigration of the Japanese to Korea has been about 12,000 a year. It was larger in the first years after the annexation when the government apparatus was growing rapidly and industrial and commercial fields were not yet completely occupied by Japanese. But, as will be shown later, there are now more Koreans in Japan than Japanese in Korea.

If one compares the data of vital statistics for Koreans and Japanese in Korea one is struck with the differences between them.

The Korean marriage rate is twice that of the Japanese in Korea; that of divorces and births almost one and a half times as great; that of deaths is higher by 27 per cent. All this shows that the Japanese, living among the Koreans, constitute a dis-

[6] Two tenths of one per cent of the total population are "foreigners," chiefly Chinese.

POPULATION

RATES OF BIRTHS, DEATHS, ETC., OF KOREANS AND JAPANESE IN KOREA
(Ten year averages, 1929-1938 per 1,000 of population)

	Koreans	Japanese
Births	32.4	24.1
Deaths	19.9	15.6
Marriages	7.5	3.7
Divorces	0.321	0.225

tinct group of people with their own customs and conditions of life. One may say that perhaps the age distribution of the Japanese population in Korea is such that the rates are not characteristically Japanese. It is true that the Japanese in Korea have a proportionately larger number of middle-aged persons, yet on the whole the age composition approaches normal, and differences between Japanese and Koreans in other respects do not, therefore, result from difference in age composition.

The difference in occupational distribution is even greater and more significant.

OCCUPATIONAL DISTRIBUTION OF THE POPULATION[7]
(in percentages)

	Korea 1920	Korea 1929	Korea 1938	Korea 1939	Japan 1930	United States 1930
Agriculture and forestry	85.6	81.9	73.6	68.3	47.7	21.4
Fishing	1.2	1.6	1.5	1.6	1.9	.5[b]
Mining			1.2	1.8	.9	2.0
Industry	2.2	2.6	3.1	3.5	19.2	28.8
Commerce			7.0	7.9	15.1	12.5
Communications	6.2	7.2	1.0	1.3	3.7	7.9
Public and professional services	2.2	3.4	3.9	4.8	6.9	8.5
Other occupations	1.7	1.8	6.9	8.3	2.0	8.2[c]
Domestic service	1.7	—	—	—	2.6	10.1
No occupation, or unrecorded	1.9	1.5	1.8	2.5	—[a]	—
	100.0	100.0	100.0	100.0	100.0	100.0

[a] The number of those who, "are not gainfully employed," excluded from the table, is 34,830,365.
[b] Fishing and forestry.
[c] Clerical occupations.
Source: For Korea and Japan—*Takumu Tokei*; for the United States—*Statistical Abstract of the U. S. A.*, 1941.

[7] Several objections may be made to the use of such comparative tables: (1) as we have seen, the current population statistics in Korea are not good; occupational statistics, which in Korea are based upon them, are naturally no better, and probably worse; (2) classifications in various countries are different; (3)

No less than 85.6 per cent of the Korean population were engaged in agriculture in 1920; in 1929 the percentage had fallen to 81.9 and in 1938 to 73.6. However, in view of the sudden rise of "other occupations," this sharp fall to 73.6 per cent may be rather a result of changes in classification. In any case, it is clear that even today at least three quarters of the population in Korea are engaged in agriculture. Those occupied in industry and mining form only 4-5 per cent of the population. It is true that in 1920 the number of those engaged in industry and mining was only about 2 per cent, but the growth is small. In both Japan and the United States the percentage of persons occupied in commerce and communications is less than that of persons occupied in industry; in Korea it is two or three times larger. This clearly indicates the backward character of Korean economy. Those in public and professional service (chiefly government employees) make up about 4 per cent of the total—a small percentage in comparison with the figures for Japan and the United States, but a relatively large one in an agricultural country such as Korea.

This table of occupational distribution reveals that there have been very few changes in the occupations of the Koreans. The remarkable changes supposed to have been brought to Korea by Japanese rule do not appear in this table. If we had a more detailed table in which the number of landlords, agricultural laborers, and servants were shown for all these years, it would clearly be seen that Japanese domination has impeded the development of the country. Only the necessity of preparing for the aggressions planned after 1932 compelled the Japanese Government to pay more attention to the hitherto neglected Korean resources.

The data given in the last table embrace the whole population of Korea. Let us now see what differences there are, if any, with respect to occupational changes between Japanese and

---

changes are introduced which invalidate all comparisons; in Korea, for example, evidently through a change in classification, the number of those in "other occupations" jumped from 352,000 in 1929 to 1,498,000 in 1932. And yet we believe that such comparisons are useful. If statistics show that the number of Koreans engaged in agriculture is about 80 per cent, that of Japanese 48 per cent and that of Americans 21 per cent, differences of such breadth cannot, of course, result only from statistical manipulations. Korea, Japan, and the United States have, in fact, as this table shows, three different types of economic development.

Koreans, the senior and junior brothers, according to official terminology.

OCCUPATIONAL DISTRIBUTION OF KOREAN AND JAPANESE
POPULATION IN KOREA
(Per Cent)

	Korean Population			Japan Population		
	1920	1929	1938	1920	1929	1938
Agriculture	87.1	81.8	75.7	11.5	8.3	5.3
Fishing	1.1	1.5	1.5	3.2	2.5	1.5
Mining	1.9	2.2	1.2 }	17.8	14.5	2.3 }
Industry			2.6			16.6
Commerce	5.6	6.3	6.5 }	33.7	30.2	23.4 }
Communications			0.9			5.9
Public and professional services	1.7	2.5	2.9	29.3	34.2	38.1
Other occupations	1.7	4.3	7.0	3.7	6.9	2.9
No occupation	0.9	1.4	1.7	1.4	3.4	4.0
	100.0	100.0	100.0	100.0	100.0	100.0

This table shows that the Koreans and Japanese in Korea are not amalgamated, do not form one people. Incomplete and distorted as these figures are, they nevertheless show the cleavage between Koreans and Japanese. The chief occupation of the Koreans remains agriculture, in which more than three quarters of the people are engaged. The chief occupation of the Japanese is government service. As many as 41.4 per cent were thus occupied in 1937; in 1938 war brought a slight drop —to 38.1 per cent,[8] while in 1920 the percentage was 29.3. Other Japanese occupations in the order of their importance are commerce, industry, and communications. Only 5 per cent are engaged in agriculture, as compared with 11.5 per cent in 1920. But even these figures understate the actual contrast. It is true that in 1920 forty thousand Japanese were occupied in agriculture; this figure rose to 44,932 in 1932 and then gradually fell to 33,638[9] in 1938. These are not only farmers, but all the employees of the large Japanese companies that rent their land to Korean farmers. The number of Japanese *farmers* who settled in Korea is about 4,000, and this in spite of all encouragement and help, grants, subsidies, low-interest loans,

[8] The group also includes those engaged in professions, but as will be seen later, there is very little room for professions in Korea outside of government service.
[9] These figures include members of the family not gainfully employed.

and other benefits lavished upon them by the Japanese Government. Those who could do so preferred to become landlords in Korea, of whom more will be said below.

Further, 585,589 Koreans and 105,184 Japanese were occupied in industry—or, excluding the members of their families, about 150,000 Koreans[10] and 25,000 Japanese. But the Japanese are owners of enterprises, engineers, accountants, and overseers, while Koreans are mainly unskilled workers.

Urbanization.

The movement of the population to the cities so characteristic of our time has reached Korea, too, despite her predominantly agricultural character. In 1910 only eleven cities had a population of 14,000 or more, and their aggregate population was only 566,000, or about four per cent of the total population. By 1939 the population of these cities had reached 1,916,000, or about 8.4 per cent of the total. However, many of the villages had become cities since 1910. Altogether in 1938 there were in Korea fifty cities with a population above 15,000; their aggregate population was 3,012,400, or about 13-14 per cent, as compared with 45.9 per cent in Japan in 1935, and 47.6 per cent in the United States in 1940 (in both countries cities with a population of 10,000 or more). The population of the largest cities in Korea may be seen from the following table:

POPULATION OF KOREAN CITIES
(October 1940 census)

Keijo........ 935,464	Kanko......... 75,320	Zenshu........ 47,230
Heijo........ 285,965	Kaijo.......... 72,062	Taiden........ 45,541
Fusan........ 249,734	Chinnampo.... 68,656	Shinshu....... 43,291
Seishin....... 197,918	Koshu......... 64,520	Gunzan....... 40,553
Taikyn....... 178,923	Moppo......... 64,256	Rashin........ 38,319
Jinsen........ 171,165	Kaishu......... 62,651	Masan........ 36,429
Genzan...... 79,320	Shingishu....... 61,143	

Source: *Asahi Nenkan*, 1942, p. 562.

But the cities are important in another respect—the Japanese concentration in them. In 1938, seventy-one per cent of the Japanese were concentrated in fifty cities (as compared with 11.5 per cent of the Koreans); and over half of the Japanese

[10] Actually the number of Koreans occupied in industry must be much higher, because factories alone employed in 1938 more than 150,000, and besides these factory hands there were numerous handicraft workers and workers occupied in construction.

were concentrated at ten points—Keijo (21 per cent of all the Japanese), Fusan (9 per cent), Heijo, Taikyn, Kanko, Jinsen, Seishin, Genzan, Taiden and Gunzan. In all cities they formed a minority of the population.

Emigration

At least ten per cent of the Korean population is now earning its bread abroad. More than one million Koreans are working in Japan, about one million are settled in Manchuria, 200,000 in the Russian Far East, and about 100,000 in all other countries (mostly in China). Almost all of this emigration is of recent origin—since the start of the "benevolent" protection of Prince Ito—and its causes are both political and economic. In 1913, there were only 3,000 Koreans in Japan.[11] In 1920 there were 40,755, in 1930—419,000,[12] and according to various estimates, their number in 1940 exceeded one million. They are chiefly unskilled workers, miners, and agricultural workers. Most of them consider Japan their temporary home, send their savings home and look forward to the time when they will be able to return. The Japanese Government formerly placed various obstacles in the way of their migration to Japan, but under the pressure of war and the shortage of manpower that resulted, it began to encourage the immigration of Koreans (as temporary workers). However, the hostile attitude of the Japanese population, difficulties in providing for the education of their children, extremely poor housing conditions, and obstacles in the way of using their savings (forcing them to buy Japanese bonds, etc.) make this migration less attractive to Koreans than it formerly was.

According to the estimates of Japanese authorities, there were 870,000 Koreans in Manchuria in 1936.[13] Today the number is probably above a million. There have been Koreans living in the frontier area of Manchuria for several centuries, especially in the Kanto (in Chinese—Chientao) region. However, the movement to Manchuria became especially strong after 1905 when so many of the opponents of the Japanese regime fled to Manchuria. Chientao, as has been mentioned, was for many years a center of anti-Japanese activity. Unfortunately,

[11] Takahashi, *op. cit.*, p. 398.
[12] *Dainippon Teikoku Tokei Nenkan*, 1939, p. 37.
[13] *Chosen Keizai Nempo*, 1939, p. 265 *et seq.*

since the occupation of Manchuria by the Japanese, the latter have strengthened their control over Chientao, and many Koreans have lost their lives there. But even now there are still bands of Koreans fighting the Japanese in Manchuria and Korea.

Life in Manchuria for the Koreans has never been idyllic. Most of them are tenants, tending rice fields; and yet economic conditions in Korea were so bad that they preferred to work as tenants in Manchuria. Many of the Koreans in Manchuria were those whose land in Korea had been expropriated by the Japanese under various pretexts. Now emigration from Korea to Manchuria is "planned," and about 10,000 Korean families are supposed to be settled annually in Manchuria by Sen-Man Takushoku Kabushiki Kaisha (The Chosen-Manchurian Colonization Corporation), the capital of which is twenty million yen. The purpose of this planned immigration is simple. Manchuria is peopled predominantly by Chinese. Japanese rule over it cannot be secure without Japanese and Korean settlement; not that the Koreans would be ready to defend the Japanese, but bitter feelings may be created between Chinese and Koreans on the "divide-and-rule" theory.

The position of the Koreans in the Russian Far East before the Revolution of 1917 was similar to that in Manchuria: they were tenants of rich farmers or unskilled workers. Collectivization of farms placed them on an equal footing with the rest of the population. They are now members of the collective farms; all schools are open to their children; every young Korean fit for military service is called to the colors; and there are Korean officers in the Red Army. There were rumors that all Koreans were removed by the Soviet Government from the Far East to the Russian Middle Asia, but this was not true. The probable basis for this rumor was the removal of the greater portion of the population, not only Korean but also Russian, from the border regions where important fortifications have been built.

The Korean population in China consists of two groups: they are either Japanese camp followers who, using their Japanese citizenship, open gambling houses, opium dens, brothels, and other disreputable enterprises in Chinese cities in which they compete with their masters; or they have crossed the line and are trying to reach the Chinese Army in order to get a chance to fight the Japanese.

In 1938 there were about two million Japanese abroad, (including Formosa and Korea), or 2.8 per cent of the total number of the Japanese at home. Most of them were officials (in Korea, Formosa, Manchuria, China, Japanese Mandates) and the rest received grants, subsidies and protection from the Empire. There are 2,300,000 Koreans abroad, or about 10 per cent of the Koreans left at home; they hold no official positions, enjoy no subsidies or grants, and very often would be more happy if Japanese "protection" overlooked them.

CHAPTER V

AGRICULTURE IN KOREA[1]

Introduction

Before entering on an analysis of agricultural conditions in Korea, we should first have a general idea of the Korean economy and the place of agriculture in it. The following table gives the gross value of production for Korea and Japan, by major categories, in 1938.

GROSS VALUE OF PRODUCTION, 1938
(million yen)

	Korea	Japan	Per Cent Korea	Per Cent Japan
Agriculture	1,398[a]	4,109[a]	46.4	16.1
Forestry	167	567	5.5	2.2
Fishing	146[b]	420[b]	4.8	1.6
Mining	165[c]	884[c]	5.5	3.4
Industry	1,140	19,667	37.8	76.7
Total	3,016	25,647	100.0	100.0

[a] This includes agriculture proper, sericulture and cattle breeding.
[b] This includes processing of fish; in order to avoid duplication, it is assumed that half of the catch was processed and its value was deducted from the total.
[c] The latest figures available are those for 1936. It is assumed in the table that the value of production for 1938 was fifty per cent above that for 1936.

This table shows that the gross value of production in Korea in 1938 was just over three billion yen[2] as compared with 25 billion in Japan, and that the per capita value was 126 yen in Korea as compared with 358 in Japan.[3] The gross value of production is not, of course, an ideal index; but in the absence of anything better it provides at least an approximation. The fundamental fact of Korean economy is the extremely low value of production. Life in Japan, with 358 yen of per capita gross

[1] More detailed official figures relating to agriculture are given in Appendix I. See also Appendix II concerning reliability of agricultural statistics.

[2] Judging by the value of many commodities the prices of which are known, the ratio Y3=U. S. $1 corresponded fairly closely to the level of prices in these two countries in 1938, and may well be used as a basis of comparison for that year.

[3] The population is estimated on the basis of the 1940 census.

production, is difficult enough. But how much more difficult is life with only 126 yen per annum—a per capita production of which an unusually large proportion is taken by the Japanese. Here we will not discuss whether the situation in this respect has deteriorated under the Japanese, or whether their regime should be held responsible for this extraordinary poverty. These and related questions will be touched upon later. But to understand other problems we must constantly remind ourselves of the central fact—the extraordinary poverty of the Korean people. The remark of Governor General Ugaki about the Korean people eating bark and roots of trees in spring reflected this essential fact. And that remark was made in what was on the whole a "good year," and not a year of catastrophic crop failure such as occurred in 1939 and 1942.

The percentages given in the above table show that in Korea agriculture is responsible for 46.4 per cent of gross production —as compared with 16.1 per cent in Japan. If we assume that the net value of agricultural production is 70 per cent of the gross value, and that in industry, it is 44 per cent of the gross value[4] and if we further assume that the number of workers per farm is 1.5, we arrive at the following estimate of the net value of production per worker in the Korean economy.

VALUE OF NET PRODUCTION PER WORKER IN THE KOREAN ECONOMY, 1938

	Agriculture	Industry
Net value, total (in million yen)	978.6	501.6
Number of occupied persons (thousands)	4,577	167[a]
Value per person employed (in yen)	214	3,000
Value per day per worker (in yen)	0.59	8.22

[a] This figure is for 1937.

The net value per day per worker in agriculture is 0.59 yen, while in industry it is 8.22 yen, or almost fourteen times as large. Thus, a second fundamental fact is the very low per capita value of agricultural output in Korea as compared with that of industry. It is not Korea that is "over-populated"; it is the agriculture of Korea that is "overcrowded." Far more extensive industrialization would seem to be the only solution for this extreme poverty.

[4] This is the ratio used by Japanese statisticians in the 1930 census. The figure of 44 per cent for industry is based on the similar corresponding figure for Japan in 1930.

The Structure of Korean Agriculture

In this analysis, Korean agriculture is considered as a whole and an average Korean farmer is compared with an average Japanese and an average American farmer. Obviously, this "average" farmer is a fiction, but it is a useful fiction because it helps to emphasize certain special features of Korean agriculture.

GROSS VALUE OF FARM PRODUCTION IN KOREA, JAPAN AND THE U.S.A. IN 1938

	Gross value of agricultural production, in million U.S. dollars[a]	Number of farms	Gross value of production per farm, in U.S. dollars[a]
Korea	466	3,052,392	153
Japan	1,369	5,519,480	248
U.S.A.	11,148[b]	6,096,799 (1940)	1,828

[a] The ratio of exchange used is Y3 = U. S. $1.
[b] For the manner in which this figure is reached see a note to the table on page 88.

From the above table we see that the number of farms in Korea in 1938 was almost exactly one-half the number of farms in the United States, but that the gross value of the output was only four per cent of the American and one-third of the Japanese. The gross value of production per farm is 153 dollars in Korea, 248 in Japan, and 1,828 in the United States. This suggests that the productivity of an American farmer is more than ten times as great as that of a Korean, and six or seven times as great as that of a Japanese. Of course, we have heard a good deal about over-population in Korea and Japan and about the remarkable achievements of their farmers in respect to crops. We have been told that their yields per unit of area are large and can hardly be increased, so that their poverty must be explained exclusively by overpopulation. American farmers, it is said, are lucky because they have so large an arable area at their disposal; their cultivation is "extensive" as compared with the "intensive" cultivation of Koreans, Japanese, and other Oriental peoples. This argument has been advanced so often that it has become almost an axiom; and the reasoning of many experts on the Far East proceeds from this assumption. But what does "intensive agriculture" really mean? Usually it means that even though, in terms of production per man, Oriental agriculture cannot stand comparison with, say, American agriculture, it is superior to American agriculture in production per unit of area. The Oriental farmers are able to squeeze from an available area more than an American farmer does.[5] The following table shows the yields for the most important crops in Korea and Japan, as compared with yields in the United States for the year 1938.

YIELDS PER UNIT OF AREA IN KOREA, JAPAN AND IN THE UNITED STATES IN 1938[a]

	Korea	Japan	United States
Wheat	92	190	100
Barley	78	141	100
Maize	40	88	100
Rice	111	156	100
Potatoes	80	140	100
Beans	56	100	100

[a] Calculated from data in the *International Year Book of Agricultural Statistics*, 1939-40.

It may be seen that Korean yields are in general below those of the United States (except those of rice, a very important crop in Korea), and Japanese for the most part above them. But here one important circumstance should be considered, namely, the relative importance of the various crops. Yields of maize in Korea, for example, are very low, but the area under maize is relatively small; yields of rice in the United States are low, but their proportion is insignificant in the total. To overcome this complication these yield ratios can be weighted by the corresponding percentages of area devoted to various crops in the different countries to give weighted average ratios. This calculation shows that if the average figure for the United States is taken as 100, the average is 92 for Korea and 156 for Japan; i.e., yields in Japan exceed yields in the United States by 56 per cent. Of course, these figures are not exact, but they show roughly that there is a great difference. It must also be noted, however, that in both Japanese and Korean agriculture

[5] John R. Orchard writes, (*Japan's Economic Position*, New York, 1930, p. 32.) "The output of rice . . . averaged 2,350 pounds per acre. In the United States it was only 1,076 pounds . . . It is difficult to see how it [Japanese agriculture] can be made much more intensive, for, after all, there is a limit to what the land can be made to produce." Writes Harold G. Moulton, *Japan*, Washington, 1931, p. 331: "The productive area of Japan has long been cultivated by the most intensive methods"; and he quotes Miriam Beard: "Japanese cultivable land has been worked with amazing intensity." (*Realism in Romantic Japan*, New York, p. 345.)

the yields represent practically the whole output from a given unit of land because crops are not diversified. This may be seen from the following table:

COMPOSITION OF GROSS VALUE OF AGRICULTURAL PRODUCTION
IN KOREA, JAPAN AND THE UNITED STATES, 1938
(in million U.S. dollars)

	Absolute data			Per Cent		
	Korea	Japan	U.S.A.	Korea	Japan	U.S.A.
Crops	432	1,142	5,814[a]	92.7	83.4	52.2
Livestock	28	112	5,334[b]	6.0	8.2	47.8
Sericulture	6	115		1.3	8.4	
Total	466	1,369	11,148	100.0	100.0	100.0

[a] In order to make these figures comparable with the Japanese and Korean, we have taken "farm values" from the *Statistical Abstract of the United States* and added from *Agricultural Statistics* only those values which were absent in the *Statistical Abstract*. The difference in some cases is substantial. Take the case of corn. Most of it is neither sold nor consumed by the farmer, but is consumed by his cattle and thus does not appear in the statistics of gross farm income. But Japanese and Korean statistics give exact equivalents of "farm values."

[b] This is taken from *Agricultural Statistics*—gross farm income—because in this case there is no such difficulty as in the case of corn. These products are either sold or consumed by the farmer's family.

Thus in the United States the gross value of production of crops is only slightly above that of livestock, whereas in Japan crops are responsible for 83.4 per cent of the total value, and in Korea for 92.7 per cent. Koreans have little knowledge of stockbreeding; theirs is almost exclusively a crop agriculture and Japanese agriculture resembles Korean in that respect. But in estimating the "intensity" of use of a given area, the products of live stock must be included. Of course, there will be some degree of duplication, (for example, corn fed to livestock should be deducted from the value of livestock) but it is clear that even if only 50 or 60 per cent of the value of livestock products represents an increase in value over and above the value of crops consumed by the livestock, the intensity of agriculture in the United States per unit of area is not below that of Japan.

E. F. Penrose has demonstrated the shallowness of the usual interpretations of intensive and extensive farming,[6] but he thinks that "there is a more legitimate sense in which it can be said that within a single cycle of the seasons the land is intensively utilized in Japan."[7] "The Japanese practice of growing

[6] His "Japan" in *The Industrialization of Japan and Manchukuo*, New York, 1940, edited by E. B. Schumpeter, p. 21.

[7] He proposes also to take as a criterion of "intensive" and "extensive" cultivation the *proportion* of labor to other factors per unit of product. This proportion can be important and significant, but why call it extensive or intensive *cultivation*?

two major crops annually on the same land over most of the country, together with the practice of sowing rice seed beds and planting out the young plants about two months later may be regarded as a response to the pressure exerted by the scarcity of arable land."

G. C. Allen goes even further. He asserts that "on the best rice land a crop of barley or of some other cereal is grown as a second crop . . . ; while the upland-fields often yield each year three or four crops of cereals, roots, and vegetables, sown in rotation. This fecundity is, however, the result of intensive cultivation . . ."[8] So, according to Professor Penrose, the Japanese raise two major crops annually on the same land over most of the country; according to Professor Allen, the best paddy land brings two crops, while the upland fields *often* yield even three or four crops a year. If the Japanese (or Korean) farmer is able to raise two, three, and even four crops from the same area in the same year, then cultivation is indeed intensive, and even the raising of livestock in the United States would not compensate for this intensity. However, the language of both writers quoted is rather indefinite. From Professor Nasu's work[9] we know that "the annual frequency of arable land utilization" in Japan is 1.28. The author's own calculation, on the basis of Japanese statistics, does not give a figure higher than 1.33-1.35.[10] This means that intensive cultivation in Professor Penrose's sense increases the results by from 20 to 30 per cent only, and comparison with production in the United States would not reveal any remarkable difference. How can it be otherwise? A poor Oriental farmer works mostly on rented land with primitive implements, without any machinery, and hopelessly in debt. How can he produce much more per unit of area—in spite of his incessant efforts—than an American farmer with the aid of machinery? In Japan and Korea the same or almost the same amount of foodstuffs could be produced with the help of machinery, with a fraction of the labor that is now being spent, and thus free a tremendous amount of human energy to raise the standards of living. It is not overpopulation that lies at the root of Korean and Japanese poverty, it is low productivity coupled with oppressive social conditions and often caused by them.

[8] *Modern Japan and Its Problems*, E. P. Dutton & Co., New York, p. 120.
[9] S. Nasu, *Land Utilization in Japan*, Tokyo, 1929, p. 133.
[10] For Korea see below, p. 99.

GROSS VALUE OF CROP PRODUCTION IN KOREA, JAPAN AND THE UNITED STATES IN 1938

	In million dollars			In percentages		
	Korea	Japan	United States	Korea	Japan	United States
Rice	254.1	724.2	33.7	58.9	63.4	0.6
Wheat, barley, oats, rye	51.2	135.1	887.5	11.9	11.8	15.3
Other cereals	33.4	11.2	1,324.5	7.7	1.0	22.8
Beans, peanuts	29.4	32.3	121.2	6.8	2.8	2.1
Vegetables, potatoes	36.2	136.6	723.6	8.4	12.0	12.4
Fruits, berries, nuts	5.3	38.4	445.1	1.2	3.4	7.7
Industrial crops	22.2	64.2	1,054.6	5.1	5.6	18.1
Hay			623.9			10.7
Other crops			600 (about)			10.3
Total	431.8	1,142.0	5,814.1	100.0	100.0	100.0

The above table shows that Korean and Japanese farming is predominantly rice farming: 58.9 per cent of the total value in Korea and 63.4 per cent in Japan were contributed by rice alone. The share of vegetables in Korea, despite the abundance of labor, was only 8.4 per cent and total production was estimated at only 36.2 million dollars; the share of fruits was also small (1.2 per cent), as was that of industrial crops. The agriculture of Korea is not diversified, and the efforts of the Japanese Government, as will be shown later, were directed toward accentuating this onesidedness. The Japanese neglected the fact that rice suffers more from periodic droughts than *awa* (millet), barley, *hie* ("Deccan grass"), and other cereals, because they were primarily interested in rice exports from Korea to Japan.

The following figures, indicating the extent to which rice and other cereals in Korea are affected by droughts, show that rice production fluctuates far more than that of other cereals.

CEREAL CROP PRODUCTION AND WEATHER CONDITIONS

	Rice crop, in 1,000 koku	Bad years as % of preceding good year	Other Cereals 1,000 koku	Bad years as % of preceding good year
1927, Good year	17,299		17,525	
1928, Bad year	13,512	78	17,423	100
1929, Bad year	13,702	79	19,383	105
1930, Good year	19,181		19,033	
1931, Bad year	15,873	83	18,059	95

AGRICULTURE IN KOREA

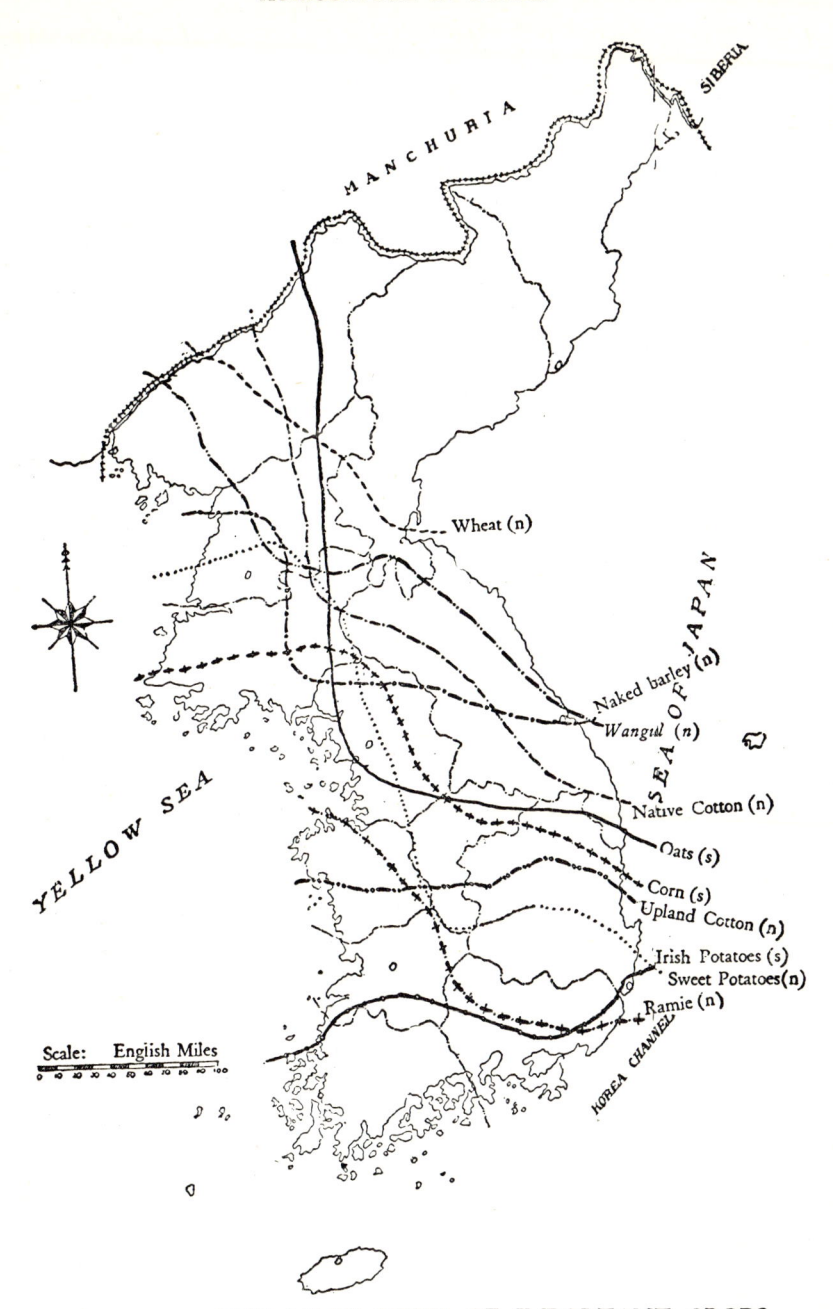

THE LIMIT LINES OF IMPORTANT CROPS.
(n. indicates northern and s. southern limit of the Crop named)

Agricultural Policy

The principles which, according to an official pronouncement, guided the Japanese Administration before 1919 were:

(1) Gradual advance;
(2) Avoidance of encouraging too many things at once;
(3) Encouragement, first, of what was easy to realize;
(4) Giving practical leadership.[11]

"Make haste slowly" was the avowed principle.

However, in 1918, there was an acute shortage of rice in Japan, and rice riots spread in the principal cities. As a result, it was decided to increase the production of rice in Greater Japan and the policy in Korea was completely changed. A thirty-year plan for increasing Korean rice production was worked out,[12] and by 1933, 118.4 million yen had been spent on work connected with this plan, as compared with a planned expenditure of 170.5 million yen; that is, the actual expense incurred was only 69 per cent of that planned. Private entrepreneurs fulfilled their quota by 85 per cent.[13] But at this point unexpected developments brought the plan to a premature end. As noted above, the aim of increased rice production in Korea was to meet the rice shortage in Japan. Between 1918 and 1930, Japanese militarists, politicians and economists tried hard to present Japan as a country under the constant threat of hunger and in need of outlets for her rapidly growing population. Most Western economists and journalists accepted the Japanese arguments and failed to notice the change that took place in the actual situation, namely that about 1930, Japan and her dependencies began to suffer from overproduction of rice. In 1933 the Korean Government-General—under pres-

[11] *Chosen Keizai Nempo*, 1939, pp. 94-95.
[12] The first part of this plan, a fifteen-year plan, provided for an increase of the area under rice of 427,000 *cho*, and an increase of output by 9,200,000 *koku*, at a cost of 169 million yen. By 1925 it became clear that because of various difficulties the plan could not be fulfilled. Then a new twelve-year plan was prepared which provided for (1) improvement works on an area of 195,000 *cho* already irrigated; (2) the changing of 90,000 *cho* from dry fields into paddy; (3) the clearing of new lands; a total addition of 350,000 *cho*, or a 2,800,000 *koku* increase in yields from this source. Moreover, it was expected to attain an increase of 1,920,000 *koku* through a larger and better application of fertilizers and better methods of cultivation, and an additional increase of 3,440,000 *koku* from improvements in cultivation of the existing 1,390,000 *cho* of paddy, a total of 8,160,000 *koku*. The plan was to be completed in 1938.
[13] For details see Hishimoto, *Chosen Bei No Kenkyu*, Tokyo, 1938, p. 59.

sure from Japan, where the landlords clamored for protection against the flood of Formosan and Korean rice and complained that the Japanese Government was financing this competition—cancelled all plans for the increase of rice production, and in May 1934 even discontinued works in progress.

Just as previously the plans for the increase of output had nothing to do with the interests of the native Koreans, so now a new plan was worked out which was again to serve the interests of Japan and not those of Korea. Korea was to become a source of industrial raw materials for the empire, especially of cotton. It was pointed out that cotton production in Korea did not threaten Japanese interests in Japan Proper, and that Japan was in need of imported cotton.[14]

In 1933, General Ugaki advanced the slogan: cotton in the south, sheep in the north, and a ten-year plan was prepared for sheep-raising. During this period their number was to be increased to 100,000 and they were to supply 3,000 tons of wool annually.[15] Actually, the number of sheep increased from 2,675 in 1933 to 27,405 in 1938, (far behind the plan) and much of this increase was achieved by the importation of Australian sheep which ceased in 1938.[16]

Plans for the "intensification and diversification" of Korean agriculture which had been worked out in 1933-34, were again overhauled in 1938-39. The change in 1933 was necessitated by the "over-production" of rice. But the war with China caused

[14] In 1933, a twenty-year plan of cotton production was worked out for Korea. According to this plan, the total area under cotton would eventually be 500,000 *cho*, and the crop 600 million *kin*. In the first ten-year period (1933-1942), the goal was 350,000 *cho* and 420,000 *kin*. The actual achievements are shown below:

COTTON CULTIVATION IN KOREA

	1929-33 (average)	1939	1942 (plan)
Area, in 1,000 hectares	180	252	347
Crop, in 1,000 metric tons[a]	28.4	39.6	84.0
Yield, in kilograms per hectare	158	157	242

[a] In terms of ginned cotton; 3 tons of seed cotton are here considered equal to one ton of ginned cotton.

The increase, according to the plan, was to result from an increase in the area under cotton and of the yield per unit of area. In both respects the actual cultivation of cotton in 1939 was far behind that provided for in the plan: production in 1939 was to have been 67.3 thousand and not 39.6 thousand tons.

[15] *Chosen Nenkan*, p. 370.

[16] In 1937 or 1938 a new plan was initiated calling for an increase of sheep to 500,000 in twelve years.

a renewed shortage of rice in Japan. So a new outlook was encouraged in Tokyo: "the program should be looked at as a whole" for Japan, Korea, Manchuria, and China, and in this program "it is better to concentrate production of raw materials for industry in China and Manchuria, while Korea should concentrate on production of rice."[17] Thus another great transformation took place; hungry Korea was resuscitated as a granary of the Empire. In 1933, General Ugaki had tried his best through his speeches to convince the Koreans that they should eat more rice; in 1939 General Minami advised them not to eat rice. In September 1938, the Korean Government-General decided to increase the production of rice in Korea by two million *koku* through improvement of seeds, increased use of farm-made fertilizers, deeper autumn ploughing, extermination of pests, and "harvesting at the appropriate time." No important irrigation or improvement works were planned. But the need grew more pressing. The plan for 1939 envisaged an increase of rice production by 1,200,000 *koku*, but actually the crop was only about half of that produced in 1938. In spite of this, a five-year plan was worked out in September 1939 to increase rice production to 3 million *koku* by 1944; and a new seven-year plan, prepared in October 1939, called for an increase to five million *koku*! This short description of the shifts in the official agricultural policy suffices to show that this policy did not have the welfare of Korea in view.

Increase of Area under Cultivation

A survey of the cultivated area in Korea concluded in 1919, revealed that this area amounted to 4,381,568 *cho*. By 1938 it had increased to 4,515,676 *cho*; a net increase in nineteen years of 134,108 *cho*, or an average of 6,610 *cho* annually. Such an increase cannot be regarded as large. The question is—can this small actual increase be sufficiently explained by the fact that the total cultivable area was already cultivated? According to estimates made by the Government in 1927-28, the cultivable area still unploughed amounted to 1,100,000 *cho*,[18] indicating that there were substantial possibilities for new development which were not utilized by the Government, probably because

[17] *Chosen Keizai Nempo*, 1940, p. 160.
[18] Quoted by Hoon K. Lee, *op. cit.*, p. 122.

most of the area was good only for dry fields, and the Government was interested mainly in rice production.

The cultivated area of Korea formed 20.3 per cent of the total area in 1938, exceeding the corresponding proportion in Japan. However, Korea is not as mountainous a country as Japan, and in this respect a comparison with Italy is more illuminating because the topography of Italy is similar to that of Korea. In Italy, 32.2 per cent of the area is under cultivation, and an additional 18.6 per cent is in permanent meadows and pastures. This suggests that there was room for expansion of the cultivated area in Korea if the Government had concentrated its attention on the development of the country and not on preparation for wars of aggression.

Kaden

In the preceding statistics, *kaden*, or fire-fields, were not included. This system is practiced by many peoples. It consists of the burning of grasses and bushes in the forest area and planting cereals or potatoes there for a few seasons and then moving to another place when the fertility of the ground has been exhausted. This primitive system is harmful in many respects: the farmers set fires to forests, and these fires often cause great losses; they disturb the virgin soil and then leave it broken, so that erosion sets in. An increase of the area given over to this type of agriculture is a sign of deterioration and not of progress. The statistics of such areas cannot, of course, be reliable, because the squatters are always on the move and try to avoid the attention of the authorities. In Korea, their activities are mainly in the northwest. It is interesting to note that in 1932 the area of firefields was estimated by the Government at 202,158 *cho* and in 1933 at 366,601 *cho*, an increase in one year by 81 per cent. This clearly indicates how unreliable these figures are. In 1938 the area of *kaden* was estimated at 442,045 *cho*.[19]

Irrigation

Conditions of rainfall in Korea are such that irrigation is of great importance for Korean agriculture. Paddy or flooded fields (*suiden* in Japanese) are irrigated fields. The increase

[19] As far as it is possible to ascertain, the crops of *kaden* are not included in current statistics of Korean crops.

of irrigated fields should be measured not only by the increase of the total area, but also by the increase of fields from which two crops of rice are taken because this demands, as a rule, additional irrigation.

IRRIGATED AREA IN KOREA
(in 1,000 *cho*)

	Paddy fields, total	Paddy fields yielding two crops
1919	1,547	247
1937	1,736	465
1938	1,751	460
	(4,292,000 acres)	(1,127,000 acres)
Increase as compared with 1919	204	213
Average increase per year	10.7	11.2
	(26,200 acres)	(27,500 acres)

This increase of 26.2 thousand acres a year is considerable, though not exceptionally large.[20] However, on further examination, the situation appears much less favorable. Of the total area of 1,751,000 *cho* of paddy fields, 522,000 *cho* depended upon rain water; 262,000 *cho* were irrigated with the help of dams, 597,000 *cho* with the help of ponds; 69,000 *cho* with the help of pumps, and 301,000 by other means. The irrigated land is divided among the following types of property:

IRRIGATION WORKS IN KOREA, BY OWNERSHIP, IN 1938

	Irrigated Area (in 1,000 *cho*)
Irrigation associations	222
Village associations	584
Individuals	320
Others	90
Total	1,216

Source: *Chosen Nenkan*, 1941.
Note: 522,000 *cho* "irrigated" by rain water naturally are not included.

This table shows that the dominant position is still occupied by village associations which, as a rule, have little capital and only primitive irrigation works. Second place is occupied by individuals—evidently, landlords and rich farmers; while the government-sponsored works, those of the irrigation associations

[20] In the United States the average annual increase of irrigated area between 1919 and 1929 was 35,600 acres.

(*suiri kumiai*)—financed by the banks—irrigate only 222,000 *cho*, or 12.7 per cent.

Dr. Lee describes irrigation associations and their functioning in the following words:[21]

"The way of organizing an irrigation association is also definitely laid down in the Irrigation Association Order. Article 3 of that order reads:
" 'When an Irrigation Association is to be organized, at least five men, according to the statement made by the Governor-General of Chosen, who wish to be the members of the said Irrigation Association, shall assume the promotion and make the articles of that association. They shall obtain a permit from the Governor-General of Chosen, after getting the approval of over one-half of the persons who are to be members and owners of not less than two-thirds of the area to be included in the association area.'
"In reality the consent from the landlords concerned and the members is obtained by implicit coercion by the Government. To form such irrigation associations is its definite policy, and the persons concerned have to follow it, whether they like it or not . . . The responsibility for paying the debts (of the association) rests on (all) the members . . . Had the work of the associations been carried out without any suspicion of scandalous graft on the part of officials and contractors, and had the prospective profit from the increased product been realized . . . there would have been no complaints from the members of the associations. On account of the poor appointments to the management of associations,[22] of ill-management, of the economic depression, of the unprecedented fall in the price of rice, and some other contributing factors about which we are prohibited to talk, write, or give information,[23] almost all of the associations have become targets of attack from the persons concerned, mostly the landlords and tenants in the association areas."

According to *Chosen Nenkan*, 1941, (p. 342) the total cost of the works of 189 *suiri kumiai* on December 31, 1938, was 112,979,000 yen, and the debt of these *kumiai* was 107,697,000 yen. This means that almost all the irrigation works were constructed with borrowed capital. If we suppose that the rate of interest on this borrowed capital is 10 per cent,[24] then the annual interest charge would be about eleven million yen, though the total gross revenue of the associations in 1938 was only 16,618,000 yen. This shows that even in a favorable year

[21] Lee, *op. cit.*, pp. 126-130.
[22] Koreans assert that the Japanese managers of these associations are "mostly corrupt, old, inefficient, and retired from the government service." Lee, *op. cit.*, p. 130.
[23] Dr. Lee is a Korean professor, living in Korea.
[24] The average rate of interest paid by one of the best *kumiai* was 8.3 per cent, so 10 per cent for all kumiai is quite probable.

in respect to rice prices the position of the associations was not very good. In years of low prices it was extremely difficult; and one should remember that the members of the associations, recruited mostly against their will and without control over the management of the affairs of the associations, are, nevertheless, responsible for the debts.

Mr. Drake has written about irrigation in Korea as follows:[25]

"But all the Korean sees is that whereas water was free, he must now pay three yen a year, and that he may only chop such wood for his house and his fire as the authorities permit. And it is useless to tell him that for three yen he has perhaps a doubled rice crop, and is completely relieved of the menace of famine . . . Well, what can you do with such a people?"

Koreans are represented here as a people who do not understand the advantages bestowed on them. Let us see how far Mr. Drake's description fits the actual situation. Take the case of an owner-farmer who has one cho of irrigated field under rice. His annual payments to the *suiri kumiai* would be not three yen, as Mr. Drake suggests, but about seventy-five yen. The Koreans may not know it, but this is more than double what the Japanese in Hokkaido pay for irrigation.[26] As to the crop, according to Choji Hishimoto the average increase of yields per *cho* is from 6 *koku* to 13.9 *koku*, or 7.9 *koku*. The wholesale price of a *koku* of unpolished rice in Korea was about 16 yen in 1931 and 29 yen in 1936. If we assume that the farmer received 70 per cent of the wholesale price—i.e., 11-20 yen in 1931 and 20-30 yen in 1936—eight additional *koku* of rice would then bring the farmer about ninety yen in 1931 and 162 yen in 1936, and after payment of irrigation fees (which we assume unchanged) he would be left with 15 yen in 1931 and 87 yen in 1936.

Nor should it be assumed that if water is available, the farmer simply opens the faucet and in the autumn collects a double yield. An irrigated field demands much additional work and much additional fertilizer.[27] We may therefore assume that in 1931 the farmer had, in all probability, a net loss from operation, and in 1936 a modest surplus, if he was an owner.

It may be said that now, when the price of rice is so much higher, irrigation works are very advantageous and the attitude

[25] Drake, *op. cit.*, p. 147.
[26] Takahashi, *op. cit.*, p. 273.
[27] The *average* cost of fertilizer per *cho* in 1933 was estimated at 52 yen.

of the population may have changed. But the high price of rice is deceptive. It results from inflation; relative to other goods the price of rice has gone down. So the construction costs now would be much higher and, correspondingly, so would the charges for water.

We therefore reach two conclusions: first, that the irrigated area in Korea can be expanded; and, second, that the Government has spent a relatively small amount on irrigation. Up to 1939, only 113 million yen had been expended on *suiri kumiai*[28] whereas in two years, 1940 and 1941, the Japanese Administration of Korea contributed more than 120 million yen to Japan's war chest. The management of *suiri kumiai* is in Japanese hands and cannot be controlled by the members, and the charges for water are high because of the excessive cost of management, high construction costs, and high interest rates.

Annual Frequency of Utilization

In a country with a mild climate, like that of Korea, it is often possible to harvest two crops or even more from the same field in the same year. According to H. K. Lee[29] the average frequency of utilization in Korea in 1930 was 1.34, that is, on 34 per cent of the cultivated area a second crop was gathered. The author's calculations for 1938, made by dividing the reported crop area by the cultivated area (6,078,000 *cho* by 4,516,000 *cho*) result in a ratio of 1.35, i.e., a figure very close to that of Professor Lee. It is interesting to note that the average frequency of utilization in Japan, according to Professor Nasu, is 1.28, that is, lower than in Korea, though temperatures in Japan are higher and rainfall is more abundant. This circumstance suggests that Korean farmers are not as lazy as they are sometimes represented: they seize every opportunity to

---

[28] This is not the sum total of the Government-General's contribution to irrigation, because (1) *suiri kumiai* borrowed money chiefly from the banks; (2) the Government had been giving grants and subsidies for irrigation purposes to individuals; (3) it invested capital in works which have an indirect relation to irrigation. But the investments in *suiri kumiai* may well serve as an index because they are the largest. According to Takahashi, the total expenditures of the Government-General on land improvements between 1911 and 1933 were only 58.2 million yen, and the *total* expenditure of the Government-General and the provinces on agriculture was 169.2 million yen in 33 years. This includes expenditure on sericulture and cattle-breeding.

[29] Lee, *op. cit.*, p. 111.

increase their crop yield. These figures are averages. Naturally, in southern provinces the frequency is higher. In southern Keisho it is 2.08 for paddy fields and 1.84 for *hatake* (dry fields). Greater frequency of utilization in Korea is difficult to achieve. Partly it is a problem of irrigation, because, as we saw, the average monthly precipitation except for the summer months is rather low in Korea.

Improvements in Seed Material

According to Japanese statistics, only 22 per cent of the area under rice in 1915 was sown with improved seeds, whereas in 1937 the proportion was 84.4 per cent. This shows that on the one hand considerable work was done by the experimental stations and, on the other, that the Korean farmers were receptive to these improvements. In 1932, the average yield per *cho* of unimproved varieties of rice was 8.86 *koku*, and of improved varieties 10.34 *koku*,[30] an increase of 17 per cent. Of course, comparison is difficult because improved varieties of rice may benefit from better irrigation facilities, and from other causes, but the figures suggest a substantial difference in yield.

Fertilizers

There is no need to dwell upon the importance of fertilizers in agriculture, especially in a country like Korea where the soil has been cultivated for several thousand years. The statistics on the use of fertilizers are the least reliable of all agricultural statistics, but since the yearly figures indicate a definite trend, it is permissible to draw certain conclusions.

USE OF FERTILIZERS IN KOREAN AGRICULTURE

	Quantities in 1,000 tons			Values in million dollars		
	Green manure	Compost	Commercial fertilizers	Green manure	Compost	Commercial fertilizers
1919	127.8	6,401	48.1	0.6	34.6	4.0
1928	814.7	15,758	285.8	6.4	91.8	21.7
1938	1,774.6	28,126	367.6	9.0	112.2	90.0
1939	....	27,680	....	...	....	...

Source: *Chosen Keizai Nempo*, 1939, and *Chosen Nenkan*, 1941.

The figures in the above table show that in the course of twenty years there has been a considerable increase in the use

[30] Calculated from data given in Takahashi, *op. cit.*, p. 262.

of fertilizers. They do not include several other farm-created fertilizers (ashes, grasses, faeces, etc.), but nevertheless the picture reveals progress up to 1939. The reliability of the figures for green manure, compost and other ingredients is, of course, open to question. Figures for commercial fertilizers are more reliable because the dealers in them make reports to government agents. *Chosen Keizai Nenkan,* 1939, ascribes an increased use of commercial fertilizers to the fact that after annexation the collection of leaves in the forests became more and more difficult, or even impossible; the amount of straw available decreased because of the manufacture of straw bags and mats, and export of cattle to Japan decreased the available amount of stable manure.[31] Shirushi likewise thinks that the amount of farm-collected manure actually declined in recent years because the forest became private property and the collection of leaves was forbidden. The strips of land along dams and ditches also became private property and the peasants were not allowed to collect grass or pasture cows there, because these activities endangered the dams.[32] For these reasons, commercial fertilizers have acquired a special importance in Korean agriculture, and it is estimated that their purchase accounts for about 50 per cent of the cash expenditures of Korean farmers.[33] The plan worked out under the pressure of war to increase agricultural production envisages an increase of yields, but it is difficult to see how this can be achieved without an increase in the use of commercial fertilizers. It is true that the production of fish manure has increased, but it goes chiefly to Japan Proper; the same is true of soybean cakes. The increase before 1938 was chiefly in sulphate of ammonia and superphosphate of lime, which are produced locally; but their shortage in Japan in 1938 compelled the government to cut its supplies to Korea in half,[34] and in order to achieve the desired increase in rice production the authorities recommended to the farmers a larger use of home-made fertilizers.

A plan to produce sulphate ammonia in the Empire (July

[31] *Op. cit.,* p. 157.
[32] *Chosen no Nogyo Chitai,* Tokyo, 1940, pp. 29-32.
[33] *Ibid.*
[34] *Ibid.* Official statistics for 1938 show a fall in the consumption of sulphate of ammonia by only 5 per cent as compared with 1937, but according to *Chosen Keizai Nempo,* 1940, p. 146, the amount consumed in 1938, as compared with 1937, fell by 30 per cent, while prices increased by 19 per cent.

1939) stipulated production of 1,210,000 tons in Japan, 460,000 tons in Korea, and 200,000 tons in Formosa but it soon became clear that Japan Proper would fall far behind the plan, so shipments of sulphate of ammonia from Korea to Japan had to be increased, with a corresponding reduction in Korean use of the chemical. It is doubtful whether the situation has improved since then.

Agricultural Machinery and Implements

With respect to Korean agricultural implements, Shirushi wrote in 1940 that "the agricultural implements used by the Koreans are most primitive."[35] The Korean Government-General, on the other hand, quotes figures to show a striking increase in the use of machinery and other implements.

USE OF AGRICULTURAL MACHINERY AND IMPLEMENTS

	Number		Per cent
	1929	1938	of increase
Oil prime movers	3,711	7,567 (1935)	104
Foot pumps	20,004	30,639	53
Mechanical pumps	772	3,539	357
Improved ploughs	41,140	288,538	601
Winnowers	59,193	93,809	59

Source: *Chosen Nenkan*, 1941.

This table shows a "rapid development"—an annual increase in some cases of 4 per cent and in the case of improved ploughs of as high as 21 per cent. But we should always keep in mind the number of Korean farmers—3,052,392 in 1938. If we compare this number with the number of pieces of machinery and implements in 1938, we see that only one out of every eleven families had an improved plough, while the others used the same primitive ploughs that their forefathers had used for hundreds of years; one family out of 863 had a mechanical pump and one out of a hundred had a stirrup pump. This clearly indicates that only a few rich farmers or landowners have such machines and implements. In the United States the average expenditure per farm on machinery and implements in 1939 was 329 dollars,[36] while the average expenditure per

[35] *Op. cit.*, pp. 28-29.

[36] 549.3 millions were spent by 1,686,609 farmers reporting, *Statistical Abstract*, p. 698.

farm in Korea for the same purpose was 1.4 yen.[37] This would indicate that Korean agriculture was still decidedly backward. During the war, with the sharp rise of metal prices and strict rationing of iron and steel, there can have been no improvement in this respect.

Livestock

Dr. Elizabeth Boody Schumpeter writes:

"The raising of livestock is also of growing importance as a subsidiary occupation for the farmer. The Korean cattle not only supply the greater part of the labor required on the farms but they are of good size and their flesh is considered very palatable. The number has increased from 700,000 in 1910 to 1,703,000 in 1936."[38]

It must be emphasized, however, that the figures for 1910 are not reliable. If, in the years after the occupation, the Government was unable to count men and to estimate correctly the cultivated area, it is most unlikely that they were able to make an accurate estimate of the number of cows and pigs. This assumption is borne out by the figures: the number of cattle (as compared with that in the preceding year in all the examples below) increased in 1911 by 29 per cent, in 1912 by 15 per cent, in 1913 by 16 per cent, in 1914 by 10 per cent, and so on. But after 1919 we note a remarkable change. The increase

NUMBER OF LIVESTOCK
(in thousands)

	1919	1929	1938
Cattle	1,462	1,586	1,717
Horses	53.2	55.8	51.6[b]
Donkeys	13[a]	7	3
Sheep	0	2	27
Goats	114[a]	22	44
Pigs	963	1,327	1,507
Fowl	4,998	6,185	7,165

[a] 1915. [b] 1936.
Source: *Chosen Keizai Nempo Takumu Tokei.*

in 1920 is less than 2 per cent, in 1923 about 0.2 per cent; in 1924 there is a decrease, and in 1925 a further decrease. It is clear from these figures that between 1910 and 1919 it was

[37] This figure is quoted by Shirushi; H. K. Lee gives 4.68 yen per investigated household (*op. cit.*, p. 210). However, the farms investigated by Dr. Lee were considerably above the average in all respects.
[38] *Op. cit.*, p. 293.

not size of the herds that was growing, but the ability of the authorities to register them.

The above table shows that there was some increase of livestock in Korea during these twenty years, especially pigs and fowl. But in order to evaluate this growth correctly it is necessary to consider its relation to the growth in the number of farms.

NUMBER OF LIVESTOCK PER FARM
(in units)

	1919	1938
Cattle	0.55	0.56
Horses	0.020	0.017
Donkeys	0.005	0.001
Sheep	0	0.009
Goats	0.005	0.014
Pigs	0.36	0.49
Fowl	1.92	2.35

The number of horses and donkeys per farm decreased, the number of cattle remained practically the same, the number of pigs rose from 0.36 to 0.49, and the number of fowl per farm family rose from 1.92 to 2.35 in twenty years. Today there is an average of one cow, one pig and five chickens for every two farms in Korea, while only a very small proportion of farms possess horses, donkeys, or sheep. According to official statistics the value of animal products formed 14.1 per cent of the value of plant products in 1915; 6.1 per cent in 1919; 6.1 per cent in 1929 and 6.5 per cent in 1938. These figures certainly do not support Mrs. Schumpeter's statement that "the raising of livestock is also of growing importance as a subsidiary occupation for the farmer."

Calculations show that only about 650,000 farms out of more than three million keep cattle of working age. Of course, the rich farmer can lend his ox or cow to a poor farmer, and so the same number of cattle can do much more work. This actually happens in Korea, and, according to Hoon K. Lee, "the labor power derived from cattle (in Korea) is the largest source of farm labor, *except the human*."[39]

Only 37,000 farms out of 3,052,400 had horses in 1938 and only 1,124,237 farms kept pigs, that is about one farm out of three. The number of farms keeping sheep was only 2,949 out of more than three million. There is no information available

[39] *Op. cit.*, p. 220, italics by the author.

with regard to fowl, but if we assume an average of one cock and four hens per farm, this would mean that only one farm out of three was sufficiently prosperous to keep them.

The Social Stratification of the Korean Village

Up to this point the problems of the Korean farmers have been discussed as if all of them were equally rich or equally poor. These average figures indicate that the net result of the Japanese administration cannot be called a success, and that what has been accomplished has been done with an exclusive view to the interests of the Japanese Government by a bureaucracy foreign to Korea. But this approach, useful as it is, does not suffice to explain the basic causes of Korean poverty. The real explanation lies in the social conditions prevailing in rural Korea. Better results might be achieved in Korea within a short time if the social conditions prevailing there could be changed. It will be noted below how Japanese domination resulted in the forcible destruction of domestic spinning and weaving in Korean villages. This is a social phenomenon, not rooted in climatic or any other natural conditions. Let us see what other social conditions stand in the way of Korea's economic development.

Japanese Seizure of Korean Agricultural Land

As we saw in the chapter on population, Japanese and Korean residents in Korea form two groups which differ greatly in their social status. Under these conditions the fact that this or that particular area of agricultural land is Japanese-owned is of great social and political importance.

The Governor-General wrote in 1914:[40]

"Formerly Japanese buying paddy and dry fields in Chosen aimed at obtaining incomes by renting them to Korean tenants or reaping profits by reselling them. Now those undertaking agricultural industry themselves are gradually increasing. Besides, as a result of the efforts put forth by the Oriental Development Company under Government directions to encourage the immigration of Japanese farmers, the number of Japanese farmers living in Chosen has greatly increased."

But as we saw before, the number of Japanese farmers has not greatly increased; only the activity of Japanese companies, landlords and speculators has really increased. Professor E. deS.

[40] *Results of Three Years' Administration of Chosen since Annexation*, by the Chosen Governor-General, January, 1914.

Brunner, who visited Korea in 1926 and carried out an investigation of rural conditions there, wrote as follows:[41]

"Government statistics show less than six per cent of the agricultural and residential land registered as Japanese in ownership. But this fact needs careful scrutiny. All land belonging to corporations with a Korean charter is classed as Korean in ownership, though the ownership of the concern may be Japanese. The holdings of some of these companies are considerable. On the other hand, some of the companies incorporated in Japan Proper have Korean stockholders.[42] Again, virtual transfer of the ownership of land, title of which is in the name of Koreans, may result through loans made by Japanese institutions or individuals. No data are available on that point. Various careful estimates of fair-minded nongovernment Japanese and Koreans place the proportion of land owned, actually or virtually, by the Japanese at a point between 12 and 20 per cent. In some counties in the south, Japanese ownership, based on tax records, is said to extend over half of the land. Thus in one county, Ikson, in south Keisho province, an investigation by a Korean landlord and educator is reported to have shown 32 per cent of the assessed property valuation in the hands of 120,000 Koreans and 68 per cent in the hands of 8,000 Japanese. Since the great part of Japanese-owned land is in the south, it is probably fair to conclude that in this section about one fourth of the land has passed out of Korean hands."

In this connection, it must be noted that southern Korea is mainly a country of paddy fields which produce almost twice the yield of dry fields; that is, the economic importance of the 25 per cent of holdings in the south is much higher than that figure would suggest. James Dale Van Buskirk writes:[43]

"It is asserted that over half the land—some say two-thirds—has passed into Japanese control . . . These statements are, of course, gross exaggerations, but there is cause for concern in the very reports, and in the underlying basis of fact."[44]

It is perhaps significant that the Government no longer publishes statistics of Japanese holdings in Korea. We know that between 1921 and 1927, the area of holdings classified as

[41] *Rural Korea*, International Missionary Council, 1928, p. 126.
[42] The number of such stockholders is extremely small.
[43] *Korea, Land of the Dawn*, pp. 71-72.
[44] These are not such gross exaggerations as Mr. Van Buskirk thinks if we take the whole country into consideration. After annexation, the Japanese Government declared the property of the Royal House, most of the forests, post lands, and other public land, government property, i.e., Japanese property. Probably, more than half of the private forests are in Japanese hands—let us say half. Then the Japanese hold the following: state forests 6,700,000 *cho*, private forests 3,700,000 *cho*, say, 20 per cent of the cultivated land in private Japanese hands 1,000,000 *cho*, state agricultural lands about 100,000 *cho*, or a total of about 11,500,000 *cho*. Thus if the Japanese control only 20 per cent of the cultivated land, their holdings would be about 11,500,000 *cho* out of a total area of the country of 22,200,000 *cho*, or more than half of the total.

Japanese[45] increased from 242,500 *cho* to 346,200 *cho*,[46] or by 43 per cent. There is reason to believe that after 1929 this process of expropriation of the Koreans peasantry was greatly accelerated.[47]

Ownership and Tenancy

The agricultural population of Korea is divided into seven groups, namely:

1. Landlords: i.e., persons who do not work on the fields and do not hire laborers to work their fields, but lease all their land to those who have none of their own, or not enough of their own, and in return receive rent. Orthodox economists have tried to justify the existence of these parasites, but without great success.[48]

2. Farmer-landlords: farmers who lease out the larger part of their land but also undertake the cultivation of a portion of it, usually with the help of hired workers. They represent a group between the purely parasitic type and the capitalistic entrepreneur.

3. Farmer-owners: those who own their land and till it themselves, that is, owners of their homes, owners of the land they farm, people deeply attached to their native soil.

4. Farmer-owner-tenants (or semi-tenants, or semi-owners); those whose own landholdings are insufficient so that they are compelled to lease some land from landlords and landlord-farmers.

5. Tenants: farmers who have no land of their own and lease the land they farm from landlords, paying rent for it.

6. *Kadenmin*: "fire-field" farmers or squatters, who do not have land of their own but cultivate clearings in Government or privately owned forests or wastelands, moving from one plot to another.[49]

[45] And, as was pointed out by Professor Brunner, Japanese corporations registered in Korea are classed as Korean in ownership.
[46] H. K. Lee, *op. cit.*, p. 146.
[47] The fact that the holdings of the Japanese are increasing does not mean in itself deterioration of tenancy conditions: the new big master may be better in some respects than was the small Korean proprietor. However, the Korean landowner in many ways was connected with Korean life, while the interests of the Japanese are in Japan. Every *cho* of land that passes into Japanese hands intensifies the pressure upon the Korean population.
[48] For those who may suspect the author of bias, the well-known Japanese economist K. Takahashi may be quoted to support this definition of Korean landowners as parasites: "The Korean tenancy system is exceptionally harsh and parasitic." *Op. cit.*, p. 187.

7. Agricultural laborers: whose main earnings come from wage-labor even if they rent a miniature plot of land to cultivate for their own use.[50]

Of course, a capitalist without land could rent land and till it with the help of laborers and be classified as a tenant, though his social and economic position would be above that of most of the farmer-owners. However, there are no such tenants in Korea. A tenant in Korea is a farmer who would be glad to accept employment for wages if he could find it and who in order to exist must rent land.[51]

The statistics of the period 1910-1918 are, as we have seen, especially unreliable. From 1919 to 1932 the agricultural population was socially constituted in the following way:

FARM FAMILIES IN DIFFERENT CLASSES OF RELATION TO LAND
(Percentages of the total number)

	1918	1928	1932
Non-farming landlords	0.6	0.7	1.2
Other landlords	2.5	3.1	2.5
Farmer-owners	19.7	18.5	16.6
Owner-tenants	39.5	32.3	25.9
Other tenants	37.7	45.4	53.8
	100.0	100.0	100.0

Calculated from absolute data given in *Chosen Nenkan*, 1939.
Note: *Kadenmin* are omitted from 1928 and 1932 because statistics for them are available only after 1926.

---

[49] One may disagree with the placing of *kadenmin* below the tenants: they do not pay rent and may appear to those who do not know the actual situation as farmers who are nearer to the category of owners. But this is how the Japanese report characterizes them: "These poor people are driven by hunger from place to place, making shelters in log cabins and keeping their bodies and souls together by planting grains and vegetables on the hillsides." (The *Annual Report on the Administration of Chosen*, 1934-35, p. 116.)

[50] Some students believe that this social ladder is an over-simplification. There may be farmers who lease out some part of the land they own and lease in other land; there may be farmers who rent land in order to sub-lease it to poorer tenants. This is true: life is not simple, and only with difficulty can its varied phenomena be classified under rigid headings. However, we must take into consideration the form in which statistics are available and make the best of it. If the statistics do not give information on the number of tenants who sub-lease the land they lease, nothing can be done about it. Moreover, the divisions named represent the main groups. Take the case of the tenant who sub-leases his rented land. The number of such tenants is small and cannot influence, for example, the general tendency of changes in tenancy. Their sharp increase, for example, could not occur without a large increase in the number of tenants. The number of owners who lease out part of their land and rent some land is small as compared with the total number of owner-tenants.

[51] Questions concerning credit and farm indebtedness will be discussed below.

In 1932 the government modified the form of its statistics. Non-farming landlords were omitted altogether; other landlords were combined with farmer-owners, and a new category, laborers, was introduced. The information on *kadenmin* is available since 1927. In order to supply a comparable basis with the preceding period, we start in the following table with the year 1932, which was the last year of the preceding table.

CHANGES IN ECONOMIC POSITION OF KOREAN FARMERS
(percentages of total)

	1932	1938
Farmer-owners	18.4	18.1
Owner-tenants	24.9	23.9
Other tenants	51.8	51.8
Kadenmin	2.0	2.4
Agricultural laborers	2.9	3.8
	100.0	100.0

The change that has taken place in Korean villages, as shown in these two tables, is striking. The proportion of landlords has increased, but, of course, it continues to be small because landlords, like rich people everywhere, never form a substantial portion of the total population.[52] The percentage of owner-tenants fell from 39.5 in 1918 to 25.9 in 1932, and another one per cent between 1932 and 1938. Non-owning tenants formed 37.7 per cent in 1918 and 53.8 per cent—more than one-half of the total—in 1932; their position remained stationary between 1932 and 1938, but the two other groups below that of the tenant in social standing increased rapidly. *Kadenmin*—those roaming dispossessed peasants who try to wrest a living from half-cleared patches in the forests—increased from two per cent of the total in 1932 to 2.4 in 1938, and agricultural workers from 2.9 per cent of the total to 3.8 per cent. (This class is, of course, least susceptible to accurate statistical reporting, and, judging from descriptive accounts, such as that of Hoon K. Lee, is probably much larger.) Tenants of all kinds, *kadenmins*, and laborers together formed 81.9 per cent of the total number of

[52] In the period of 1928-1932—the latest about which we have data—the number of landlords who do not manage any agricultural enterprises increased by 12,153 and the number of landlords who do some management of their estates fell by 12,426 in the same period; i.e., the landlords of Korea were becoming more and more parasitic. Figures are taken from *Chosen Keizai Nempo*, 1939, pp. 96-97.

farmers in 1938. Those who did not even have one patch of their own land formed 58 per cent of the total number of agricultural families, as compared with 37.7 per cent in 1918. It is clear from these figures that a rapid process of dispossession is taking place among Korean farmers which turns them first into owner-tenants, then into tenants, and finally into proletarians, squatters, beggars, and vagabonds.[53]

We have shown that the assertion that "over half of the Korean land has passed into Japanese control" is not a "gross exaggeration," when the total land area of Korea is considered. It would also seem that such assertions are not far from the truth even with respect to the cultivated land. The proportion of farmer-owners fell from 22.2 per cent of the total in 1918 to 18.1 per cent in 1938,[54] and the proportion of owner-tenants fell from 39.5 per cent to 24 or 25 per cent. This means that tens of thousands of farmers were dispossessed and that other tens of thousands of the younger generation could not acquire land in spite of the increase of the cultivated area. All of this increase, together with a large portion of the old cultivated area, went to a relatively few landlords. Were these landlords Koreans or were they Japanese? The official silence on this question is in itself eloquent. Why was the publication of land statistics by nationality discontinued? "The probable reason" in the opinion of the Korean economist, Hoon K. Lee, "is that this kind of publicity would irritate the Koreans and might cause an outbreak of a revolutionary movement like that in 1919."[55]

Let us look at the question from another point of view. We have seen that Japanese agricultural policy in Korea was directed towards an increase in the production of rice. It is natural to expect, then, that the process of dispossession of farmers advanced farther in rice-producing regions than in

[53] Of course, the sequence may be changed, and an owner may become a laborer directly, but usually a farmer fights tenaciously for his position and descends the social ladder gradually.

Many writers on Korea have mentioned the efforts of the Japanese, beginning with General Terauchi and ending with General Minami, to stop this process of dispossession and even to reverse it, but it would seem that these efforts were far from adequate.

[54] The figures, as has been shown, are not strictly comparable, yet the mistake made in direct comparison is very small.

[55] *Op. cit.*, p. 144.

others. When we investigated the density of the population, we divided the area of Korea into three regions: (1) the paddy region where paddy fields form from 50 to 100 per cent of the cultivated area; (2) the mixed area, with paddy fields occupying from 20 to 50 per cent of the area; (3) the dry field region, where paddy land forms less than 20 per cent of the cultivated area. The ownership of land in these three regions is shown in the following table.

OWNERSHIP RELATIONSHIP IN THREE ECONOMIC AREAS, 1937
(percentages)

	Paddy region	Mixed region	Dry-field region
Owners............	13.7	16.5	31.3
Owner-tenants......	25.2	23.9	21.8
Tenants............	55.8	52.6	40.7
Kadenmins..........	0.3	4.0	5.1
Laborers...........	5.0	3.0	1.1
Total........	100.0	100.0	100.0

Note: Calculated from the official data given in Hishimoto's *Chosen bei no Kenkyu*, Tokyo, 1938, p. 91.

This table shows that in the paddy region the owners make up only 13.7 per cent of the total number of farmers and the laborers 5 per cent; in the dry-field region, the owners are still 31.3 per cent of the total, laborers are few, but the number of *kadenmins* is large, 5.1 per cent. Thus in the most important regions, from the Japanese point of view, independent farmers are a small minority.

The Government-General does not publish statistics of land owned by non-farming landlords, by farmer-owners, and by owner-tenants. However, we can make some calculations which give an insight into the picture. The table presented below is based on certain assumptions.[56] It cannot claim great accuracy, yet it helps to give a better understanding of Korean conditions.

[56] The assumptions are as follows:
1. The number of absentee landlords is the same as in 1932, i.e., 33,000.
2. The number of landlords who cultivate a portion of their land is 50,000, and the average area which they cultivate is five *cho*.
3. The owner-tenants who in the official statistics are termed "chiefly owners" are supposed to own 75 per cent; and those "chiefly tenants"—25 per cent of the land they cultivate.
4. The average size of the farm in each class given in the official statistics is at the midpoint of each class interval.
5. No farmer-owner leases his land.

LAND DISTRIBUTION IN KOREA, AN ESTIMATE

Category	Number	Area owned (in 1,000 acres)	Percentages of Totals Number	Area
Landlords............	83,000	7,198	2.7	63.9
Owner-farmers........	502,320	2,888	16.3	25.7
Owner-tenants........	729,320	1,174	23.6	10.4
Tenants..............	1,583,435	0	51.3	.0
Kadenmins............	71,187	0	2.3	.0
Laborers.............	116,020	0	3.8	.0
Total....	3,085,282	11,260	100.0	100.0

In this estimate the share of the wage-earner, *kadenmin*, and tenants is, of course, zero. The area owned by landlords is a good approximation. We see from this table that less than three per cent of the total number of families own about two-thirds of the cultivated area; 16.3 per cent own 25.7 per cent of the area, and the remaining 81 per cent own 10.4 per cent. Furthermore, it is extremely difficult for a landless person to buy land in Korea. Agricultural wages in 1939 were about 15 yen per month. If the agricultural worker can save half this amount, he would be able to buy one *cho* (2.45 acres) of dry field after working twenty-four years.[57] Under these conditions it is clear that for the majority of the landless farmers it is impossible to become owners. The Korean farmer is "free" to buy land and enjoy the blessings of ownership, but actually he cannot buy it.

As to the renting of land, there are two important questions: first, how many competitors are there, and second, the amount of rent. The two questions are closely related because the greater the number of competitors, the higher the rent and the smaller the plot which can be rented.

If the entire cultivated land in Korea were distributed equally, the average holding would be 1.48 *cho* or 3.6 acres. This is very small by American standards, but it would permit a modest existence under Korean conditions. However, from table 5 in Appendix I, one can see that almost half a million farmers (17 per cent) till less than 0.74 acres, most of them as tenants or owner-tenants. Another 21.4 per cent of the farmers each till an area of between 0.74 and 1.26 acres. We have heard

[57] One *cho* of paddy was valued in 1938-39 on the average at 2.160 yen and one *cho* of dry field at 750 yen. (*Kokusei Gurafu*, a Japanese Monthly, July 1940, p. 500.)

much about the smallness of plots in Japan, but the situation in Korea is no better in that respect.

COMPARISON OF FARM SIZES IN KOREA AND JAPAN

Percentage of total number of farms

	Korea (1938)	Japan (1937)
Less than 0.5 cho	38.4	33.8
0.5-0.99 cho	24.9	34.2
1-1.99 cho	19.7	22.7
2-2.99 cho	10.9	5.7
3-4.99 cho	4.7	2.3
5 or more cho	1.4	1.4
Total	100.0	100.0

Source: *Kokusei Gurafu*, February 1939, p. 106.

This table indicates that in Korea the poorest farmers form a larger part of the total than in Japan. And those of them who are tenants are in a much worse situation than the farmer-owners because they must pay rent.

There are five common forms of rent in Korea, three under which the tenant pays with the produce of the rented land or with its substitute, and two under which he pays in cash. Rents in kind are (1) a fixed rent, when the tenant surrenders a previously agreed amount from his crop; (2) a rent fixed after the harvest; (3) rent in which a previously agreed share of the harvest is paid. Cash rents are of two kinds: (1) real cash rent, i.e., when the amount of rent is fixed in advance in money; (2) equivalent cash rent, when the amount is fixed in kind, but the tenant pays its equivalent at current values. Cash rents are relatively rare in Korea. As to the rents in kind, the fixed rent is prevalent[58] in two provinces; the "after-harvest" rent is prevalent in three, and share rent is prevalent in nine provinces. The share of the harvest which is taken by the landlord may be seen from the following table:

SHARE OF HARVEST GOING TO THE LANDLORD IN 1930 IN KOREA
(As per cent of total harvest)

	Fixed rent	"After-harvest"	"Share" rent
Highest	58-90	50-79	50-80
Common	40-51	45-60	50-55
Lowest	20-39	30-44	30-50

Source: Hishimoto, *Chosen bei no Kenkyu*, Tokyo, 1938.

[58] I.e., it is met more often than the other two forms of rent in kind.

Thus the most common share of the rent is 50 per cent of the crop; but in view of the fact that rents rise as high as 90 per cent, while the lowest falls to only 20 or 30 per cent, it is reasonable to suppose that the average rent is above 50 per cent, and may be as high as 60 per cent.

In addition, the tenant usually pays the land taxes;[59] he pays for water to *suiri kumiai*; he delivers the grain (and when the landlord lives in a city, this may be quite expensive); pays fees for inspection of rice; supplies animal power, seeds, fertilizers; and makes presents to the landlord. Moreover, most of the landlords are absentee owners; they have their agents on the place who, according to K. Takahashi, compel tenants to bring them presents, and to work for them; who order harvesting at a time convenient to themselves, increase rent to their own advantage, and burden the tenants in other ways.[60] As a result of all this, tenants are left with only a small portion of their crop. According to Shirushi the tenants in Kogen province are left with only 18 per cent of the rice crop and those in the Kimpi region with only 25 per cent.[61]

Most of the tenants make only oral agreements. According to Hishimoto, only 27 per cent of rent contracts are in written form.[62] An investigation in 1930 showed that 81 per cent of rent contracts had no fixed term;[63] i.e. the landowner could evict the tenant at any time. In the case of a fixed term, this was usually one or three years.

These are the conditions of tenancy in Korea as described by Japanese authors writing in 1935, 1937, and 1940. All Japanese economists agree that these conditions are bad. Yet we find the following statement in the work of the American investigator, Paul H. Clyde:

[59] "After annexation it was decreed that land tax should be borne by the landowner, but in view of the force of old custom, public taxes and imposts are still often shifted to the tenants, and this is extremely prevalent in Chusei, Zenra, Keisho." Hishimoto, *op. cit.*, p. 122.

[60] This information is taken from the work of K. Takahashi, *op. cit.*, pp. 187 *et seq.*; also from Hishimoto, *op. cit.*, p. 116 *et seq.*

[61] *Op. cit.*, p. 14-15. Shirushi was writing in 1940. But in 1926 E. DeS. Brunner wrote: "In one village in the south a careful investigation by W. Lyon, of Taiku, showed that the renter's actual *net* share was 17 per cent—a condition by no means exceptional in that part of the country." (*Op. cit.*, p. 127.)

[62] The year is not given. His book was written in 1938.

[63] *Op. cit.*, p. 124.

"To protect farmer tenants, as differentiated from owner cultivators, the Government completed regulations in 1928 by which the tenant is protected in his tenancy of land, in maintenance of the land's fertility, in methods of payment of rent and taxes, and in the settlement of disputes. These regulations have produced beneficial results at a time when agricultural distress had been aggravated by the world-wide depression."[64]

If this is true, then the Korean farmers have been protected since 1928 and have enjoyed the beneficial results of these regulations. Unfortunately, this assertion is based on a misconception. The number of landlord-tenant disputes in Korea began to rise sharply in the 'twenties. As has been shown above, a very large part of leased land in Korea is in Japanese hands. To quote H. K. Lee:

"When a dispute begins between Japanese landlords and Korean tenants, it easily grows serious beyond the immediate economic issue at stake because of the national and racial feeling."[65]

Chosen Nenkan also points to the dangers of these disputes in view of their influence on public opinion.[66] To meet this situation, the Government-General in 1928 established a Temporary Committee for the Investigation of Tenancy (*Rinji Kosaku Chosa I-inkai*). This committee "made investigations, worked out—on the basis of these investigations—a plan for the improvement of tenancy customs, and lent administrative guidance to begin this improvement."[67] The ground was then prepared for publication, in December 1932, of a Decree on Tenancy Arbitration, and this decree became effective in February 1933. This law did not exist in 1929-1933, so it is difficult to see how its "beneficial results" could have been observed by Professor Clyde. Hoon K. Lee, writing in 1935 or 1936, noted that "how the order will affect the actual situation remains to be seen."[68] Hishimoto wrote in 1937: "Though the results of the *Nochirei* [the more comprehensive law of 1934, see below] are not yet apparent because only a few years have passed, yet it will contribute."[69]

In April 1934, on the basis of investigations by the Tempo-

[64] *Op. cit.*, p. 446.
[65] *Op. cit.*, p. 176.
[66] *Op. cit.*, p. 307.
[67] *Takumu Yoran*, 1939, p. 184.
[68] *Op. cit.*, p. 180.
[69] *Op. cit.*, p. 137.

rary Committee mentioned above, the Government-General published *Nochirei*, or the Law on Agricultural Land which became effective in October 1934. Takahashi notes that the law passed over the opposition of landowners, and that in the regulation of tenancy problems Korea found itself ahead of Japan.[70] The official *Takumu Yoran*, 1939, describes this law in the following terms: it "stabilizes the position of the tenants, regulates the activities of the landlords' agents, helps to avoid friction between landlords and tenants and supports peace in the villages . . . protects not only the interests of tenants, but also the just interests of landowners, and it can be hoped that in a spirit of harmony and cooperation between landowners and tenants agriculture will develop and farmers will progress."[71]

The Law on Agricultural Land, however, did not apply to leases of mulberry tree fields, forests, salt fields, or to perpetual leases—important exceptions as far as Korean agriculture was concerned. As to the landlords' agents, it stipulated that they should be registered with the local Committee on Tenancy which would see whether the agents were fit for this work or not. The failure to comply with this regulation could result in a maximum fine of 300 yen. As to the term of the contract, the goal was set as three years; if neither party notified the other three months before the expiration of the contract, it was to be considered renewed. Disloyalty and other causes were sufficient for the landlord to refuse renewal. With respect to the most important problem—the amount of rent—the law merely recognized that this was an "exceptionally difficult question," and stated that in case of dispute at the time when the rent was due, the dispute was to be settled by mediation. Yet if the amount of rent is not determined by law, it is clear that all the other provisions of this law mean little, because the landlord can evict any tenant by demanding excessive rent.[72] Moreover, much depends upon the Tenancy Committee and the Courts which are in Japanese hands. Thus it is difficult to see any significant change in the position of the tenants as a result of the publication of this law.

[70] *Op. cit.*, p. 198.
[71] *Takumu Yoran*, 1939, p. 185.
[72] Writing in October 1940, *Toyo Keizai* notes that "some landlords—bad landlords—recently very often change their tenants."

The Japanese cannot change the situation for two reasons. First, they cannot very well undermine the medieval land relations in Korea while the same system still prevails in Japan itself. One can hardly expect a country to be more liberal in its colony than at home. Secondly, this system coincides with Japanese needs. For the Japanese, Korea is primarily a source of raw materials and foodstuffs.[73] The Korean farmers eat less and less rice because rice must be exported to Japan Proper. The tenancy system, together with the taxation system, is an important instrument for pumping rice out of Korea. Korean farmers, after paying rent and taxes, are left with only a small fraction of the rice they produce. Let us see how this system works in practice. In 1932, an investigation was made in Korea by the Japanese authorities to determine the marketable surplus of rice. The results of this investigation are embodied in the following table:

DISTRIBUTION OF RICE PRODUCED IN KOREA AMONG AGRICULTURAL CLASSES OF POPULATION

Economic class	Total output of rice (in 1,000 koku)	Rice available per member of the family, koku
Landlords	6,486	11.43
Owner-farmers	2,578	0.99
Owner-tenants	4,892	1.21
Tenants	3,440	0.41
Total	17,398	1.88 (average)

Source: *Chosen Beikoku Keizairon.*
Note: The rice available to owner-tenants and tenants is actually less than the amount shown because in the investigation only rent was taken into consideration.

This table shows how misleading it is to speak solely in terms of averages. The average is 1.88 *koku* per person; but landlords have 11.43 *koku* and tenants (more than half of the total) have only 0.41 *koku*. It also shows how rice is pumped out of Korea. Farmers have very little rice left, especially if the payment of taxes, payments for fertilizers, and other expenses are taken into consideration. They have not enough for themselves; but the landlords have a substantial surplus and this surplus goes to Japan.

[73] *Toyo Keizai* (The Oriental Economist) wrote in its issue of October 20, 1940: "Because of her geographical position—being a military base for the continent—the part of Korea as a supply depot for military materials and foodstuffs is very important. Her contribution to the Empire's demand for rice ... also is very great."

Now we can better appreciate the "general trend toward greater consumption."[74] Omitting the year of crop failure, 1939, let us see how these "improving conditions" and the "general trend toward greater consumption" affected the Korean population as a whole.

PER CAPITA CONSUMPTION OF RICE IN KOREA
(in *koku*)

Average for	Amount	Index
1915-1919	0.707	100
1920-1924	0.638	90
1925-1929	0.512	72
1930-1933	0.449	63
1934-1938[a]	0.396	56

Source: For 1915-33, *Chosen Keikoku Keizairon:* for 1934-38 calculated by the author.[75]

[a] Figures of crops for 1936-1938 as corrected, see Appendix II.

The trend is unmistakable, but it is quite different from the "trend" discovered by Dr. Schumpeter. The average consumption of rice in Korea was almost halved in twenty years, and was 0.396 *koku* in 1934-38 as compared with 1.089 *koku* in Japan in 1939.[76] [77]

But, one may ask, why should Koreans eat rice? Millet is as good for them. Dr. Schumpeter writes, for example:

"They (the Koreans) consume their own barley, wheat, and millet and also import millet from Manchuria. The small Korean farmer sells[78] his rice and buys or raises cheaper millet for his consumption."[79]

[74] Schumpeter, *op. cit.*, p. 292.

[75] The method of calculation (the same as that used by the Japanese) is as follows: (1) the crop of, say 1937, is considered as consumed in 1938; (2) the figures for exports are taken from *Chosen Keizai Nempo,* 1940, p. 52; (3) the figures for population are those of current statistics (with census figures consumption would be less), but the figures for 1936-37 production were "recalculated" in order to make them comparable with those for the previous years. (The reasons for this are explained in Appendix II.)

[76] *Nogyo Nenkan,* 1941, p. 270.

[77] One objection may be made to these calculations—"the absence of any accurate statistics of stocks and carry-over" (E. B. Schumpeter). However, this absence does not invalidate the conclusions. The capacity of the Korean rice warehouses in 1934-36 was about one million and a half *koku*; movement of rice to and from them may change the picture for a particular year by 5-10 per cent, but it cannot seriously influence a five year average, because if at the beginning of the period the warehouses were full and at the end completely empty (or vice versa), this could influence a five year average only by 2-3 per cent, but it is clear that the warehouses at both points were neither completely full, nor completely empty.

[78] We have seen above that "the small Korean farmer" cannot sell his rice because all his surplus is taken from him.

[79] *Op. cit.*, p. 290.

However, if we examine the consumption of all kinds of cereals in Korea, as shown in the following table, we find that not only the consumption of rice but the consumption of all cereals is on the decline.[80]

PER CAPITA CONSUMPTION OF CEREALS AND BEANS IN KOREA
(in *koku*)

	1915-1919	1930-1933
Rice	0.707	0.447
Millet	0.303	0.325
Barley	0.430	0.411
Beans	0.190	0.142
Others	0.402	0.343
Total	2.032	1.668

Source: *Chosen Beikoku Keizairon.*

The available figures indicate that this "trend" continued up to 1938, that in 1939 there was an unprecedented crop failure, that the 1940 crop was poor, that the 1941 crop was about equal to that of 1938, and that in 1942 there was another serious crop failure.

Japanese economists have admitted this trend (in Japanese language publications). Hishimoto, Takahashi, Shirushi, Ogawa, Tobata, Fukui, and others whose works are quoted in these pages are officials whose duty it is to investigate and report on what they find. The Government-General has shown itself aware of the plight of the Korean farmers.[81] But it could not change the social system of Korea while the same system prevailed in Japan. It could not suddenly invest vast amounts of capital in Korean agriculture. Armaments, and preparations for war were absorbing all available resources. It could find money for the production of sulphate of ammonia because this

[80] The average consumption of cereals, as given above at 186 kg. per *koku* gives a daily per capita consumption of cereals in Korea at 1.87 lb. A part of this goes as fodder to the animals; a part is used as seeds; another part is used in making alcohol; and, in addition, the consumption by the rich (including Japanese) is much above the average. The average per capita daily consumption of meat in Korea was about 0.02-0.03 lb. in 1938.

[81] In 1929, an official investigation reported 837,000 families having no means of subsistence (Takahashi, *op. cit.*, p. 201); in the spring of 1930 (which was not a year of crop failure) 1,253,000 families had no food and were gathering grass and bark of trees. The government report of 1935, mentioned above, gave as representative Korean farmers, three individuals, each with a deficit of cash and a shortage of cereals; Shirushi, writing in 1940, presents a striking picture of the gradual impoverishment of the Korean village and of the return to a natural economy, because the farmers have no means to buy anything.

meant explosives for use in time of war. It could find money for steel mills, because they were important for the prosecution of war. But there was no money for reclamation, for agricultural improvements, or for construction of dwellings. What could the Administration do under such circumstances? Under General Ugaki it organized the Movement of Rural Revival with emphasis on self-help, self-reliance, and spiritual mobilization. This movement was started on January 1, 1934, at the lowest point of the depression, and was designed to give some hope to the villagers. The main slogans were:

> Achieve self-sufficiency in foodstuffs, each household!
> Repay your debts!
> Balance your income and expenditure (in other words, stop buying manufactured goods).[82]

Some model villages were selected and in these a concrete plan was worked out for each family showing how, in five years, it might raise itself materially and spiritually through self-awakening, self-effort, and spiritual mobilization. An investigation of one such model village was made. It was found, for example, that the village had eight cows of which two were borrowed. The advice was to increase the number to twenty. Also, improvement in fodder, and in harness was recommended. It was calculated that if the villagers increased their production by so much they would have—assuming that the prices remained the same—such and such cash income and would pay off their debts first of all; then they would buy land and the tenants would become proprietors. The benevolence of the landlords was mentioned as a contributing factor. The number of working days was to be increased from an average of 95 to 100, and the surplus of labor was to be used for cultural advancement.[83]

---

[82] K. Takahashi was troubled a little by this particular slogan: it threatened the profits of capitalists. (*Op. cit.*, pp. 79-85).

[83] K. Takahashi, (*op. cit.*, pp. 85-86) also mentions the necessity of (1) more work by women outside the home; this would give a cheap supply of labor for industry; (2) stopping the cooking of fodder for horses and cows—a custom which takes so much time, wastes so much precious firewood, and wastes straw needed for making compost fertilizers. Professor Brunner, writing earlier than Takahashi, mentioned the following causes of rural depression in Korea: (1) the agricultural depression throughout the world; (2) transitional period in Korea (from agriculture to industrialization); (3) lack of resourcefulness; (4) improvidence; (5) the political situation. The last cause is not elaborated, and landlordism is not mentioned in this connection.

General Ugaki promised that by such means as these the abject poverty of Korea would be eliminated in ten years and the inner regeneration of the Korean population accomplished; and then in another ten years the Koreans might even be ready for self-government and become subjects (Shimmin) of the Empire.[84] Writing in 1939, Fukui notes that "five years have now passed since the start of this movement; and though the results are not small, yet it depended too much on guidance by the officials."[85]

War conditions have brought no improvement in the situation. As we have seen, the mass of the Korean farmers have no marketable surplus of cereals because it is taken from them through rents, taxes, and other charges, so that favorable prices, if any, do not help them. It is true that they are now making their own straw shoes and use rape-seed oil instead of kerosene, but a complete return to a natural economy is impossible because home spinning and weaving are being destroyed by the Government system of compulsory sales and the destruction of looms, and because the burden of taxes and duties on such enterprises is increasing.[86]

The supply of commercial fertilizer is not increasing; the labor force in the villages is drained by military necessities (armament works, mines, construction of roads, airfields, and, more recently, conscription); and the production of implements has declined because of the shortage of steel. The only hope is that the burden of usury (about which more will be said later) may be alleviated through the depreciation of currency, but even this is doubtful because the loans bearing especially high rates of interest are, as a rule, short-term, and the usurers under-

[84] K. Takahashi, *op. cit.*, p. 572.
[85] *Chosen Keizai Nempo*, 1939, p. 104. J. Dale Van Buskirk (*Korea, Land of the Dawn*, in a section entitled "Efforts to help the people," p. 74) enthusiastically describes one model village, Turimyi. "The annual income for Turimyi families is over $400, more than two and a half times the average for that part of Korea. The people have so prospered that they have been able to buy land, and now there are 28 owner-cultivators and 18 part-owners among the householders; only fourteen are tenants. The various associations [of this village] have over $7,500 in cash and property. They lend money to their own villagers at 18 per cent, while charging outsiders the prevailing 36 per cent." A nice model village charging 36 per cent interest to the outsiders and only 18 per cent to its own members! But if all villages must become usurers in order to become prosperous, one wonders where eventually the victims will be found.
[86] Sadanao Shirushi, *op. cit.*, pp. 33-34.

stand better than the farmer the dangers of depreciation. They can demand conversion to payment in kind, and no government regulations can save the farmer because he is dependent upon the usurer. The usurers can also insure themselves from depreciation by storing cereals and buying up land, and it is known that the price of land is sharply rising. To all this should be added the consequences of the crop failure and famine in 1939.

CHAPTER VI

FORESTRY AND FISHING

Forestry

The achievements claimed by and for the Japanese Government in Korea in the matter of afforestation have been widely publicized. The purpose of this chapter is to evaluate these achievements.

KOREA'S FOREST AREA
(in 1,000 *cho*)

1910	15,850
1930	16,601
1938	16,317

Source: Government General of Korea, *Annual Report for 1910-11*, and *Takumu Tokei*, 1938.

This table suggests that the forest area, which now is about 74.6 per cent of the total area of Korea (that of Japan is about 63 per cent), rose during the first twenty years by seven to eight hundred thousand and then fell by three hundred thousand *cho*. But this comparison is of doubtful value. In 1910 the forest area was divided in the following manner: 5,123,000 *cho* were listed as covered with "regular forest," 6,619,000 *cho* with "young trees" and 4,107,000 *cho* "without standing trees"; but such a division is not available for the later periods, and without it the comparison has no meaning. However, we have estimates of the volume of standing timber since 1927.[1]

VOLUME OF STANDING TIMBER

	In million *shakujime*	In million cubic metres
1927	824.7	247
1930	747.8	224
1933	719.9	216
1936	569.2	198
1938	673.2	202

Source: *Chosen Keizai Nempo*, 1939, and *Chosen Nenkan*, 1941.

[1] There may be information for previous years, but the author has been unable to secure data previous to 1927.

This table shows that in eleven years the volume of Korea's standing forests fell from 824.7 million *shakujime* to 673.2 million—a decrease of 18.4 per cent. One may ask how this is possible when almost all works dealing with Korea praise the Japanese achievements in the field of afforestation. The answer is: (1) tens of thousands *cho* of good forest are destroyed by fire each year; (2) 30,000 to 40,000 *cho* each year are burned by *Kadenmin*[2] who, as has been mentioned, move from place to place burning forests to clear land for their fields; (3) from year to year Japanese companies have felled larger and larger amounts of timber:

TIMBER FELLED IN KOREA
(in million cubic metres)[a]

1910	0.673	1936	2.269
1920	0.890	1937	2.436
1930	1.250	1938	2.649
1935	2.265	1939	2.780

[a] Ratio used is one shakujime equals 0.333 cubic metres. Calculated from *Chosen Keizai Nempo*, 1939, and *Chosen Nenkan*, 1941.

Thus, according to official information, timber felled in the last few years forms 1.3 to 1.4 per cent of the standing timber. But the actual volume of felling is probably much larger, because the official figures are based on the licenses granted, but felling in private forests (which constitute by now the larger part of the forests) is difficult to estimate, and fellings in state-owned forests often exceed the amount shown in licenses. In addition, there are large amounts of forest used annually for firewood, charcoal and other forest products, the amount of which is given in weight, so it is difficult to compare it with other figures. Moreover, large amounts of forest are destroyed by accidental fires and by fires caused by *Kadenmin*. All this clearly shows that the Government's successes have not been remarkable: while some afforestation (and this chiefly by private efforts) has been achieved in the south and center, deforestation has proceeded rapidly in the northern provinces, the only ones where good stands of forests can be found. Before 1937 the Government spent less than two million yen annually on forests, while the value of forest products in 1939 was almost 200 million yen. Even the plan of 1939, which is to run for

[2] K. Popov, *Economica Yaponii*, p. 389.

fifteen years, calls for the expenditure of only 76.6 million yen, or about 5 million yen annually, and provides for afforestation of only 230,000 *cho* or 15,000 *cho* each year. But during these years felling is certain to increase tremendously because of extensive industrial construction and, more important, because Japan is now cut off from her foreign supplies of timber and pulp, while her needs in connection with the war have sharply risen, and Korea is her nearest source of supply.[3]

Another development with respect to forests should also be noted: the changing character of ownership. Before the coming of the Japanese there were very few state forests: forests were in private hands and in the hands of the king. After annexation not only the king's lands but also private forests became Japanese property:

"After the annexation of Korea by Japan, in 1910, most of the privately owned forest land was taken over by the government as state land, because the owners had failed to register it under the law of 1908. By doing this the government acquired more than four-fifths of the entire area under forest."[4]

However, after this confiscation of forests the policy was reversed. First, some of the forests taken over from Korean owners were returned (about 3.5 million *cho*). Forests which were "generally uncared-for" or "barren" were also "widely scattered" and their adequate care by the State was difficult. On the other hand, to dispose of them in any other way than to hand them back to the former owners would be a threat to their livelihood.[5] In other words, they were returned because it was impossible to utilize them. But there were also many good forests transferred to private hands:

[3] The program mentioned above was supplemented by a new program in 1938 at a total cost of 27 million yen, to be completed in twenty years. The measures to be taken were (1) reforestation of cleared lots; (2) protection of young plants; (3) afforestation of barren lots or those with scattered trees only; (4) seeding each year of 20,000 *cho* for pulp, bring the total area to 400,000 *cho*; (5) establishment of 150 forest districts; (6) development of the population's love for forests, etc. But in 1939 a new plan was adopted: to plant one million *cho* in twenty years at a cost of twenty million yen. This over-production of plans reflects how rapidly the destruction of forests has proceeded since the start of the war and casts doubt on the figures of slight increase in the volume of standing timber in 1937 and 1938 over 1936, as shown in the above table.
[4] H. K. Lee, *op. cit.*, p. 183.
[5] *Annual Report*, 1936-37, pp. 127-128.

"Among other things the new law also provided a way by which unreserved state forest land might be leased to private persons for the purpose of afforestation and ultimately be transferred to those who might show success in this work. Japanese as well as Koreans took advantage of the opportunity."[6]

Unfortunately, the Government transferred forest land to Japanese owners not only "for the purpose of afforestation," but also for purposes of deforestation. The scale on which such gifts were made may be seen from the following example: on September 1, 1937, Chosen Ringyo Kaihatsu Kabushiki Kaisha (Corporation for the development of forest exploitation in Korea) was organized with a subscribed capital of twenty million yen and a paid up capital of two million yen. The purpose of the corporation was to exploit state forests and give "help" to the owners of private forests. This corporation received from the Korean Government-General 500,000 *cho* of the best timber land in Korea for nothing—about one-fourth of the remaining good forest in Korea. Moreover, the company was to receive a subsidy from the Government—7.4 million yen in annual installments up to 1946.[7] It was reported significantly that now "Korean forestry from a stage of simple protection and planting reached a stage of utilization and exploitation."[8] We have seen that Korean forestry even before 1937 was not limited to "simple protection and planting." More destruction than planting of forests went on.[9] Now, evidently, the time had come for a more reckless exploitation of the remaining forests of Korea. Between 1927 and 1937 the volume of standing timber in state forests fell from 588 to 338 million *shakujime*, while that of private forests increased from 210 to 288 million *shakujime*; in other words during this period a considerable part of the state forests was transferred to private ownership. Unfortunately, the Government-General does not publish statistics of land—agricultural and forest—owned by the Japanese, though it possesses such statistics.

The total value of the forest products in 1939 was 192.6 million yen and was made up of the following items:

[6] H. K. Lee, *op. cit.*, p. 183.
[7] *Chosen Keizai Nempo*, 1940, p. 185.
[8] *Ibid.*, 1939, p. 177.
[9] This is the opinion of the Japanese themselves: "Increment [of forest] has a tendency to diminish each year because felling and planting are not kept in balance." (*Chosen Keizai Nempo*, 1940, p. 179).

FORESTRY AND FISHING

VALUE OF FOREST PRODUCTS, 1939

Product	Volume of weight	Value (in million yen)
Timber	2,780,000 cub. mt.	37.6
Firewood	4,670,000 mt. tons	42.2
Branches and leaves	4,090,000 mt. tons	28.8
Grass (1938)	850,000 mt. tons	3.3[a]
Materials for composts (1938)	5,170,000 mt. tons	14.7
Others including grass and materials for composts		84.0
Total		192.6

Source: *Chosen Keizai Nempo*, 1940; *Chosen Nenkan*, 1941.
[a] Excluded from the total.

If these official data are correct, then the Koreans pay more for firewood, leaves and grasses than the Japanese companies pay for timber! Grass mentioned in this table is used for manure.

Fishing

The coast line of Korea, including the innumerable islands, bays, and inlets, is very long—about eleven thousand miles (that of Japan 17.5 thousand miles). Moreover, on the coasts of Korea cold and warm sea currents meet—a condition favorable for fishing grounds. There are some 75 kinds of edible fish in Korean waters, 20 kinds of shell-fish, 15 algae and ten kinds of other sea animals and plants. In order of importance the following fish should be mentioned: *iwashi* (a kind of sardine), *mentai, saba* (mackerel), *guchi*, and *tachi*.

Since the annexation of Korea, fishing has undergone a rapid development. According to official estimates, the value of sea products caught in Korean waters increased from 8.5 million yen in 1912 to 87.1 million yen in 1938. Though statistics for 1912 can hardly be considered reliable, yet, even as compared with 1919 the value of the catch doubled and the quantity approximately quadrupled. In 1939 the quantity of fish caught in Korean waters was 1,596,000 tons and, including shell fish, sea-weed and other marine products—1,758,100 tons, as compared with 2,425,900 tons caught in Japanese waters. Thus the catch in Korea amounts to almost 73 per cent of the catch in Japan, which leads the world in this respect. The question remains, however, whether this remarkable growth has resulted from the reckless plunder of fishing resources without any thought of the consequences.

The expanded volume of the Korean catch was due chiefly to a tremendous increase in the catch of *iwashi*, namely from 275,900 tons in 1932 (23.6 per cent of the total) to 1,388,200 tons in 1937 (65.5 per cent of the total). In 1938 there was a sharp fall in the catch of *iwashi*—to 975,500 tons. This fall may of course be a temporary phenomenon, but members of fishing associations in southern Korea have complained that there are no fish in their lots any more. The catch per vessel, for example, was only at 3,600 yen in South Keisho, as compared with 127,000 in Northern Kankyo, which has only been recently developed. The difference between the catch of vessels in these two provinces cannot be due to a difference in quality of equipment since all these vessels belong to Japanese entrepreneurs.

Recently the manufacture of sea products has assumed great importance. At least three-fourths of all fish caught in Korean

DEVELOPMENT OF SEA PRODUCT MANUFACTURES
(Value in million yen; quantity in 1,000 tons)

	Quantity	Value
1918	...	19.1
1923	...	29.6
1928	...	44.9
1933	...	35.6
1937	556	93.4
1938	453	96.8

SEA PRODUCTS MANUFACTURED IN 1938

	Quantity (in tons)	Value (in 1,000 yen)
Dried fish	34,800	12,832
Salted dry fish	7,300	1,779
Boiled dry fish	15,600	6,745
Salted fish	42,500	6,400
Canned fish, 1,000 boxes	2,019[a]	4,178
Salty fish (*shio karai*)	12,900	3,217
Seaweeds (laver, etc.)	10,200	6,915
Other foods	12,600	2,595
Sub-total: foods	135,900	44,661
Fertilizers	198,900	28,926
Fish oil	116,000	21,979
Other products	2,500	1,252
Total sea products	453,300	96,818

Source: *Takumu Tokei*, 1938.
[a] Not included in the total.

FORESTRY AND FISHING 129

waters are used for other than food purposes, while 91 per cent of the catch of *iwashi* in 1937 was processed further, chiefly into oil and *iwashi* cakes. *Iwashi* oil is used in the production of hard oils, glycerine, fatty acids, gunpowder, medicines, soap, candles, and margarine, while the cake is used for fertilizer.[10]

The last table shows that 54 per cent of the manufactured products are not used as food, and some of them serve important war purposes.

Mention should also be made of fish-breeding in the interior waters of Korea. In 1938 the value of fish caught in these waters was 5.9 million yen and the quantity—6,400 tons.

It would appear that a catch of almost two million tons of fish might be a substantial supplement for the Korean diet—almost 220 pounds per head of the population. Unfortunately this is not the case. As has already been mentioned, less than one-fourth of the fish caught and less than one-half of the manufactured sea products are used directly for food purposes. But even this is not the end of the story. Parallel to the development of fishing in Korea a rapid growth of exports of fish from Korea took place, mainly to Japan, as may be seen from the following table:

TRADE IN SEA PRODUCTS
(in thousand yen)

Year	Imports Value	Imports Quantity (in 1,000 tons)	Exports Value	Exports Quantity (in 1,000 tons)	Net Exports Value
1926	1,895	11	25,672	103	23,777
1929	2,994	12	36,404	159	33,410
1932	2,870	13	22,016	161	19,146
1935	2,951	14	42,215	248	39,264
1938	5,519	21	81,862	510	76,343

Source: *Chosen Nenkan*, 1941.

This table shows that (1) imports of sea-products into Korea as compared with exports are very small (3-4 per cent in quantity in recent years); (2) exports in twelve years increased almost five times in quantity and more than three times in value; (3) at least five-eighths of the fish and other sea-products are exported; this shows that the increase in quantity of fish caught brought very little benefit to the Korean population. This,

[10] *Chosen Keizai Nempo*, 1939, p. 183 *et seq.*

again, shows how dangerous it is to consider an increase in the value of products "an impressive record," and to believe that "all . . . statistical measures point to improving conditions," as did Dr. Schumpeter.[11]

Altogether about half a million persons are engaged in fishing, and thirty thousand in processing fish-products. The capital invested in the industry is estimated at forty million yen —an important industry under Korean conditions. Unfortunately it presents the same picture as do other forms of enterprise in Korea: there are both Japanese and Koreans in this industry, but they have little in common. The number of Japanese fishermen in Korea was 29,063 in 1915 and 15,931 in 1932 (the latest figure available); that is, it fell by one-half in seventeen years, while the number of Korean fishermen rose from 242,000 to about 450-480,000. In the same year, 1932, the value of catch per Korean fisherman was 102 yen, per Japanese —1,910 yen, or nineteen times more. This was not because the Japanese were more skillful in catching fish than the Koreans but because they got the best lots and had better equipment. In 1932, the value of equipment per Japanese fisherman was 265 yen, or seventeen times as large as that of Korean fishermen which was 15 yen, 20 sen. Furthermore, there was one boat for each two Japanese fishermen, as compared with one boat (and, of course, a very small one, with primitive equipment) for every thirteen Korean fishermen. It is clear then, that Japanese "fishermen" are actually entrepreneurs using Koreans as a labor force. If the Koreans wish to borrow money, equip vessels and make good profits, they must go either to Japanese banks or to Korean usurers. In both cases the situation is similar. K. Takahashi points out that Koreans fish mainly along the coast because their vessels are small. They are dependent upon merchants. A considerable part of their "capital" is borrowed at 30 per cent per year, or ostensibly with no interest at all but with the obligation to surrender their catch only to their creditors and at low prices.[12] In some cases, however, the position of even the Japanese entrepreneurs is not easy because three purchasers of raw fish—Nippon Yuhi, Chosen Chisso and Chosen Yuhi—dominate the market.

[11] *Op. cit.*, p. 289 on the value of marine products, and p. 292 on "statistical" measures.
[12] *Op. cit.*, p. 314 *et seq.*

CHAPTER VII

POWER AND MINERAL RESOURCES

Power Resources of Korea and Their Exploitation

Wood, coal, water power, oil, and wind constitute Korea's sources of power for industrial and mining enterprises. In domestic industry, labor and animal power are used extensively, but modern industry cannot be created on this basis. Wood under Korean conditions is too expensive as a source of power, and no large use of wind is made. A special company has been carrying on a survey for oil since 1935,[1] but no discoveries have been reported and imports of oil are small. Thus coal and water power are at present the only power resources of importance in Korea.

In 1932, H. F. Bain estimated Korea's coal reserves at 42 million tons.[2] Since then substantial discoveries have been made and in 1939 the reserves of anthracite were estimated at 1,340 million tons and of soft coal at 410 million tons. These reserves are not large, though with an annual consumption rate of only two million tons (in 1936), they would be sufficient for more than eight hundred years. It is quite probable that new discoveries will give an even higher figure. Korea is not richly endowed with coal, but she is better supplied than, for example, Italy, and a very considerable part of her reserves consists of anthracite. Coal production increased sharply between 1930 and 1936 as indicated in the following table; production figures since that date have not been published.

OUTPUT OF COAL IN KOREA
(in thousand tons)

1910	78
1920	289
1929	938
1930	884
1936	2,282

Source: *Chosen Keizai Nempo*, 1939.

[1] K. Popov, *op. cit.*, p. 393.
[2] Bain, *Ores and Industry in the Far East*, 1933, p. 40.

DISTRIBUTION OF COAL RESERVES
I. Anthracite

Province	Coal Field	Reserves (in million tons)
Kogen	Neietsu field and Sanchoku	374
Heian, southern	Southern part	300
	Northern part	491
Kankyo, southern	Bunsen and Kogen	125
Keisho, northern	Bunkei	27
Heian, northern	Kokai	20
Zenra, southern	Wajun	3
Total		1,340

II. Soft Coal

Province	Coal Field	Reserves (in million tons)
Kankyo, northern	Along the Tumen Kisshu	373
Heian, southern	Neisen	20
Keisho, northern		10
Kokai		5
Kankyo, southern		1
Total		409

This table shows that only the northern and east central part of Korea have rich coal deposits. These regions also possess great water-power and iron-ore reserves, and so are destined to become the seat of Korea's heavy industry.

As to the actual production of coal, in 1936 it was distributed among the provinces as follows:

Province	Output (in 1,000 tons)
Heian, southern	966
Kankyo, northern	945
Kokai	175
Kankyo, southern	86
Heian, northern	58
Zenra, southern	35
Kogen	9
Keisho, northern	8
Total	2,282

Source: *Chosen Nenkan*, 1941.

This table shows that the output was concentrated almost entirely in two provinces—in Southern Heian, near Heijo and Kaisen, and in Northern Kankyo, near the Russian border. The Kogen fields are being rapidly developed, however, and the Japanese say that the quality of their coal is equal to that of Indo-China.

The chief producers of anthracite are the Korea Anthracite Company, the Oriental Development Mining Company, and the Japanese Navy and Mitsubishi Mining Company. Production of soft coal is in the hands of the Korea Coal Industry Company, the Korea United Coal Mining Company, the Meiji Mining Company and the Japan-Korean Mining Company— all of which are Japanese concerns.

Many experiments have been made with the liquefaction of Korean brown coal which, it is said, can easily be turned by the dry process at low temperatures into tar, heavy oils, volatile oils and paraffin. The Korea Nitrogen Fertilizer Company (Chosen Chisso Hiryo Kabushiki Kaisha) started the construction of a plant for these purposes in Eian in 1938 or 1939 and the Korea Coal Industry Company (controlled by Chosen Chisso) started the production of oil for the navy from the coal of Agochi coal field.

In 1937 a five-year plan for increasing coal production in Korea was introduced and it was said to have worked well; but the vast increase in the demand for coal in Korea and in Japan caused a great strain. Before 1937 Korea was a net importer of coal, though the quantities imported were insignificant. But after 1937 the wartime expansion of Japanese heavy industry created a greatly increased demand for Korean anthracite. However, the rapid expansion of the Korean coal industry was retarded by a shortage of materials and labor, and, in many cases, by the inability of the railway feeders to cope with the situation. There were also complaints that the prices for coal established by the government were too low and did not take into account conditions in particular fields. Yet in spite of all these difficulties a significant rise in coal production as compared with 1936 was reported and some experts predicted that the output of coal in 1943 would reach 6.5 million tons, as compared with 2.3 million tons in 1936.

Water Power and Generation of Electricity

From 1911 to 1914 the Korean Government-General conducted an investigation of water power resources which resulted in the conclusion that the potential capacity was only 57,000 kw. At that time the great variation in the volume of water in periods of drought and flood during the same year was considered the chief obstacle. A second investigation conducted between 1922 and 1926 estimated the water power potential to be 2,250,000 kw. It is said that the change in the estimate was due to possibilities created by new techniques—higher dams, tunnels through the ridges and larger reservoirs. All this is true, but probably not to the extent of a forty-fold increase. More recent investigations have raised the estimates of potential capacity to five million kw. including one million kw. which can be generated by the frontier rivers Yalu and Tumen (actually two million, but half of it would go to Manchuria).[3]

Moreover, investigations are being conducted to determine the use of differences in sea level during the tides and it is estimated that a hydro-electric station using the difference of levels of the tides at Kinsen could generate one million kw. Korea thus ranks relatively high among the countries of the world with regard to hydro-electric power resources, and if all this power were used, it would generate more electricity than was generated in either Italy or France in 1937.

This circumstance is of tremendous importance for the future of Korea. Her forest reserves, as we have seen, are rapidly being depleted; her coal reserves, as they are known now, are modest; but her water-power resources would permit the development of substantial large-scale industry.

DEVELOPMENT OF ELECTRIC STATIONS
(in 1,000 kw.)

	In Operation				Under Construction		
	Water	*Coal*	*Other*	*Total*	*Water*	*Coal*	*Total*
1910............	...	1.7	...	1.7	...	...	...
1917............	0.1	6.5	1.4	8.0	...	...	...
1923............	3.5	18.6	3.3	25.4	22.6	...	...
1929[a].........	13.4	34.5	...	...	...	...	...
1931[b] (March)..	109.4	53.4	...	162.8[b]	274.9	0.1	274.9
1938 (March)...	722.3	145.8	...	668.1[b]	798.3[c]	50.2	848.5

Source: *Chosen Keizai Nempo*, 1939.
[a] *Takumu Tokei* gives for 1929 a total of 112,434 kw.
[b] *Takumu Tokei* gives for 1931 a total of 234,532 kw. The difference may be due to difference in date: its figures appear to relate to December 31.
[c] Including 320,000 kw. of the Yalu station.
[d] It is est'mated that the capacity of electric stations in Korea will reach two million kw. by the end of 1943.

[3] *Chosen Keizai Nempo*, 1939, p. 238.

COMPARISON OF CAPACITY OF ELECTRIC STATIONS

	Year	Capacity (in 1,000 kw.)	Per cent of water power
Korea	1938	668.1[a]	78
Japan	1937	7,166.5[b]	55
United States	1940	41,639.0	28

Source: For Japan—*Dainippon Teikoku Nenkan*, 1939.
For the United States—*Statistical Abstract*, 1941.
[a] Some estimates for the end of 1943 go as high as two million kw.
[b] Some estimates for the end of 1943 go as high as 13.2 million kw.

Full utilization of these resources, however, is still a problem for the future. The foregoing tables show the extent to which they had been developed by 1938.

The first of the above tables shows that before 1930 there was a very slow development of electric power in general and of water power in particular. In 1929 the capacity of water power stations was only 13,400 kw. as compared with the 34,500 kw. capacity of electric stations using coal. The first large development—in 1931—came ostensibly as a result of the need for nitrogen fertilizer; but since nitrogen products are important for war purposes as well as for agriculture, it may be assumed that the development took place primarily as a result of pressure from the Army. Korea was to become a powerful economic base for future military adventures on the continent (*Tairiku heitan kichi*), and for this purpose the rapid development of electric power under Government supervision was considered essential. Accordingly, a law was published in 1932 stipulating that construction of new stations must be approved by the Government-General, which was to draw up the blueprints; that the Government-General was to exercise general control over all electric stations, and that it must approve the senior administrative and technical personnel of the electric companies.[4]

This clearly indicated that the rapid development of power resources after 1931 was not a purely "spontaneous" move on the part of private interests. The table given above shows that by March 1938 stations in operation had a capacity of 668,100 kw., while stations with a capacity of 848,500 kw. were under construction. Water power had come to occupy a dominant place—522,300 kw. in operation and 798,300 kw. under construction in 1938. These figures show, however, that the capac-

[4] K. Popov, *op. cit.*, p. 392.

ity as of March 1938 was only 9.3 per cent of the total capacity of Japanese stations in 1937 and only 1.6 per cent of the capacity of the United States stations in 1940. They also show that there was still room for further development in Korea even after completion of all projects under construction at that time. It was expected that before 1940 water power stations would increase their capacity by 710,000 kw. and that 40,000 kw. would be added by stations working on coal. Some estimates for the capacity of electric stations by the end of 1943 give a total figure of two million kw.

All stations are in the hands of private corporations with the exception of a station in Kenjiho which is municipal. These corporations possess large capital. In 1933 there were 63 corporations, but through mergers the number was reduced to 18 (1939); of these only three have a capital of less than one million yen each; thirteen corporations have ten million yen each or more and three of them have a capital above 50,000,000 yen each. These corporations are thus bigger than those in Japan, where only 13-14 per cent of all electric corporations had a capital of ten million yen or more each.

The paid-up capital of electric corporations in Korea increased as follows:

Year	Capital in million yen
1919	10.2
1929	34.5
1934	100.4
1937	267.6

Source: *Chosen Nenkan*, 1941.

Among the most important stations, finished and under construction, the following should be mentioned:

(1) Fusenko, finished, with a capacity of 180,000 kw. belongs to Korea Nitrogen Fertilizer, the power being used at its huge plant at Kanan. The cost of construction was 55 million yen. The area of the reservoir—9 square miles; the height of the dam—87 meters; the head of the first fall—707 meters; of the second—216 meters; the third—94 and the last 41. The total capacity of the stations (when the fourth is finished)—202,000 kilowatts.

(2) Choshinko, under construction, with a final capacity of 325,000 kw., owned by Choshinko Electric Power Company;

planned cost—60 million yen; electric current was expected by the end of 1941; volume of water in the reservoir—1,059 million cubic meters, effective volume—840 million cubic meters; height of the dam—48.5 meters, length—733 meters; the head of the first station (144,000 kw.) 465 meters; of the second—(106,000 kw.) 313 meters; of the third (47,000 kw.)—142 meters; of the fourth (118,000 kw.)—92 meters. In the first station there will be four turbines of 36,000 kw. each.

(3) Yalu. The final capacity of the seven stations on the Yalu is estimated at 1,580,000 kw. and their cost will be 354 million yen; but for the time being only the largest one, at Shuifengtung, is under construction by the Manchurian Yalu Water Power Company and the Korean Yalu Water Power Company, each supplying fifty million yen. On the "Korean" side the money is to come from the Chosen Electric Power Transmission Company and others. The capacity of this station now reported in operation is 640,000 kw. with a maximum volume of water, but 445,000 with an average volume, half of which is to go to Korea. The height of the dam is to be 94 meters, breadth, 80 meters at the base and 8 meters at the summit; the area of the reservoir is to be 300 sq. km., or half of the famous Lake Biwa in Japan, and the volume of water 7,300 million cubic meters. One of the turbines is to be 92,000 kw. The construction was expected to be finished by the end of 1941[5] but several floods caused delay.

(4) Kasen and Seihei, owned by Kanko Water Power Electric Company, were started in February 1939; the first part (Seihei) 170,000 kw., was expected to be finished by December 1941, the second (Kasen)—by June 1942.

(5) Two Kokai stations about 200,000 kw.

(6) Funei station first generated electricity in November 1939 for the chemical industry of Northern Korea.

(7) Neietwu, working on anthracite, southeast of Keijo (Seoul) and Genshu, with a capacity of 100,000 kw., was to have been ready in 1940.

(8) A station was planned in Tokusen, (Southern Heian province), upstream from Heijo.

Total, including others, is 1,493,360 kw. for hydroelectric

[5] Details for Fusenko, Choshinko and Yalu River projects are taken from Seiichi Kojima, *Sen-Man-Shi Shinko Keizai*, pp. 70-77.

stations, and 517,000 kw. for stations using coal, or a total of 2,010,360 kw.

It is expected that in a few years one grid will cover all of Korea and permit equalization of supply and demand.[6] This is especially important in view of the "unprecedented" increase in demand from industrial enterprises, which necessitated control over the distribution of electricity.

In time of war and inflation the question of the price charged by these corporations is not as important as in peacetime. Yet it is worth mentioning because it shows the policy of the big Japanese corporations which monopolize the generation of electricity. In 1937 the average revenue per kwh in the United States was 4.3 cents for non-farm-residential and domestic sales, and 1.7 cents for non-farm commercial and industrial sales; in other words the price charged to residential consumers was 2.52 times greater than the price charged to industrial users. In Korea the average price charged to industrial users was about 2 sen and to residential consumers 15-16 sen or 7-8 times more. Moreover, the prices charged to industrial users differed according to the volume of demand, so that the price charged to small industrial consumers was 4-5 sen per kwh and to large ones 1.4-2.20 sen. Thus small entrepreneurs paid at least twice as much per kwh as the large ones, and, as will be shown later, the large ones are exclusively Japanese. To the advantages enjoyed by Japanese enterprises over Korean in respect to credit, taxation, etc., one should add that of cheaper power. At one time some economists hoped that electricity

[6] The development of the electric power transmission lines may be seen from the following table:

LENGTH OF TRANSMISSION LINES
(in miles)

	1931, March	1938, March	1939, October (planned increase)
66,000 v.	125	1,490	450
110,000 v.	83	409	...
154,000 v.	...	423	...
220,000 v.	...	...	2,022
Total	208	2,322	2,472

Source: *Chosen Keizai Nempo*, 1939.

Thus, it was planned to more than double the transmission in one year.

would destroy the advantage of large enterprises over small ones, but, at least in Korea, it has increased this advantage.

In conclusion let us compare the number of families using electric light in Korea and Japan:

FAMILIES HAVING ELECTRIC LIGHT
(percentage of total number)

	Year	Per cent of total
Korea	1939	12.5
Japan	1937	90-91

Thus, while in Japan nine tenths of the homes are supplied with electricity, in Korea, in spite of all development, only one eighth of the population enjoys its benefits.

Mining

The development of mining in Korea may be seen from the following table:

VALUE OF MINING PRODUCTS
(in 1,000 yen)[a]

1910	6,068	1929	26,488
1915	10,516	1931	21,746
1920	24,205	1936	110,430
1922	14,503	1937	150,000[b]

Source: *Chosen Keizai Nempo*, 1939.
[a] Including the value of coal.
[b] Given in a round figure in *Chosen Keizai Nempo*, 1939, p. 195.

This table shows (1) rather slow development before the Mukden incident; (2) a fall in 1921-1922 and 1930-1931 due to depression; (3) rapid rise of output after 1931. Of course, a certain proportion of this rise is illusory, being due to the rise of prices, yet, on the whole the large increase is real. This is indicated by the fact that the number of miners increased from 36,000 in 1931 to 140,000 in 1936, and to 220,000 in 1938.

PAID-UP CAPITAL OF MINING CORPORATIONS
(in million yen)

1914	9.6
1933	24.5
1938	183.6

Source: For 1914, *Annual Report*, 1913-14; for 1933, K. Takahashi, *Gendai Chosen Keizairen*; for 1938, *Kokusei Gurafu*, April, 1940.

All data point to the rapid growth of mining in Korea after the Mukden incident. K. Takahashi enumerates the following causes: (1) depreciation of the yen and, consequently, the rise of yen prices and the gold "rush"; (2) partially as a result of the first—the discovery of other ores; (3) the demand of munition factories for metals and ores; (4) the development of new light metals; (5) the cheapness of electricity and encouragement by the Korean Government-General.

Takahashi's second and fourth reasons can be disregarded because metals other than gold and iron have so far played a small part, and the development of the light metals, aluminum and magnesium, is the direct result of the demand of the Japanese armament industry. As to encouragement by the Government-General—it was not an all-round encouragement, but followed a certain plan, and this, as can easily be seen, was closely related to military plans. The largest subsidies were given to the gold producers, and those who have noted the export of gold from Japan to the United States to pay for imports of scrap iron, copper, zinc, etc., can easily see the reasons behind this encouragement. Next to that given gold producers, the most substantial encouragement—in money, tax exemptions, and so on—was given to the producers of aluminum and magnesium, so much needed for the production of airplanes. In other words, the feverish expansion of mining and *some* branches of industry in Korea was only a step in preparation for the big war.[7]

It is estimated that 200 minerals and ores are found in Korea, of which 137 are now used industrially. Korea has little or no sulphur, copper, chrome, tin, or manganese. In considering the development of mining by-products, we shall investigate first iron ore and the production of iron and steel; then gold, aluminum and magnesium, and then thirteen other products.

Iron Ore—Korean iron ore is of great importance for Japan. In 1929, 551,814 tons of iron ore were mined in Korea and in 1936, 234.4 thousand tons. Since that time no data have been published, but it is known that there have been important discoveries of additional ore deposits, and that strenuous efforts have been made to exploit them. Experts estimate that production in 1943 may have reached 6,300,000 tons, or slightly more than production in Manchuria and six times as large as Japanese production for the same year. Though these esti-

[7] According to *Chosen Keizai Nempo*, 1940, p. 199: "Formerly considerations of commercial profit stood in the way of development of some of the ores."

POWER AND MINERAL RESOURCES

mates appear to be too "optimistic" yet there is no doubt that a great increase in production has taken place.

It is estimated that Korea has about twenty million tons of iron ore of a high iron content and more than one billion tons of low grade ore. (Manchurian reserves are estimated at 800 million tons.) The most important source of low grade ore is Mosan, on the Manchurian frontier about one hundred miles from the Russian frontier. Its reserves alone are now estimated at one billion tons. The site was known long ago and in 1925 was estimated to contain several billion tons, but its ore, magnetite, contains only 32 per cent of iron. Its development was started by Mitsubishi, and recently the Mitsubishi Mining Company, Japan Iron Manufacturing Company, and Japan Iron Mining Company formed the Mosan Mining Corporation for its exploitation. Iron ore is also found in five places in Kokai province, especially at Kenjiho, near Tsinnanpo; in southern Keian at Kaisen; in southern Kankyo at Tigen (near the seashore, a very rich deposit recently discovered) and also at Tansen; at Jijo, near the Yalu in northern Keian; and two deposits in Kogendo. In 1936 the demand for steel by the countries of the yen bloc was estimated at six million tons, of which only fifty per cent was met from iron ore (through pig iron) and the rest from scrap from the United States, a source which could not be relied upon in war. The demand of the yen bloc area in 1941 was estimated at twelve million tons of steel, for which at least 24 million tons of iron ore were necessary, and the Mosan deposit was expected to play an exceptionally large part in supplying the yen-bloc area with iron ore.

Turning now to the question of pig iron and steel, we notice the following development:

PRODUCTION OF PIG IRON AND STEEL
(in 1,000 tons)

	Pig iron	Steel
1917	0.002	...
1918	42.7	...
1923	99.9	...
1925	101.9	...
1929	155.5	...
1931	147.9	...
1934	175.5	59.7
1935	147.8	97.4
1936	155.5	87.0

Source: *Chosen Keizai Nempo*, 1939.

Since 1936 no official data on production of pig iron and steel have been published, but it is known that a considerable development has taken place and it was estimated that in 1943 production of pig iron would reach 800,000 tons and production of steel—300,000 tons.

The Mosan Mining Development Corporation was expected to produce its first pig iron at the end of 1939 through a German process, while the Korean Nitrogen Fertilizer Company received permission in February 1938 to produce iron from iron sulphides. The Chosen Metal Corporation received a permit in March 1939 to produce steel in Jinsen (Chemulpo). In May 1939 the first blast furnace of the Mitsubishi Seishin plant started work, while the plant of the Japan Iron Company in Seishin was expected to be ready by April 1941. Thus beside Kenjiho, which for twenty years was the only center of production of pig iron and steel (Mitsubishi, later Nippon Seitetsu), several other centers of production have presumably begun operation, of which the most important is Seishin (a port, about 60 miles from the Russian frontier).

Gold and gold ores—Production of gold in Korea increased in value from 317 million yen in 1910 to 3.9 million in 1923 and 9.0 million in 1931; then it underwent a rapid development and reached 49.9 million yen in 1936,[8] and 69 million in 1937. General Ugaki's plan for the development of gold mining was replaced under the pressure of war by a new five-year plan. The 1937 output (20 tons) was to be increased each year by 10 tons and to reach 75 tons in 1942. When the plan was adopted it was considered quite feasible. The government lavished grants and subsidies[9] on the large producers[10] and spent tens of millions for this purpose.

[8] According to K. Takahashi (*op. cit.*, p. 323) this is only a part of the actual output, because great quantities of gold are smuggled out of the country.

[9] Twenty-five million yen were assigned for this purpose (including improvement of mining roads and electric transmission) in the 1939 budget. *Chosen Keizai Nempo*, 1940, p. 201.

[10] Since the start of the Pacific war, there has been no use for Japanese gold, and the large investments made in this industry are for the time being profitless. That is why we give less place to gold-mining than it would otherwise deserve; but the questions of policy have considerable historical interest. Subsidies were given to those companies (1) who had already been in business at least three years; (2) the value of whose production was about 10,000 yen a year, and was expected to increase; (3) to those who possessed approved mining lots (a measure directed against Koreans); (4) to those who used drilling machines. In 1931, 55.7 per cent of the total output was produced by entre-

The plan was not fulfilled in the first year (1938). The producers complained about the difficulties of obtaining necessary materials, shortage of labor and natural calamities. As for the second year of the plan, it was said that the result "does not permit optimism." The government then ordered the population to surrender all personal gold ornaments. At the same time the last foreign mining companies were squeezed out and one American company which had operated since 1899 at Unsan (Northwest) was bought out on July 14, 1939. Japanese officials claimed that foreign enterprises had tried to obstruct the development of gold-mining in Korea.

There were four gold refineries: (1) at Chinnampo (Kuhara's) (2) at Konan (Noguchi's) (3) at Choko (Chusei nando), Chosen Seiren Company, capital ten million yen; (4) at Bumpei (Sumitomo's), and two were under construction, one at Kaishu, Kokaido, to be ready by June 1940 and a second at Ryogampo (at the mouth of the Yalu), to be ready by October 1940 (Mitsui affiliate).

Aluminum—Production of aluminum in Japan was about 14,000 tons before the war and was in the hands of five corporations (including Sumitomo). But this industry had no domestic source of raw materials, so special attention was paid to Korea in that respect. On the seashore and on the islands near Moppo (Zenra Nanko) there are twenty-thirty million tons reserve of alunite, containing 20-35 per cent of aluminum. In 1939 this was mined and sent to Japan, but Korea Nitrogen Fertilizer Company has now built a plant for the exploitation of ore from Kasa island, Zenra Nando, and is producing 99.5 per cent pure aluminum.

In the coal fields at Heijo alunite shale is found in layers alternating with coal. It contains 40-50 per cent of aluminum and the reserve is estimated at 40 million tons. It was formerly used only in the production of fire-resisting materials, but a plant for the production of aluminum from this ore was being built at Chinnampo by Chosen Riken Kinzoku Kabushiki Kaisha. In 1940 the Korea Nitrogen Fertilizer Company in

---

preneurs with an output of Y500,000 or more and 20.4 per cent by those whose output was Y200-500,000. Small producers were also to receive help in the form of "technical advice." Recent reports from Japan indicate no new developments in gold mining and attention has shifted to other metals needed for war purposes.

Konan had almost completed an aluminum plant, and it was partially in operation. It is probable that production of aluminum in Korea in 1943 was not much below the 10,000 ton mark.

Other Minerals

Magnesite—Surface deposits of magnesite in Korea at Tansen (on the seashore, Kankyo Nando) are estimated at 650 million tons and another deposit is estimated at three billion tons; reserves at Kisshu (Kankyo Hokudo, south of Seishin) are estimated at tens of millions of tons. Korea thus ranks high in respect to reserves of magnesite. The first corporation to exploit magnesite was organized in 1934 by the Korean Nitrogen Fertilizer Company and some American capitalists with a plant at Konan. In 1935 the Japan Magnesium Chemical Industries Company started to build a plant in Seishin. The Chosen Riken Kinzoku Company has built a plant in Chinnampo and in 1939 the government established a special company for the exploitation of newly found deposits. Several other plants for the production of magnesium were under construction in 1939-1940. It was planned to mine 130,000 tons of ore in 1940.

Barytes—Deposits of barytes in Korea are numerous and among the best in the world. Barytes are used in dyes, cosmetics, and for military purposes. According to S. Kojima "The demand (for Korean barytes) sharply increased after the Manchurian incident."[11]

Copper—No copper ores of importance have been found in Korea. The copper which was produced (2-3,000 tons a year) was a by-product of gold and silver ores. It was estimated that in 1943 production of copper would exceed 10,000 tons.

Fluorspar—Fluorspar is used in the production of iron, glass, cement, and aluminum. Its production in Japan is insignificant. Mining in Korea started in 1928 and production reached 8,740 tons in that year. After that a large deposit (of about one million tons) was discovered in Kokaido which is now exploited by Mitsubishi. It is also mined in Kogen and Southern Kankyo provinces.

Graphite—Japan possesses only negligible amounts of this mineral, so important in the electrical industry, but Korea has extensive reserves of graphite which are found in all provinces.

[11] *Op. cit.*, p. 107.

Production in 1936 was 41,000 tons, chiefly in southern Kankyo and northern Keisho. But as only 10 per cent of it is scaly (the kind most needed by the refining industry) new surveys are being made.

Lead—Lead ores are found in southern Heian and southern Kankyo and its output rose from 824 tons in 1927 to 2,737 tons in 1936. It is said that lead ore reserves are such that in the future Japan may not need foreign imports of lead. Production of lead in 1943 was expected (by American experts) to reach 10,000 tons.

Lithium—(The lightest metal.) Rich deposits of lithium ores are found in Northern Chusei, in the Tan-yo district.

Mercury—It is found in several provinces and has been mined for many centuries, but the annual output is below one ton.

Mica is used as an isolator in the electrical industry and also in the glass industry; its uses are rapidly increasing. Production in Japan is small. Production in Korea is 70-80 tons annually. The most important mines are Toyo Kirara in Northern Heian; Kinko Kirara in Southern Heian (white mica); Hoshu and Rindo in Northern Kankyo.

Molybdenum, used in production of special steels, is almost absent in Japan Proper. Mining of molybdenum ores is rapidly increasing in Korea under the pressure of war, and the entire production is exported to Japan. Deposits are widespread. Annual production is estimated at 100 tons.

Nickel—Ores are found and mined by Sumitomo in Kogendo, Kinka district and by the Army and Government-General in Tansen district, Southern Kankyo (25-35 per cent metal content). Nickel is also found in Southern Chusei, etc. It is believed that future production will be sufficient to cover Japan's needs.

Silver—Ores are found in Korea chiefly as a compound with gold or gold and copper. Production in 1936 was 59 tons.

Iron Sulphides—At Tansen (Southern Kankyo) deposits have been worked since 1925 and recently additional important discoveries were made. The output is used by the Korean Nitrogen Fertilizer Company in its Kanan plant for the production of sulphuric acid. In addition, this corporation received a permit in December 1938 for the manufacture of iron from sulphide dregs.

Tungsten—Ores are found in many places in Korea. Production started during the first World War, but after the war the prices fell and production stopped. It was renewed in 1927 and from five tons in that year rose to 152 in 1933 and 1,706 tons in 1936. After that it continued to rise under the spur of war demands, but no figures of output were published. Some estimates put production in 1943 at 2,500 tons.

Zinc—Japanese domestic production of zinc ores is barely sufficient to cover one-fourth to one-third of the demand. This lends special importance to Korean zinc ores. Besides zinc ores, a rich combination of zinc, lead, copper, gold and silver is found in North Keisha. It is assumed that with the increase of mining, production may cover Japan's needs. The output of zinc ores in 1936 was 5,571 tons all of which was exported to Japan. Production in 1943 was expected to reach 18,000 tons.

This list of products mined in Korea is, of course, not complete, but it gives a sufficient picture of Korea's importance to Japan's war effort. The rapid development of mining can be clearly traced to war needs. Encouragement, subsidies, exemption from taxes, guarantees from losses—every means was used for this purpose. Landowners on whose lands ores were found became millionaires overnight. The number of mining applications grew by leaps and bounds. It was 5,200 in 1933; 15,700 in 1938. However, only a small proportion of the applicants received permission to mine. In 1933, 728 permits were granted (14 per cent of the number of applications for that year), in 1938—1,466 permits (9 per cent of the applications). Of course, many applications did not deserve serious consideration, but this was nevertheless a powerful weapon at the disposal of the Japanese government to prevent Koreans from going into business. Furthermore, it is one thing to get a permit and another to start a business. In 1936, for example, 1,268 permits were given, but new enterprises launched numbered only 500, since many Koreans lacked sufficient capital to go into business. The Japanese government then organized, in July 1939, a special corporation for the exploitation of dormant permits. But among those who had already started mining many were unable to continue, so they either shut down or sold out to big corporations. In this way big firms—branches of Mitsubishi, Sumitomo, etc.—secured control of the mining industry. As to the European and American mining enterprises, there were

41 of them in 1910, eleven in 1921, two in 1937 and none in 1941. A mining law in 1916 forbade new foreign enterprises.

Thus in the mining industry we find the same situation as elsewhere in Korea—domination by Japanese capital. In 1933 the value of mining products of Japanese enterprises was 35.9 million yen, of Korean—7.8 million. On December 31, 1938 the paid-up capital of 121 Japanese corporations occupied in mining in Korea was 171.1 million yen; on the same date there were only 29 Korean corporations occupied in mining and their capital was 12,449,000 yen, or 7.3 per cent of the capital of the Japanese corporations. With few exceptions, Koreans are employed only as laborers in the mining industry.

As to labor conditions in Korean mines, H. B. Drake wrote:

"There was no eight-hour day there [in a coal mine in Northern Korea], we learned, but two twelve-hour shifts. The workers . . . looked pale and seedy. They seemed to live in single-roomed houses, where the families swarmed together like rabbits. And always the price of coal increased, Father Calistus told me, and the wages decreased."[12]

In March 1939 the mining entrepreneurs in Korea held a second conference.[13] They faced a difficult situation. The government demanded increased production from them, but they were faced with a shortage of machinery and tools, shortage of materials, and shortages of skilled labor. The conference asked for additional grants, for the lowering of the price of materials, further reduction of railway tariff rates on ores, etc., from the government. But they did not forget the workers. They recommended:

(1) Cultivation among them of a spirit of work and patriotism.
(2) Improvement of *treatment* of workers.
(3) The negotiation of an agreement concerning control over workers.
(4) Training for workers.

Wages and hours were not mentioned.

[12] *Op cit.*, p. 196.
[13] *Chosen Keizai Nempo*, 1940, p. 211.

CHAPTER VIII

INDUSTRIAL DEVELOPMENT

Size, Character, and Distribution of Industry

Industrial statistics in Korea are deficient in more than one respect. First of all, as to the capital invested, there is relevant data only for the corporations, represented in Korea mainly by big enterprises, and even these statistics refer chiefly to "subscribed" capital and "paid-up" capital which in many cases are only remotely related to the present state of investment. With respect to production we have only statistics of the gross value. The number of workers is available only for enterprises with five or more workers or with a prime mover. All this makes for an incomplete picture. Furthermore, in some cases statistics are not comparable: the number of workers relates only to factory workers while the figures for gross value of output include household industry. In the opinion of K. Takahashi, Korean industrial statistics in general are exaggerated because there are no taxes in industry which would provide reliable data, while local officials like to show good results which they may claim as due to their own encouragement.[1] However, since he wrote this numerous taxes have been introduced in Korea, so that this criticism is no longer valid.

Of course, all these defects do not make the data valueless;

DEVELOPMENT OF INDUSTRY

Year	Number of employees in thousands	Gross value of industrial production in million yen
1922	46	223.3
1929	94	351.5
1933	120[a]	367.2
1937	207[a]	959.3
1938	231[a]	1,140.1
Japan, 1938	3,215	19,667.0

Sources: *Takumu Tokei*, 1938; *Chosen Keizai Nempo*, 1940.

[a] This is the number of employees; the corresponding number of workers was 108.8 thousand in 1933, 166.7 thousand in 1937 and 182.8 thousand in 1938.

[1] *Gendai Chosen Keizairon*, Tokyo, 1935, pp. 104-105.

important conclusions may be reached if due care is exercised. For the purpose of this analysis the year 1922 is used as a starting point because only since then has the value of production of domestic industry been calculated with any accuracy, and in that year the value of state and public enterprises was included in the total for the first time.

This table shows that in a fifteen year period the number of employees increased from 46,000 to 207,000 or by 163,000—eleven thousand a year on the average—but in 1938 jumped by more than 24,000 (because of the rapid increase of armament works). However, even in 1938 the number of industrial employees was only 7.9 per cent of the number of workers in Japan Proper, though the population of Korea formed about 33 per cent of the population of Japan.

The subscribed capital of industrial corporations increased from 382.2 million yen in 1936 to 663.0 in 1938 and to 728.7 million in 1939,[2] but even in 1938 it was equal to only 4.4 per cent of the subscribed capital of industrial corporations in Japan.

The figures for the gross value of production are not comparable with the figures for employees, because they also include the value of products of household industry. They show a growth from 223.0 million yen in 1922 to 1,142.6 million yen in 1938. However, a change in the price level should be taken into account. If these figures are divided by the index of wholesale prices (Keijo), the results would be somewhat different, as shown below.

GROSS VALUE OF INDUSTRIAL PRODUCTION
Corrected for changes in the level of prices
(in million yen of 1933)

1933	367
1937	672
1938	690

This table suggests that the physical increase over 1933 was just over 80 per cent, and the increase in 1938 over the previous year was very small despite the large increase in the number of workers.

If we exclude the production of household industry, the

[2] Including the capital of gas and electric enterprises. *Chosen Keizai Nempo,* 1940, pp. 239-240.

gross value of Korean industrial production was only 858.5 million yen in 1938, or 4.4 per cent of the figure for Japan, 19,667 million yen. This clearly shows that industry in Korea is still very backward in spite of its growth since 1929.

In 1929, the food industry occupied first place in Korea with textiles as a poor second. Other branches of industry existed, but only insofar as their presence was an absolute necessity even in a colony (repair shops, printing of government publications, some gas service, etc.). Gradually, however, the chemical industry expanded until it occupied first place, accounting for one-third of the total value of production in 1938. The food industry was second, the textile industry third, and the metal industry fourth (see Table I, Appendix III).

HOUSEHOLD INDUSTRY
PART OF HOUSEHOLD INDUSTRY IN TOTAL INDUSTRIAL PRODUCTION
(per cent of gross value)

Year	Per cent
1933	40.1
1935	33.1
1937	27.1
1938	24.7

The household industry of Korea, *i.e.* industry conducted at the home of the "entrepreneur" and by members of his family usually in their spare time[3] was responsible for 40.1 per cent of the total gross value of industrial production in 1933, and even as late as 1938 it was still responsible for one quarter of the total. This indicates, of course, not so much a remarkable development of household industry, as the undeveloped state of factory industry. The gross value of production of household industry increased as follows:

GROSS VALUE OF PRODUCTION OF HOUSEHOLD INDUSTRY
(in million yen)

Year	Value
1933	147.1
1935	200.1
1937	260.2
1938	281.7

Source: (1) *Chosen ni Okeru Katei Kogyo Chosa.*
(2) *Chosen Keizai Nempo,* 1940.

Taking into consideration the rise of prices in the same period, this indicates a growth of about fifteen per cent over

[3] See the definition in *Chosen ni Okeru Katei Kogyo Chosa,* Keijo, 1937.

the level of 1933. Of course, statistics of household industry are even less reliable than manufacturing statistics, yet a tendency of growth is apparent. This is to be expected in view of the unsatisfactory situation in the rural communities which compels the farmers to supplement their meager earnings from the land. The expansion of household industry may be attributed almost exclusively to the ability and tenacity of the Koreans because neither subsidies, grants, concessions, exemptions nor any other "encouragements of industry" were lavished on household industry. This fact is important because so often Japanese economists represent the Korean worker as a lazy, incapable person.[4]

Household industry predominates in the food industry, lumber industry and "others." In the textile industry, household work was responsible for 21.9 per cent of the total value of production in 1938; in machinery and tools for 15.6 per cent, and in ceramics for 26.5 per cent. Even in the chemical industry it was responsible for 10.7 per cent. (For details see Table II, Appendix III.) In the textile industry, the household was strongly represented in processing the cocoons of wild silk worms and silk refuse, and in weaving rayon and hemp. In the metal industry it prepared kitchen utensils. In the machine and tool industry it made agricultural implements and simple machinery, carts and boats. In ceramics it manufactured earthen utensils, bricks and tiles; the predominant position of factory industry in ceramics was due to the fact that cement and enamel utensils were produced only in factories. In the chemical industry it was strongly represented in medicines (made of domestic herbs), in products of vegetable oils and animal fats, in the making of fish oil, paper, fish fertilizers, and coal bricks. In the timber industry the home predominated in the making

[4] K. Takahashi, for example, attributes the following defects to the Korean worker (*op. cit.*, p. 402): no desire to advance; laziness; no desire to use intellect in work; very weak sense of responsibility. He mentions as positive qualities (*op. cit.*, p. 403): low wages and low standard of living; sufficient strength; "ability corresponding to the work to be done!" However, Takahashi noticed during his visits to the factories (*op. cit.*, p. 404) that the Korean workers who have obtained an education are very efficient though their sense of responsibility is still weak.

Seikaku Ito (*Chosen ni Okeru Katei Kogyo Chosa*, p. 216) points out the following "good points" (biten) of Korean workers: health, ability to withstand long hours of monotonous work, and their natural submissiveness. In Ito's opinion the defects of the Korean workers are: lack of inventiveness, indifference to technical improvements, and dislike of rules.

of furniture, casks, tubs, *gota*, lathework, etc.; in the food industry in making unrefined *sake* and other alcoholic beverages, soy, *miso* (bean paste), flour, candy, bread, fish products, etc. Among "other" products, the core of village industrialization as envisaged by the Korean Governors-General—we find willow ware, bamboo ware, paper ware, rattan ware, rush ware, and reed ware, wild grass ware, straw ware, needlework, footwear, etc.

This enumeration shows that household industry in Korea as elsewhere can exist only as long as the farmers and artisans can obtain raw materials, or where raw materials are almost a free gift of nature difficult to monopolize, such as wild grasses, reeds, and clay for pottery. This is a significant fact. It means that once export trade or big industry monopolizes these raw materials, the corresponding domestic industry comes to an end.[5] Even before the beginning of the Sino-Japanese "incident," legislation and administrative measures were applied in cases where for some reason the development of Korean household industry was considered undesirable. After the "incident," police power and the law were used even more energetically in reducing the supplies available for household industry.

Modern Industry

In contrast to the household industries with their primitive tools, there are very modern factories in Korea which can be compared with the best in the world. The new corporations organized in Korea after 1929 were connected with the houses of Mitsui, Mitsubishi, Sumitomo, and Yasuda, and were built on a larger scale than the corresponding enterprises in Japan Proper. For example, the Korea Nitrogen Fertilizer Corporation, a subsidiary of the Japan Nitrogen Concern, had in 1937 a capital of 62.5 million yen, and its fertilizer works in Konan claimed to be the second largest in the world. Production of sulphate of ammonia by the Japan Nitrogen Concern in Japan Proper

---

[5] It is interesting to note that in this struggle for raw materials the Japanese administration applied unusual methods. According to Sadanao Shirushi (*Chosen no Nogyo Chitai*, Tokyo, 1940, pp. 22-28), in some places it forbade the use of handlooms in villages, while in others handlooms were rendered useless by the obligation to use not more than ten *kin* (13 pounds) of yarn per person. Looms were often confiscated either outright or through fines imposed upon the owners. This policy was ruthlessly and successfully pursued in respect to cotton and silk which were to be sold to Japanese agents at prescribed prices (*kyohansei*).

was only 80,000 tons, while the annual capacity of the plant of the Korea Nitrogen Fertilizer Corporation was 500,000 tons.[6] Such enterprises are, as a rule, incorporated; so the growth of industrial corporations may serve as a good index of the growth of modern factory industry in Korea.

GROWTH OF INDUSTRIAL CORPORATIONS
(Including mining)

	1929	1932	1935	1938	1939
Number of corporations	484	563	717	1,203	App. 1,300
Subscribed capital, million yen	189.9	260.9	287.9	656.3	728.7
Paid-up capital, million yen	76.7	143.6	198.1	430.1	App. 510
Paid-up capital of all corporations in Korea, million yen	310.6	373.3	591.3	1,028.1	...
Industrial as per cent of total	24.7	38.2	33.5	41.8	...
Average capital per industrial corporation, Y 1,000	158	255	276	358	App. 390

Source: *Takumu Tokei*, 1938 and *Chosen Keizai Nempo*, 1940.

This table shows that the paid-up capital of industrial corporations (including mining) increased from 76.7 million yen in 1929 to about 510 million in 1939. Mining was responsible for about one-third of the total. The table also shows that the proportion of industrial capital in the total increased from 24.7 per cent in 1929 to 41.8 per cent in 1938, and that the average capital per corporation increased from 158,000 yen in 1929 to 390,000 yen in 1939,[7] while the average capital of a mining corporation was more than two million yen in 1938. Japanese economists stress the point that the growth and shift from one industry to another were planned (*keikaku sui-i*), and subsequent events showed that these changes were planned as part of war preparation.

For data on the distribution of industry in Korea in 1937, see Appendix III.

Textile Industry—In 1938 the gross value of production in the textile industry accounted for only 14.4 per cent of the total, but the industry employed more than 21 per cent of the workers in 1937 (namely 35,558 in enterprises with five and more workers). Its development is rather recent. In 1917 the Korea Spinning and Weaving Corporation was organized at Fusan with a capital of five million yen. But for some reason

[6] Seiki Miyake, *Shinko Kontsuerun Tokuhon*, pp. 75 and 143-144.
[7] Part of the increase is due to the rise in prices.

the factory began operation only in 1922 or 1923. In 1919, the Keijo Spinning and Weaving Corporation was established in Eitoho (a suburb of Keijo, across the river) with a capital of one million yen. However, even these two companies led a precarious existence due to competition from Japanese industry, and had to be subsidized by the Government-General. The industry began to expand only in 1933 when the Toyo Bosoki (Spinning) Corporation opened a mill in Jinsen. This expansion can be explained by the fact that taxation in Japan Proper was increasing, as were various industrial controls, while Korea in this respect was a capitalist's paradise—taxes on business were almost non-existent, legislation to protect the workers was completely absent, and wages were less than one-half of the wages in Japan Proper. As a result, the number of spindles in Korea increased from 15,000 in 1934 to 213,000 in 1939. The gross value of production in 1935 and 1937 was made up of the following items:

GROSS VALUE OF PRODUCTION OF TEXTILE INDUSTRY
(in thousand yen)

	1935	1937
Raw silk	16,788	21,626
Cotton yarn	15,022	37,662
Cotton goods	27,053	50,972
Silk goods	5,724	6,534
Hemp goods	7,438	8,793
Rayon goods	1,671	3,455
Goods mixed with rayon	1,752	2,322
Knitted goods	3,957	5,746
Other goods	2,922	4,044
Total	82,328	141,154

Source: *Takumu Tokei*, 1938.

This table suggests a rapid growth, but a part of this seeming increase must be attributed to the rise of prices: the price of cotton yarn, for example, increased by 39 per cent in the same period. The relatively small size of the Korean textile industry is shown by the fact that in 1937 Korea produced 2,148 tons of raw silk and 27,021 tons of cotton yarn, while corresponding figures for Japan were 37,132 tons of raw silk and 721,904 tons of cotton yarn. As has been mentioned before, 21.9 per cent of the production (in value) was made up of goods produced by household industry.

Among the ginning-houses there were six employing more

INDUSTRIAL DEVELOPMENT 155

than two hundred workers—three in Moppo, one in Taikyu, one in Masan, and one in Jinsen. One was planned in 1940 for Tetsugen.

Large-scale filatures were located in Keijo, Seishu, Taiden, Zenshu, Koshu, Taikyu, Tenkai, Shariin, Heijo, Kanko and Tetsugen. Twenty enterprises (among 74 in 1938) employed more than two hundred workers each (chiefly girls), the largest ones being owned by Kanegafuchi, Katakura and other large Japanese firms. The share of household industry in total production may be seen from the following table:

SILK REELING, 1938

Factories, *number*	74	Households, *families*	350,421
Basins	9,204	Basins	339,295
Production, tons	1,392	Production, tons	769

A list of firms engaged in spinning and weaving in 1938 is given in Appendix III.

The textile industry is concentrated at Fusan and Keijo. Fusan is a port, the oldest Japanese settlement and only 120 miles from Shimonoseki, while Keijo is an important trade center and labor market.

In 1938, large mills producing knitted goods were located in Fusan, Keijo, and Heijo, but they worked chiefly for export. The manufacture of hemp goods on a factory scale took place only in the plant of the Empire Hemp Corporation (Teikoku Seima), although Kanegafuchi planned to establish one in Taiden. Teikoku Seima had opened one mill in Jinsen for Army needs and planned five mills in Northern Korea for the processing of flax, though its production in 1938 was still very small. Two big mills (one in Fusan and one in Seishin) produced ropes and twine. Rayon was produced by the Kanegafuchi mill in Heijo, its daily capacity being ten tons of rayon and 27 tons of staple fiber. The Dainippon Boseki mill in Seishin had a daily capacity of 24 tons of rayon and five tons of staple fiber. Tayo Rayon in Konan, under construction, was to have a daily capacity of twenty tons; and a plant was planned for Gunsan with a capacity of ten tons daily.

However, the rapid expansion of the textile industry in Korea came to an abrupt end in 1939. One of the reasons was that the war compelled the Japanese administration to increase the taxation of business in Korea. This circumstance alone would not in itself have been decisive because taxation continued to be lower than in Japan, and labor costs were very low. But soon the shortage of cotton and of raw materials in general became a retarding factor. In 1938 and 1939 the expansion of the cotton industry was stopped by government decrees, and only one plant was permitted to continue construction. Restrictions on the use of cotton, obligatory mixture of cotton goods with staple fiber, and the difficulties of the link system for exporting firms—all contributed to the decline of the textile industry beginning in 1939,[8] and it is unlikely that this situation has improved, especially since Japan is now cut off from her cotton and wool supply sources and from a considerable part of her pulp supply for the production of rayon.

Metal Industry

This industry contributed 8.1 per cent of the gross value of Korean industrial production in 1938 and employed 6,805 factory workers in 264 plants. The share of household industry in the gross value of production was 20.2 per cent in 1935, but fell to 4.3 per cent in 1938 because new mills started work for the Army and because the small shops were refused raw materials. The recent development of the industry may be seen from the following table.

METAL INDUSTRY IN KOREA

	1935	1937	1938
Pig iron, 1,000 yen	5,948	11,704	....
Pig iron, 1,000 tons	217.2	237.5	....
Castings, 1,000 yen	2,907	4,059	....
Gold, Silver manufactures, 1,000 yen	3,279	2,511	....
Other metals and manufactures, 1,000 yen	14,834	32,493	....
Total value of output, 1,000 yen	26,989	59,766	91,966

The growth in yen, as will be seen, was very rapid: in three years the value of production increased 3.4 times. But there was no corresponding increase in the volume of production. In 1937 production of pig iron increased in value over that of 1935 by 97 per cent, but the increase in quantity was only 9 per cent.

[8] But "decline" does not mean that profits decreased. The net profits of the largest textile corporations in Korea in 1939-40 were 49-50 per cent. (*Toyo Keizai,* October 11, 1941).

Toward the end of 1939 the following plants were in operation:

1. Nippon Seitetsu (Japan Iron Manufacturing) Corporation in Kenjiho, Kokaido, producing pig iron and steel;
2. Nippon Koshuha Jukogyo (Japan High Frequency) Corporation in Seishin, producing electric steel.
3. Mitsubishi Kogyo (Mining) Corporation, using the Krupp method for enrichment of Mosan iron ores. This plant was not yet in full operation in 1940.

Under construction were:

1. Nippon Seitetsu Corporation in Seishin, to produce pig iron and steel; a part of this plant was expected to be in operation shortly (1940).
2. Chosen Chisso Hiryo (Korea Nitrogen Fort.) Corporation in Konan, producing special steels by Passe (?) method.
3. Chosen Riken Kinzoku Kogyo Corporation in Jinsen, to produce special steels by means of rotary kilns.

Gold refining plants have already been enumerated in the chapter on mining.

Machine and Tool Industry (Including Vehicles and Vessels)

The development of this industry may be judged from the following figures:

MACHINE BUILDING INDUSTRY

Year	Number of Establishments	Number of Workers	Production,[a] 1,000 yen	Production,[b] million yen
1929	221	3,400	4,543	....
1933	272	3,967	3,010	....
1935	324	6,490	11,525	8.3
1937	417	9,542	16,565	12.9
1938	533	17,058	26,799	22.6
Japan	11,135 (1937)	377,398 (1937)	....	3,558.7 (1938)

Sources: *Chosen Nenkan,* 1941; *Takumu Tokei,* 1938; *Kokusei Gurafu,* January 1941.
[a] Excluding household industry.
[b] Including household industry.

The development after 1933 was very rapid, but even in 1938 the gross value of this industry's production constituted only 2.3 per cent of the total industrial production of Korea. Household industry accounted for 15.6 per cent of the value of production in 1938.

Before 1935 there were only three large plants in this industry, two of them employed more than two hundred workers each, and one about two hundred,—The Ryuzan Kosaku Corporation (south-west of Keijo) producing rolling stock; the Chosen Shoku Corporation, producing agricultural machinery and implements, and the Chosen Keiki Corporation making weights and measures. There were also numerous small plants producing small ships with internal combustion engines, agricultural implements, electric bulbs, etc. However, after 1935 the development was rapid. This growth was a planned one, and its purpose was preparation for war.[9] A list of corporations engaged in machine building is given in Appendix III.

The list of new machine and tool building plants shows (1) that attention was directed chiefly towards the production of mining and electrical equipment and vessels; (2) that the future centers of machine building were to have been Jinsen, Keijo and Jusan. Later reports indicate that difficulties of supply restricted activity, especially of small producers, many of whom were faced with the necessity of closing their plants.

Ceramics

This industry employed 9,666 workers in 1937, but in 1938 more than a quarter of the gross value of its production was contributed by household industry. Half of its output (in value) consisted of cement, production of which reached 676,500 tons in 1937. The large cement works belong to three Japanese groups:

(1) Ohno concern, has three plants—in Heijo, Sonnairi (northwest of Genzan) and Komosan (north-west of Seishin), with a total capacity of 800,000 tons;
(2) Chosen Cement Corporation, Ube concern, plant near Kaishu, capacity 500,000 tons;
(3) Chosen Asano Cement Corporation, in Hosan (Shariin, south of Keijo), capacity 180,000 tons.

The total capacity in 1939 was 1,560,000 tons, but this was considered insufficient. Ohno was building a plant in Sanchoku (south-east of Kogen), and the Yalu Denki Corporation was building one plant in Heijo, which was to be ready in 1940. But even this was not enough to meet the planned demand, and it was proposed to move idle equipment from Japan.

[9] "The concrete problem before us is creation of military industry," said Shibuya, the director of Chosen Kogyo Kaisha, echoing words of Kawai, of the Chosen Bank: "The present undeveloped state of the machine-building industry is our most fatal defect." Kojima, *Sen-man-shi Shinko Keizai*, Tokyo, 1938, p. 118.

As to ceramics proper, there was only one large-sized plant—the Nippon Koshitsu Toki Corporation, exporting its ware to Manchuria and China, but because of war-time conditions and shrinking exports it ran into difficulties. All the other enterprises are small.

In the production of common bricks Korea is self-sufficient. One hundred and fifty plants were working at full capacity before the war; one of them, at Eitoho, employing more than two hundred workers. But shortage of coal may have reduced their operations. Fireproof bricks are produced by the Nittetsu plant in Kenjiho and by the Nippon Magnesite Kagaku Kogyo Corporation. No sheet glass is produced in Korea, though small works make household goods.

In recent years enamel manufacture has been included under ceramics (formerly in the metal industry). The first plant to produce enamelware was built in Korea in order to avoid restrictions applied in Japan. Cheapness of labor attracted other entrepreneurs, and eight plants were eventually opened. Among them, the Korea Enamel Works has a large modern plant, but war-time restrictions have paralyzed this industry.

Chemical Industry

The chemical industry, now the most important in Korea, presents a strange picture: on the one hand there are numerous small enterprises with primitive techniques, making fish oil and fish fertilizers, pressing vegetable oils, etc.; on the other hand, there are a few giant plants with the most modern techniques. But there can be no doubt as to the industry's future.

GROWTH OF CHEMICAL INDUSTRY

Year	Number of Establishments	Number of Workers	Gross value of production[a] (thousand yen)	Gross value of production[b] (thousand yen)
1929	393	9,378	17,412	....
1933	820	20,883	51,992	....
1935	1,161	34,412	117,983	147,834
1937	1,581[d]	50,871	269,599	304,948
1938	1,588[d]	47,059[c]	319,683	352,819
Japan, 1938	6,146	322,398	3,657,419	....

Sources: *Chosen Keizai Nempo*, 1939, 1940; *Chosen Nenkan*, 1941; *Takumu Toke*, 1938; *Kokusei Gurafu*, January, 1941.

[a] Excluding household industry.
[b] Including household industry.
[c] This figure, showing a decrease in the number of workers, is given in *Kokusei Gurafu*; *Chosen Nenkan*, 1941, gives the figure 65,381 which appears more probable.
[d] There may be a misprint in the source: the figure for 1938 was misplaced.

Already in 1938 household industry was responsible for only 10.7 per cent of the gross value of production in this branch.

As to the larger enterprises (five and more workers), their development may be seen from the foregoing table.

The growth shown in these figures is rapid and substantial, yet it appears too early to assert that "with cheap and abundant water power and abundance of anthracite Korea will be the center of fertilizer production for all of Eastern Asia."[10] The composition of the chemical industry is as follows:

VALUE OF PRODUCTS OF CHEMICAL INDUSTRY
(in thousand yen)

	Values		Quantities, tons	
	1935	1937	1935	1937
Drugs and medicines	4,768	4,111	....	....
Hemp oil	1,592	1,937	2,539	2,709
Cotton seed oil	854	1,315	2,632	3,389
Castor oil	230	256	614	486
Other vegetable oils	1,900	3,443	....	....
Iwashi (fish) oil	17,359	26,872	119,738	140,321
Other oil and fat	2,891	1,184	....	....
Mineral oil	2,674	21,546	....	....
Rubber footwear	10,522	17,036	531,737[a]	36,677
Paper	7,248	9,200	....	....
Fertilizers	55,046	90,558	....	....
vegetable	2,434	6,481	....	....
animal (fish mainly)	14,488	26,840	....	....
sulph. of ammonia	28,226	35,771	452,934	421,057
other mineral fertilizers	8,675	3,844	....	....
other fertilizers	1,223	17,621	....	....
Coke	3,478	12,377	285,932	352,491
Briquettes	2,545	3,507	203,999	215,465
Other chemical products	36,728	111,605	....	....
Total	147,834	304,948		

Source: *Takumu Tokei.*
[a] A misprint in the source, probably 31,737.

This table reveals that by 1937 production in the chemical industry had already shifted from peace-time to war-time requirements. Production of fertilizers for agriculture was reduced, while "other chemical products" increased by more than three times.

These figures also indicate that production of fertilizers

[10] *Chosen Keizai Nempo,* 1940, p. 272. The editor adds immediately after this statement that the fertilizer industry is important from the military point of view.

INDUSTRIAL DEVELOPMENT

occupies the most important place in the chemical industry. Large-scale production of fertilizers in Korea was initiated by the "young" Japanese concern, Japan Nitrogen Corporation, which had a paid-up capital of ninety million yen in 1937, and controlled twenty-seven other companies with a paid-up capital of almost two hundred million yen, among them:

1. Chosen Chisso Hiryo—Korean Nitrogen Fertilizer Corporation, paid-up capital sixty-two and a half million yen plus seventy million yen worth of bonds; holdings of Japan Nitrogen—one hundred per cent;
2. Chosinko Suiden (Electric Plant on the Choshin River, northern Korea), 45 million yen; holdings of Japan Nitrogen—one hundred per cent;
3. Chosen Sekitan Kogyo (Korea Coal Industry)—two and a half million yen, holdings of Japan Nitrogen—one hundred per cent;
4. Shinko Tetsudo (Shinko Railway), 1,520,000 yen; holdings—one hundred per cent;
5. Tampo Tetsudo (Tampo Railway), 500,000 yen; holdings—one hundred per cent;
6. Chosen Building, 500,000 yen; holdings—one hundred per cent;
7. Chosen Chisso Kayaku (Korea Nitrogen Gunpowder), 250,000 yen; holdings—one hundred per cent;
8. Chosen Maito (?), 50,000 yen; holdings—one hundred per cent;
9. Yuki Denki (Electric Station in Yuki), 625,000 yen; holdings—seventy per cent;
10. Chosen Sodon (Korea Power Transmission), six million yen; holdings—fifty per cent;
11. Chosen Sekiyu (Korea Mineral Oil), two and a half million yen; holdings—twenty per cent.

In view of the remarkable interest in Korea shown by this corporation and its head, Mr. Noguchi, it deserves more detailed consideration. The largest holders of shares in Japan Nitrogen are Noguchi, (also the president of Korea Nitrogen Fertilizer Corporation, Yalu Hydroelectric Power Corporation, and many other corporations in Korea) and Iwasaki, of the Mitsubishi interests. The chief reason for their extensive activities in Korea, apart from their "breadth of vision" and "ability" to direct the affairs of twenty-seven corporations in three countries at the same time, is the fact that in Japan their Japan Nitrogen Corporation was making only 11-13 per cent net profit, while in Korea the net profit of Chosen Chisso Hiryo was 31-33 per cent in 1936. The invasion of Korea by this powerful concern proceeded in the following manner:

1926 —Establishment of the Korea Water Power Corporation, with a capital of twenty million yen.
May, 1927 —Establishment of Korea Nitrogen Fertilizer, with a capital of ten million yen.
Nov., 1929 —Opening of the first part of the project of Fusenko Water Power Station.
Jan., 1930 —Nitrogen Fertilizer Plant in Konan started operation. Konan formerly was little more than a small hamlet; now it is a city of 60,000; Water Power Corporation and Nitrogen Fertilizer merged.
June, 1930 —Fusenko Power Station ready; Konan works—second installation—completed.
July, 1930 —Establishment of a plant at Eian for carbonization of coal at low temperatures.
Dec., 1932 —Capital of Nitrogen Fertilizer increased to sixty million.
May, 1933 —Harnessing of the Choshin River started; capital of the new enterprise twenty million yen.
June, 1934 —Establishment of Korea Magnesium Corporation, with a capital of 4.2 million yen.
March, 1935 —Establishment of Korea Coal Corporation, with a capital of ten million yen.
April, 1935 —Establishment of Korea Nitrogen Gunpowder Corporation, with a capital of one million yen.
April, 1935 —Establishment of Soya Bean Chemical Industry, with a capital of ten million yen.
May, 1935 —Liquefaction of coal started. Yearly capacity of works for gasoline, 50,000 tons, planned to increase to 200,000 tons. Establishment of Korea Building Corporation, with a capital of two million yen.
Nov., 1936 —First installation of Choshinko Water Power Plant completed.
June, 1936 —Korea Nitrogen Fertilizer Corporation merged with Soya Bean Chemical Industry; combined capital seventy million yen.
July, 1936 —Establishment of Korea Nitrogen Gem Corporation, with a capital of 500,000 yen for production of artificial gems.
Oct., 1936 —The capital of Chochinko Suiden increased to seventy million yen.[11]

Developments after 1936 cannot be presented in the same chronological order, but it is known that the range of activities of Noguchi and Mitsubishi (or, better, Mitsubishi and Noguchi) has expanded considerably since then.

The corporation's Konan plant has a producing capacity of 500,000 tons of sulphate of ammonia. The Japan Iron Corporation (Nippon Seitetsu) also produces sulphate of ammonia in its

[11] These details are taken from Miyake's *Shinko Kontsuerun Tokuhon*, Tokyo, 1937, pp. 118-120.

plant in Kenjiho as a by-product. The Sanchoku Kaihatsu Corporation, the third producer, has a plant with a capacity of 30,000 tons of sulphate of ammonia and also produces lime nitrogen (presumably in Bunkei, north-west of northern Keisho). Nippon Chisso Hiryo produces superphosphate of lime in Honkyo.

In addition, the following plants were under construction in 1939:

1. Chosen Kagaku Kogyo Corporation (Korea Chemical Ind.) in Jinsen (north-east of Heijo), for production of *nyoso sekko* (urea gypsum?).
2. Nissan Kagaku Kogyo Corporation, in Chinnampo, to produce superphosphates of lime.
3. Plant of Chosen Kagaku Corporation in Kogen, to produce sulphate of ammonia.

Enterprises planned:

1. Plant of Kanegafuchi Chemical Corporation[12] in Kunsan (west of Northern Zenra), for production of lime nitrogen and carbide.
2. Plant of Katakura Fertilizer Corporation[12] in Jinsen, for production of superphosphates of acid.
3. Plant of Kokai Suiden Kaisha at Kokai (eastern part of Northern Heian), for production of sulphate of ammonia.
4. Plant of Chosen Yalu River Water Power Corporation, for production of sulphate of ammonia.

If all these plants were in operation, the Japanese chemical industry in Korea would suffer from overproduction and would be in need of export markets, though this does not mean that *under changed conditions* there would be overproduction.

Among chemicals other than fertilizers the following should be noted:

Gunpowder—Before 1933, the Japanese government in Korea did not permit the establishment of any gunpowder factories in Korea.[13] But with the start of adventures on the continent this prohibition became harmful to the military effort. Now two corporations produce it—the Korea Nitrogen Fertilizer Corporation, with a plant in Konan[14] which has been in operation since July 1936, and the Chosen Kayaku Seizo Corporation, a subsidiary of Niho Kayaku Sezo. The gun-

---

[12] These are examples of textile corporations entering the chemical industry. Kanegafuchi is a subsidiary of Mitsui.
[13] K. Takahashi, *op. cit.*, p. 338.
[14] The original capacity of the plant was ten tons daily.

powder plant of Chosen Asano Corporation (a subsidiary of the Asano Cement Corporation) was partially in operation in 1939 and two plants were under construction—one for the Chosen Oils and Fats Corporation and the other for the Mitsubishi Mining Corporation. It was expected that after the completion of these plants Korea would have a surplus of gunpowder "for export."

Absolute alcohol—So important in the production of explosives, is produced from sawdust by a subsidiary of the Totaku concern in Shinkishu (Northern Heian) in a plant with an annual capacity of 30,000 *koku*; another plant is planned on Quelpart Island using potatoes as raw materials.

Leather—There are two large leather works in Korea—Chosen Hikaku Corporation in Keijo, and Taiden Hikaku Corporation in Taidon (Southern Chusei).

Matches—There are ten match factories in Korea—one each in Keijo, Heijo, Jinsen, Shingishu, Seishin, Moppo, Suigen (South of Keijo), Yokuho (North Zenra), and two in Fusan. In March 1939 the producers, in order to avoid competition among themselves and to meet competition from Japan, organized a *kumiai* (association) and reached an agreement concerning quotas and prices. But the domestic market was too narrow for them and they looked for markets abroad.

Bean Oil—There are many small-scale bean oil plants. Among the largest plants, which not only press oil but also produce many chemical products from soya beans, are the mills in Seishin (a Mitsui enterprise) and in Shingishu, and one in Konan[15] (Soya Bean Chemical Industrial Corporation of Korea Nitrogen Fertilizer Corporation). They used Manchurian beans but since 1939 have experienced difficulty in getting them.

Cotton Oil is produced by two large plants, one in Moppo (owned by the Dainippon Celluloid Corporation), and another in Fusan.

Fish Oil—Production in Korea, according to the table given above, was more than 140,000 tons in 1937. By far the largest part of it was produced in small and medium-sized establishments (there are more than one thousand of them in Korea). Among the modern ones two should be mentioned—Kyuhon Shoten (presumably a subsidiary of Korea Nitrogen Fertilizer Corporation) and Rinken Shoten. Production of fish oil is

---

[15] Its daily capacity in 1937 was one hundred tons of soya beans.

closely connected in these two plants with production of hard oils.

Hard Oils—The biggest plant is that of the Korea Nitrogen Fertilizer Corporation in Konan (capacity 20,000 tons of hard oil a year in 1933 and since that time considerably expanded). There is one in Seishin, and another, that of Chosen Kyodo Yushi Kaisha (affiliated with Mitsui) in Sanchoku. Kogen, which had a capacity of 12,000 tons in 1934 also produced glycerine and fatty acids.

Other Non-Mineral Oils—There is a corn-oil plant in Heijo (with starch as a by-product) a rice-bran oil plant; and the firm of Teikoku Seima has a flex-oil plant. There are also many small plants.

Synthetic Oil—There is one plant in Eian with a capacity of 50,000 tons and another plant at Agochi; they use the "Navy's method" for liquefaction. In general, cooperation between the Chosen Nitrogen Fertilizer Corporation and the armed forces is complete. Through their cooperative research a new method of liquefaction of anthracite was discovered and plant capacity was to increase to at least 200,000 tons of oil a year. Besides gasoline the plants produce paraffin, semi-prepared coke, metanol, formalin, artificial resin, urothropin. Semi-prepared coke is used in the generation of electricity in Ranan, Seishin, and Joshin. There is also a plant in Ryoken owned by the Nissen Kogyo Corporation, which uses the dry method at low temperatures.

Oil Refining—The Chosen Sekiyu (Mineral Oil) Corporation[16] has had a refinery in Gunzan since 1935, making heavy oils, gasoline, kerosene, light oils, and machine oils. The paid-up capital of this corporation was 6,250,000 yen in 1937, and its plant had an annual capacity of 280 million litres. The Rissoki Shoton Seiyu plant in Fusan refines light oils and machine oils, and has a capacity of ten million litres. These capacities are not sufficient to meet Korean needs.

Paper and Pulp—For some years the Oji concern (a subsidiary of Mitsui) made pulp and wrapping paper in its plant in Shingishu and two or three other mechanical mills. Production of the Shingishu plant was 16,400 tons in 1937. In April 1935 the Hokuson Seishi Corporation (North Korea Paper Manufactur-

---

[16] Controlled by Japan Nitrogen (Mitsubishi and Nogano), Totaku and Mitsui Bussan.

ing Corporation), with a paid-up capital of ten million yen, was established by Oji and other interests for the exploitation of larch and other forests around Paitoushan (Hakutosan) in an area of 800,000 *cho* (1,960,000 acres). The corporation has its own railways which are of considerable length. At the time of its organization its capacity was planned at 20,000 tons of pulp, but under the pressure of war it was increased to 30,000 tons (1939). The plant is at Kisshu, south of Seishin. Ryozan Kosaku and Chosen Keishi produce Japanese paper. A plant for the production of pulp from reeds was built in Shingishu by the Kanegafuchi Corporation, and it was expected to begin operation in 1940. Many small plants manufacture Korean-style paper.

Rubber Goods—The availability of cheap labor has induced many industrialists to open rubber-goods factories. There were about sixty corporations in 1938, chiefly small and middle-sized, some of them Korean-owned. In view of the sharp competition, a tendency developed to merge small plants. The largest enterprises were (1) Sanwa Gomu Kaisha, (2) Asahi Gomu Corporation in Fusan, (3) Nissei Gomu Kogyo Corporation in Taikyu, (4) Chosen Riken Gomu in Jinsen—rubber reclamation, (5) Chosen Gomu Kogyo Muniai Rengokai in Keijo—rubber reclamation.

Soap—The largest plants are in Konan, Keijo, Fusan and Heijo. A considerable portion of the product is exported.

Lumber Industry

This industry is largely a household industry in Korea (51 per cent of gross value of production in 1938 and 60.3 per cent in 1935). There are 120 saw mills, of which the largest is in Shingishu.

Printing

In 1939 there were 300 printing establishments, most of them small, concentrated mainly in Keijo. The largest were the Chosen Insatsu Corporation and the Chosen Shoseki Insatsu Corporation. Later, because of a shortage of type, ink, oil and paper, all of them experienced great difficulties and production was curtailed.

Food and Beverages

The food industry has receded to second place (after chemicals); but its importance is still very great, and the proportion of household industry in it is very large—48.4 per cent of the gross value of production in 1938 and 54.8 per cent in 1935. Its development may be seen from the following table:

FOOD INDUSTRIES[a]

	1929	1933	1935	1937	1938
Number of establishments..	1,958	2,183	2,326	2,273	2,399
Number of workers.......	24,756	32,293	34,957	34,999	37,929
Value of Product A[b] (thousand yen).........	....	....	76,507	....	141,500
Value of Product B[c] (thousand yen).........	223,412	122,729	169,420	238,032	274,400[d]

Source: *Takumu Tokei*, 1938; *Chosen Nenkan*, 1941.

[a] Production in 1936 in *Chosen Keizai Nempo* is given at only 20 million yen, and this misprint is repeated in the next issue. We have corrected some of the obvious errors.
[b] Excluding household industry.
[c] Including household industry.
[d] In *Kokusei Gurafu*, January, 1941, yen 277,208,000.

The table, apart from changes in the level of prices, suggests a rather slow growth, and the reasons for this are not difficult to see: it is a consumers' goods industry, while the efforts of the Government and of the large concerns were concentrated on preparation for war.

The principal products of this industry are shown in the following table:

	Values, 1,000 yen		Quantities, tons unless stated otherwise	
	1935	1937	1935	1937
Beer, hectolitres................	3,672	6,952	72,640	133,714
Unrefined sake, 1,000 hectolitres....	31,989	49,843	3,534	4,123
Refined sake, 1,000 hectolitres......	7,057	11,307	174	262
Shochu (strong drink)............	21,732	27,412	1,419	1,016
Other wines and sake............	7,507	3,276	....	....
Total wines and sake........	71,957	98,790	....	....
Soy, 1,000 hectolitres.............	21,282	31,184	4,136	4,587
Miso (bean paste)	8,500	10,726	79,940	132,044
Wheat flour.....................	9,299	11,737	56,375	56,337
Other flour.....................	2,224	1,994	....	....
Soft drinks.....................	944	1,751	....	....
Candy.........................	8,458	10,334	....	....
Starch.........................	2,348	4,218	....	....
Sugar..........................	8,522	10,547	....	....
Canned goods...................	2,752	4,465	....	....
Salt............................	2,631	2,503	98,663	90,129
Seaweeds, prepared..............	2,866	4,312	....	....
Bread..........................	3,249	3,764	15,198	15,080
Other products..................	24,388	41,710	....	....
Total.....................	169,420	238,033		

Source: *Takumu Tokei*.

It is interesting to note that almost half of the "food" products are made up of alcoholic beverages: sake, beer and wine. Production of all other foods was valued in 1937, a year of "prosperity," at 139 million yen. If we assume that each Japanese in Korea consumed an average of ten American cents' worth of such foods daily, this would mean an annual expenditure by the Japanese population of 69 million yen and would leave for the twenty-two million Koreans less than one-third of an American cent per day per person. Taking into consideration that among the Koreans there is a well-to-do group whose standards of living would approach that of the Japanese, the rest of the population would be left with next to nothing in manufactured food products. These calculations do not pretend to give a real estimate of consumption; they only attempt to show that the production of manufactured foods in Korea is relatively insignificant in comparison with the size of the population.

Alcoholic Beverages

Beer—In 1933 Dainippon Beer established a subsidiary, Chosen Beer, in Korea with a capital of 1.5 million yen, and Showa Kirin Beer built a brewery in Eitoho (a suburb of Keijo) at a cost of 1.2 million yen. But since most Koreans do not drink beer, and the Japanese population is not large, the capacity of these two plants is larger than the demand for beer in Korea.

Korean Alcoholic Beverages—Koreans do not take kindly to Japanese sake and still prefer their national drinks, produced by numerous small enterprises. The government has lately encouraged mergers among them because the fewer the number of such enterprises the easier it is to control them.

Refined Sake—There are 130 plants in Korea producing refined sake for the benefit of the Japanese population, or one plant for each 5,000. The owners are the same as in Japan. Production is sufficient for the demand of the Japanese population.

Distilled spirits are produced chiefly by many small and middle-sized enterprises using primitive methods. Recently, however, several large plants have been built by the Japanese.

Canning—The annual value of production is from three to four million yen. There are many plants on the eastern coast where fish (almost the only material available for canning) are caught; but the domestic demand is very small and the products are exported.

Confectionery—Korea consumes between thirteen and fourteen million yen worth of confectionery each year—more than the country produces. The chief producers are the Hokoku Seka Corporation and the Keijo Seka Corporation.

Soft Drinks—The annual value of production is about one million yen, with ten concerns engaged in their manufacture.

Starch—The largest concern is the Nippon Kokusan Kogyo Kaisha, a subsidiary of Mitsubishi. The capital was originally ten million yen, but was later reduced to 7.5 million. The plant (in Heijo) uses corn as raw material for the manufacture of starch. The annual capacity is 45,000 tons of corn starch, but the product is chiefly exported.

Sugar—During the World War Chosen Seito Kaisha (Korea Sugar Manufacturing Company) was organized to make sugar from beets, and constructed a plant in Heijo with a capacity of 50,000 tons. But, unfortunately, there were no sugar beets in Korea at that time, and the plant was sold to the Nippon Seito Corporation which started refining imported cane sugar. Some time ago the government included in its program for the development of North Korea the cultivation of sugar beets and pushed it with great vigor and enthusiasm but no information regarding sugar beet production can be found in the statistical reports.

Rice Cleaning—In a country where rice is a staple product it is natural to find about six thousand mills for cleaning rice; that is, as many enterprises as all others put together. But lately mergers have been numerous and the Japanese are rapidly taking over this last stronghold of native capital.

Wheat Flour—The first modern flour mill was built in Chinnampo in 1919, by Manshu Seibun; the second in Keijo, in 1921, by Hokoku Seibun. Now there are seven mills in operation; the Chosen Seibun Corporation has one in Chinnampo and the Nippon Seibun Corporation has mills in Keijo and Jinsen. The capacity of these mills is 5,000 barrels, which is not enough for the Korean market, the deficit being met by imports from Japan.

Gas and Electricity

Generation of electricity has been described elsewhere, and here only the production of gas will be discussed.

The first gas company was organized in Korea in 1908 (Japan-Korea Gas), but later this and other gas companies were merged with electric corporations. Production of gas in 1938 by value was only about three million yen and by quantity—25 million cubic meters. The amount of capital invested was small (two to three million yen), but net profits were good—15 per cent. Plants are located in Keijo, Fusan, Heijo, and Taikyu, and new plants had been planned for Seishin, Yuki, Ranan, Rashin, and Jinsen. But all these gas works were to operate with coal, and with the shortage of coal since the start of the war (as well as shortages of other materials) the production of existing enterprises has declined while expansion and new construction have been stopped by a government decree.

In Keijo, gas is produced in two slant and seven horizontal ovens with a capacity of 31,500 cubic meters; there is also a gas tank with a capacity of 5,700 cubic meters, as a reserve. In Fusan there are four ovens with a capacity of 9,000 cubic meters, and two tanks of 500 and 2,260 cubic meters. Heijo has two ovens with a capacity of 1,428 cubic meters each, and a gas tank of 1,500 cubic meters. In Taikyu (a municipal enterprise) there are two ovens of 1,100 cubic meters each, and one gas tank of 1,100 cubic meters. Shingishu has no gas works of its own and obtains its gas from Antung across the Yalu by high-pressure gas pipe. Its gas tank is only 300 cubic meters.

CONSUMPTION OF GAS BY NATIONALITY OF THE CONSUMERS

City	Number of consumers Japanese	Number of consumers Korean	Number of families per stove Japanese	Number of families per stove Korean
Keijo	15,757	1,187	2	103
Fusan	4,023	237	3	147
Heijo	1,549	50	3.8	905
Taikyu	1,176	67	4	448
Shingishu	400	40	5	205

Source for the absolute figures, *Chosen Keizai Nempo*, 1939.

The above table reveals an interesting situation. In Keijo one out of every two Japanese families used gas; but only one out of every 103 Korean families. In Fusan, in Taikyu, and in Shingishu the picture was the same, while in Heijo the ratio was even worse for the Koreans. In Keijo one Korean family out of 103 used gas and in Heijo—one out of 905. This difference is easily explained: the richest Korean families, those who can afford to have a gas stove, are concentrated chiefly in Keijo. According to an official source, "the demand for gas in Korea is almost exclusively from Japanese or foreigners."

The Problem of Nationality in Industry

We have seen that industry is growing in Korea, at least in some branches; and their growth would be considered good even by European standards. The question remains whether this progress represents Korean enterprise or Japanese. If sulphate of ammonia is produced in modern plants which are in Japanese hands, and then exported to Japan and if the proceeds are invested in new Japanese enterprises in Korea, what advantages do the Koreans derive from such an industry? The usual argument is that they receive wages. To what extent this opportunity of employment for wages is beneficial for the Koreans will be discussed later. Here we shall first concern ourselves with benefits other than wages. In the first place, it must be noted that even if the fertilizers produced in Korea are not exported to Japan but are sold in Korea to Korean farmers and thus serve to raise the yield of Korean fields, it does not follow that the development of the chemical industry in Korea, by the Japanese, is beneficial to the Koreans. It is true, they are able to raise two stalks of rice where formerly they raised only one. But if this increase in yield results only in increased exports of rice to Japan and a *fall* in consumption of rice in Korea—what advantages did the Koreans gain from this growth of industry? Of course, it is possible to find some cases in which they actually obtain some advantages. Everything that the rulers do in a colony is not in itself bad. For example, increased production of vaccine that prevents the spread of smallpox is an undeniable benefit to the native population.[17] But this does not justify the uncritical and enthusiastic attitude on the part of those writers on colonial problems who see in each newly constructed factory further proof of increased welfare for the natives. The question of the nationality of the owners of indus-

[17] However, the natives would probably be able to prepare such a vaccine themselves. If Turkish, Russian, or Mexican doctors are not in need of foreign masters in that respect, why should the Koreans be?

trial enterprises in colonies is of tremendous social and political importance.[18]

There are no good statistics on the nationality of owners of individual enterprises in Korea. Yet the available information may help us to arrive at some general conclusions.

K. Takahashi gives the following data for 1928:

INDUSTRIAL PRODUCTION BY NATIONALITY, 1938

	Japanese	Koreans	Total (including others)
Establishments, number	2,144	2,652	4,836
Gross value of production, million yen	244.5	90.1	339.9
Gross value, percentages of the total[a]	72.0	26.5	100.0

Source: K. Takahashi, *Gendi Chosen Keizaron*, p. 348.
[a] The last line is calculated by the author.

According to this table, nearly 75 per cent of Korea's industrial production (based on gross value of production) was produced in Japanese enterprises, and one quarter in Korean, in 1928, i.e. before the development of modern large-scale industry in Korea. However, this table is misleading in one respect; the number of enterprises includes only those which have five or more workers, but the value also includes the value of production of household industry. If we exclude household industry, the Korean part would shrink by at least one-half and perhaps by three-quarters. Unfortunately, in none of the available publications does the Japanese government give data on the nationality of ownership in industry.[19] But we have statistics of corporations for 1938 and inasmuch as all medium-sized enterprises and many small ones in Korea are now incorporated, these statistics are a good index of the position of Koreans in industry. In order to avoid later repetition, figures are given

---

[18] K. Takahashi, undoubtedly an able Japanese economist, understands the importance of nationality in this question; he expresses the desire for the continued existence of Korean enterprises in Korea, but for peculiar reasons. He knows that Korean enterprises are small or medium-sized only. Now, if there were no Korean enterprises, big Japanese capitalists would face masses of Korean workers, and there might appear national animosity in their attitudes toward employers as such. But if small and middle-sized Korean enterprises continue to exist, working conditions in them, of course, would be worse than those in large-scale Japanese enterprises, and the Korean workers, comparing conditions in Japanese and native enterprises, would feel differently. (*Gendai Chosen Keizairon*, p. 67.)

[19] Judging from the fact that K. Takahashi, writing in 1935, could not publish such data, we may assume they have been intentionally withheld.

INDUSTRIAL DEVELOPMENT

here not only for industry but for all branches of Korean economy. The position of Korean corporations in 1923 and in 1938 is shown in the following table:

CAPITAL AND NUMBER OF CORPORATIONS UNDER KOREAN MANAGEMENT

	Number of Corporations		Paid-up Capital in thousand yen	
	June, 1923	Dec. 31, 1938	June, 1923	Dec. 31, 1938
Banks	12	3	11,950	5,481
Other financial institutions	20	94	1,472	4,627
Insurance	1	1	125	125
Commerce	75	846	6,983	23,395
Industry:				
Textile	4	37	975	6,075
Metals and machinery	..	58	...	1,852
Brewing	7	32	167	12,054
Medicine and drugs	4	33	301	1,676
Ceramics	3	12	131	432
Rice cleaning, etc.	3	94	110	2,526
Foodstuffs	..	17	...	217
Lumber	1	19	50	594
Printing	6	44	717	625
Chemicals	1	37	125	2,954
Others	7	68	498	1,193
Total industry	36	740	3,075	30,198
Electricity	3	...	240	....
Agriculture	12	81	1,855	13,344
Forestry	1	5	62	107
Fishing	4	27	1,632	915
Mining	..	29	...	12,449
Railways	..	...	...	....
Motor transport	5	87	187	4,012
Water transport	1	17	37	458
Conveyances	12	138	159	2,163
Warehouses	3	16	285	767
Publishing	7	25	502	2,616
Real Estate	4	75	5,159	18,942
Contracts	1	36	1	1,128
Others	5	58	328	1,933
Grand total	202	2,278	34,055	122,660

Source: *Kokusei Gurafu*, April 1940.

In analyzing these figures, three facts must be borne in mind: (1) Between 1910 and 1920 a corporation law was in effect which made it difficult even for a Japanese to open a new business in Korea, while for the Koreans it was next to impossible. Thus the number of corporations in 1923 was less than it would otherwise have been, since only three years had passed since the publication of the new law and the movement for incorporation had just begun.[20] (2) The appearance of many corporations between 1923 and 1938 does not signify that genuinely new enterprises were started. In many cases already existing enterprises preferred to assume corporate form. Thus the increase in the number of corporations and in the amount of their paid-up capital meant in many instances only a change in form. (3) Some of these corporations were actually owned both by Koreans and Japanese. Government statistics of corporations show this. Before 1930 they distinguished between three types of corporations: Japanese, Korean and Korean-Japanese (mixed). Statistics for 1925, for example, show 22.6 million yen as the paid-up capital of Korean corporations and 12.9 million yen as that of mixed corporations, or a total of 35.5 million yen which closely corresponds to the figure in our table of 34.1 million yen in 1923. No mixed corporations are shown for 1938. A considerable portion of the corporations shown as Korean are probably mixed, and some proportion of their capital is Japanese.

Bearing in mind these qualifications, we see that Korean banks decreased in number and in paid-up capital (though there was at the same time some development of credit cooperatives, to be discussed later); that Korean insurance companies, electric enterprises, forestry and fishing companies, water transport and warehouses were practically non-existent in corporate form; that the capital employed in commerce amounted to 23.4 million yen, but that the average per corporation in 1938 was only 28,000 yen (in 1923—113,000 yen). There are some relatively large corporations in mining, the result of the new policy in respect to gold mining. Agricultural corporations, naturally, represent only a change in form in most cases and irrigation works in a few cases. Motor transport is represented by 87 small corporations that operate lines connecting remote places with provincial centers. As to industry, an increase of capital from 3.1 million yen to 30.2 million yen represents for the most part a change of juridical form and not a growth of industry (especially in brewing, medicines and drugs, ceramics, rice cleaning,

[20] The paid-up capital of all Korean corporations in 1917 was less than seven million yen.

chemicals, *i.e.* chiefly fish processing and the manufacture of Korean paper). Only in textiles, metals, and in the chemicals represented by the rubber industry is the growth probably genuine because the size of the corporations suggests relatively large enterprises.

The share Korean corporations had in the total capital of corporations in 1938 is as follows:

STATISTICS OF CORPORATIONS DECEMBER 31, 1938

	Korean corporations paid-up capital, 1,000 yen	Japanese corporations paid-up capital, 1,000 yen	Korean as per cent of the total	Capital (Paid-up) per corporation, 1,000 yen Korean	Japanese
Financial Institutions	10,108	75,455	11.7	104	994
Insurance	125	1,250	9.1	125	1,250
Commerce	23,395	65,754	26.2	28	63
Industry	30,198	214,705	12.3	41	267
Electricity	....	213,065	...	...	13,300
Agriculture and Forestry	13,451	51,563	20.6	156	288
Fisheries	915	13,686	6.3	34	198
Mining	12,449	171,120	6.8	429	1,415
Transportation	7,400	90,901	7.5	29	332
Others	24,619	61,234	28.6	127	112
Total	122,660	958,733	11.3	54	306

Source: *Kokusei Gurafu*, April 1940.

In commerce, agriculture, and "others," the share of Korean corporations was more than one-fourth. In all others it was slightly less than one-tenth. Furthermore, the paid-up capital of the average Japanese corporation was six times as large as that of the average Korean. Actually the difference is considerably greater, because so many Japanese corporations issue debentures in the Japanese market, which is easy for them in view of their connections with the big Japanese concerns, while the Korean corporations rely almost exclusively upon their own capital. For example, the Korea Nitrogen Fertilizer Corporation, with 62.5 million yen of paid-up capital, has issued seventy million yen worth of debentures, and this is not an isolated case. Thus it is probable that the capital of the Korean corporations constitutes only about five or six per cent of the capital of all corporations. The paid-up capital of Korean and Japanese corporations in various branches of industry is compared in the following table:

CAPITAL OF INDUSTRIAL CORPORATIONS, DECEMBER 31, 1938
(thousand yen)

	Korean corporations paid-up capital	Japanese corporations paid-up capital	Korean as per cent of the total	Capital per corporation (paid-up only) Korean	Japanese
Textile	6,075	23,103	20.8	164	593
Metals and machinery	1,852	23,654	7.3	32	249
Brewing	12,054	13,772	46.6	38	107
Medicines and Drugs	1,676	934	64.2	51	37
Ceramics	432	15,791	2.7	36	395
Flour mills and rice cleaning mills	2,526	9,860	20.4	27	141
Foods	217	9,621	2.2	13	128
Lumber	594	10,553	5.3	31	129
Printing	625	1,461	29.8	14	35
Chemicals	2,954	100,736	2.9	80	1,340
Others	1,193	5,220	18.6	18	39
	30,198	214,705	12.3	41	267
Electricity	....	213,065	...	...	13,300

Source: *Kokusei Gurafu*, April 1940.

These statistics show that brewing, preparation of medicines, rice cleaning and other processing of agricultural products were still, to a considerable degree, in the hands of Koreans, but even in these branches the size of Japanese corporations, as shown by the paid-up capital, was several times as large as that of the Korean. Moreover, though in the printing industry Korean corporations represent (in capital) almost 30 per cent of the total, this does not mean that they supply anything like that proportion of the total demand, because the Japanese printing industry in Japan Proper supplies the greater part of Korean needs, and the 30 per cent of paid-up capital represented by Korean corporations merely indicates that only a small proportion of books and newspapers are published in the Korean language.

It is clear from these figures that the proportion of Korean capital in industry, as in other forms of enterprise, is very small. Since the Korean enterprises are small and numerous, their market is, as a rule, a highly competitive one in which prices are kept down to a minimum and as a result profits are low. The Japanese corporations, on the other hand, are large and either monopolize the whole market or enter into agreements with competitors, which is made easy by the fact that competitors are few and as a rule are associated in one way or another among themselves. This permits profits of 20, 30 and 50 per cent and secures for the Japanese corporations the lion's share of the total profits. The fact that the Japanese have not squeezed the Koreans completely out of industry which they could easily do, may be due to political considerations, such as those suggested in the Statement of Takahashi quoted above (see page 172).

Labor Conditions

Just as the existence of a corrupt Korean government 37 years ago permits some foreign professors to proclaim that "it is the general conclusion of students competent to judge that, since 1919, Korea has possessed the best government she has ever known," so the existence of small and often inefficiently run Korean enterprises permits Japanese industrialists to point with pride to their own "benevolent" treatment of Korean workers. But the information available about labor conditions precludes any belief that the evils of sweating, low wages, and poor working conditions are limited to Korean enterprises. The figures given below refer primarily to workers in Japanese enterprises. In the first chapter it was pointed out that of a total of 4,271,308 Korean families in 1938, 116,020 were those of agricultural workers. The number of daily, seasonal, or casual agricultural workers in Korea is much larger, as many of them combine work on their own fields or on rented fields with work for some one else and are enumerated in other categories; but these 116,020 are real wage-earners, that is persons who have no means of production of their own and who exist by selling their labor. *Kadenmins* are not included in this number because, though their economic status may be below that of the workers, they nevertheless cling to the idea of ownership; they still hope that somehow they will be able to become respectable farmers again. This hope may be elusive and eventually they will swell the ranks of the workers, but for the time being they are not wage-earners. For the same reason, we may exclude those tenants who try to eke out a precarious existence on a plot of land of 0.5-0.7 acres and who annually swell the ranks of the workers by tens of thousands in the event of a crop failure, a fall in prices, or some other circumstance beyond their control. They are the labor reserve of Korean economy but they are not yet employed laborers.

In 1938, the number of workers employed in mining was 224,000, the number of workers in industry 273,000,[21] and in construction 193,000. The number of fishermen who in 1938 were not members of *kumiai* but wage-earners pure and simple may be estimated at 60,000; at least 150,000 were employed in transportation and communications; and at least twenty or thirty thousand in commerce (that is, excluding the owners of stores and members of their families). Thus the total number of workers in Korea in 1938 was presumably between one million and one million one hundred thousand.[22] As there were about 4,200,000 families in Korea in 1938, approximately one quarter of the families included a wage laborer. This shows that the labor problem in Korea is already one of major proportions. We used to think of Oriental countries as countries of independent farmers. It is time to change this notion. There are more than one million wage workers in Korea, a country with a total population of between 23 and 24 million; and their standard of living cannot be a matter of public indifference.

Nationality of Workers

For each ten workers of Korean nationality in industry there is one Japanese worker. One Japanese economist advocates a great increase (up to three or four million) in the number of Japanese residing in Korea.[23] But these hopes would appear to be illusory. The reason that today there is only one Japanese worker for every ten Koreans is because their pay is much better than the pay of the Koreans. As a rule they get wages that are twice as high,[24] although their productivity is certainly not

[21] This is enterprises of five and more workers, but between household industry and census industry there should also be a considerable contingent of workers in enterprises with from one to five hired workers.

[22] Official statistics give 1,053,154 "employed" in 1936 and 1,173,285 in 1938 (*Chosen Nenkan*, 1941, p. 590).

[23] K. Takahashi, *op. cit.*, p. 65.

[24] In a special investigation of large-scale enterprises (with fifty and more workers) made by the Government-General in 1933 it was found, for example, that the daily pay of a Japanese worker was Y1.93 and that of a Korean, Y0.92; Japanese women were paid one yen, the Korean women half a yen. Official statistics for 1939 give Y2.32 per day for a Japanese worker and Y1.10 for a Korean worker in large-scale industry; wages in small-scale industry were much lower.

double that of the Koreans. It is obvious, therefore, that the hiring of Japanese workers by Japanese enterprises is done on other than economic grounds, and that it would be impossible to increase their numbers from one hundred thousand to one million without endangering all the "advantages" which Japanese factories and other establishments in Korea enjoy. When Japanese economists start to evaluate these advantages, they invariably mention (1) low wages, (2) the absence of labor legislation hampering the bold imagination and initiative of the Japanese entrepreneurs, (3) long hours of work, (4) the possibility of having night shifts. No international labor conventions have ever been applied in Korea; from this point of view the country is a paradise for Japanese industrialists.[25] Under these conditions they cannot permit a large increase of Japanese workers.

According to an index compiled by the government in Korea (July 1910-100), wages in April 1940 stood at 210; that is, in thirty years the money wages of Korean workers appear to have more than doubled. But if prices are taken into consideration, as in the following table, we find that after thirty years of uninterrupted "progress" the real wages of the workers in 1940 were

INDEX OF WAGES AND PRICES IN KEIJO, KOREA
July 1910 = 100

	Wages	Prices	Real wages (relative to prices)
1916, average	76	129	59
1920, "	239	305	78
1929, "	224	207	108
1933, "	149	160	93
1936, "	161	191	74
1937, "	181	206	88
1938, "	197	237	83
1939, "	210	274	77
1940, April	210	312	67

Source: *Chosen Keizai Nempo*, 1939, 1940; last column calculated by the author.

one-third less than their 1910 level, and that only once during this entire period, in 1916, were they lower than this. Of course,

[25] The only traces of labor legislation which it has been possible to unearth are (1) some laws concerning safety published in 1938 in view of "rapidly growing accidents" especially in mining; (2) a decree published presumably in 1940 limiting (but not forbidding) the use of juvenile labor, which provides so many exceptions that it is doubtful whether it has been successfully applied; (3) assistance to workers in peace-time industries which the Government ordered closed, so as to help the workers transfer to war industries.

it is difficult to make comparisons over a period of thirty years, and to make exact estimates of changes in prices and wages; nevertheless this is at least a rough "statistical measure," and it does not point to "improving conditions."

Moreover, difficulties in making comparisons and drawing up indices are not as great as they are in other countries and under different conditions. The level of wages in Korea is known. The character of consumption has not changed much. Of necessity a Korean worker is not interested in too many prices. In the United States we may be puzzled by the problem of whether a 1938 model motor car, the price of which might enter an index of living costs, represents the same amount of satisfaction as the odd-looking car made in 1910, and whether whole wheat bread enriched with vitamin A can be considered the same bread as that used in 1910, and so on. However, Korean conditions are so simple that problems of different makes of cars, radios, refrigerators, or enriched bread, do not exist. Taking as a basis the year 1936, for which we have comparatively full data for Keijo, the capital, we see from the table given above that real wages in 1940 were lower than in 1936 and there can be little doubt that in 1942 they were lower still. In December of 1936, the wage of workers without special skills was one yen a day. Let us suppose that a worker of this type worked twenty-eight days a month (a common state of affairs, see below) and earned twenty-eight yen; let us also suppose that no fines were imposed upon this worker, no taxes, no deductions whatever. Let us suppose further that he had a family of five—an average family for Korea; namely, his wife and three children. Knowing the retail prices for 1936, the best pre-war year, we can construct an imaginary budget for such a worker. We shall put rent per month at five yen—this is not too high a rent for Keijo conditions. Let us also suppose that the family is in need of eight pounds of firewood a day for heat and preparing food —again not an excessive quantity (no other fuel is cheaper). This would make Y2.55 per month. Let the family consume five pounds of rice per day, or 150 pounds per month, or about $361/2$ *sho*—Y11.96. One quarter of a pound of *miso* (a special food made of beans, rice, flour, sugar) per person would make Y2.25 per month. Let us suppose that the average family's need of textiles for all purposes is one hundred yards a year—again a very modest amount, or eight yards a month, four yards of cotton and four of hemp cloth—a total of Y1.56. Let us add to this one pound of tea and four pounds of sugar (*i.e.* 0.8 pound per person per month)—Y1.48. Electricity (kerosene is more expensive)—one yen a month; tobacco—one yen and a half, and soap—36 sen a month. This makes a total of twenty-eight yen, or the total wage of our worker. If any further expenditures are necessary, these amounts would have to be decreased. Meat is omitted entirely because one pound of it costs 73 sen (60 sen for one hundred *momme*).

Furthermore, this hypothetical budget makes no provision for fish, alcoholic beverages, salt, thread, needles, paper, shoes, matches, amusements, expenses of births, burials, etc.—all of them expenditures which no worker, however low his earnings are, can avoid. Their inclusion would necessitate cutting down other items. Of course, the worker may forego rice and use Manchurian *awa* (millet), but this would save him only Y2.16 per month (one *sho* of rice was 33 sen and one *sho* of awa—27 sen). It would be interesting to see what budget showing "improving conditions" could be constructed with these wages and prices. The only logical conclusion possible in these circumstances is that these wages are not sufficient to support a family. This conclusion is borne out by an investigation conducted by the Japanese Government in 1929, which showed that the *expenses* of a single coolie in Korea per day were 54 sen, while his earnings were seventy sen. It is clear that under these conditions a worker can exist only by remaining single or when two or three members of the family are working.

But if the wage situation is so bad, why do farmers leave the villages and flock to the cities? There were some workers whose wages in 1936 were above one yen a day; there were some farmers who left their villages because conditions in the cities were better than those at home, or they supposed that conditions were better, or were escaping other evils of rural life, so that the consideration of wages was not paramount in their mind. But the main body of workers leave their villages not because the standard of the wage worker's living is higher, but because they *have* to go, either because their families are in need of money (to pay taxes, to pay debts, to pay for fertilizer, etc.) or because their land has been taken away, their house and farming implements have been sold in order to cover their debts and tax arrears, and they have become "free." In 1932, in one year, the number of farmer-owners decreased by 12,228; the number of owner-tenants decreased by 110,809. These families did not all become tenants or *kadenmins*. Many of them were forced to seek employment as wage laborers in the cities. They were compelled to move by the economic forces that are at work in Korea; and these forces are not merely blind economic forces. They are influenced, transformed, and in many cases guided by the political arms of the Japanese rulers. Manufacturing and mining industries in Korea, as elsewhere in the world, are ostensibly motivated by considerations of an economic character based on production costs, so that each enterprise covers at least its costs and if it cannot do so goes out of business. And yet, the most important factor in industry—labor—is not paid its cost of reproduction. The Korean worker cannot support his family. Moreover, he was not, as a rule, brought up in a worker's family, but in a farmer's family, so that the expenses of his rearing were borne by agriculture, by that "backward" village economy which the captains of industry consider only as a market for their products.[26]

Trade unions do not exist in Korea and attempts to form them have been suppressed with an energy equal to that used in the suppression of Communism and the eradication of "dangerous thoughts." Information on labor disputes is not published, but since the start of the Sino-Japanese "incident," a Labor Patriotic Front (*Kinro Hokoku Undo*) has been sponsored by the police as part of a "Spiritual Mobilization" program conducted by the police, gendarmerie, and Army.

Women and Children in Industry

At the end of 1938 the workers in factories were divided by age and sex as follows:

---

[26] One should add to this the fact that big enterprises in Korea consistently yield net profits of 15, 20, 30, and even 50 per cent a year. How much truth is there then in the contention that the free movement of prices in the market regulates production, and that abolition of the free market would make normal production impossible, because planners would have no guide for decisions? Of course, one may reply that conditions in Korea were far from normal. If so, why then did those who happened to write about Korea (and they were brought up on the theory of the free market) not only not notice this, but on the contrary, were delighted with the economic progress made there? Even such writers as F. A. McKenzie and H. M. Vinacke, who on political or humanitarian grounds criticize Japanese rule in Korea, have nothing but praise for the economic side of the picture.

COMPOSITION OF KOREAN WORKERS BY AGE AND SEX, DECEMBER 31, 1938
(percentage of the total)

Industry	Children (below 16)	Workers from 16 to 50	Workers over 50	Women[a] 1931	1932
Textile	22	78	..	79	81
Metal industry	5	94	1	2	5
Machinery, vehicles	9	91	..	1	4
Ceramics	9	90	1	8[b]	26[b]
Chemicals	4	95	1	30	26
Lumber	5	94	1	1	1
Printing	6	93	1	4	3
Foodstuffs	4	94	2	30	..
Gas and Electricity	..	99	1	1	3
Other industries	16	82	2	29	31[c]
Total	9	90	1	35	30

Calculated from data given in *Chosen Nenkan*, 1941.
Data for 1931—K. Takahashi, *Gendai Chosen Keizairon*, 1936, p. 420.

[a] In the first three columns the data for males and females are combined.

[b] One of these figures must be caused by a misprint in the original source, because such a rapid change in the same industry in seven years is hardly possible under Korean conditions.

[c] It is impossible to determine the percentage for food industries through misprints in the original: in the source, the number of men in food industry is given as 39,048; the number of women —88,744, and the total—7,922. In 1931 the percentage of women in industry was 30 and, judging by other branches, the changes since that time have not been large.

[d] Because of misprints mentioned in the footnote above, and the absence of totals in the source, we must assume that the proportion of women in the food industry in 1938 was the same as in 1931 (30), and on this basis calculate the total.

This table shows that child labor is used extensively in Korea: it makes up almost ten per cent of the total. Neither men nor women above fifty can be found among the workers, and thirty per cent of the workers in industry are women. In 1938 nine per cent of all workers in Japan were below the age of sixteen, *i.e.*, the same or almost the same percentage as in Korea,[27] while in the United States, according to the census of the population of 1930,[28] the percentage was about 0.2.

In Korea the workers over fifty years of age constituted only one per cent of the total; in Japan, two per cent, and in the United States (1930 census) twenty per cent. The reasons for the difference are premature death and earlier discharge. Without the necessary data we cannot say which of these two causes is the more important; the fact remains that in Korea (and to a lesser degree in Japan) industry does not bear either the full

[27] The figures for Japan are taken from *Kojo Tokeihyo*, 1938, published in 1940.
[28] The figures for the United States are taken from the *Statistical Abstract of the United States*, 1941.

costs of maintaining the workers' families or those of old age—it throws the workers out at a relatively early age and thus considers its obligations at an end.

As to the use of female labor, there is still a lingering idea in publications dealing with Oriental society that the Oriental woman in general and the Korean women in particular does not work outside her home or her family's fields. Yet, as we have seen, in 1938 thirty per cent of industrial workers in Korea were women; in Japan during the same year the proportion was 38 per cent, and in the United States (1930 census) 13 per cent. This clearly shows that in the Orient women play a much larger part in industry than they do in the United States. According to the table given above, the percentage of women among the Korean workers fell from 35 per cent in 1931 to 30 per cent in 1938, but this is not to be explained by a decreased desire on the part of the Korean women to work. In absolute figures their numbers increased in the same seven years in almost all industries; but there was an important change in the composition of industry, from branches traditionally employing women to those which employ but few.

Hours of Work

As to hours of work, the men in large-scale enterprises in 1939 worked on an average ten hours a day, and women and children ten hours fifteen minutes and ten hours and twenty minutes respectively. In 1938, the working day of women and children was eleven hours. The decrease in 1939 was due not to governmental interference, but to the fact that women and children were occupied mainly in peace-time industries which, because of the shortage of materials, worked shorter hours. It is interesting to note also that Japanese workers in Korea worked on the average fewer hours than Koreans. In small and medium-sized enterprises, the working hours reach twelve and even thirteen hours a day. All hours given above are exclusive of time for lunch recesses. With respect to holidays, the usual arrangement is two rest days a month, though in 1931 an investigation of enterprises with ten workers and more revealed that 35 per cent of these enterprises had no rest days whatever.

CHAPTER IX

TRANSPORT AND COMMUNICATIONS

We have seen that in agriculture, industry and commerce the corresponding figures for Japan are considerably higher than those for Korea. Let us see how Korea fares in respect to transportation facilities.

RAILROAD TRANSPORTATION IN KOREA AND JAPAN
(including government and private railways)

Year		Korea	Japan	Korea as per cent of Japan
1940[a]	Length of railways, km.	5,671	24,955	22.7
	in miles	3,524	15,497	22.7
1937	Population,[b] thousands	22,355	71,253	31.2
1937	Passengers transported, millions	47.3	1.789	2.6
1937	Freight, million metric tons	14.0	130.8[c]	10.7
	Passengers per 1,000 population	2,110	25,100	8.4
	Freight, tons per 1,000 population	626	1,835	34.1

Sources for absolute figures: *Takumu Tokei*, 1938.
Dainippon Teikoku Tokei Nenkan, 1939.

[a] For Japan—1938.
[b] Current statistics.
[c] The corresponding figure for the United States for the same year was 1,928,444,000 tons of 2,000 pounds.

The railway network of Korea—5,671 km.—is less than a quarter the length of the Japanese railways, although the Korean population is one-third that of Japan. Compared with the much greater discrepancy in other economic indices, however, this is a relatively favorable development. Furthermore, though the paid-up capital of all industrial corporations in Korea was only 244,903,000 yen, the investment in railways was valued in 1938 at 644.7 million yen for government railways and 147.6 million for private railways, or a total of 792.3 million yen. These two figures—244.9 million yen for industry and 92.3 million yen for railways are not exactly comparable,[1] but they indicate that the Japanese considered railway construction in Korea more important than the expansion of industry. This was not because Korean railways have a large number of passengers or a large

[1] Paid-up capital of private railways was 54.5 million yen on the same date.

volume of freight to carry. In 1937 the number of passengers carried by the Korean railways was only 2.6 per cent of the figure for Japanese railways, and the amount of freight only 10.7 per cent,[2] and even if these figures are reduced to a per capita basis, Korea is still far behind Japan. The explanation is that military rather than economic considerations governed the construction of Korean railways; they served "to advance Japan's continental policy."[3] Today they provide the quickest route from Japan to Manchuria, to the Russian frontier and to Peking. Three days are necessary to reach Dairen from Japan by sea, while the journey by train through Korea takes only a single day. The Korean railroads assume additional importance because of the shortage of Japanese shipping and the dangers to which ships plying between Kobe and Dairen or Tsuruga and Seishin would be exposed in case of war with Russia; while a crossing of the Tsushima and Korean straits demands only seven hours and thirty minutes. Statistics of railway transportation in Korea after 1937 are misleading precisely for this reason: a large portion of the increase in traffic results from an increase of passengers and freight *through* Korea.

Up to 1940 the railway system of Korea had one serious defect. Troops sent from Japan could disembark in Korea at Fusan, Masan, Reisui, Moppo and Kunsan[4] and railway lines extended to the north or northeast from each of these ports. However, they all converged at Suigen and from Suigen to Keijo there was only one line. Again, three lines crossed the Manchurian frontier, but Keijo remained the bottleneck of this system. The Japanese General Staff anticipated this difficulty and planned the construction of two additional lines— one connecting Fusan with Keijo through Eisen and Genshu, and another connecting Fusan with Genzan skirting the eastern shore. These lines will pass through sparsely populated and mountainous areas; so under no circumstances can their construction be attributed to economic motives. If they have been completed, Keijo and Genzan would remain the bottlenecks

[2] In Japan coastal transportation is very well-developed and probably carries more freight than railways, while in Korea coastal transportation is relatively modest.

[3] *Chosen Keizai Nempo*, 1940, p. 298.

[4] Of course, the number of ports is larger, but we take only the nearest ones for disembarkation, otherwise the advantages of rapid movement would be lost.

of the system. Moreover, two northern lines pass near the Siberian frontier; and this may be, under certain circumstances, a liability rather than an asset.

The per capita annual average number of trips in Korea in 1937 was 2.1; that in Japan was 25.1, twelve times as many. If only 69,000 workers commuted to work every day, 341 days a year, this would account for the 47 million trips made in Korea in 1937. This clearly shows how little the life of Koreans is affected by the railways.[5]

It is interesting to note that the average fare paid by passengers in Korea was 78 sen as compared with 22 sen in Japan. This difference is not explained by the fact that the Koreans are richer than the Japanese and travel first or second class, as may be seen from the following:

PASSENGERS TRANSPORTED BY KOREAN RAILWAYS IN 1937 BY CLASSES
(thousands)

I class passengers	9
II class passengers	231
III class passengers	35,666
I and II class passengers as percentage of the III	0.7
The same in Japan in 1937	0.8

Only one out of every 150 passengers in Korea is able to travel in I or II class, though second class tickets cost only 80 per cent more and the difference in conveniences offered is substantial.[6]

The freight carried by the state railways in Korea (the state railways are the most important; private railways are virtually nothing but feeders for the state railways) increased in the following manner:

[5] One may object to this method of reasoning: in the U.S.A. by the same reasoning only 666,000 persons out of 130,000,000 might have used the railway to make up the actual number of trips paid for; but in the U.S.A. there are tens of millions of buses and private cars carrying passengers (including owners), while in Korea there were only a few thousand motor cars, buses and motorcycles in 1938 which carried fewer passengers than did the railways, and, of course, over shorter distances.

[6] F. G. Carpenter writes (*op. cit.*, p. 294): "The first-class passenger cars of Korean railways are patronized chiefly by foreigners and high officials, and the second class by the well-to-do. The third class cars, which have only wooden benches for seats, are exceedingly rough. They are used by the people of the poorer classes." He adds: "Practically all the conductors and trainmen were Japanese."

INDEX OF FREIGHT MOVEMENT ON THE KOREAN STATE RAILWAYS

```
1932............... 100
1934............... 124
1936............... 164
1938............... 217
```

In six years the freight carried by state railways more than doubled. The causes of this increase were (1) expanded production in the chemical industry; (2) increase in the output of mining products; and (3) increase in the volume of military freight.

RELATIVE CHANGES IN CLASSES OF FREIGHT CARRIED ON THE KOREAN RAILWAYS
1934-100

	1934	1936	1938
Agricultural products	100	98	105
Forest products	100	161	178
Mining products	100	149	235
Fish and other sea products	100	98	106
Industrial products	100	172	189
Various	100	134	182
Railways' own freight	100	109	198
Total	100	132	175

Calculated from percentages given in *Chosen Keizai Nempo*, 1940.

This table shows that the volume of agricultural and sea products hardly changed in the five year period; the transportation of mining products increased 2.35 times and that of industrial products 1.89 times. It is not known whether military freight is included under "mining" or "industrial" products.

Description of Railways[7]

Government Railways
A. Keifu (*i.e.* Keijo-Fusan)
  1. Fusan-Keijo (connecting Fusan and Japan with the capital), 280 miles.
  2. Taikyu-Eisen (South of N. Keisho), 24 miles.
  3. Keijo-Jinsen (connecting the capital with the nearest sea port), 19 miles.
B. Keigi (Keijo-Shingishu) Railway.
  4. Keijo-Antung (connecting the capital with Manchuria, Antung is on the Manchurian side of the river, across the bridge), 310 miles.
  5. Daidoko (South of Heijo)—Shokori (connects Heijo with coal mines), 14 miles.

[7] Includes all lines and branches over 20 km. (12.5 miles) long.

TRANSPORT AND COMMUNICATIONS 189

  6. Heijo-Chinnampo (connects Heijo with its port), 34 miles.
C. Konan Railway.
  7. Taiden-Moppo (serves southwest; Moppo is a port), 162 miles.
D. Gunzan Railway.
  8. Riri-Gunzan (Gunzan—the capital of N. Zenra and a port), 15 miles.
E. Kankyo Railway (passing through North and South Kankyo).
  9. Genzan-Yujo (the line skirts northeastern shore; beyond Yujo, which is a station west of Seishin, the Korean lines are in charge of the South Manchurian Railway), 331 miles.
F. Keizen Railway (connecting the provinces Keisho and Zenra).
  10. Sanroshin-Shinshu (connecting Fusan through Sanroshin with the southwest, intended to join eventually the Taiden-Moppo line), 68 miles.
  11. Shogen-Chinkai (Shogen, a station on the Sanroshin-Shinshu line, near Masan; the line connects the Japanese naval base with main railway lines), 13 miles.
  12. Junten-Shoteiri (Shoteiri—a station on the Taiden-Moppo line; between Junten and Shinshu is a gap), 84 miles.
  13. Koshu-Tanyo (in South Zenra), 13 miles.
G. Zenra Railway.
  14. Riri-Reisuiko (connecting Riri, mentioned before, on Taiden-Moppo line with a port in Reisui in the south), 123 miles.
H. Tokai Railway (skirting the Eastern Sea).
  15. Fusan-Keishu (connecting Fusan with southern part of Northern Keisho), 70 miles.
  16. Taikyu-Eisen-Kakuzan (connecting main line Keijo-Fusan with eastern shore), 24 miles of normal gauge (to Eisen) and 46 miles (Eisen-Kakusan)—light railway.
  17. Ampen-Joyo (a part of the projected line which should connect Genzan and Fusan, the gap between Joyo and Kakuzan, or nearby Hoko, was not filled in 1940), 120 miles.
I. Keisho Railway (connecting the capital with Keisho).
  18. Keisho-Eisen, 21 miles.
  19. Eisen-Yuho, 25 miles.
  20. Keijo-Yokei, 33 miles.
  These three lines (17-19) will form one line connecting the capital with the southeast.
J. Heigen Railway.
  This line should provide an additional cross-connection from Chinnampo (and Heijo) to Kogen, north of Genzan; but it was not yet finished in 1940. Its eastern section was
  21. Kogen-Jonai, 12 miles; its western section—
  22. Saiho-Yotoku, 77 miles.
K. Mampo Railway.
  The purpose of this railway is to establish an additional connection between Heijo and Manchuria (Mampotin—a point on the Korean side of the Yalu).

23. Junsen-Mampo (Junsen—a station on the line 21, north of Heijo) 186 miles.
24. Shinanshu-Kaisen (an additional connection of The Railway 11 with Railway 2), 18 miles.

L. Keizan Railway (additional connection in the North with Manchuria), Keizanchin (a town on the upper Yalu).
25. Kisshu-Keizanchin, 88 miles.
26. Kakugan-Yuhodo (would finally connect the line 24 with Mosan Iron Mines), 62 miles.

M. Kyogen Railway (connecting Keijo with Genzan in Kogen).
27. Ryuzan-Genzan, 139 miles.

Lines operated by the South Manchuria Railway:
28. Seishin-Yujo-Kainel-Yuki, 204 miles.

Total enumerated	2,615 miles
Small branches not enumerated	38 miles
Total	2,653 miles

Private Railways

A. Chosen Railway Corporation (a Mitsubishi subsidiary).
29. Chotin-Seishu-Chuchu (in North Chusei), normal gauge, 58 miles.
30. Kinsen-Anto (North Keisho), normal gauge, 74 miles.
31. Lines in Kokaido province, gauge 2'6", 178 miles.
32. Lines in North Kankyo, connecting with Mosan Iron Mines, gauge 2'6", 27 miles.

B. Chosen Keinan Railway Corporation.
33. Lines in Keiki, gauge 2'6", 78 miles.

C. Kongozan Electric Railway.
34. Electric line in Kogen, connecting with Diamond (Kongo) Mountains, normal gauge, 73 miles.

D. Shinko Railway Corporation (a subsidiary of Korea Nitrogen Fertilizer Corporation).
35. Lines in South Kankyo, connecting chemical enterprises, electric stations, lumber camps, mines, gauge 2'6", 107 miles.

Total enumerated	743 miles
Not enumerated	31 miles
Total Private Railways	774 miles[8]
Total Private and State	3,427 miles[9]

Among the new construction projects should be noted (1) double tracking of important lines (figures not given); (2) construction of a tunnel nine miles long connecting Yuki with

[8] This does not include the 50 miles of six tramway lines, namely in Keijo, Fusan, Heijo, one in South Zenra and two in Keiki province. It is interesting to note that along these fifty miles more than twice as many passengers were carried in 1938 as over the 3,391 miles of private and government railways.

[9] There were under construction at the end of 1938, 542 miles of state and 480 miles of private railways, or a total of 1,022 miles. The annual combined average of railway construction by state and by private corporations has been 93 miles in the last ten years.

Rashin, an important naval base in the north; (3) construction of fourteen bridges across the Yalu and Tumen rivers between 1935 and 1942; (4) increase of rolling stock.[10] The latest information concerning rolling stock is as of March 1933, when the number of locomotives in Korea was 360, passenger cars 900, and other cars 3,992. Since that time the figures have probably doubled. However, the traction capacity of the locomotives is small: passenger trains consisted on the average of eight cars, and freight trains of fourteen to fifteen cars.

An important shortcoming of the railway system was that the gauge in Japan Proper was different from that in Korea, Manchuria and China (in Japan 3'4"; on the continent 4'8.5") so that no locomotives or cars could be transferred from one region to another. However, a recent plan, involving the expenditure of more than a billion yen, envisaged a change to the standard gauge in Japan Proper by 1943. Whether this plan has been realized, in view of the shortages of metals and manpower, is not known. It should also be noted that in 1939 the Japanese Government started an investigation of an ambitious project to connect Japan with Korea by tunnel, the cost of which was tentatively estimated at one and a half billion yen. At present a ferry service runs between Shimonoseki and Fusan, taking seven and a half hours to cross the straits. This route is served by six steamers with a total capacity of 28,104 tons; but storms make crossings difficult, and in time of war submarines can make them perilous. The projected tunnel crossing would run from Kyushu to Fusan through the islands of Iki and Tsushima. The total length of the line would be 123 miles, of which 42 miles would be on the islands and 81 miles under the sea in three tunnels, each from 20 to 30 miles long. The construction of these three tunnels would considerably strengthen Japan's grip on Korea and Manchuria.

Roads

The road system of Korea has not developed as much as the railway system.

There are in Korea only 0.17 miles of road per square mile as compared with 4.5 in Japan Proper. There is no information available concerning the character of the roads, but along most of them regular bus traffic is carried on. Two of the least

[10] The repair shops are in Fusan, Keino, Heijo, and Seishin.

ROADS IN KOREA AND JAPAN
(in thousand miles)

	Korea, 1938	Japan, 1935	Korean as per cent of Japanese
I and II class in Korea; I, II, III in Japan	7.4	97	7.6
III class in Korea;[11] IV in Japan	7.3	500	1.5
Total	14.7[12]	597	2.5

Source: *Chosen Nenkan*, 1941.
Note: (1) Only completed roads are given.
(2) In Korea the roads are divided into three classes, in Japan into four.

populated provinces in Korea have a disproportionately large percentage of first-class roads: North and South Kankyo. Their combined population was only 10.5 per cent of the total, but their net-work of first class roads was almost one-third of the total in 1939. These provinces are adjacent to the Soviet border.

In 1938 the buses in Korea carried 47.1 million passengers and 2,668,719 tons of freight. But the use of roads by trucks and buses is largely confined to the Japanese.

STATISTICS OF VEHICLES IN KOREA, 1938

	Number
Horse and cow carts	158,117
Pushcarts (moved by manpower)	38,049
Rickshaws	1,540
Bicycles	533,277

Source: *Takuma Tokei*, 1938.

To a person not well acquainted with transportation these figures may not suggest much. In the following table they are converted into ratios and compared with figures for Japan.

NUMBER OF VEHICLES PER 100 OF POPULATION, 1938

	Korea	Japan
Bicycles	2.4	11.8
Horses and cow carts	0.7	0.67
Pushcarts	0.17	2.0
Rickshaws	0.007	0.019
Motor cars (passenger)	0.011	0.105
Motorcycles	0.007	0.097
Total	3.3	14.7

Note: Data for 1939; includes *all kinds* of motor cars.

[11] The width of III class roads in Korea is 12 feet (F. V. de Fellner, *Communications in the Far East*, 1934, p. 223) i.e., this class corresponds to class IV in Japan Proper.

[12] More recent information places the total mileage at 19,000 miles of which 7.8 thousand are state roads (a new classification) and 11.2 thousand local roads. State roads are roads connecting important centers, roads of military importance and roads of economic importance.

In Chapter III we quoted an author who was astonished to find good roads almost deserted in Korea. Now we can see the reason for his astonishment. The Koreans do not use the roads because they have no vehicles (and nothing to carry in the vehicles). Only one family out of ten has a bicycle; only one family out of thirty has a horse or cow cart, and the number of pushcarts, motorcars and motorcycles is exceedingly small. Only one out of every 2,000 families has a motor car.

And this is not just the usual, inevitable Oriental poverty, about which nothing can be done, for we see that in Japan the comparable figures for vehicles, with the exception of horse and cow carts, are at least ten times as high as in Korea.

Ports and Communications

The movement of ships to and from Korean ports and in coastal shipping is relatively large. In 1939, for example, it was more than twice as large as in Australia and three times as large as in French Indo-China, the population of which is about the same as that of Korea. But the years of war brought an acute shortage of bottoms, with the result that the tonnage

TONNAGE OF SHIPS ENTERING KOREAN PORTS
(in thousand tons)

1936	15,716
1937	15,214
1938	12,618

Source: *Chosen Keizai Nempo*, 1939.

in 1938 was only three-fourths of the volume in 1936, even though mining and industrial production for military needs was rising. This shortage led to a sharp increase in shipping rates. The rate for carrying 100 koku of Korean rice from Jinsen to Japan, for example, was 65 yen in August 1936; it was 95 yen in August 1937 and 136 yen in February 1939, *i.e.* it more than doubled; and this upward movement has presumably continued because the war in the Pacific and the spread of operations have undoubtedy intensified the shipping shortage. As to the relative importance of Korean ports of call, we have no data in tons, but only the value of goods exported and imported through them.

This table underestimates the importance of the northern ports because it shows only statistics of the trade of Korea, whereas Yuki, Rashin, Seishin, and to a lesser degree Shingishu,

DISTRIBUTION OF KOREAN TRADE AMONG THE PORTS, PERCENTAGES OF TOTAL

	Exports 1935	Exports 1938	Imports 1935	Imports 1938	Absolute figures for 1938, in million yen Exports	Absolute figures for 1938, in million yen Imports
Fusan	21.8	23.8	31.1	30.9	209.4	326.4
Chinnampo	18.4	15.4	7.3	8.6	135.5	91.0
Jinsen	12.0	14.8	20.9	20.3	129.9	214.7
Gunsen	11.5	7.1	3.6	2.5	62.8	26.3
Shingishu	5.1	6.7	6.5	4.6	58.7	49.0
Moppo	5.3	4.6	2.4	1.9	40.8	19.7
Seishin	3.8	4.4	4.6	6.8	38.7	71.9
Yuki	2.5	1.1	2.4	1.1	9.3	11.2
Genzan	1.4	2.4	4.3	4.5	21.1	47.5
Others	18.2	19.7	16.9	18.8	173.6	198.3
Total	100.0	100.0	100.0	100.0	879.6	1,055.9

Source for absolute figures: *Takumu Tokei*, 1938.

handle a substantial volume of sea-borne transit trade. Nevertheless, Fusan and Jinsen are by far the most important ports, being responsible for more than half of the imports and about two-fifths of the exports. In the four years accounted for in the table the importance of the southeastern ports decreased and that of the northeastern ports increased. The facilities of these ports are described below.

Fusan

Before 1940 about fifteen million yen were spent by the Japanese administration on improvement of the port, and in 1936 a new program of construction was worked out, to be finished in 1944, at a total cost of eighteen million yen. The port handles several million tons annually and has accommodations for ships of 7,000 tons; a breakwater shelters the harbor from the north. The area of the port is 3.8 square miles (2,834,000 *tsubo*).

Chinkai

It is the southern naval base, and information concerning it is unavailable.

Masan

The cost of constructing this port was two million yen. The port is important because being well sheltered it is safe from storms and does not freeze even in the coldest winters.

Reisui

A rapidly growing commercial and fishing port of South Zenra—its harbor is open to southern winds; a breakwater to cost about three million yen was expected to be ready by 1940.

Shingishu

Shingishu is not a sea port, being situated eleven miles from the mouth of the Yalu. The sea port is on the island at the mouth, which is now connected by an embankment with the Korean shore and is to be connected by rail with Shingishu. Works under construction (at a cost of two million yen) would permit the handling of 500,000 tons yearly. The port is not frozen in winter.

Jinsen

The port of Keijo, fifty minutes distance from Keijo by rail, protected by islands and free from ice. Its construction cost about nine millions, and since 1935 a new program costing nine million yen has been under way and was to be completed in 1944; the capacity of the port will then be five million tons a year. A special feature of the port is its double lock-gate dock (a second one is under construction) made necessary by the great tidal range here.

Chinnampo

A sea and river port with the river nearly one mile wide; its construction cost four million yen; experiences the same difficulties as Jinsen (high tides); ten thousand ton ships can be accommodated.

Kunsan

The construction of this port cost three million yen, and since 1933 a new program costing 1,230,000 yen has been under way. The port has accommodations for 3-4,000 ton ships which moor to floating pontoons instead of quays because of high tides. Anchorage is well sheltered from wind and sea but needs dredging because of river silt.

Moppo

The port has a good natural harbor, for which reason only one million yen was spent upon improvements. In view of the high tide, the ships moor at pontoons (ships of 2,000 to 3,000 tons). Anchorage about 1.5 miles long. Water area 2,700 acres.

Genzan

A good natural harbor with an area 2,500 acres and depth 32-45 feet; improved by works costing four million yen; accommodations for vessels of 3,000 tons.

Joshin

Located at the boundary line between North and South Kankyo; about three million yen was spent upon its improvement (the port was not naturally sheltered from storms). Construction of a paper mill and of magnesium and other plants guarantees its future development.

Seishin

Seishin is an important port for northeastern Korea and for Manchuria. It is connected with Tsuruga in Japan Proper by a shipping line with a daily schedule of sailings. More than eight million yen were spent on the improvement of its commercial and fishing harbors, and seven ships of from three to six thousand tons can be accommodated at the same time at its quays.

Rashin

This port is well sheltered by two islands; its area is 0.65 square miles (500,000 *tsubo*), the anchorage is deep, and its water does not freeze in winter. The port is divided into two parts, commercial and military: it is the naval base for northern Korea, important in view of its proximity to Vladivostok. The development of the commercial port was to proceed in five stages (at a cost of sixty million yen). The last one is scheduled to be completed by 1948 at which time the capacity of the port would be nine million tons, capable of handling twelve eight thousand ton ships, 24 seven thousand ton ships, and twelve four thousand ton ships. In 1939 the first stage was completed, and the capacity reached three million tons. Now the second stage, an additional two million tons, is being realized. The port is connected by a tunnel 9.5 miles long with the nearby port of Yuki.

Yuki

Yuki has a deep natural harbor. Construction work costs more than a million yen. The port serves as a supplementary port to Rashin.

Besides the enumerated ports there are about 160 fishing and commercial harbors with modest facilities.

With such a development of Korean ports one might expect the existence of a good-sized merchant marine, not, of course, approaching that of Japan with her 5,140,450 tons of shipping in 1938, but something paralleling the development of the ports. However, the total shipping of Korean registry had a tonnage of only 298,000 tons in 1938. Two special features mark the development of this fleet. (1) The number of vessels in 1938 was 15,908; thus on the average the capacity of a vessel in that year was 18.7 tons. Unfortunately, the statistics of the ships of the heavily subsidized Japanese companies are unavailable, but their tonnage is about 100,000 tons.[13] This means that the average for Korean vessels is thirteen tons, *i.e.* they are nothing but fishing boats of a primitive type. (2) Sixty-three per cent of the ships' tonnage and 88 per cent of their number were sailing vessels. With the exception of Japanese-owned tonnage, all Korean vessels are small fishing boats of the same type as those used in the previous century. Thus the excellent harbors of Korea with their modern facilities have been built mainly in order to serve Japanese shipping. They have little to do with so-called *Korean* shipping.

Air Lines

Since 1929 the Government-General of Korea has paid subsidies to the air companies in order to encourage aviation; but all aviation lines in Korea, except one, are in the hands of companies registered in Japan, and the only one in Korea belongs to the Japanese. The most important air line connects Japan with Dairen through Korea. It leaves Japan at Fukuoka (Kyushu) and enters Korea at Urusan (North of Fusan), passing through Taikyu, Keijo,[14] and Shingishu. Another line connects

---

[13] The tonnage of vessels used on the routes prescribed by the Government-General was 74,612 tons in 1938 (*Chosen Keizai Nempo*, 1940, p. 313).

[14] It may be of some interest to note that the landing field in Keijo was improved in 1932 at the expense of 200,000 yen and this operation was shown as "expenditures for rural revival" (noson shinko jigyohi) (*Takumu Yoran*, 1939, p. 377).

Keijo with Seishin through Genzan and Kanko and then crosses into Manchuria. These lines operate a daily service. Keijo is connected with Koshu through Riri (three times a week service). The routes are supplied with beacons, lighthouses and radio stations. The latest figures available for Korean civil aviation are for 1936. In that year 2,339 flights were made, total passenger arrivals were 1,922; and 5,000 tons of freight and 130,000 postal pieces were carried.

The passenger planes used in 1939 had a *usual* speed of 180-190 miles per hour and a cruising range of 930-1,050 miles. Cargo planes had a speed of 90-100 miles and a cruising range of 500-620 miles.

Post, Telegraph, Telephone, Radio

Korea has a well-developed network of post-offices and telegraph lines. In 1938 there were 1,031 post-offices, 1,019 of which were also equipped to send telegrams. Nine thousand miles of roads, 3,400 miles of railways and 33,000 miles of water routes were used to collect and distribute mail. The length of telegraph lines was 5,600 miles, 117 miles of which were cable lines. The length of telephone lines was 7,100 miles. In the same year the post-offices handled 385 million letters, 3,238,726 parcels, 11,710,575 telegrams; and deposits in the post offices reached in 1938 a sum of 187,552,404 yen. All these are high figures which may appear remarkable. However, as in previous instances,

POST OFFICE STATISTICS IN KOREA AND JAPAN, 1938

	Korea	Japan
Number of post offices, per 10,000 population	0.47	1.75
Pieces of mail handled per person	17	67
Parcels per person	0.14	1.25
Telegrams per person	0.52	1.07
Telephones per 1,000	2.4	14
Radio receiving sets, per 1,000	1.8[x]	58
Postal savings, yen per person	8.3	46.0

Note: This figure is only for the Korean population in Korea. Its source is *Chosen Keizai Nempo*, 1940.
Source for the Table: Calculated from the data in *Takuma Tokei*, 1938.

these figures are hardly indicative of any remarkable progress unless they are shown in their relation to the population and are compared with those for other countries. Then and only then may we correctly estimate the stage of progress reached.

This table shows that in respect to post offices Korea's facilities are only one-fourth those of the Japanese. We also see that persons living in Korea send only one-fourth the number of letters sent in Japan. The relative situation in respect to parcels, telephones, radios, and postal savings is even worse. The picture is clear: Korea is inadequately supplied with these facilities, because her population is so poor that it has no means of using them to any greater extent.

Unfortunately, the actual situation in respect to the use of communication facilities is even worse than the table given above suggests. The figures given above combine figures for the Japanese and the Korean population, and they include also the use made of the facilities by the Japanese administration. The Japanese form only a small proportion of the population but their activities and those of the Japanese Government strongly influence these statistics. The average Japanese in Korea is many times wealthier than a Korean; and the Japanese Government in Korea is a bureaucracy which is fond of mailing circulars and sending telegrams. The fact is that in 1938, 2,206,779 telegrams out of a total of 11,710,575 were sent *muryo, i.e.* without charge because they were official telegrams,—one-fifth of the total. A handful of bureaucrats succeeded in sending as many telegrams as 4,300,000 of the population.

Now let us compare figures of communication statistics for the Japanese and Korean population in Korea, as far as they are available. The 53,000 telephones in Korea in 1938 were distributed among 14,484 Koreans and 37,972 Japanese. This means that one out of 306 Korean families and one out of four Japanese families had a telephone, or that telephones in Korea are used almost exclusively by the Japanese.

We have no separate statistics of postal savings for Koreans and Japanese since 1933, but in that year they were as follows:

POSTAL SAVINGS STATISTICS, 1938

	Total	Korean	Japanese
Total savings, in 1,000 yen....	97,297	7,423	89,874
Per capita of population, yen..	4.68	0.37	165

Source: Calculated from the data in *Takumu Tokei*, 1938 and *Chosen Keizai Nenkan*, 1940.ˣ

ˣ *Chosen Keizai Nenkan* supplied absolute data under the heading "Rise of the economic power of the Koreans," p. 513.

Thus, in 1933 the per capita postal savings of Japanese were 165 yen and those of Koreans only *thirty seven sen*. This again shows that the attempt to separate these two groups of the population is justified, that their economic circumstances are completely different, and that combining the average for these two groups is extremely misleading.

MAIL AND TELEGRAMS SENT BY KOREANS AND JAPANESE

	Koreans per capita[x]	Japanese in Korea per capita[xx]
Letters sent in 1937	0.56	522
Telegrams sent in 1937	0.13	12.3

[x] Given in *Chosen Keizai Nempo*, 1940, p. 514.
[xx] Calculated by the author on the assumption that after the deduction of letters and telegrams sent by the Koreans the remainder were sent by the Japanese.

This table shows that the average Korean sends only one letter every two years and one telegram in eight years.

CHAPTER X

MONEY AND BANKING

The money in circulation in Korea consists of banknotes issued by the Bank of Korea and subsidiary coins. But as the latter only constitute about five per cent of the total amount of currency in circulation, we may say that the money of Korea consists of paper notes issued by the Bank of Korea. The Bank of Korea is a private bank, the stock of which is owned by Japanese banks and large corporations, and its governors and vice-governors are appointed by the Japanese Government for a term of five years. Not one of them has ever been a Korean. Before 1924 the bank was under the control of the Governor-General, but in 1924 control was transferred to Japan's Minister of Finance. The development of the bank's activities was rather slow until 1917, but war and the preoccupation of the Western powers and the United States with Europe in 1914-1918 permitted the bank to become the spearhead of Japanese penetration in Manchuria, the Russian Far East and China. It opened branches in all important commercial centers in Manchuria and in the Russian Far East, as well as in Tsingtao, Shanghai, Tientsin, Peking, Tsinan, and an agency in New York, the purpose of which was to secure American loans and deposits to finance Japanese plans for expansion. The notes of the bank circulated far beyond the frontiers of Korea so that it would be difficult to say whether at any time there were more of the bank's notes within or outside of Korea. The bank bought, sold, and invested money in all sorts of enterprises. In 1921 its deposits and loans were distributed in the following manner (in million yen):

	Deposits	Loans
Korea	39.0	90.2
Japan	69.7	54.6[a]
Manchuria	34.0	118.4
Elsewhere	19.8	10.6
Total	162.4	373.7

[a] A misprint; should be 154.6.
Source: A. Ireland, *op. cit.*, p. 301.

However, Russian territory soon was virtually closed to foreign financial penetration; European and American banks became more active in the Far East; and Chinese banks also increased their activity in Manchuria. The war and post-war boom came to an end, and the bank found itself in difficulties. Its capital was cut in half and a policy of retrenchment and caution was inaugurated. In 1936, Manchuria (except the Kwantung Leased Territory) was closed to the bank and its notes, and the bank's external activities were limited to China Proper, where new agencies were opened in Tai-yuan and Kalgan.

Money and Prices

The bank's issue of notes and the changes in the level of wholesale prices in Korea are given in the following table:

MONEY ISSUED IN KOREA AND THE LEVEL OF PRICES[a]

	Notes issued by the Bank of Chosen, million yen	Subsidiary coins, million yen	Index of prices in Keijo (July 1910-100)
1911	25.0	0.3	112
1913	25.7	...	120
1914	21.9	...	110
1915	34.4	...	109
1916	46.6	...	129
1917	67.4	...	173
1918	115.5	11.0	235
1919	163.6	13.0	296
1920	114.0	13.0	305
1921	136.4	9.0	230
1928	132.4	8.5	214
1929	118.7	13.0	207
1930	90.6	8.1	180
1931	100.9	7.2	145
1932	124.6	8.0	144
1935	220.8	9.2	180
1936	210.7	9.6	191
1937	279.5	10.5	206
1938	322.0	12.3	237
1939	444.0	...	274
1939, April	289.5	...	259
1940, April	448.5	...	312

Source: For prices and notes—*Chosen Keizai Nempo*, 1940 and 1941.
For subsidiary coins—*Annual Report on Administration of Chosen* and *Chosen Nenkan* 1940.
[a] For issues—end of year unless stated otherwise; for prices—averages.

Before the annexation of Korea the money in circulation consisted of copper, nickel, and gold coins, and some notes, issued chiefly by a Japanese bank. But the excessive issue of nickel coins, according to the Japanese, "brought the credit of the coin to the ground, and the stability of commodity prices was destroyed."[1] The monetary system was reformed at a cost of "less than eight million yen—an extremely small price to pay for the manifold advantages of a stable currency."[2] Thus, "the mischievous nickels"[3] were withdrawn and "stable" currency was introduced. But, as one may see from the last column of the table given above, the level of prices in Korea rose from 100 in July 1910 to 305 in 1920, *i.e.* trebled in ten years. In another twelve years it fell by one half and in another eight years it increased 2.2 times. There can be little doubt that by the time the present war ends prices will have skyrocketed and the value of money will have undergone a depreciation similar to that in some European countries in the 'twenties. In short, under the former inefficient Korean Government the situation in respect to the *stability* of money was incomparably better, because one could not produce large-scale inflation with "mischievous nickels" and coppers.

When the Bank of Chosen began operations in Korea, its paid-up capital was ten million yen; now it is twenty-five million. As of April 1940, the bank's reserve was equal to 42 per cent of the total note issue and consisted only of paper notes of the Bank of Japan, another Japanese private institution now hurriedly printing more and more notes. This creation of money with the help of the printing press has aided the Japanese in acquiring Korean property and labor, and has served as an important instrument in the process of dispossessing the Koreans.

CHANGES OF WHOLESALE PRICES
(Keijo, 1936-100)[a]
(as of April 1940)

Cereals	168.7
Other foods	159.7
Textiles	190.8
Metals	240.0
Fertilizers	154.1
Average	180.3

[a] The index includes ten groups and eighty commodities. It is calculated by the method of simple geometric averages. Five other groups (building materials, fuel, etc.) are omitted here.
Source *Chosen Keizai Nempo*, 1940.

[1] *Annual Report*, 1926/27, p. 63.
[2] A. Ireland, *op. cit.*, p. 281.
[3] *Annual Report*, 1926/27, p. 63.

The above table shows that prices almost doubled between 1936 and 1940, and that the prices of agricultural products were lower than those of the commodities which the farmers buy (except fertilizers, see below). In order to stop inflation, the government froze prices, though the issue of notes and inflation of banking credit continued at an accelerated tempo. This brought about the disappearance of many commodities from the open market and increased dealings on the black market. The official index of prices shows only a slow rise in 1940, but it does not reflect the actual situation. Fertilizers were simply unavailable. According to Shirushi,[4] the agricultural prices as shown in the index reflect the actual prices because here a method of common sales is applied: the farmer or the landlord is compelled to surrender his grain at an official price. But industrial goods were mostly unavailable, except through the black market. One example: rubber-soled shoes cost 60 to 70 sen in 1936; according to the official statistics, the price index in 1940 was 205.3 (1.23-1.43 yen); but at this price one could not get them, and in the black market their price was 2.50 yen.

Banks in Korea

The banking system of Korea consists of the following: (1) special banks—the Bank of Chosen with thirteen branches, Chokusan Ginko ("Industrial Bank") with 67 branches, and the Oriental Development Corporation.[5] They are called special because their task is not only a purely business one; they also serve as instruments of official policy, each in its own sphere; (2) ordinary banks—six in number; (3) saving banks (one); (4) credit cooperatives; and (5) others (trusts, *mijins*). Besides six ordinary banks registered in Korea, three Japanese banks are represented in Korea—Daiishi ("the First"), Yasuda and Sanwa.

We see from the table that the concentration of banking in the hands of a few corporations was progressing rapidly—only nine banks (not counting Japanese branches) were left in the entire country in 1940. Furthermore, their paid-up capital and reserves constituted a smaller and smaller percentage of their

[4] *Op. cit.*, p. 12.
[5] This is not exactly a bank, but it is engaged in some banking operations and plays an important part in the credit system of Korea.

SOME STATISTICS OF BANKS IN KOREA[a]
(in 1,000 yen)

	1932	1938	1940, May	1938 as per cent of 1932	1940 as per cent of 1938
Banks with main offices in Korea	15	9	....	60	...
Branches	172	204	....	119	...
Paid-up capital	60,971	71,931	....	118	...
Amount borrowed from government	73,824	83,665	....	113	...
Reserve fund	18,522	33,104	....	179	...
Debentures	260,992	389,572	....	149	...
Deposits, million yen	255.7	624.3	1,231.2	243	197
Loans, million yen	529.6	1,053.3	1,988.6	199	189
Net profits	6,210[b]	9,414	....	151	...
Net profits as per cent of paid-up capital	10.2	13.1[c]	....	130	...

[a] This includes only groups (1) and (2), but does not include Totaku the debentures of which amounted to 317.6 million yen in December 1938 and to 375.2 million yen in April 1940. The debentures of the Industrial Bank were equal to 517.6 million yen in April 1940.

[b] The profits of the banks for 1936 (3,979,000 yen) as shown by the *Annual Report* for 1936-37 and other years, are "underestimates" because they show profits only for the *second* half of the years and thus make the net profit appear only half as large as it actually is.

[c] The rate of net profit for banks other than the Chosen Bank was 15 per cent.

Source: *Chosen Nenkan*, 1941. Percentages calculated by author.

transactions (in 1938 they formed only ten per cent of the amount of outstanding loans, and in 1940 probably only five per cent). The gap between loans and deposits was broadening: in 1938 it was 429 million, in 1940, 757 million yen. The difference was covered by debentures for which the banks paid higher interest rates than for deposits. Deposits appeared to be growing faster than loans, but this, as will be shown below, did not signify a healthy tendency. Bank profits increased in six years by thirty per cent, but prices increased by 65 per cent, so this seeming prosperity was a mirage of inflation. In seventeen months—from December 1938 to May 1940—the loans outstanding doubled and increased by one billion yen, though there is no evidence of a corresponding growth in the actual volume of production and commerce in the country. This would indicate that the banks were becoming more and more deeply entangled in the inflationary process.

The character of the deposits that have grown so rapidly in recent years is illustrated in the following table.

This table shows that the share of fixed deposits fell from 49.2 per cent in 1932 to forty per cent in 1940; that the share of current deposits rose from 14.9 per cent to 20.4 per cent;

CHANGE IN THE STRUCTURE OF DEPOSITS IN THE BANKS OF KOREA
(percentages of the total)

	1932	1938	1940, May
Fixed	49.2	46.3	40.0
Current	14.9	18.4	20.4
Special current deposits	15.6	15.7	20.6
Others	20.3	19.6	19.0
Total	100.0	100.0	100.0

Source: calculated from data in *Chosen Nenkan*, 1941.

that of special current deposits rose from 15.6 per cent to 20.6 per cent and that of others fell slightly. However, a fixed deposit by definition is one which can be withdrawn only after the expiration of a certain period. In Korea the coefficient of turnover of fixed deposits (total sum deposited in the year divided by the average amount or, in case of absence of data, by the balance at the end of the year) was not quite 2 in 1938; but the coefficient of turnover of the current deposits, used chiefly by business men, was 99 in the same year, and the coefficient of turnover of special current deposits was slightly above 10. Special current deposits represent chiefly the monthly salaries of clients and their coefficient—10—approaches the figure of 12 (*i.e.*, when the client deposits his salary each month and then draws it out in small sums, but not with checks).

Thus the change in the character of deposits in Korea means a faster and faster turnover of bank deposits. The average coefficient for all deposits in 1932 was 19; in 1938 it was 22.5 and probably reached 25-26 by 1940. Thus not only was the amount of deposits larger, but their circulation was also more rapid. This means that the current deposits represented credits rather than savings. The Bank of Korea issued paper money; other banks issued debentures; the clients received credit from the bank guaranteed by the same debentures and received new notes to spend; but because of the rise of prices they were in need of larger and larger credits, and the inflationary spiral started its course. In peacetime it is possible to stop this spiral movement at the cost of depression, but this is impossible during a major war when the State is in need of larger and larger amounts of munitions and other products. Thus, currency expansion continued in Korea; the stability of money, which was previously of a doubtful character, was further undermined, and the inflationary spiral was accelerated.

Besides the banks, which are chiefly in Japanese hands, there are in Korea credit cooperatives (*kin-yu kumiai*) which have developed into strong banking institutions, and supply credit to farmers and small business men in the cities. Their membership was 1,934,000 on December 31, 1939; but their paid-up capital was only 15.1 million yen (an average of 7.8 yen per member). They work chiefly with capital borrowed from Shokusan Ginko (Industrial Bank) and with capital supplied by their depositors who are predominantly non-members and who are attracted by the government guarantee of deposits and by high interest rates. Deposits with them totalled 283.5 million yen and their loans amounted to 306.5 million yen in 1939,[6] thus representing a substantial addition to the credit facilities in Korea.

Interest Rates

Since 1932 the Japanese Government has pursued a policy of low interest rates in Japan and applied the same policy in Korea. In 1929 the banks in Korea paid 5.1 per cent on fixed deposits; in 1938 the rate fell to 3.6 per cent. In 1929 they charged 9.1 per cent for loans on collateral; in 1938 they charged only 6.6 per cent. However, in Korea (as in many other countries) there is great disparity between the rates charged to clients. This rate depends not only upon the institution, the kind of security offered, and the purpose of the loan, but also upon the nationality of the borrower, Koreans paying as a rule 25 per cent more than Japanese. The credit cooperatives pay 4.3 per cent on deposits, *i.e.* 0.7 per cent more than the banks, but on the average they charge 9.1 per cent for loans, with a different rate for members and non-members. Loans for certain purposes, approved by the Government, bear a lower rate of interest; interest rates on loans for agricultural improvements, for example, are only 6.7 per cent if secured and 7.7 per cent if not secured. The Government can insist on and carry out this policy because the credit cooperatives are dependent upon the Government in three ways: (1) the administration of *kumiai* must be approved by the Government; (2) credit cooperatives are in debt to the Government; (3) they use many millions of yen borrowed from the Industrial Bank. Unfortunately the amounts available for such loans are limited

[6] *Chosen Nenkan*, 1941.

and because of this the prevailing rates continue to be high. For example, the rate charged for loans without security to the members of rural *kumiai* was 11.3 per cent in September 1939, and rates of 18 per cent and more to non-members were not exceptional. Loans to members who can supply security may not exceed 1,000 yen; to those without security 200 yen. According to an estimate of farmers' indebtedness made in 1932, only 17.4 per cent of the loans to farmers were supplied by *kumiai*, and 26 per cent were supplied by private persons, mostly usurers, who charged from 30 to 48 per cent. Since most of the farmers are tenants, they lack the only security available in villages—land.

Since 1932 the loans made by credit cooperatives have doubled, but the need, in view of the sharp rise of prices, has probably also doubled, so that the problem of rural credit remains unsolved.[7] Total rural indebtedness was estimated at 491.2 million yen in 1932, and there is no more recent estimate. But even the estimate for 1932 appears to be too low. Of course, the figures of loans offered by banks and *kumiai* are known to the Government and the margin of error on that account should be small; but the amount borrowed by the farmers from private persons was probably underestimated. In 1932 it was given as 128 million yen, or 26 per cent of the total. However, several investigations conducted among the farmers in 1933 showed that loans from individuals made up more than 60 per cent of the total. Shirushi,[8] writing in 1940, asserts that at that time 1,400,000 families, or more than 40 per cent of the total number of farmers, did not have enough foodstuffs, and that the average debt per family was about two hundred yen. This would suggest a total agricultural indebtedness, including the debts of the irrigation associations, of 700 to 800 million yen. Of course, the fact that loans from usurers constituted 60 per cent of the total does not mean that the usurers supplied 60 per cent of the loaned capital. Because of the high rate of interest charged, the farmer, as a rule, is unable to repay his debt; he is always in arrears, and the debt keeps increasing.

[7] An investigation conducted in 1933 in South Kanyo revealed that though the rate charged by the banks was 8.8 per cent and by the credit cooperatives 9.8 per cent (*i.e.* rates approaching those of 1939), loans from private individuals bore a rate of 35.2 per cent, and the weighted average for all loans gave a rate of 25.2 per cent. (Takahashi, *op. cit.*, pp. 219-226).

[8] *Op. cit.*, p. 36.

The tragedy of the situation is that because he must borrow to buy food, especially in springtime, the farmer is unable to borrow for productive purposes and thus cannot break the vicious circle. According to the same investigation in South Kankyo, the purposes of the loans investigated were as follows (percentages of the total):

	per cent
for food	39
for productive purposes	23
for marriages and burials	15
after calamities	9
for repayment of debts	5
for other purposes	6
Total	100

In short, less than one-fourth of the loans were made for productive purposes which would increase the ability of the farmers to repay debts. In almost all other cases this ability either remained the same or was impaired (especially in view of the high rate of interest).

Thus, though there have been certain improvements in regard to rural credit in Korea, it is doubtful whether the problem will disappear as long as the majority of the farmers remain tenants.

CHAPTER XI

PUBLIC FINANCE

In the preceding chapter we have shown how their control of currency and credit permitted the Japanese to acquire Korean land and labor with the help of the printing press. In this chapter we shall see how the taxation apparatus was used for the same purpose.

GROWTH OF PUBLIC FINANCE IN KOREA AS REFLECTED IN THE BUDGETS OF THE GOVERMENT-GENERAL
(in million yen)

Year	Revenue	Expenditure	Growth of debt and borrowings	Indices, 1911-100 Revenue	Expenditures
1911	52.3	46.2	45.6[a]	100	100
1920	146.3	122.2	147.6	280	260
1932	220.3	214.5	431.8	420	460
1935	330.3	284.0	516.7	630	620
1938	590.3	500.5	674.8	1,130	1,080
1939	704.5	708.0	845.6	1,350	1,530
1940	866.6	866.0	1,035.1	1,650	1,880

[a] Year 1910.
Note: For 1911-38—actual budgets; for 1939-40—budget estimates.
Source: *Chosen Keizai Nempo.*

The above table reveals that in thirty years Korean revenue increased from 52.3 million to 866.6 million yen, or 16.5 times; that expenditures increased from 46.2 million to 866 million yen, or almost nineteen times; and that the debt of the Government-General had risen from 46 million to 1,035 million yen (estimate) by the end of the 1940-1941 fiscal year.

According to some writers, this growth in indebtedness was achieved at considerable expense to the Japanese Imperial Government. The welfare of Korea grew, so to speak, at the expense of the Japanese at home. Professor H. Moulton, writing in 1931, noted that

"The contributions from the Central Government for the support of the colonies have shown a steady increase since pre-war days. The Central Government provides in its general budget for military and naval protection of the colonies. From a fiscal point of view, therefore, the colonies as a whole have thus far clearly been a liability rather than asset."[1]

In this respect the Japanese economist K. Takahashi is in complete agreement with Professor Moulton. He thinks that the Japanese Treasury still carries a great burden because of Korea on three accounts: (1) expenditures on the Army and Navy, (2) grants to the Korean Government, and (3) payments of interest on some debts connected with Korea.[2] He even presents a table in which these expenses are calculated to the last yen. According to Takahashi, the Japanese Government between 1907 and 1931 spent 343,263,000 yen upon military and naval protection for Korea, and 159,537,000 yen upon grants and payments of various obligations, or a total of 651,424,000 yen. If we assume that the expenditures on the army and navy continued at the level of 1931, the total for 1907-1938 would be 1,272,354,000 yen.

The subject of grants will be touched on later. As to military expenditures, it is questionable that they were caused by the annexation of Korea. The two divisions that were stationed in Korea would have been deemed necessary in any case for the defense of Japan and would have cost more if they had been stationed in Japan. And it is difficult to prove that the occupation of Korea resulted in larger expenditures for the Navy.

The analysis of Korean public finances requires, in the first place, a comparison of the revenue of the Government-General with that of the provincial governments.

REVENUE OF THE GOVERNMENTS IN KOREA
(in million yen)

		1932	1936	1939
A.	Government-General	220.3	384.5	656.1
B.	Provincial Governments	63.9	77.4	103.9
	B as per cent of A	29	20	16

Source: *Takumu Tokei*, 1938.

The above table shows that the revenue of the provincial governments forms only a relatively small part of the total

---
[1] *Op. cit.*, p. 234. Moulton adds that full appraisal of the economic importance of the colonies "cannot be [made] . . . without reference to their commercial relations with Japan Proper and without consideration of their value as outlets for the surplus population." According to P. H. Treat (*op. cit.*, p. 392), "these improvements were stimulated by Japan, who advanced many millions of dollars which were charged against the home budget."
[2] *Op. cit.*, p. 441.

revenue, and that its share decreased rapidly between 1932 and 1939, *i.e.*, public finances were becoming more and more centralized. Moreover, since twenty to thirty per cent of the provincial governments' revenue consisted of grants from the

THE REVENUE OF THE KOREAN GOVERNMENT-GENERAL
(in thousand yen)

Fiscal year beginning March 31,	1936	1937	1938	1939	1940
Taxes, duties, monopolies[a]	121,964	137,670	143,276	162,836	228,650
Railways (net)[b]	23,756	31,675	31,375	37,014	50,133
Communications (net)[b]	3,840	5,709	5,101	4,634	4,832
Forests (net)[b]	2,440	3,576	4,321	9,372	10,296
Weights and measures	951	1,383	1,942	2,182	2,583
Income from prisons	2,489	2,710	3,815	3,689	4,250
Sales of Government property	570	571	469	1,826	942
Fines and confiscation	218	263	280	290	309
Income from hospitals	760	829	968	1,002	1,260
Gifts from the population	525	34	81	17	6
Grants from the Japanese Treasury	12,918	12,913	12,909	12,904	12,899
Loans	31,620	65,000	106,000	164,868	199,500
Borrowings	....	....	....	6,000	....
Miscellaneous	2,250	2,623	2,628	7,278[c]	32,332[c]
Total	204,301	264,956	313,165	413,912	547,992
Transfers from preceding years	14,208	22,182	26,369	26,612	3,011
Grand total	218,509	287,138	339,534	440,524	551,103

THE SAME AS PERCENTAGES OF THE TOTAL[d]

Taxes, monopolies	59.5	52.0	45.8	39.3	41.8
Railways (net)	11.7	11.9	10.0	9.0	9.1
Communications (net)	1.9	2.2	1.6	1.1	0.9
Forests (net)	1.2	1.3	1.4	2.3	1.9
Weights and measures	0.5	0.5	0.6	0.5	0.4
Prisons	1.2	1.0	1.2	0.9	0.8
Sale of property	0.3	0.2	0.2	0.4	0.2
Fines and confiscations	0.1	0.1	0.1	0.1	0.1
Hospitals	0.4	0.3	0.3	0.2	0.2
Gifts	0.3	0.0	0.0	0.0	0.0
Grants from the Japanese Treasury	6.3	4.9	4.1	3.1	2.3
Loans and borrowings	15.5	24.6	33.9	41.3	36.4
Miscellaneous	1.1	1.0	0.8	1.8	5.9
Total	100.0	100.0	100.0	100.0	100.0

[a] For details see below.
[b] Only "ordinary" expenditures were deducted, but not new constructions and extensions.
[c] Increase in these two years was due to the borrowings ("transfers") from the special capital account.
[d] Transfers from the preceding years are excluded from the totals.
Source: Compiled from data in *Takumu Tokei*, 1938, and *Chosen Nenkan*, 1941.

central government, their own revenue formed only about ten or fifteen per cent of the combined revenue.

The Korean Government-General is the biggest entrepreneur on the peninsula. It runs the railways, post offices, telegraphs, and telephones, and manufactures salt, tobacco, opium, and morphine.[3] The financial aspects of these operations are reflected on both sides of the ledger—on the side of revenue and also on the side of expenditure—a method which understates the importance of taxes in the total revenue. A more accurate picture can be obtained by reducing the figures for monopolies, railways, and other income producing enterprises to *net* revenue figures (or expenditures, as the case may be); the net revenue figures from fiscal monopolies may also be combined with taxes, because that is in effect what they are. The particular form in which they are collected is caused by considerations of stricter control. In the foregoing table the revenue of the Government-General is given for the five years 1936-1940 inclusive.

This table shows that by reducing the revenue from monopolies, railways, forests, and communications to a *net* basis, the total becomes much smaller. The largest contribution to revenue is made by taxes and net receipts from monopolies which almost doubled their amount in these five years: from 122 million yen in 1936, a pre-war year, to 229 million yen in 1940. In the total figures, however, their proportion fell from 59.5 per cent in 1936 to 41.8 per cent in 1940, this fall being caused almost exclusively by the failure of ordinary revenue to keep pace with the sharply increased needs of the Japanese Government during the war.

The poverty of the Korean population has already been described. Now we see that from this population the Government received 122 million yen in time of peace and 229 million in time of war. In one year, 1940, the Government took more in taxes than it had spent on agriculture in Korea since the annexation.

For purposes of analysis, it may be assumed that the land tax, income tax, war-time profit tax, tax on interest, corporation tax, and inheritance tax were levied only upon the more wealthy (though this is not entirely true in respect to the land tax). The

---

[3] Consumption of opium and morphine is a "privilege" of Koreans and Formosans, of which the Japanese in Japan Proper and in the colonies are deprived.

REVENUE FROM TAXES AND MONOPOLIES OF THE KOREAN GOVERNMENT-GENERAL
(in thousand yen)

Tax or Monopoly	1936	1937	1938	1939	1940
Land tax	13,313	13,827	13,431	13,502	13,618
Income tax	9,023	10,187	16,546	21,341	33,988
War time profit tax	....	....	2,663	8,447	17,129
Tax on interest on capital	484	1,313	1,180	1,359	3,364
Tax on the capital of corporations	....	....	811	783	1,335
Special corporation tax	....	....	....	....	6
Tax on distribution of dividends	....	....	175	775	466
Tax on public bonds	....	....	70	74	65
Inheritance tax	293	333	475	765	1,197
Mining tax	2,147	2,577	2,164	2,577	3,897
Business tax	2,251	2,580	2,541	3,027	5,774
Tax on fishing	442	616	756	....	....
Capitation tax	1,084	2,840	....	....	....
Stock Exchange tax	984	1,152	844	875	1,543
Tax on note issue	145	255	27	2	27
Tax on alcoholic beverages	21,756	24,067	21,854	24,086	24,132
Tax on non-alcoholic beverages	....	....	329	565	836
Tax on consumption of sugar	3,218	3,597	4,165	4,108	5,547
Tax on textiles	325	410	441	....	....
Tax on tobacco	....	1,983	1,297	....	....
Tax on port clearance	129	265	139	429	435
Customs duties	16,814	12,800	15,404	9,707	9,987
Tonnage duties	58	69	44	55	63
Stamp duties	20,939	19,788	20,622	18,791	24,156
Monopolies, net revenue	25,634	31,468	33,479	35,625	54,039
Tax on benzine	....	....	1,553	1,580	2,420
China Incident tax	....	....	563	....	....
Transportation ticket tax	....	....	1,017	1,029	1,750
Admission tax	....	....	131	195	512
Commodity tax	....	....	4,441	9,867	14,692
Tax on construction	....	....	....	172	82
Tax on amusements and restaurants	....	....	....	3,030	7,590
Other taxes	....	1,474	....	....	....
Total taxes	121,964	137,670	143,276	162,836	228,650

Source: Compiled from *Takumu Tokei*, 1938, and *Chosen Nenkan*, 1941.

total receipts from these sources amounted to 71,168,000 yen in 1940, or to thirty-one per cent of the total amount of taxes; while sixty-nine per cent was borne by the whole population. This was not because there was not a sufficiently large wealthy class to provide more revenue. The income of individuals liable to income tax was estimated by the taxation office at 478.9 million yen in 1938 and may be assumed to have been at least two hundred million yen more in 1940.[4] We must therefore conclude that those who drew large incomes were treated with greater consideration than the poorer sections of the population.

The land tax showed no significant increase during this period, probably because the Government preferred to reach landowners through income taxes: out of the 478.9 million yen of taxable income in Korea in 1938, 152.8 million yen were shown as income from dry-fields and paddy. Moreover, the land contributes heavily to local finances (10.7 million yen to provinces and probably as much as that to *fu* and to *yu-men*). As to the income tax on individual incomes, the rates in 1940 were one per cent on incomes of 1,000-1,200 yen; ten per cent on ten-fifteen thousand yen; twenty-seven per cent on incomes between one and two hundred thousand yen, etc. Rates of inheritance tax were also relatively low for those in the upper income groups. Inheritances valued at less than 5,000 yen paid one per cent; ten to twenty thousand—one and one-half per cent; 100 to 150 thousand—eight per cent, and one to two million—twenty-two per cent. These rates were much lower than the rates on articles of consumption. Sugar consumed in 1939 in Korea was valued at about six million yen, and the excise tax on sugar was expected to bring in 4.1 million yen in 1939 and 5.5 million yen in 1940 (the rate in 1940 was thirteen sen per *kin*—1.3 pound). Textiles, beverages, and other commodities were treated in the same way. Tobacco, ginseng, salt, opium, and morphine are government monopolies and produced 54 million yen net revenue (estimates for 1940-41). The sale of morphine was made a government monopoly after it was discovered that opium addicts turned from the high-priced government opium to cheaper morphine. Drug consumption is rapidly increasing, as may be seen from the following estimate of receipts.

The next important item in revenue is the *net* income from the railways. It increased from 23.8 million yen in 1936 to 50.1 million yen in 1940 as a result of the increase in traffic and the raising of rates. As compared with the capital invested in railways, this represented less than a five per cent return in 1938—

---

[4] The income of persons and corporations whose domicile is in Japan Proper was presumably not included in this total. Gross value of industrial production in Korea in 1941 was 1,873,000,000 yen, as compared with 955 million yen in 1937; profits have increased at least at the same rate.

GROSS REVENUE FROM OPIUM AND MORPHINE MONOPOLY
(in thousand yen)

Year	Receipts
1931	294
1936	449
1937	618
1938	2,488
1939	3,330
1940	6,690

Source: *Chosen Nenkan*, 1941.

a surprisingly small return for Korean conditions. This confirms the view that the railways were built primarily for military purposes, rather than for immediate profits.

The revenue from the forests increased substantially, from 2,440 million yen in 1936-37 to 10,296 million yen in 1940-41. It has been pointed out that the Japanese authorities now consider that the forests of Korea have reached the stage of exploitation rather than that of conservation, and this increase in revenue shows that the process of intensive exploitation is well under way.

Weights and measures represent a government monopoly in Korea and the revenue from this source is treated as such. It is interesting to note that "gifts from the population" decreased from 525,000 yen in 1936 to 81,000 yen in 1938, and that the government did not expect much more than 6,000 yen from this source in 1940-41. The annual subsidy from the Japanese Government remained on the same level after 1932 and formed only 2.3 per cent of the total in 1940-41.

After the beginning of the war with China, the Japanese Government in Korea was not able to raise enough in taxes and other kinds of revenue to finance its ambitious military plans, and resorted more and more to the issue of loans. In 1936 the amount of loans was 31.6 million yen, or 15.5 per cent of the total revenue; but by 1940-41 it had risen to 199,500 million yen, or 36.4 per cent of the total revenue.

Turning now to the expenditure side of the ledger, let us see what use the Korean Government makes of the funds at its disposal. The following table gives the expenditures of the Government-General in Korea for the five-year period, 1936-40 —one pre-war year and four years during the period of the China "incident." The figures are official and no changes have been made in them, with the exception of some combinations of various items under a general title, for economy of space.

EXPENDITURES OF THE KOREAN GOVERNMENT-GENERAL
(estimates, in thousand yen)

Fiscal year beginning April 1,	1936	1937	1938	1939	1940
Japanese shrines[1]	72	74	79	247	381
House of Li	1,800	1,800	1,800	1,800	1,800
Government-General, Office	5,886	11,391	7,140	6,865	7,714
Courts and Prisons	9,204	10,296	11,497	11,677	12,783
Ideology,[2] conversions,[3] mobilization of spirit	118	385	272	608	816
Police	20,694	21,200	21,525	21,987	24,343[4]
Military purposes[5]	895	13,346	28,574	43,665	54,669
Other expend. on local affairs sections[6]	7,185	7,696	7,997	7,758	7,758[4]
Grants to local governments	300	484	858	1,093	11,059
Pensions	7,328	7,639	7,989	8,081	8,405
Taxation, monopolies,[7] customs	5,513	3,164	7,066	7,705	8,884
Debt service	38,012	29,764	31,709	35,219	41,693
University	1,927	2,196	2,237	2,487	3,875
Schools and libraries[8]	10,189	11,661	13,280	15,719	18,044
Encouragement of Korean language	53	53	53	48	48
Compilation of Korean history	80	81	35	34	34
Social affairs	490	531	1,040	1,226	1,632
Health[9]	1,404	1,601	1,550	2,051	2,149
Expenditures on Koreans abroad	976	1,709	2,001	1,882	2,474
Experimental stations, laboratories, investigations	2,648	2,929	3,087	3,149	5,029
Grain Grading Station	1,929	2,100	2,323	2,640	2,754
Agriculture[10]	5,732	7,108	4,729	10,735	14,323
Economic control of all kinds	2,296	4,315	5,429	8,150	12,312
Ports, docks, shipping	5,238	10,174	11,299	13,576	17,487
Telegraph, telephone[7]	2,060	6,310	3,678	4,979	3,865
Railway construction[7]	35,562	65,182	105,842	150,728	178,848
Air transport	301	2,167	2,580	3,405	3,765
Meteorological stations	....	....	1,340	1,570	1,242
Road construction	2,675	2,675	2,662	3,038	4,233
Total transport and communic.	45,836	86,508	127,401	177,296	209,440
Construction and repairs	2,870	3,622	3,060	3,528	4,791
Floods and sands, prevention of	7,225	6,700	6,737	6,372	6,364
Forests, encouragement of new planting	839	877	877	917	1,557
Construction of salt fields	810	850	850	650	1,314
Subsidies for gold production	....	445	11,022	21,145	57,468
Subsidies to other mining	....	....	657	860	1,549
Subsid. to other private interests[11]	13,996	18,097	20,172	25,317	28,915
Reserve	3,500	3,500	5,500	8,000	9,000
Miscellaneous	668	567	2,040	801	1,280
Total revenue	200,075	262,689	340,586	439,712	564,657

THE SAME AS PERCENTAGES OF THE TOTAL

	1936	1937	1938	1939	1940
Japanese shrines	0.0	0.0	0.0	0.1	0.1
House of Li	0.9	0.7	0.5	0.4	0.3
Office of the Governor-General	2.9	4.4	2.1	1.6	1.4
Courts and Prisons	4.6	3.9	3.4	2.8	2.3
Ideology	0.1	0.1	0.1	0.1	0.1
Police	10.3	8.1	6.3	5.0	4.3
Military purposes	0.4	5.1	8.4	9.9	9.7
Grants to provinces and local gov.	3.7	3.1	2.6	2.0	3.3
Pensions	3.7	2.9	2.3	1.8	1.5
Taxation	2.7	1.2	2.1	1.7	1.6
Debt service	19.0	11.3	9.3	8.0	7.4
Subtotal—Government	48.3	40.8	37.1	33.4	32.0
University	1.0	0.8	0.7	0.6	0.7
Education	5.1	4.5	3.9	3.6	3.2
Encour. of Korean language	0.0	0.0	0.0	0.0	0.0
Compilation of Korean history	0.0	0.0	0.0	0.0	0.0
Social affairs	0.2	0.2	0.3	0.3	0.3
Health	0.7	0.6	0.5	0.5	0.4
Koreans abroad	0.5	0.7	0.6	0.4	0.4
Subtotal—Culture and Welfare	7.5	6.8	6.0	5.4	5.0
Exper. stations, labor investig.	1.3	1.1	0.9	0.7	0.9
Grain Grading Station	1.0	0.8	0.7	0.6	0.5
Agriculture	2.9	2.7	1.4	2.4	2.5
Economic controls	1.2	1.6	1.6	1.9	2.2
Communications	22.9	33.0	37.4	40.3	37.1
Construction and repairs	1.4	1.4	0.9	0.8	0.8
Floods and sands, prevention of.	3.6	2.6	2.0	1.4	1.1
Forests, encouragement of	0.4	0.3	0.3	0.2	0.3
Salt fields	0.4	0.3	0.2	0.1	0.2
Subsidies for gold production	...	0.2	3.2	4.8	10.2
Subsidies, other mining	...	...	0.2	0.2	0.3
Subsidies to other private int.	7.0	6.9	5.9	5.8	5.1
Subtotal—Expand. of ec. char.	42.1	50.9	54.7	59.0	61.2
Reserve	1.8	1.3	1.6	1.8	1.6
Miscellaneous	0.3	0.2	0.6	0.2	0.2
Total	100.0	100.0	100.0	100.0	100.0

Notes: [1] Expenditures on Japanese shrines are put first on the list by the officials.
[2] "Guidance of education."
[3] i.e., "Prevention of ideological crimes."
[4] Estimated; it is assumed that expenditures of the Local Affairs Section other than on police were on the same level as in 1939-40.
[5] Includes expenditures for the encouragement of horse breeding (corresponding figures in thousands 62; 195; 302; 346; 618), to increase the supply of horses for the Army.
[6] These are expenditures of the Local Affairs Section, but insofar as they were chiefly on the police force, the cost of the police is deducted from them and combined with other expenditures on police (training, etc.).
[7] Only those expenditures which represent *new* investments; ordinary expenditures were deducted from the receipts and the balance is shown in the table of revenue.
[8] These are expenditures (chiefly in the form of grants) of the Government-General; there are in addition expenditures on education under provincial authorities, municipalities, school district organizations, and foreign Christian missions.
[9] These are expenditures of the Government-General only, see further for expenditures of local government.

This table is far from complete: if complete figures of expenditures were available, it is certain that expenditures on the police, Army and other instruments of force would be considerably larger than they appear in the table; but even in the form in which they are given they are substantial.

For the purpose of this analysis, expenditures have been divided into four groups (1) those for the maintenance of the government apparatus; (2) those which are appropriated for culture, health, and other social services; (3) those which are of an economic character; (4) others.[5]

(1) Expenditures for the maintenance of the government apparatus. Included under this category are:

1) Expenditures on Japanese shrines because they are recognized by the Japanese Government itself as instruments of policy, used to make Koreans conscious of being subjects of the Empire. The native population has practically no followers of Shintoism and these expenditures are absolutely unnecessary for them; but, as one may see from the table, the construction of these *jinja* has been accelerated in time of war.
2) The expenditures on the former Royal House of Li represents nothing but an attempt to give an appearance of legality to the seizure of Korea by the Japanese. The members of the House of Li do not perform any functions in Korea; they are married to Japanese princesses and princes and have lost all connection with the Korean people.
3) Expenditures on the Government-General's office and construction of its buildings.
4) Courts and prisons.
5) Expenditures on "mobilization of spirit," "guidance," prevention of "ideological crimes," etc.
6) Expenditures on police.
7) Expenditures for military purposes.
8) Grants to provinces and local administrations.
9) Expenditures on the collection of revenue and debt service.
10) Pensions to government functionaries.

These ten items may accurately be described as expenditures to maintain the Japanese government and administration in Korea, and we see that in time of peace 48.3 per cent of the

[5] Inasmuch as the items making up each of these groups are given, the reader can check the correctness of this classification or try out other combinations.

---

[10] Some expenditures on agriculture (chiefly on experimental stations) are included in "Experimental Stations, Laboratories, Investigations."
[11] To industry, shipping, private railways, oil, forest, and other corporations.
Source for absolute figures: compiled from *Chosen Nenkan*, 1941.

total expenditures went for this purpose, but that in time of war the proportion fell to 32 per cent. This happened not because social services were proportionately enlarged, but because modern war is primarily economic, and so the economic functions of the government expanded tremendously. Actually, the expenditures on the government apparatus during these five years almost doubled (rising from 97 million yen in 1936-37 to 180 million in 1940-41). Especially remarkable was the rise of expenditures on war-contributions to Japan's war chest. They increased from almost nothing in 1936-37 to 180 million yen in 1940-41. These tens of millions were exacted chiefly, as we have seen, from the masses of the Korean population.

But though the Japanese Government in Korea is generous to its bureaucrats, police, prison, and army, it is miserly with respect to social services for the native population, services which in other parts of the world are now generally considered part of the primary functions of government. These expenditures made up 7.5 per cent of the total (15.1 million yen) in 1936-37 and five per cent (28.3 million yen) in 1940-41, not quite as much as was spent on the police alone.

In addition to the expenditures of the Government-General there are, of course, the expenditures of the provinces and municipalities. But even if provincial budgets were combined with the budget of the Government-General, the general picture would not be changed: almost all expenditures are for the bureaucracy, police, and war, with little remaining for social services.

The Imperial University, as will be shown later, is primarily for Japanese students. At least one third of the expenditures on education in Korea is spent on Japanese students there, though they form only about six per cent of the total number of students. The expenditures on hospitals, small as they are, likewise are mainly expenditures for the benefit of the small Japanese population.

As to "Social Affairs" or "Social Welfare" services, it may be noted that among the duties of the Social Affairs Section is the promotion of "patriotic" organizations, the spiritual mobilization of the population, aid in shifting workers from peace-time to war-time industries, and help to the families of Japanese residents mobilized for war[6] (this latter item alone was responsi-

---

[6] The allowance for the family of the mobilized Japanese appears to average 29 yen per month.

ble for almost thirty per cent of all such expenditures in 1939 and probably for a larger share in 1940). In 1938 this section rendered help amounting to 65,000 yen a year to 4,000 needy Koreans, an expenditure of one yen per month per person. Expenditures on Koreans abroad are included in this category because there seems to be no better place for them. It is true that such expenditures include sums spent on schools and hospitals for Koreans in Manchuria and China, but they also include expenditures on policing and "protecting" them and there is no doubt that most Koreans abroad would be very happy not to enjoy this sort of protection.

This almost exhausts "social welfare" expenditures. But mention should be made of 48,000 yen appropriated for the encouragement of the Korean language and 34,000 yen for the compilation of a Korean history.

Expenditures of an economic character increased from 42.1 per cent of the total in 1936 to 61.2 per cent in 1940 or, in absolute figures, from 84.2 million yen to 345.8 million yen. A small proportion—on experimental stations, laboratories, and some investigations—was incurred to improve agriculture, but other large sums were spent on mining investigations, the development of liquid fuels, and substitutes for scarce materials and many other expenditures directly or indirectly connected with war and preparations for war.

The next item in the table—expenditures on the Grain Grading Station—is expenditure on grading rice exported to Japan. Of the expenditures on agriculture, 2.9 million yen in 1940-41 were to be spent directly for increase of rice production; 5,400,000 on land improvements; 1,899,000 on rural "revival," and 3,507,000 on help to the victims of calamities (very often in the form of construction of military airfields, strategic roads, or the like).

The expenditures on economic control of all kinds (including "economic police," the function of which is to unearth the numerous violations of war-time economic regulations) rose from 2.3 million in 1936-37 to 12.3 million yen in 1940-41, indicating the degree to which the economic life of the colony was regimented during this period.

The next item—"communications"—increased from 22.9 per cent of the total (45.8 million yen) in 1936-37 to 37.1 per cent (209.4 million yen) in 1940-41. This increase may seem remarkable, in view of the fact that communications bring a lower rate of profit than other branches of economic activity in the peninsula; that passengers are few, travellers on the roads are scarce, and the volume of freight relatively modest. The explanation of this greatly increased expenditure on railway construction and air transportation, however, lies in the geographical position of Korea. It is the bridge between Japan and the continent; it is also a depot for supplying the armies in Manchuria and China, and its communications are therefore of the greatest importance for Japan's war machine.

Among other expenditures for economic purposes two items deserve attention: subsidies for gold production in various forms, and subsidies for other private enterprises. Subsidies for gold production reached the remarkable figure of 57.5 million yen in 1940-41, and subsidies to other private enterprises (railways, mines, manufactures, and others) increased from 14 million yen in 1936 to 30.4 million yen in 1940-41. And it is not only the Government-General which is so liberal with "subsidies," "encouragements," "helps," "supports," and comforts of all kinds to private entrepreneurs and corporations; local governments are not far behind the central government in this respect. The provincial governments were to spend for the same purposes eleven million yen in 1940; the governments of *fu* and *men* more than two million yen in 1939 out of their more than modest means, and the municipal governments several millions. The chief beneficiaries of this government activity are, of course, the Japanese business men and financiers who control virtually all large-scale economic enterprises in Korea. In comparison with the amounts spent on the encouragement of Japanese enterprise and the support of Japanese war measures, the twelve million yen subsidy given annually by the Imperial Treasury to the Japanese Government in Korea appears insignificant. Certainly it would seem that, contrary to the assertions of Professor Moulton and Takahashi, Korea has not been a financial burden to Japan.

The pattern shown in the following table is familiar: an increase in the relative importance of loans, and a decline in the percentage of revenue spent on social services, from 33 per cent of the total in 1936 to eight per cent in 1940. Unfortunately,

PUBLIC FINANCES OF THE KOREAN PROVINCES, 1936-40
(unit-1,000 yen)

Revenue Fiscal year beginning April 1	1936	1937	1938	1939	1940
Taxes:					
Land surtax	9,252	....	....	9,881	10,724
Income surtax	477	....	....	668	....
House taxes	6,447	....	....	7,603	7,908
Business surtax	452	....	....	805	1,483
Slaughterhouse tax	743	....	....	694	628
Fishing tax	402	....	....	536	1,058
Mining surtax	90	....	....	13	169
Carriages, tax on	1,353	....	....	1,608	1,543
Forests, tax on	1,240	....	....	1,281	1,493
Real estate, taxes on	2,847	....	....	2,682	3,063
Others	13	....	....	126	4
Total taxes	23,316	22,649	24,735	25,897	28,073
Imperial gifts	945	941	879	873	865
Transfer from preceding year	10,639	13,909	2,966	4,310	2,883
Grants from the Government-Gen.	17,688	18,804	24,648	19,286	54,519
Loans	12,897	15,179	20,223	24,302	35,724
Commissions and rentals	4,212	4,560	5,213	5,576	6,838
Other revenue	7,752	8,832	9,502	13,391	28,430
Total revenue	77,449	84,555[1]	88,761[2]	103,682[3]	157,332
Expenditures					
Engineering works (*doboku*)	12,750	20,786	20,202	25,119	36,522
Health	3,383	3,429	3,800	7,141	4,859
Encouragement of business	14,029	17,747	14,129	9,843	11,017
Employment service	615	947	1,001	820	880
Education	15,461	16,372	18,132	5,765	7,189
Social Welfare	1,952	2,203	908	621	648
Provincial assemblies	79	83	83	87	90
Offices	1,975	2,127	2,361	2,502	2,705
New Construction	1,940	4,011	3,596	5,187	9,626
Debt service	5,130	10,017	11,823	14,275	20,073
Reserve	525	585	598	601	629
Others	5,328	6,222	3,536	34,234	63,092
Total expenditures	63,167	84,917[4]	88,768[5]	103,382[6]	157,332

[1] If the items are correct, the total should be 84,874,000 yen.
[2] The same—88,166,000. *Takumu Yoran* gives a total of 93,233,000 yen.
[3] If the items are correct, the total should be 93,365,000 yen.
[4] The same—84,529,000 yen.
[5] The same—80,169,000 yen. *Takumu Yoran* gives a total of 93,233,000.
[6] The same—106,195,000 yen.
Source: *Chosen Nenkan*, 1941.

there is no information as to what is included in the 63.1 million yen expenditure in 1940, classified as "others."

The figures for *fu* (municipalities) are available only for 1938.[7] They are as follows:

[7] The total revenue (or expenditures) of twenty municipalities in 1940-41 (estimates) was 70,138,000 yen.

PUBLIC FINANCES OF MUNICIPALITIES
(in thousand yen)

Revenues		Expenditures	
Taxes	5,948	Offices	2,300
Rents and commissions	5,790	Engineering	14,940
Grants and subsidies from the Treasury	1,629	Water Works	4,873
		Garbage	1,050
Borrowings	14,738	Debt Service	4,338
Others	8,010	Others	8,776
Total	36,076	Total	36,076

The figures for *yu* and *men* (something like towns and townships) are as follows:

PUBLIC FINANCES OF KOREAN *YU* AND *MEN*
(unit—1,000 yen)

Revenue Fiscal year beginning April 1	1936	1937	1938	1939
Taxes	16,098	17,102	17,852	19,366
Revenue from property	1,358	1,446	1,573	1,785
Commissions and rentals	2,078	2,341	2,543	2,782
Subsidies (*kofu*)	1,273	1,308	1,390	1,534
Transfers (*kurikoshi*)	2,012	1,848	2,089	2,347
Subsidies (*hojo*)	2,190	2,230	2,170	2,575
Transfers (*kuri-ire*)	333	306	325	326
Loans	1,001	1,680	1,082	393
Others	1,214	1,570	1,546	2,091
Total revenue	28,178	30,539	31,416	34,279

Expenditures	1936	1937	1938	1939
Offices	14,422	15,326	16,205	17,709
Engineering (*doboku*)	2,140	2,649	2,328	2,305
Health	900	981	1,004	1,066
Water Works	1,243	1,116	1,223	917
Encouragement of business	1,888	1,925	1,816	2,314
Guards	436	455	536	605
Management of property	317	338	358	346
Reserve	395	468	474	605
Subsidies	360	218	415	594
Debt service	5,170	5,968	5,939	6,748
Others	907	1,095	1,118	1,250
Total expenditures	28,178	30,539	31,416	34,279

Source: *Chosen Nenkan*, 1941.

The average population of one *yu* or *men* is about ten thousand persons. According to this table the average expenditure per *yu* or *men* per month for all its needs was only 1,220 yen. Fifty-two per cent of the total was spent for administration, pure and simple; twenty per cent for payment of interest on debt, seven per cent on maintenance of buildings and for similar purposes, six per cent on encouragement of business and two per cent on subsidies.

Public Debt

In the year of annexation, the debt of the Korean Government stood at 45,590,106 yen. By 1938 it had risen to 673,968,148 yen, and by now, judging by the trend of borrowings in 1937-1941, it must be not less than 1,500,000,000 yen. As to debts of the local governments, on December 31, 1938, they were as follows:

Provincial	¥157,399,448
Municipal	48,661,419
Yu and *men*	8,721,208
Others	2,723,017
Total	217,505,092[a]

[a] The total as on December 31, 1938 should be greater because the debts of *yu* and *men* are given as on December 31, 1937.
Source: *Takumu Tokei*, 1938.

This debt too has probably doubled by now because borrowings have been at the rate of 50 million yen a year.

CHAPTER XII

THE EXTERNAL TRADE OF KOREA

The table below shows a rapid development of Korea's external trade between 1910 and 1940: imports increased from 39.6 million yen to 1,388.4 million yen, or thirty-five times, while exports increased even faster: from 19.9 million yen to 1,006.8 million yen, or almost fifty-one times.

DEVELOPMENT OF THE EXTERNAL TRADE OF KOREA
(in thousand yen)

			Indices	
Year	Imports	Exports	Imports	Exports
1910	39,783	19,914	100	100
1915	59,695	50,220	150	250
1919	283,077	221,947	710	1,110
1920	249,287	197,020	630	990
1925	340,012	341,631	860	1,710
1929	423,094	345,664	1,060	1,730
1930	367,048	266,547	920	1,340
1935	659,403	550,796	1,660	2,800
1936	762,417	593,313	1,920	2,980
1937	863,552	685,542	2,170	3,440
1938	1,055,927	879,606	2,660	4,400
1939	1,388,448	1,006,794	3,500	5,050
Jan.-Sept. 1939	1,007,488	749,707		
Jan.-Sept. 1940	1,176,121	700,848		

Source: 1910-1935, *Chosen Keizai Nempo*, 1939; 1936-1939, *Chosen Nenkan*, 1941.

Even if we take into consideration the fact that the price level in 1940 was almost three times the level of 1910, the results are still impressive; so impressive that almost all writers on Korea have been struck by this development. Some were amazed by the speed and magnitude of development, others jumped at once to the conclusion that the welfare of the Koreans was increasing as rapidly, or almost as rapidly, as Korea's external trade. Thus, Professor E. deS. Brunner writes:

"It is sometimes maintained that the increase in [Korea's] foreign trade represents very largely the business of Japanese and is not a fair measure of the economic strength of Korea. Undoubtedly, the Japanese, who form two per cent of the population, have greater per capita wealth than the

Koreans. But the total foreign trade of Korea (exports and imports) has increased twelve times as fast as the Japanese population. One cannot but see in these figures evidence of increased resources on the part of the Koreans."[1]

The proof given by Professor Brunner for his contention is not very convincing, for is it not also possible that the wealth of the Japanese residents has grown much faster than their numbers? And do trade statistics accurately reflect the wealth of the residents? On this subject of Korea's foreign trade, H. M. Vinacke states that:

"In the field of trade the Japanese predominance is due primarily to her need for Korean products and her ability to supply Korean needs, coupled with the natural advantage of geographical proximity; and only secondarily to a deliberate attempt to monopolize Korean trade."[2]

It is not quite clear what Professor Vinacke had in view when he spoke of "Korean needs," but evidently this part of his statement was intended to refer to the needs of the Korean people. Thus Professor Vinacke sees a mutually beneficial exchange: Japan gets raw materials from Korea and the Koreans' needs are supplied by Japan. In his view, however, this exchange is based primarily on the fortunate coincidence that Japan needs what Korea produces and is so near to Korea, and only secondarily on the Japanese political domination of Korea.

EXTERNAL TRADE OF KOREA BY COUNTRIES FOR 1911 AND 1939
(Absolute figures in thousand yen)

| | Absolute figures |||| Percentages ||||
| | Exports || Imports || Exports || Imports ||
	1911	1939	1911	1939	1911	1939	1911	1939
Japan	13,341	736,883	34,058	1,229,417	70.8	73.2	63.0	88.6
Manchuria	....	205,149	....	80,459	...	20.4	...	5.8
China	3,009	33,566	5,422	10,334	16.0	3.3	10.0	0.7
Asiatic Russia	1,511	0	49	2	8.0	0.0	0.1	0.0
Netherlands Indies	....	635	360	3,392	...	0.1	0.7	0.2
British India	....	476	82	8,846	...	0.0	0.2	0.6
United States	953	3,646	4,261	23,522	5.1	0.4	7.9	1.7
Great Britain	1	171	7,929	1,338	0.0	0.0	14.6	0.1
Germany	20	337	1,311	3,940	0.0	0.0	2.4	0.3
Other countries	22	25,931[a]	596	27,198[a]	0.1	2.6[a]	1.1	2.0[a]
Total	18,857	1,006,794	54,088	1,388,448	100.0	100.0	100.0	100.0

[a] It is difficult to ascertain what is meant by these "other countries." Figures for Hongkong, Malaya, French Indochina, and Canada are given, and they are very small. It is possible that these figures represent chiefly exports and imports to the Japanese Leased Territory of Kwantung.
Source for absolute figures: (1) *Statistical Survey of the Foreign Trade of Japan*, 1935.
(2) *Keizai Nenkan*, 1940, published by Toyo Keizai Shimbunsha.

[1] *Op. cit.*, pp. 116-117.
[2] *Op. cit.*, p. 366.

To estimate the validity of this contention, we must examine the development of Korea's trade with Japan and with foreign countries since the country's annexation by Japan.

This table shows that trade with all the countries named (except trade with Russia and imports from Great Britain) increased absolutely, but that the *share* of almost all the countries with the exception of Japan and Manchuria declined. Japan's share of exports rose from 70.8 per cent to 73.2 per cent; but together with Manchuria (and for all practical purposes Manchuria is now a part of the Japanese Empire) it was 93.6 per cent in 1939. Exports to China in that year formed only 3.3 per cent of the total, but this was to that part of China occupied by the Japanese, a member of the "yen-bloc."

Thus exports to yen-bloc countries formed 96.9 per cent of the total in 1939, and exports to the other countries named, only about one per cent of the total; imports from Japan in the same year formed 88.6 per cent of the total and from Japan *and* countries occupied by Japan, 95.1 per cent. Only imports from the United States amounted to more than one per cent (1.7 per cent) in 1939, and this was due almost entirely to purchases of much-needed American machinery.

Thus it is clear that the Japanese monopoly of Korean trade is virtually complete. But it is also clear that this monopoly is not the result merely of geographic proximity and other factors independent of political control. For example, Korean exports to China (including Manchuria) amounted in 1930 to 21.6 million yen. After the occupation of Manchuria in 1933, exports to China were only 1.6 million yen, and those to Manchuria were 40.6 million yen. The geographic proximity was the same; the needs of the population had hardly changed, yet exports to "Manchukuo" were twice as high as the combined exports to China and Manchuria in 1930. In 1936 when the Chinese coast was still in Chinese hands, exports to China from Korea amounted to 3.7 million yen; in 1939 when the entire coastal area of central and northern China was occupied by Japanese forces, they jumped to 33.6 million yen, or nine times those of 1936. Imports from Germany were valued at only 1.0 million yen in 1936, but after the conclusion of the anti-Comintern pact they began to grow and reached 3.9 million yen in 1939. Imports from the United States were valued at 9.2 million yen in 1936; after that year the rapid construction of war industry caused a demand for machinery which Japan was unable to satisfy, and imports from the United States rose to 23.5 million yen in 1935. The influence of Japanese political control on Korean trade was exercised not only through the tariff wall which guarded Korea against the intrusion of non-Japanese goods (goods from Japan entered duty-free), but through the control of the country's entire economic life. Industry, banks, communications, and the government machinery were in Japanese hands. Under these conditions it was inevitable that the decisions as to what to import or what and where to export were taken by Japanese import and export firms, and that these decisions were influenced by official Japanese policy. After 1937 this control became complete and all-embracing, and the external trade of Korea was pressed into the service of the government's war plans.

EXPORTS AND IMPORTS OF LIVING ANIMALS, CEREALS, FLOUR, BEANS
(in thousand yen)

	1929	1936	1937	1938	1939
A. Exports of this kind	177,091	285,203	272,156	360,696	228,250
B. Total Exports	342,745	591,258	679,842	877,394	1,003,455
A as per cent of B	51.6	48.3	40.1	41.2	22.7
C. Imports of this kind	54,038	69,257	58,154	46,634	97,723
D. Total Imports	421,930	760,324	859,328	1,052,917	1,383,924
C as per cent of D	12.8	8.9	6.5	3.9	6.6
C as per cent of A	30.5	24.3	21.4	12.1	42.8

We see from this table that the animal and agricultural products named form the largest percentage of exports from Korea; in 1929 they accounted for 51.6 per cent, and in 1938 for 41.2 per cent of all exports. These exports consisted chiefly of rice, the most important single export commodity of Korea; the value of rice exports making up 35 per cent of the total in 1938. Other commodities in the order of their importance in this group are beans, cattle, and wheat flour.

Korea also imports agricultural products. From the table given above it is seen, however, that such imports formed a small and a diminishing part of the total imports (12.8 per cent in 1929 and only 3.9 per cent in 1938) and also that imports of these products amounted to 30.5 per cent of exports in 1929 and only 12.1 per cent in 1938. In other words, Korea was exporting more and more agricultural products and importing less and less. The year 1939 has been omitted from the analysis because it was a year of exceptional crop failure, when it was natural for exports of agricultural products to fall sharply and for imports to increase. The effect of this crop failure was felt in both 1939 and 1940.

EXPORTS AND IMPORTS OF FOODSTUFFS, DRINKS, TOBACCO
(figures are given in thousand yen)

	1929	1936	1937	1938	1939
Exports	33,576	37,684	42,674	56,425	91,449
Imports	37,010	57,421	64,065	74,168	93,941

Imports of foodstuffs, drinks, and tobacco normally exceed exports, though in 1939, the year of famine, exports almost doubled and equalled imports. Fish and other sea products are the chief items of export; imports include sugar, Japanese liquor (*sake*), beer which is not drunk by the masses of the Korean population, confectionery products, jams, jellies, Japanese sauces (*soy*), fresh vegetables, fresh fruits, condensed milk, and canned goods. In other words, with the exception of sugar and a few other commodities, these are chiefly foodstuffs for the Japanese population and for the upper class Korean. According to the author's observations and the testimony of others who have visited Korea, 80-90 per cent of the Korean population never eat imported fresh fruit, or imported fresh vegetables, or drink condensed milk or Japanese *sake* or beer. Thus, Korea exports food products for mass consumption and imports products for consumption by the upper class of the native population and by Japanese residents. The case of sugar must be examined in greater detail. Korea does not produce sugar to any large extent, so a comparison of imports and exports should help us to arrive at an approximate estimate of the domestic consumption.

KOREA'S TRADE IN SUGAR
(in thousand tons)

	1929	1936	1937	1938	1939
Exports	30.0	33.0	32.5	22.1	12.5
Imports	52.8	66.4	66.5	55.5	57.4
Net imports	22.8	33.4	34.0	33.4	45.4
Per capita consumption in pounds	2.58	3.32	3.35	3.26	4.2
Consumption in Japan, pounds[a]	28.8	32.5	31.0	...	...
Consumption in U. S., pounds[b]	107.6	102.1	92.3	96.4	107.7

[a] Source: *Keizai Nenkan*, 1940.
[b] Source: *Statistical Abstract of the United States*, 1941.

The case of sugar provides an excellent example of how difficult it is to interpret changes in consumption through trade figures. The figures in this instance show a great improvement in the situation: the total net imports increased from 22,800 tons to 45,400 tons, or almost doubled in eleven years; and per capita consumption increased from 2.6 pounds in 1929 to 4.2 pounds in 1939. Though even in that year it was only one-tenth of the Japanese per capita consumption, yet it had increased, and this might be considered a clear proof of an improvement in the general level of consumption. However, let us look at the same problem from another point of view. There were in Korea in 1939 650,000 Japanese, as well as a small group of relatively prosperous Koreans. If we assume that their consumption of sugar was the same as the average annual consumption of sugar in Japan, that is, 32.5 pounds, this would mean that the per capita annual consumption of sugar by the great mass of the Korean people was still very low. Taking into consideration the fact that the Japanese in Korea consume more than the per capita average in Japan,[3] it would appear that the bulk of the Korean population consumes practically no sugar.

Another group of imports chiefly for consumption is that of textiles, including raw materials, yarns, tissues, and clothing. The respective value of exports and imports of the enumerated textiles changed in the following way:

KOREA'S TRADE IN TEXTILES
(in million yen)

	1929	1936	1937	1938	1939
Exports	55.4	62.2	90.6	102.4	144.6
Imports	125.8	193.9	211.2	267.7	318.1
Net imports	70.4	131.7	120.6	165.3	173.5

Again we see a "clear" case of increased consumption: imports increased two and a half times in value in eleven years, and net imports increased similarly. From 125.8 million yen in 1929 the imports of textiles increased to 318.1 million yen in 1939. Is this not a proof of an improvement in Korea's eco-

[3] That an average Japanese in Korea is more wealthy than the average Japanese in Japan may be seen from the following comparisons: the number of telegrams sent, the number of telephones per family, the amount of deposits in the banks, and others. All these indices were higher for Japanese in Korea than for Japanese in Japan.

nomic situation? Let us take tissues, the largest component of this group, and compare the quantities exported and imported.

KOREA'S TRADE IN TISSUES
(in million yards)

	1929	1936	1937	1938	1939
Exports[a]	8.6	47.5	142.5	128.7	67.4
Imports[b]	192.7	286.5	278.4	333.3	192.4
Net imports	184.1	239.0	135.5	204.6	125.0
Per capita net imports, yards	9.5	10.8	6.1	9.0	6.5

[a] This includes cotton tissues and rayon tissues.
[b] This includes tissues made of cotton, wool, hemp, silk, rayon, and staple fibre.

These statistics, even if they do show a rapid increase in the value of imports and also in the volume of imports up to 1938, cannot serve as a proof of increased consumption unless the figures of domestic production and other data are also given. Imports of tissues increased in value from 71.2 million yen to 184.2 million yen in eleven years—a rather rapid increase. The per capita increases of imports was much smaller and then, with the war, gave way to a decrease. In 1929, per capita net imports of tissues of all kinds amounted to 9.5 square yards; in 1936 it was 10.8 square yards; in 1937—6.1; in 1938—9.0; and in 1939 only 6.5 square yards.

KOREA'S NET IMPORTS OF TISSUES
(imports minus exports)
(in million square yards)

	1929	1936	1937	1938	1939
Cotton tissues	139.0	129.9	31.5	−11.8[a]	−23.3[a]
Hemp tissues	13.3	8.4	8.9	5.9	2.3
Woolen tissues	4.2	10.0	7.7	8.5	8.5
Silk (pure)	15.8	10.1	8.8	15.7	30.8
Rayon	11.8	82.6	74.4	155.9	38.6
Staple fibre	...	...	4.2	30.4	58.1

[a] Net reports.

This table shows that in the thirties imports of cotton and hemp tissues were decreasing, while imports of woolen, silk, and rayon tissues were rapidly rising. This can hardly mean that Koreans generally wanted to wear silk and woolen tissues instead of cotton, for if the net per capita imports of all tissues was only 6.5 yards in 1939, it is obvious that the increase in imports of woolen and silk tissues had nothing to do with the

THE EXTERNAL TRADE OF KOREA 233

wishes of the masses of the population. With regard to domestic production, the value of cotton tissues produced in Korea in 1937 was 51 million yen, of silk tissues—6.5; of hemp tissues—8.8; of rayon—2.3; or a total of 68.6 million yen. Of this total at least 32.8 million yen worth of tissues were exported.[4] In the same year the value of imports of tissues was 89.4 million yen. This suggests, first, that the domestic production of tissues is smaller than the volume of imports; second, that per capita consumption of tissues cannot very much exceed the figures of per capita net imports, and is in general very low; third, that imports chiefly satisfy the demands of the Japanese residents and rich Koreans, and, last, that exports of tissues from Korea do not represent a "surplus" exported after the satisfaction of the elementary needs of the Koreans, but on the contrary merely indicate the low level of domestic consumption.

The "remarkable" increase in the value of Korea's trade, as far as consumers' goods are concerned, may be explained by four factors.

1. *Price increases.*
   In 1929 one *kin* (0.6 kilogram) of imported rice cost 8.6 sen; in 1939—16.4 sen; the price of one square yard of cotton tissues was correspondingly 25 and 56 sen; one square yard of silk tissues—88 and 145 sen, and so on.
2. *Transition from natural economy to exchange economy.*
   What was produced at home is now bought in the market, and the market is supplied by Japan.
3. *Increase in number of the Japanese.*
   The number of Japanese residents in 1910 was 171,500; in 1939 it was 650,000. If per capita expenditures on imported goods by the Japanese population were only one hundred yen a year, Korea's imports would increase by 47.9 million yen, if 200 yen—they would increase by 95.7 million yen through this one factor alone. Now, every Japanese is, of course, anxious to buy Japanese goods, especially because in Korea it is impossible to buy locally many things to which Japanese consumers are accustomed. The financial circumstances of the Japanese in Korea are such that they can afford to buy these goods brought from Japan.

[4] Probably more, because we have figures only for cotton and rayon tissues.

4. *Improved conditions of the Japanese and the upper strata of Korean society.*

These groups are richer on the average than they were in 1910. The paid-up capital of Korean-controlled corporations increased in fifteen years from 34.1 million yen to 122.7 million yen and a certain portion of this increase was real and not simply a change in juridical form. Many landowners became rich overnight because ores were found on their land or because a port was built on a hitherto empty coast. In 1910 Korean bank deposits were 3.9 million yen, in 1938 they had risen to 104.9 million yen, and again a portion of this increase represents a real increase in the wealth of rich Koreans. The probability that the wealth of the Japanese in the same period increased faster than their numbers may be seen from the following facts. In 1910, Japanese investments in Korea were less than one hundred million yen; in 1940 they were estimated at 5 to 6 billion yen,[5] an increase of 50 to 60 times. In 1910 the deposits of the Japanese residents in the banks were 12 million yen. In 1938 they amounted to 358.6 million yen, an increase of thirty times, though the Japanese population during the same period increased by only 3.7 times. These increases, exaggerated as they are by the change in the purchasing power of money, are nevertheless real and substantial; but they cannot serve as indices pointing to "improving conditions" of the Korean population as a whole. They point only to the improving conditions of two relatively small groups: the Japanese and the small group of rich Koreans.

Another category of imports comprises goods for production purposes; their share of total imports has been increasing and they are especially responsible for the rapid growth of Korean foreign trade.

IMPORTS OF CONSUMPTION AND PRODUCTION GOODS, 1929-1939
(in per cent of the total)

	1929	1936	1937	1938	1939
I. Living plants, animals, cereals, drinks, tobacco, textiles	51.5	42.0	38.7	36.6	36.8
II. Chemicals, machinery, metal mfrs., minerals, ores, metals	25.2	33.9	38.5	41.1	43.6

[5] *Chosen Keizai Nempo*, 1940, p. 514.

This table shows that the proportion of a group of commodity imports destined mainly for consumption fell in eleven years from 51.5 per cent of the total to 36.8 per cent, and the proportion of a group of imports mainly for production purposes rose in the same period from 25.2 to 43.6 per cent of the total or, in absolute figures, from 106.6 million yen in 1929 to 604.2 million yen in 1939. It is true that the first group does not consist exclusively of consumption goods: ginned cotton is not a commodity for direct consumption, and only a part of cotton imports is used for making clothing. The figures also include fishing nets, gunny bags, and other goods for production purposes. On the other hand, the second group contains bicycles and enamel ware—goods for consumption. But the contrast is nevertheless convincing. Moreover, the remaining share of the imports also contains goods used chiefly for production (such as fertilizers, timber, and dyes).

Thus even in 1929 production goods were responsible for more than 25 per cent and in 1939 for more than 44 per cent of the total value of Korean imports. This was to be expected in view of the development of Korea as a military base. We saw how relatively large were the investments of the Japanese Government in railways, ports, roads, air communications, explosive works, production of sulphate of ammonia, glycerine, hard oils, mining and electric works. The military base in Korea was carefully and methodically prepared; and the construction of such a base demands, of course, large imports of metals, metal manufactures, cement, glass, paint, machinery, and timber. But imports of this character, which were responsible for so large a part of the total, contributed relatively little to the welfare of the Korean population.

The growth of exports from Korea to Japan and Manchuria, which were responsible for 94 per cent of the total exports in 1939, was a result not so much of the peculiar suitability of Korean products to Japanese needs as of the necessity of using every available resource in preparation for the coming struggle for Japanese supremacy in the Pacific. The rice of Indo-China or Burma was cheaper than Korea's; Malayan iron ores were better than Korean; American mineral oil was many times less expensive than oil from Korean oil; but considerations of this kind were not decisive in the minds of the Japanese. Tariffs, subsidies, grants, "encouragements," and outright discrimination were instruments by which foreign competition was kept out. Formerly Korea's exports consisted mainly of raw materials and foodstuffs; more recently fertilizers, pulp, gold, hard oils, explosives, and other manufactures and semi-manufactured goods were added in increasing amounts. The gross value of production in Korea (mining, fishing, forestry, agriculture, industry) was estimated by the Japanese authorities in 1938 at 3,180 million yen. But the net value of Korea's total production, estimated according to the coefficients which the Government Bureau of Statistics in Japan used for the census of 1930,[6] was only 1,700 to 1,800 million yen, while total exports from Korea in 1938 amounted to 877.4 million yen. There are few countries in the world, even among the colonies, where such a large portion of the goods produced is taken out of the country. This is not only a matter of concern for the Korean people; it also shows the ability of Japan's leaders to make all the resources available to them serve their designs. With the modest resources of Japan Proper, Korea, and other Japanese colonies, they were able to challenge simultaneously the United States, Great Britain, China, and Australia. The great increase in exports from Korea to Japan was nothing to rejoice in or admire; it was a grave warning to other nations bent on peaceful pursuits.

In connection with Korea's external trade, however, one may point out that during the whole period 1910-1939 Korea had a total unfavorable balance of trade amounting to 1,888 million yen, i.e., Korea's merchandise imports during this period exceeded exports by that amount.

This fact calls for further explanation. In the first place, exports of specie and bullion from Korea must be taken into account. From 1910 to 1936, the net exports of specie and bullion from Korea amounted to 434.2 million yen. Data for 1937-1939 are not available, but many indirect statements and the sums spent by the Government for the encouragement of gold production indicate that it could hardly have been less than three hundred million yen during these three years, or, adding to the total for 1910-1936, about 730-740 million yen. This reduces Korea's excess of imports during this period to 1,150-1,160 million yen. Several other facts must also be considered in this connection.

[6] The coefficients are given in *An Inquiry into the National Income of Japan*, by the Research Division of the Japan Economic Federation, Tokyo, 1939.

1. For many years a large portion of the gold mined in Korea was smuggled into neighboring countries.[7]
2. Korea was for many years a base for Japanese smuggling into Chinese provinces of Shantung and Manchuria. Estimates of "duty-free" imports[8] from Korea ran into many millions annually.
3. Approximately one million Koreans worked in Japan in 1939-40. Horozaki, in an article on the immigration of Koreans into Japan,[9] gives examples of Koreans making monthly remittance to Korea of 20 to 30 yen and, in addition, making substantial savings. In view of the fact that among them were also women and children (though forming only a small part of the total) we may assume that the per capita remittance to Korea were ten yen per month. This would mean that each year these workers remitted about 120 million yen to Korea, and this sum could be used to pay for imports. There are also about 1,200,000 Koreans in Manchuria and North China and though their earnings are smaller than those in Japan, yet it is quite possible that their remittances amount to about 60 million yen annually. All this tends to show that on balance it was Korea which paid hundreds of millions of yen abroad, and not vice versa. Moreover, as has been mentioned, Japanese investments in Korea at the time of annexation were less than one hundred million yen; by 1939-40 they reached five billion to six billion yen; finally, many of the imports were for the benefit of the 650,000 Japanese in Korea who maintained a standard of living which for the majority of them was much higher than what they would have had in Japan.

Taken all together these items show that the aggregate net merchandise imports into Korea for the whole period 1910-1939 was in fact much less than the recorded figure of 1,888 million yen, despite heavy Japanese capital invesments during the last decade.

[7] K. Takahashi, *op. cit.*, p. 380.
[8] The term "smuggling" can hardly be applied after 1931. Exports were made with the connivance of customs authorities on both sides of the frontier, because in both cases the officials were Japanese. The purpose of these "secret" exports was to preserve the appearance of independence in "Manchukuo," a country which admits goods from all countries on a footing of equality. K. Takahashi mentions that "not a small part of increase of imports [into Korea] is due to smuggling." *Op. cit.*, p. 383.
[9] *Shakai Seisaku Jiho*, August 1940.

CHAPTER XIII

THE GOVERNMENT OF KOREA

The Government General[1]

The Japanese Government of Korea is administered through the Governor-General. He is appointed by the Emperor; but this does not mean that in the eyes of the Japanese government Korea occupies an exalted position recalling the country's sovereign rights in the past. The Governor-General's rank is that of a *shin-nin,* or minister, and a person of this rank is entitled to report directly to the Crown.[2] He may be entitled to report directly, but actually he cannot report even to the Japanese Cabinet, but must submit his reports through the Ministry of Colonies. Thus Korea has been made an administrative subdivision in the structure of the Empire. Theoretically, the post of Governor-General is open to Japanese civilians as well as to generals and admirals, but during the thirty-two years that have passed since the annexation of Korea, no civilian has ever held this office.

But whatever his rank and power may be in Tokyo, in Korea the Governor-General is virtually an absolute monarch; he is the head of the administration, including the police; and he is also the law maker. It is true that he does not have complete power over judges, but he has the power to imprison anyone in Korean territory for a term not exceeding one year, and the power to impose a fine up to 200 yen without trial; and Korean history shows that it is possible for a man to be kept in jail year after year without being tried, merely at the Governor-General's direction. This does not, of course, mean that rule by the Governor-General is purely arbitrary;[3] it simply

---

[1] Important reforms were made in the administration of Korea, Formosa, and southern Sakhalin in 1942, the purpose of which was to bring these regions under greater control by Tokyo. However, in view of the lack of information it is impossible to describe these new reforms.

[2] *Japan Manchukuo Year Book.*

[3] The fact that Japan's colonial rule is not arbitrary does not mean that it is humane, moral, expedient, or beneficial, as A. Ireland sought to represent it in his *New Korea,* (pp. 12-13, *op. cit.,*). This author writes: "It seems to me that these two factors, morality and expediency, act with greater effectiveness

shows that the Governor-General is in practice the source of all authority in the peninsula. Only the Army stationed in Korea might perhaps be considered as independent in its jurisdiction; but insofar as all governors, except one, have been generals who in the past had occupied important positions in the Japanese Army, serious friction between the Governor-General and the Commander of the Japanese Army in Korea cannot easily arise. Moreover, the Governor-General has the right to demand the use of troops when he considers it necessary.

Departments and Bureaus

The Governor-General rules in Korea through the Government-General which consists of the secretariat and seven departments (*kyoku*), namely Home Affairs, Finance, Business,[4] Agriculture and Forestry, Education, Justice, and Police. The "sections" into which each department is subdivided may be seen from the following scheme:

	Sections	Secretaries
	Office of the Secretary:	Interpreters
		Army and Navy Commissioners
	Office of Investigations:	Officials in charge of them
Secretariat.........	Personnel	
	Archives	
	Resources	
	Census...............	The chief of this section is at the same time the chief archivist.
Department of Home Affairs......	Local Administration	Keijo
	Social Affairs	Fusan
	Public Works (*doboku*), at	Heijo
		Shingishu
		Seishin

in colonial dependencies than in self-governing countries . . . Furthermore, the Colonial Governor looks for his advancement to the distant authority of a Secretary of State at the national capital. Promotion and other rewards will depend upon the way in which he administers his charge. He is little likely to earn them if . . . his territory fails to advance it its health, prosperity, and general social condition; he is almost certain to miss them if, in consequence of harsh and incompetent administration, the people rise in revolt against his rule," yes, if the people rise against his rule; but what if they rise, as they usually do, against foreign rule? Moreover, will the Governor be dismissed because of harsh rule, if no revolt follows? Will he miss his promotion if he starves natives in order to feed Japanese, or if he squeezes the colony dry for the benefit of Japanese arms in southeast Asia? It is true that "the success of his rule will be the measure of his personal success." But what is the yardstick for his success?

[4] *Shokusan* is often translated as "industry." But the term is broader than industry in the narrow sense since it also includes commerce, fishing, and mining.

Department of
Finance..........
 Taxation
 Customs
 Budget
 Management of Finances

Department of
Business..........
 Commerce and Industry
 Fuel Production
 Mining
 Gold Production
 Fishing
 Adjustment of Commodities and Prices
 Fuel Laboratory
 Museum for Encouragement of Commerce and Industry
 Training Institute for Rock-drilling
 Weights and Measures

Department of
Agriculture and
Forestry..........
 Agriculture
 Cattle Breeding
 Rural Revival
 Rice Production
 Investigation of Foodstuffs
 Irrigation and Drainage, Reclamation
 Forest Products
 Forestry, with Forest Experimental Station

Department of
Justice............
 Criminal Affairs
 Civil Affairs
 Prisons

Department of
Education.........
 Education
 Social Education
 Compilation of Textbooks
 Observatory

Department of
Police.............
 Police
 Protection (*Bogo*)
 Economic Police
 Safety
 Censorship
 Health Section

Besides these departments and sections there are a number of bureaus and institutions under the direct administration of the Government-General. They are:

Central Council

Bureau of
Foreign Affairs..... Foreign Affairs
 Emigration

Planning Bureau.... With four sections

 General Affairs
 Supervising
 Management
 Engineering
 Electric Works, two sections

THE GOVERNMENT OF KOREA 241

Department of Communications....
- Marine Affairs
- Insurance supervision
- Insurance application (*Un-yo*)
- Insurance Affairs
- Aviation
- Air-fields (Keijo, Taikyu, Shingishu, Seishin, Koshu, Kanko)
- Training Center for Communications Officials
- Branches of Marine Affairs (Jinsen, Fusan, Chinnampo, Shinishu, Genzan, Seishin, Rashin, Runsan)
- Savings Supervising Office (Keijo, Fusan, Heijo, Seishin, Central Telegraph Office in Keijo, Central Telephone Office)

Department of Railways..........
- Investigation
- Supervision
- Traffic Section
- Operating Section
- Construction Section
- Railway Guards
- Improvements
- Mechanical Section (*kosaku*)
- Management of Electricity of................
  - Fusan Railway
  - Taiden
  - Keijo
  - Heijo
  - Junten
  - Genzan
  - Seishin
  - Kokai
- Construction.................
  - Keijo
  - Heijo
  - Antung
  - Koryo
- Improvements................
  - Fusan
  - Keijo
  - Heijo
- Keijo Hospital

Department of Monopolies........
- General Affairs
- Business Section
- Accounting (*keirika*)
- Manufacturing
- Salt and Ginseng
- Investigations
- Branches (Keijo, Zenshu, Taikyu, Heijo)

Department of Taxation Control...
- Keijo
- Koshu
- Taikyu
- Heijo
- Kanko

Custom Houses
Meteorological Stations
Serum Manufacturing Station
Police Training School
Grain Grading Station
Central Research Institute

Agricultural Experiment Stations
Forest Experiment Stations
Fishery Experimental Stations
Fish Products Experiment Institute
Stud Farms
Sheep Farms
Leper Hospitals
Asylums for Orphans, Deaf and Mutes, Blind

Provincial Offices...
- Secretariat of Internal Affairs
- Business
- Police
- Fire Brigades
- Hospitals
- Schools

Municipalities (*fu*)
Counties (*Gun*)—*yu, men*
Islands (*Shima*)—*men*

Public Procurator—Procurator of Courts of Appeal—Local Courts Procurators

Supreme Court—Courts of Appeal   Local Courts

Office of Security Bonds
Prisons   for adults
                for juveniles

Political Offenders Prisons[5] and Council of Investigation

Marine Court
Council of Inquiry into Custom Appeals
Keijo University

Government Schools
- Special Schools (Colleges)
- Teachers' Seminary
- Professional Schools

Government Library

Training Center for Korean Army Volunteers

Jinsa (Shinto shrines)..........
- Keijo
- Ryotozan
- Taikyu
- Heijo

This long list of government organs and institutions is probably not exhaustive, but everything of importance is included. It presents a picture of a well-developed and orderly society, in which police, courts, prisons, reformatories, as well as public and semi-public enterprises and institutions are well represented. There is, for example, the Police Department which consists of a Police Section, an Economic Police Section, a "Protection" Section, a Peace Preservation Section, a Censorship, and a Health Section.

[5] This is termed in the English edition of the *Annual Report*: "Political Offenders' Probation Office"; but in Japanese it does not sound like that: *shisohan hogo-kansatsujo*—places for detention and investigation of political criminals.

However, even a cursory survey of these institutions shows a few striking features. In a country with a population of more than twenty-four million people, there is only one university; but there are fifteen prisons for adults, three prisons for juvenile offenders, seven special prisons for political offenders, and eleven branch prisons. Further, we know that from 70 to 75 per cent of the population of the peninsula are occupied in agriculture, and yet, in the combined Department of Agriculture and Forestry, only four of the eight sections are devoted to the Korean peasant. Two are given over to forestry, one deals with rice and another with foodstuff investigations; that is, these bureaus are concerned not with native Korean agriculture, but with the production and export of rice to Japan. One section is devoted to "Rural Revival" and, as has been shown in a previous chapter, is more concerned with incantations than with real help to farmers.

Civil Service

Another striking characteristic of this huge administrative apparatus is the fact that all positions of importance in these government institutions, departments, bureaus, sections, etc., are occupied exclusively by Japanese. The personnel of the department of Agriculture and Forestry provides exceptionally convincing proof of this assertion because this department has more to do with Korean welfare than any other and because service in it has no political implications such as, for example, service in the Department of Police or in the Department of Justice. The Department of Agriculture and Forestry—*Norinkyoku*—had the following officials in 1941: the chief—a Japanese official of the first grade—was Tatsujiro Yumura, graduate of the Law Faculty of the Tokyo Imperial University; formerly Chief of the Accounting Section of the Secretariat; then Governor of Southern Kankyo and of Keiki, who has occupied his present post since 1937. Among the other 58 higher officials in the department there was only one Korean, and he was only of sixth grade rank. In all other institutions and government organizations the situation was the same.

The Central Council

There is, however, one institution in the Government in which Koreans predominate, namely the Central Council, an advisory body to the Korean Government-General. The only Japanese in this Council is its President, the Vice-Governor-General, who is the second-ranking official in the administration; all other are Koreans selected from among "prominent" and "influential" persons. Because of this, it is interesting to see how this advisory body functions. Besides the Vice-Governor-General, who is ex-officio President of the Council, it has one vice-president, five advisors, and 65 councillors, all of them selected by the Governor-General and appointed by the Japanese Cabinet for three years. Twenty-four of the councillors are selected from among the provincial assemblymen, who are elected (see below), so that the principle of popular representation is not wholly ignored. However, there are several features which clarify the real role of the Council. First of all, its technical staff is extraordinarily small: there is a Chief of the Secretariat, a Secretary, seven clerks, seven interpreters and their chief. Second, though the terms of the councillors is for three years, anyone may be released from duty by the Governor-General before that term is ended. Third, the "who's who" of a few of these councillors is extremely revealing. (1) Viscount Hei-Seki Bin, one of the five advisors, was in 1938, the date to which our information refers, the Lord Steward to His Majesty, the Korean Emperor. (2) Marquis Eiko Boku, the Vice-President, 77 years old, was Chairman of the Board of Directors of the Keijo Spinning Company, President of the Chosen Book Printing Company, Director of the Chosen Land Improvement Company, etc. (3) Baron Yin-Yo Li, advisor, 84 years old, was Minister of War in 1904, Household Minister in 1907, and Household Councillor after that date. (4) Councillor Ei-tetsu Boku, 67 years old, was formerly a Cavalry Major in the Korean Army, then Director of the Chosen Trust Company and Chosen Railway Company. (5) Councillor Sei-ken Cho, 64 years old, was an officer in the Korean Army (dissolved in 1907); (6) So-ryn Kan, 58 years old, was Chairman of the Board of Directors, Chosen Trust Company, President of the Chosen Life Insurance Company, Director of the Chosen Marine Insurance Company, President of the Kanjo Bank, Vice-Chairman of the Keijo Chamber of Commerce, advisor to the Oriental Development Company, etc.

These few examples indicate that the members of the Council are either elderly persons formerly connected with the old retime in Korea, or men closely connected in their business affairs with the Japanese, or a combination of both these types. We have seen in a previous chapter, for example, what the activities of the Oriental Development Company in Korea are, and it is clear that only Koreans of the Quisling type could become advisors of a company the purpose of which was the settlement of Japanese in Korea and the concentration of Korean real estate in Japanese hands. In short, the members of the Central Council are for the most part men who have never raised any objection even to the worst abuses of the conquering power.

Finally, the questions which the Governor-General from time to time submits for the Council's consideration have to do almost exclusively with the interpretation of old customs and beliefs. The main topic submitted to them for the year 1935 was: "Subjects for revival of native beliefs, promotion and guidance of existing religions" (original translation, *Annual Report*). In other words, the Council has been used by the Japanese as a tool in support of their reactionary policy. Just as its personnel is recruited from the most reactionary groups in the Korean population, so the resolutions of this Council are used for reactionary purposes. The Council does not possess an iota of real authority and there is not one member in it who can be considered a representative of popular Korean interests.

The Army in Control

Korea, in short, is governed by a bureaucracy with the Governor-General at its head. The latter is usually an important member of the leading militarist group in Japan. Terauchi, the first Governor-General and simultaneously War Minister of Japan, was one of the foremost militarists of his day, just as Marshal Hasegawa, the second Governor-General, was one of the most cruel; Yamanashi was several times War Minister; Minami before his appointment to Korea was the dictator of Manchuria (combining three posts, that of Commander-in-Chief of the Kwantung Army, Ambassador to Manchukuo, and Governor-General of the Kwangtung Leased Territory); Koiso, the present Governor-General, was chief of staff of the Kwantung Army and later Commander of the Army in Korea. The only exception was Admiral Saito, several times Minister of the Navy. It was while he was Premier that Japan occupied Manchuria and left the League of Nations.

Provincial Administration

Korea is divided into thirteen provinces, each ruled by a Governor. However, "in July, 1920, an important revision was made in the local system, and advisory bodies were established throughout the country. These organs were meant as the first step toward realization of local self-government, since conditions did not justify immediate enforcement of a complete system of local autonomy"[6] The Annual Report states further that in the local bodies "the people have gradually obtained experience in its operation"; "on the other hand, it was felt that the political aspirations of the people should be satisfied, by improving the present system in accordance with the policy already formed"; "the provincial system is now changed into a Provincial Council vested with executive power"; "the Provincial Councils, hitherto advisory organs to the governors, became self-governing bodies from April 1, 1933, and in May the first general election was held throughout the country."

This may lead one to believe that there is now local autonomy in Korea and that the Provincial Councils express the will of the people. Unfortunately, nothing could be farther from the truth. The provinces are still ruled by governors appointed by the Japanese Government and subordinate to the Governor-General. These governors administer the affairs of the provinces through their secretariats and through the Departments of Internal Affairs, Police Affairs, and Production. They have the right to imprison any person in the province for a period up to three months, or fine them up to one hundred yen without recourse to the courts; they control all local bodies; and they are authorized to issue local ordinances. They cannot use troops without asking for the approval of the Governor-General, but in certain cases they may directly request local commanders of Japanese Army detachments to use their troops against the Korean population. What, then, are the functions of these "self-governing bodies"—the Provincial Councils?

Provincial Councils

The number of members in the Provincial Councils is determined by the Governor-General. For the time being it is be-

[6] *Annual Report on the Administration of Chosen*, for the year 1936-37, pp. 202-210.

tween 21 and 45. One third of the members of the Councils are appointed, mostly from among the resident Japanese; the rest are elected. The voters must be at least twenty-five years of age, male, resident in the province for at least one year, of independent means, and pay a stated minimum in local taxes. Five yen, which is the minimum tax payment required in city (*fu*) elections, may seem such a small sum that practically everyone should be able to vote. But in 1936, for example, the municipal population paid the following sums:[7]

	Japanese	Koreans
Municipal population, thousands	330.1	1,399.7
Average taxes paid per household, yen	24.0	4.48

This means that probably every Japanese resident had the right to vote, but presumably only a small minority of the Koreans could exercise that right.

Moreover, the number of representatives to be elected from each voting district is apportioned by the Governor. As a result of these restrictions, Japanese residents managed to secure 29.6 per cent of the total number of seats in the Provincial Councils in the 1933 elections, although their proportion of the population was only 2.6 per cent. No figures are available for the 1937 and 1941 election, but it is known that the number of Japanese members increased. However, despite these limitations, the Councils could do useful work if they had anything like real power. We have seen that the administration of the provinces is in the hands of the Japanese Governors, and that all the important posts in the Government are filled by Japanese.[8] What, then, are the duties of the Councils? According to the Annual Reports, they control "local finance." Unfortunately, the revenue of the provinces consists mainly of surtaxes, the rates of which are established by law, and of state subsidies, while the expenditures are narrowly circumscribed. The budget of a province is a so-called compulsory budget (*kyosei yosan no seido*). There is, therefore, very little in local finances over which these elected citizens can exercise any control. Nor are these Councils "self-governing" bodies even in their internal

[7] The *Annual Report* for 1936-37, p. 208.
[8] In the province of South Zenra, for example, among twelve high officials there were no Koreans. It is stated in *Takumu Yoran*, 1939, that in each province the Governor has a Korean adviser, but in this province even the adviser was a Japanese, named Oyama; in Kogendo it was Matsumoto, in Keiki—Hiramatsu, in Northern Keisho—Takeyama, etc.

organization. The chairman of the Provincial Council is none other than the Governor himself.

City (fu), County (gun) and Island (shima) Organization

The organization of *fu, gun,* and *shima* is similar to that of *do,* the province: each is governed by a government official called, correspondingly, *fu-in, gunshu,* and *toshi.* The municipal council of the *fu* (there were in 1939 eighteen *fu,* 218 *gun* and two *shima*) is elected on the same basis as the Provincial Council, and is similar in its organization: the chairman of the municipal council is the *fu-in*: the election law is the same. There are two differences, however: there are no appointed members; and at least one-fourth of the elected members must be Japanese and one-fourth Koreans. It may be of some interest to note that out of a municipal population of about 1,700,000 in 1936, only 56,687 persons were registered as voters.

Even in the school system we find the same division. Within each municipal council there are separate committees for Japanese and for Korean schools. The reason for this is not a difference in program, but a very considerable difference in the financing of the schools: the schools for the Japanese are incomparably better equipped in all respects than are the schools for Koreans.

Towns and Townships (Yu and Men)

In 1940 there were in Korea 76 towns and 2,262 townships, and most of the Korean population was concentrated in these, while most of the Japanese were concentrated in *fu,* or cities. Thus, *yu* and *men* (which as a matter of fact are identical in their organization, the term *yu* being given to more populated or more important districts) are the local governments for the masses of the Korean population. The heads of *yu* are, with few exceptions, Japanese; but most of the heads of *men* are Koreans because there are no Japanese to be found to work in small out-of-the-way places and for a niggardly compensation. In *yu* and *men* there are councils whose organization and functions are similar to those of the municipal councils, though the tax requirements are lower: if a five yen minimum were imposed, there would only be one or two voters in most *yu* and *men.* But even with the lower minimum, less than one in ten of the male population above twenty-five years of age has the right to vote.

With all these limitations, it may seem surprising that the Japanese should bother with these "elective" organs since all real power obviously remains in the hands of the Japanese bureaucracy. Apparently, however, the purpose of these "reforms" is to win over the wealthier section of the Korean population by showing them that they are recognized as almost equal to the Japanese. There is no information to indicate the extent to which the Japanese rulers have been successful in attaining this exceedingly limited objective.

CHAPTER XIV

COURTS, PRISONS, POLICE

There are three sources of law in Korea: (1) Special Japanese laws published for Korea, e.g., the Korean Banking Law, the Law concerning Subsidies to the Korean Private Railways, and General Provisions (Tsuho); (2) the Laws of Japan applied in Korea, e.g., the Patent Law, Financial Law, Postal Law, Peace Regulations; (3) the Decrees, Statutes and Regulations published by the Government-General, such as the Korean Government-General's Court Law, the Korean Criminal Law, the Commercial Law, the Bankruptcy Law, the Civil Procedure Law, and the Criminal Procedure Law. All these codes are copied from the corresponding Japanese codes with slight modifications in which Korean customs find some recognition. This enumeration shows that the laws applied in Korea are, in the main, Japanese laws.

Courts

Law Courts are built under the system of "three instances"—Local Courts, Courts of Appeal, and the Supreme Court. Local Courts deal with the first hearing of both civil and criminal cases. The hearing is held by a single judge; but if a civil suit involves a sum of ¥1,000 or more, and in some other cases of importance, three judges sit at the hearing. There is no jury system. A Court of Appeal considers appeals against the judgment rendered by a Local Court; it consists of three judges. The

NUMBER OF COURTS AND PERSONNEL

	1910	1923	1938	Judges, 1938
Supreme Court	1	1	1	10
Courts of Appeal	3	3	3	35
Local Courts	..	11	11	103
Branches	..	..	48	77
Sub-branches	..	..	173	..
Number of judges	254	..	225	225
Number of procurators	60	..	109	..
Number of clerks and interpreters	437	..	880	..

Sources: (1) *Annual Reports on Administration of Chosen.*
(2) *Chosen Nenkan*, 1941.

Supreme Court presided over by five judges considers appeals against a judgment rendered by a Court of Appeal and performs the functions of the highest tribunal.

Thus despite a large increase in the number of cases (see below) the number of judges has decreased. As to the nationality of the judges, official reports give the impression that a large proportion of the judges and procurators are Koreans.

"The competency of Korean judges and procurators was formerly limited to the handling of cases, civil or criminal, in which Koreans only were involved. But such limitations being thought no longer necessary, revision of the regulations for courts of justice was again made in March, 1920, with the object of doing away with all such objectionable discrimination between Korean and Japanese on the bench."[1]

Unfortunately, although Korean judges may now handle all kinds of cases, there are few Korean judges left in the Courts of Korea. These were taken over by the Japanese before the formal annexation, so that as early as 1909 there were 192 Japanese and only 88 Korean judges. In 1912 there were 161 Japanese and 38 Korean judges; in the same year there were 54 Japanese and only 3 Korean procurators. Since that time the English-language official reports do not give any figures on the nationality of judges. However, in the list of judges on September 1940, as given in *Chosen Nenkan*, there is not one Korean judge in the Supreme Court; in the Courts of Appeal there are not more than four Korean judges out of 35; and only ten per cent of the judges in the local courts are Koreans; finally, there are no Koreans among the procurators. Thus the situation in this respect is now worse than it was in 1912. With regard to Korean judges, H. B. Drake notices the following:

"There may be two Korean judges on a tribunal of three; but the third is Japanese, he is president of the Court and has the power of absolute veto. The Koreans are not encouraged to meddle in legal matters."[2]

Thus the Koreans are judged in Japanese Courts by Japanese judges according to Japanese laws. This might not be so bad because there are good and honest judges among the Japanese. But most Koreans do not know the Japanese language; most of the judges do not know the Korean language, and the legal procedure is in Japanese. Anyone who has had the misfortune of being tried or of trying a case in a Court, the

[1] *Annual Report on Administration of Chosen*, 1936-37, p. 191.
[2] *Op. cit.*, p. 10.

language of which he does not understand, knows how difficult it is to obtain justice and impartiality under such conditions. Whatever the quality of the judges may be, Korean courts in the laws they use, in the nationality of their procurators and judges, and in the official language of legal procedure, reveal the same features that characterize Japanese rule in Korea—complete neglect of the interests of the natives.

THE ACTIVITY OF COURTS IN KOREA AND JAPAN, IN 1938

	Korea	Japan	Korea as per cent of Japan
Civil cases examined in local courts, (thousands)	56.1	429.1	13.1
Criminal cases examined in local courts, (thousands)	44.4	105.1	42.2
Prisoners	19,328	50,442	38.3
Population in 1940, (thousands)	34,326	73,114	33.2

Source for absolute figures: (1) *Takumu Tokei, 1938.*
(2) *Tokyo Gazette,* July 1941.

We see from the above table that the number of civil cases in Korea is much smaller not only in absolute but also in relative terms than that in Japan, while the number of criminal cases and the number of prisoners in Korea is, relative to the population, considerably larger than in Japan. Yet the laws in Japan and Korea, as we have seen, are almost identical, the judges are trained in the same schools; many of them start their work in Japan and finish in Korea or start in Korea and finish in Japan, so there is at all times a constant interchange of personnel, ideas, and interpretations. Why then is there such a difference? It is important to note that civil cases are instituted at the request of the interested parties, while criminal cases with few exceptions are instituted at the intiative of the government. Thus, when Koreans are left to themselves, they either do not like to apply to the courts or have less cause for litigations than the Japanese have in their homeland. The Koreans *en masse* are poor. A Korean worker or a Korean tenant often has no means of undertaking litigation, and he also has no great faith in the justice of the Japanese court. As a result, the Korean population turns to the courts only in extreme cases. In respect to criminal cases the situation is different: here the Japanese government prosecutes, and if there are relatively more criminal cases in Korea than in Japan, this means that either the Koreans have among them more persons addicted to crime, or the Japanese government acts more energetically in Korea than in Japan.

Crime

As to possible criminal tendencies among Koreans, the following table may be of interest.

IMPORTANT CRIMINAL CASES[3]

	1911	1923	1938
Gambling, lottery	1,542	3,455	1,920
Dispossession	339	845	746
Larceny	3,981	3,439	5,630
Fraud, blackmail	1,358	1,545	1,631
Forgery, perjury	263	344	444
Injury	430	1,618	5,647
Robbery	1,182	514	280
Murder	263	240	210
Seizure, abduction	264	140	67
Others	...	10,237	27,825
Total	7,900[4]	22,377	44,400

Source For 1911 and 1923: *Annual Report on Administration of Chosen*, 1922-24. For 1938: *Chosen Nenkan*, 1941.

Of course, during a twenty-seven year period many changes in the law might suffice to produce a substantial change in the number of cases tried or of convictions, yet the general impression from this table is that while robbery, murder and kidnapping[5] have decreased, other crimes have greatly increased, and this is supported by official statements (relating to different periods):

"Pocket-picking which was almost unknown in old Korea, is fast becoming one of the most prevalent crimes among present-day Koreans."[6] "Intellectual crimes on the other hand, such as fraud, forgery, perjury, have yearly increased, and the tendency is for greater skill to be shown in committing them."[7]

Also:

"Lately, however, instigated by the ideas of "gang" violence in Japan Proper such crimes are again on the increase."[8]

[3] "Tried and decided." Under Korean court practices this usually means conviction.

[4] In the source the total is given as 7,900 (p. 155); but the items enumerated add up to 9,622.

[5] In many cases seizures and abductions in 1911 and 1923 were of a special character: they often represented the carrying-off of young widows.

[6] *Annual Report*, 1915-16, p. 40.

[7] *Annual Report*, 1936-37, p. 196.

[8] *Annual Report*, 1936-37, p. 196.

From these official statements it appears that crime increased in Korea after the annexation of that country by Japan, and that the influences, at least for some crimes, came from Japan Proper. However, in view of the fact that the population in Korea is mostly rural and that only from one-quarter to one-third is engaged in non-agricultural pursuits, it is difficult to escape the conclusion that the relatively larger number of crimes in Korea as compared with Japan should be explained by the special treatment accorded Koreans. This view is supported by the following evidence. In the group of "other crimes" given above, the most important numerically are "felling forest trees by stealth" and "breaches of taxation laws." In 1911, eighty-one cases of illegally "felling forest trees by stealth" were brought into court, in 1936 their number was 5,570. In 1912 only forty-four cases of "breaches of taxation laws" were considered; in 1936 such cases numbered 19,050. These two examples indicate that the crimes of the Koreans—if they be considered such—are chiefly of an economic nature and probably reflect the growing impoverishment of the population on the one hand and the growing pressure of the government on the population in respect to taxes on the other.

In 1909, when Korean prisons were transferred to Japanese control, the number of prisoners was about 5,300; in 1942 it was 19,328, a four-fold increase, notwithstanding frequent amnesties. The figure 19,328 probably does not include the inmates of the seven political prisons (they are called in Japanese *hogo kansatsu so*—protective observation places, or, as Government officials render it in English, "Political Offenders Probation Offices") in Keijo, Kanko, Seishin, Heijo, Taikyu, Shingishu and Koshu.

As to prison conditions, "improvements were steadily introduced in their [prison] building and equipment to cope with the annual increase in prisoners."[9] It is also stated that after 1933 the prisons discovered a new market, namely the Manchukuo government offices and the Kwantung Army, and were making large quantities of goods for them.

Police System

The Police system of Korea is organized in the following way: under the Government-General there is a Police Depart-

[9] *Annual Report*, 1936-37, p. 198.

COURTS, PRISONS, POLICE

ment—*keisatsu kyoku*—under which are thirteen Police Bureaus—*keisatsu bu*—one in each province; under the Police Bureaus is one police office—*keisatsu sho*—for each municipality (*fu*), county (*gun*) or island. Under police offices there are police stations, one or two for each *yu* or *men*. All these offices are completely independent of the local authorities:—the police system as a whole is self-contained and centralized. The only exception is that the governors of the provinces have control over the Police Bureaus in their respective provinces; but as they themselves are under the control of the Governor-General, this system can hardly be called a decentralized one.

The Police Department at the center and the Police Bureaus in the provinces consist of the following sections: Police; Safety; Protection; Economic Police; Censorship; Health. Their functions are as follows. The Police section is in charge of ordinary police affairs. However, it may exercise summary jurisdiction and usually does: the number of cases tried by police officers each year is more than 100,000. According to A. Ireland these are "trivial offences":

"Such cases are, for the most part, connected with gambling, simple assault, violation of the traffic regulations, and so on. No offender can be tried by summary jurisdiction unless he assents to that process; and if he assents to it and is then dissatisfied with the result he can appeal the decision in one of the ordinary law courts. The right is seldom exercised, as first offenders in petty cases are usually let off with a warning. Although the chief of a police station may inflict a penalty as severe as three months' penal servitude, he usually imposes a fine of not more than one hundred yen, or simply detention for not more than three months.

In the year 1921 there were 73,262 cases decided by the summary police jurisdiction. Of these, 71,802 ended in a conviction of the defendant; and against these decisions there were only 54 appeals, of which 42 resulted in confirmation of the sentence, and 12 in reversal."[10]

The police of Korea is presented here as an organization which saves Koreans the trouble of going to the courts, while the official sources justify the existence of this system of police jurisdiction on the pretext that it saves expenses for the accused, and because "the Koreans have habitually little conception of legal rights, so that they may hardly appreciate the difference of being arraigned before a law court or before an ordinary administrative office."[11]

[10] *The New Korea*, New York, 1926, p. 161.
[11] *Annual Report, 1910-11*, p. 70.

Unfortunately, this is not the case. We have seen that Koreans are as a rule much poorer than Japanese. However, in Japan, crimes of violating administrative ordinances are punished with imprisonment for a period not exceeding one month or a fine not exceeding twenty yen, while in Korea the corresponding limits are three months and one hundred yen. Here it is difficult to see anything but a desire to intimidate the local population.

A. Ireland affirms that "first offenders in petty cases are usually let off with a warning." This is not exactly accurate. Before 1919 the customary means used by police in such cases was not a warning, but flogging or a fine; now it is arrest or a fine. In 1937, eighty-two persons received imprisonment with hard labor; thirty-two imprisonment; 19,012 detention; 85,369 a fine of twenty yen or less, and 20,744 a fine of one hundred yen or less. It is clear what a fine of one hundred yen or even twenty yen means under Korean conditions where the daily wage is often below one yen: it often signifies economic ruin and may be regarded as a potent weapon in Japanese hands for dispossessing the native population.

Another notable feature of these summary judgments is the extraordinarily high percentage of convictions. In the year 1921, for which data are given by A. Ireland, the defendants were found guilty in ninety-eight cases out of a hundred, and in the remaining two cases they were not acquitted or found innocent, but were "pardoned." It is true that any offender dissatisfied with the results of the summary judgment can appeal the decision, and the fact that the percentage of cases appealed against summary judgments is less than one in a thousand might seem to indicate that the offenders admitted their guilt. It must be noted, however, that before undertaking such an appeal, a Korean has to consider the chances of acquittal in a *Japanese* court after being condemned by a *Japanese* policeman, as well as the expenses connected with it, which only the wealthier members of the community can afford.

The government no longer publishes figures on the number of Japanese and Koreans in the police force, but the list of the twenty-seven highest officials in the police force of Korea does not include one Korean; thus the situation in that respect has become worse than in 1919 when there were a few Korean police inspectors. Koreans, as in other departments of the administration, occupy the lowest positions.[12] The number of policemen was 20,642 in 1937, or slightly less than the number of teachers in all schools in 1938 (24,068).[13]

The safety section of the police in Korea is concerned primarily with so-called high police duties or political affairs. (It is also in charge of recruiting labor for industry.) Its task is not only to detect and exterminate "dangerous thoughts" and the carriers of such thoughts, but also to combat active Korean revolutionaries who despite all efforts by the Kwantung Army still manage to cross into Korea from Manchuria. According to *Chosen Nenkan*, 1941, the activities of communist groups in Manchuria had greatly increased since 1936 and they had organized a northeastern Anti-Japanese United Army (*Tohoku konichi Rengun*) of which Korean groups had become a part. Their power in the northeast and in the frontier districts of Southern Manchuria had increased, and they became especially active after the start of the Sino-Japanese "incident" ("presented extraordinary activity in every direction"). In this connection the following official statistics are of interest.

"During 1938 there were 3,898 cases of appearance of [Korean] bandits from the opposite [Manchurian] bank of the river; the number of men involved was 235,787; the number of men killed 391, wounded 539 and abducted 3,642."[14]

Even if we assume that each "bandit" crossed the frontier ten times a year, the number of "bandits" would still be above

[12] It may be of interest to compare the following changes in the composition of the police force in Korea. (Source—the *Annual Reports*, but for 1937—*Dainippon Teikoku Nenkan*, 1939).

	Japanese	Koreans	Total Force	Koreans as percentage of total
1910 (including gendarmes)	3,272	4,440	7,712	57.6
1918 (including gendarmes)	6,138	8,220	14,358	57.2
1919	8,383	8,500	16,883	50.3
1930	11,398	7,413	18,811	39.4
1937	....	....	20,642	...

As to Koreans who have changed their name to a Japanese name, such changes have been permitted only recently and the procedure for the change is complicated, so that it may be assumed that relatively few have taken advantage of this permission.

[13] Source—*Takumu Tokei*, 1938. This figure does not include college professors and teachers of *sohtangs*, i.e. private schools of the old type where the pupils study only Chinese ideographs.

[14] *Takumu Yoran*, 1939, p. 114.

20,000; and this was in 1938, when the Japanese were not yet busy introducing "the new order in Southeast Asia" and could concentrate more forces in Korea and Manchuria. This fact is of great importance: the Japanese themselves admit that far in the rear of the Japanese Army there are sizable forces "centering around the Korean revolutionary army" already fighting against the Japanese. With proper help and guidance they might achieve marked results.

As for the economic police, its functions have been increasing since 1936; and the number of crimes committed against regulations of an economic character now runs into many thousands annually. The censorship section is charged with preventing the appearance of dangerous thoughts in any form; not only are books, magazines, newspapers, and films censored, but also phonograph records and library books.

The protection section of the police is in charge of anti-aircraft defense, fire brigades, and measures for the prevention of floods. The number of fires in Korea varies between three and five thousand a year, and annual losses from them between three and seven million yen. As for anti-aircraft defenses, interest in them started after the establishment of Manchukuo. In November 1937 a special law on anti-aircraft defenses was published, and the new section was formed in February 1939. In October 1939, special police detachments for air defense were organized from the civilian population. Propaganda on a large scale and extensive research were also conducted.

The Health Section is concerned with registration of physicians, dentists, and pharmacists, and the prevention of epidemics among men and cattle. The more important statistical data in this connection will be discussed in the next chapter.

CHAPTER XV

HEALTH, EDUCATION, AND RELIGION

Health

According to its own official reports, Korea is one of the most advanced countries in the world in respect to medical services.

"On the advent of the present regime, further measures were taken for improvement of the existing system, and not only was the Government Hospital . . . enlarged, but similar organs were set up in the provinces also. Public health officers were appointed to the remote districts, special physicians engaged for circuit work in parts difficult of access . . . The service along this line did not stop here, for care was taken that even those Koreans living in the remote borderlands might have medical facilities within easier reach of them."[1]

"Free treatment of the needy sick is undertaken by each government hospital in Keijo and provincial towns as part of its work, and for the remote parts of the country."[2]

Judging by the official reports, the results are really striking. In 1938, for example, the following number of infectious disease cases per million persons was registered in Korea:

COMPARISON OF STATISTICS OF SOME INFECTIOUS DISEASES IN KOREA AND IN JAPAN
(number of cases per million of population)

	Korea, 1938	*Japan, 1937*
Dysentery	219	1,099
Typhoid	258	541
Paratyphoid	27	63
Diphtheria	110	281

Source for absolute figures: *Takumu Tokei*, 1938.

This table shows that infectious diseases in relation to the size of the population are from three to five times more frequent in Japan than in Korea. But now let us compare the number of hospitals, physicians and other health officers in the two countries.

[1] *Annual Report*, 1936-37, p. 180.
[2] *Ibid.*, p. 106.

MEDICAL PERSONNEL IN KOREA AND JAPAN

			Per million of population	
Number of	Korea, 1938	Japan, 1937	Korea, 1938	Japan, 1937
Hospitals[a]	149	3,045	6.6	42.7
Physicians	2,931	61,799	129	866
Native practitioners[b]	3,783	none shown	167	none shown
Dentists	879	22,072	38.8	310
Pharmacists	494	28,156	21.8	394
Midwives	1,935	61,732	85.5	865
Nurses	1,843	124,402	81.4	1,745

[a] Includes state, municipal and private.
[b] Untrained in colleges.
Sources for absolute figures: *Takumu Tokei*, 1938.

This table shows that the number of hospitals in Japan per million of population is 6-7 times greater than in Korea and the number of trained physicians in Japan is seven times as great. The situation in respect to midwives, dentists, pharmacists, and nurses is even less favorable in Korea than in the case of physicians. In other words, medical facilities in Korea still do not exist for the majority of the population. Unfortunately, the actual situation is even worse than these figures suggest. In 1938 the central and provincial government hospitals treated the following number of patients:

NUMBER OF PATIENTS OF GOVERNMENT HOSPITALS BY NATIONALITY, 1938

Japanese	334,438
Korean	389,739
Foreigners	904
Total	725,081
Inmates	42,423
Out-patients	682,658

Source: *Takumu Tokei, 1938*.

Assuming that each patient was treated only once, one Japanese out of two and one Korean out of fifty-six was treated in these hospitals. In other words, the hospitals serve the Japanese first of all, while the Koreans receive much less modern medical attention. J. Dale Van Buskirk writes on this subject:

"The poverty of the [Korean] people is so great that the cost of proper medical care seems more than they can afford; and at best, country practice offers little encouragement to young doctors after they have spent years and money in securing a medical education."[3]

[3] *Korea, Land of the Dawn*, New York, 1931, p. 112.

HEALTH, EDUCATION, AND RELIGION

But what about the statistics of infectious diseases, which seem to show that Korea is a healthier country than Japan? The fact is that these statistical data prove only how badly medical service is organized: the number of infectious diseases recorded in Korea is so small not because Koreans are so healthy or so well cared for, but because most sick Koreans never see a hospital or a physician and thus lie outside of the domain of statistics.

Education

Superficially, education represents one of the activities of which the Japanese may be proud. The following table gives figures dealing with education since the annexation.

NUMBER OF REGISTERED STUDENTS IN SCHOOLS
(in thousands)

Type of Schools	1910	1919	1930	1937
Primary (for Japanese)	15.5	42.8	67.4	89.8
Common (for Koreans)	20.1	89.3	450.5	901.2
Middle (for Japanese)	0.2	2.0	5.8	7.8
Higher Common (for Koreans and Japanese)	0.8	3.2	11.1	15.6
Girls' High Schools (for Japanese)	0.5	1.9	8.3	11.9
Girls' Higher Schools (for Koreans)	0.4	0.7	4.4	7.1
Teachers' Seminaries	...	...	1.3	3.8
Industrial Schools	1.0	2.8	12.1	20.3
Elementary Industrial Schools	0.1	1.7	3.2	6.3
Colleges	0.4	0.9	2.5	4.0
University Preparatory Courses	...	...	0.3	0.4
University	...	...	0.6	0.5
Non-standardized schools	71.8	39.2	47.5	142.6[b]
Total	110.8	184.5	614.4[a]	1,211.4

[a] The items give a total of 615.0.
[b] Includes 60,077 students of the short-course elementary schools.
Source: *Annual Reports*.

This table shows that in twenty-seven years the total number of students increased almost eleven times (from 110,800 in 1910 to 1,211,400 in 1937). Of course, there can be no doubt that whatever Korean government had existed, the number of students would have increased many times during these twenty-seven years; nevertheless, the fact remains that education under the Japanese as measured by the number of students made great progress in this period. However, this fact calls for serious qualifications. In the primary schools of Korea[4] there were in

[4] Excluding the short-course schools mentioned in the note above.

262   MODERN KOREA

1939 1,218,367 Korean students and 92,842 Japanese students.[5] This means that almost every Japanese boy or girl of school age was in primary school, but that only one out of three Korean children was in school. In other words, however great the achievements may be, more than sixty per cent of the Korean children still do not attend school.

Attendance in the high schools (all of which correspond to American high schools), was divided according to nationality as follows:[6]

> Japanese students........ 21,266
> Korean students......... 28,878
> Total............. 50,144

The number of Japanese students in the primary schools was only 7.1 per cent of the total number of students; the number of Japanese students in high schools was 42.2 per cent of the total number. This suggests that something like one-half of the Japanese of high-school age were in high schools, but among the Koreans only one out of every twenty or thirty was as fortunate.

The nationality of students in professional schools (excluding colleges) was as follows:

> Japanese............... 7,854
> Koreans............... 26,155
> Total............ 34,009

It may be thought that here the situation in respect to the Koreans is more favorable. But this is due only to the fact that few Japanese study in agricultural schools. If we exclude these schools the numbers are as follows:

> Japanese students........ 6,923
> Korean students......... 13,924
> Total............. 20,847

Professor Clyde is of the opinion that

"the greatest contribution made by the system of education which Japan has given to Korea has been in the field of agriculture . . . Courses in agricultural guidance are given to graduates of common schools in the rural districts, while groups of selected students receive further training at the government experimental stations in the provinces."[7]

[5] Public and private. Source for statistical data: *Chosen Nenkan*, 1941 and *Takumu Tokei*, 1938, unless otherwise stated.
[6] This includes the students of *all* schools, government, public, and private.
[7] *A History of the Modern and Contemporary Far East*, New York, Prentice-Hall, Inc., 1937, p. 444.

Unfortunately, the actual situation does not warrant undue optimism. The agricultural population of Korea is about fifteen million persons; there were in agricultural schools of *all types* in 1939 only 12,231 Korean students, and many of these schools have courses of only one year or even less. In general, agricultural and professional education was so undeveloped that the Japanese themselves felt this defect acutely after the start of the Sino-Japanese "incident." The plan of turning Korea into a military base of supplies ran into difficulties because of the extreme shortage of trained labor. In order to meet this crisis the Government started various types of short-term professional schools in 1939 (machine, electric, and mining courses); but it ran into another difficulty—shortage of teaching personnel, textbooks, and equipment. Japan's educational policy in Korea thus proved to be a boomerang: the failure to provide advanced training for Koreans became an obstacle in the realization of Japanese plans of aggression.

As for college education (including teachers' seminaries and preparatory courses at the university), the students were divided in the following way:

Japanese	4,674
Koreans	6,313
Total	10,987

When we come finally to the crown of the edifice, the Keijo Imperial University, the figures are as follows:

Japanese	350
Koreans	206
Total	556

Here Japanese students are in a majority. Theoretically, all schools in Korea are open to everyone regardless of nationality, on the basis of merit, as determined by the results of the entrance examinations (except primary schools and a few others). The programs of the schools are the same, the knowledge of Japanese is about the same (education in the Korean schools is conducted in the Japanese language from the first grade). How then does it happen that the number of Japanese students is almost equal to that of Koreans in the high schools, special schools and colleges and is greater than the number of Korean students at the university, while Japanese residents are only 2.9 per cent of the total population of Korea? All available testimony shows that the Korean students are in no way inferior to the Japanese, and yet the Japanese fill 63 per cent of the vacancies at the university. This question is important because the answer to it has a direct bearing on all spheres of human activity in Korea, including the economic. One is free to open an enterprise in Korea and to compete with the Japanese corporations; but somehow the Japanese occupy the field completely. Koreans are free to publish newspapers, after fulfilling some formalities; but somehow the newspapers fail to appear. In order to pass an entrance examination for the university one need not have a large fortune, credit in the bank, or exceptional skill, such as is often necessary in launching an enterprise. And yet even in this sphere the Koreans do not receive the equal treatment solemnly guaranteed them

NUMBER OF STUDENTS IN ALL TYPES OF SCHOOLS PER THOUSAND OF POPULATION IN KOREA AND JAPAN

	In Korea		
	Korean students per 1,000 of Korean population, 1939	Japanese students per 1,000 of Japanese population in Korea, 1939	In Japan, 1936
In primary schools.......	55.2	142.8	164.5
High schools............	1.31	32.7	17.9
Professional schools.....	1.18	12.1	6.2
Colleges and teachers' seminaries[a]..........	0.27	7.2	1.28
Universities............	0.0093	1.06	1.03
Total............	58.0	195.9	190.9[b]

[a] Including preparatory courses for the university in Korea and Koto Gakko in Japan.
[b] This does not include students of Youth Schools (*seinen gakko*) whose number per thousand of the population was 27.9 in the same year.
Source: Calculated from the data given for Korea—in *Chosen Nenkan*, 1941; for Japan—in *Dainippon Teikoku Tokei Nenkan*, 1939.

twenty-three years ago. The Koreans know it; they are subject to discrimination every day everywhere, and there can be no doubt as to how they feel about it. But the Japanese administration evidently considers secondary and university education harmful for Koreans.[8]

[8] The policy of the Japanese Government in keeping Koreans out of the secondary schools is shared by some non-Japanese writers. Writes H. B. Drake: "There are not nearly enough appointments, official or otherwise, to go round, and you can see that the High Schools and the Universities are aggravating the problem of unemployment; aggravating it in a particularly insidious way by loosing upon a simple and primitive people an increasing band of conceited

This table shows that education in Korea is virtually limited to primary education. Students other than those in primary schools were only 2.8 per thousand of the population, as compared with 55.2 per thousand in the primary schools. In Japan the number of students in primary schools per thousand of the population is three times as high; in high schools per thousand of the population—fourteen times; in universities—one hundred eleven times.[9] The higher we climb the ladder, the greater is the difference. This clearly reflects the aims of education in both countries. The relative number of Japanese students in Korea is considerably higher than in Japan Proper.[10] This supports the view that a Japanese in Korea is on the average considerably better off than in Japan Proper.

Much of the credit for actual achievements in Korean education belongs not to the Japanese Government but to private organizations, especially Christian missions. The following table shows how large a part is played by private organizations in Korean education.

PRIVATE ORGANIZATIONS IN EDUCATION IN 1939
(Students in their schools as per cent of the total number of students in the country for this type of school)

Primary schools	2.5
High Schools	26.2
Professional schools	15.5
Colleges[a]	56.5

[a] Excluding teachers' seminaries and preparatory courses for the university which are in the hands of the Government.
Source: Calculated from the data in *Chosen Nenkan*, 1941.

---

young men, talented in their own manner, with a prestige of learning, naturally fluent and forceful in speech, and hankering for an upheaval in the expectation of plunder in the form of lucrative offices in the new State that is to be . . . Can one be surprised that the police are instructed to arrest at sight anyone suspected of 'dangerous thought'?" . . .

"After all, Korea is a country of farmers. Why bother them with our Western learning, so fruitful of unsettlement, so ill-adapted to their needs? It might even be better to return to that little village school with their half-dozen scholars crying out their characters at the full stretch of their lungs" . . . *(Korea of the Japanese*, London, 1930, pp. 138-139).

[9] One of my critics has pointed out that every country would appear in an unfavorable light if reduced to per capita averages, percentages, etc. But this is not so. Throughout this book all Korean data have been compared not with some imaginary, ideal state of affairs, but in almost all cases with Japan, a country which is not famous for its wealth. A comparison of the first and third columns of this table shows what might have been done in Korea and what was actually done.

[10] Except for the primary schools and this is probably due to smaller ratio of the lower age groups among the Japanese in Korea.

In short, more than a quarter of the students in high schools and more than one-half of the college students study in privately established schools. This proportion would have been much higher had it not been for the restrictive policy of the Japanese Government which, fearing lest democratic ideas be introduced through these channels, imposed upon such schools all kinds of crippling restrictions. Endless patience was necessary to keep these private schools open. They were not only the road to learning for thousands of Koreans—especially girls to whom all avenues would otherwise have been blocked—they were the only means by which Koreans were brought in contact with the ideals of Christianity, democracy, and freedom. Just as in the field of medicine, where 95 of the 149 hospitals existing in Korea in 1938 were established by private organizations, so in the field of education their work was of immense importance.

The number of women in Korea is only slightly below that of men, but this is not reflected in educational statistics.

DISTRIBUTION OF KOREAN STUDENTS IN KOREA BY SEX IN 1939

	Girls	Boys	Total
Primary Schools	306,000	912,067	1,218,367
High Schools	9,535	19,343	28,878
Professional Schools	915	25,240	26,155
Colleges and Teachers' Seminaries	1,131	5,182	6,313
University	....	206	206

Source: Calculated from data in *Chosen Nenkan*, 1941.

This table shows that even in the primary schools the number of boys is three times as large as that of girls, and the discrepancy in other schools (with the exception of high schools) is even greater. This is not only because of the ignorance and prejudices of the parents, but also because of the reactionary policy of the Japanese Government in Korea. Co-education does not exist in any Government schools or privately run colleges, or professional schools; and the university does not admit girls.

But there is another important problem in Korean education —the nationality of the teachers. Teaching is conducted entirely in Japanese, a language strange to the ear of the Korean child. This might be mitigated to some extent by Korean teachers who would probably give some explanations in the Korean language; but Korean teachers are not numerous, as may be seen from the following table:

NATIONALITY OF THE TEACHERS IN KOREA, 1938

	Number of Korean teachers	Number of Japanese teachers
Public Primary Schools for Koreans..	8,520	5,745
Public High Schools...............	112	446
Government Colleges..............	70	184
University.......................	145	474

Source: *Chosen Nenkan*, 1941.

Unfortunately more detailed figures are unavailable, otherwise we would certainly see that in all these schools Korean teachers occupy only inferior positions. The discrimination goes further than the filling of vacancies in favor of Japanese. In 1938, Japanese teachers in the primary schools were paid on the average ninety-nine yen a month, and Korean teachers fifty-six yen; Japanese women teachers were paid eighty-one yen, Korean forty-seven yen. This shows that while Japanese teachers draw very modest salaries, Korean teachers earn less than a rickshawman working twenty-eight days a month.

Discrimination between Koreans and Japanese does not stop here: it permeates the entire social fabric. The primary and high schools in Korea are separate for Korean and Japanese children, though in all these schools the same language serves as the medium of instruction. It is true that children of Korean officials or merchants may with special permission of the authorities enter the school for Japanese, but this permission is given reluctantly and only to children whose parents show special alacrity in serving Japanese interests. In 1939, out of the total number of 95,500 students in primary schools for Japanese, only 3,900 were Koreans; while in the schools for Koreans there were only 640 Japanese children out of a total of 1,159,500. This is not accidental: Korean and Japanese children are kept apart in their most formative period when there is no racial prejudice and when friendships formed so often become friendships for life.

The Government spends forty-nine yen per year for every Japanese child in a primary school and only eighteen yen for every Korean child.[11] In public high schools for boys, the Japanese form almost half of the students, and the annual expenses per student are 112 yen; in the government colleges Koreans

[11] *Chosen Nenkan*, 1941, p. 546.

make up only one-third of the student body, and the annual expense per student is 770 yen; at the university it is 3,362 yen.

Inasmuch as 95 Korean students out of every hundred do not go beyond the primary grades, the curriculum in the primary schools is of special importance. The aims which the authorities have set themselves in this respect are formulated as follows in an official document:[12]

"The fostering of loyalty and filial piety shall be made the radical principle of education, and the cultivation of moral sentiments shall be given special attention . . . It is only what may be expected of a loyal and dutiful man, who knows what is demanded of a subject and a son that he should be faithful to his duties . . ."

In other words, these schools must first of all prepare loyal subjects of the Japanese Empire, who make obeisance before the portrait of the Emperor, believe in the divine origin of the Japanese Empire and are ready to be silent serfs in this Empire (not giving themselves to "vain arguments"). To this end they must first of all understand the language of their master and forget their own or, at least, neglect their own. That this is not an exaggeration may be seen from the following description of the Primary School Curriculum with a six-year course:[13]

Morals. One hour a week for the whole course, on the essential point of morals.
National language. Ten hours a week for the first year, twelve for the second, third and fourth, nine for the fifth and sixth.
Korean language. Four hours a week for the first and second year, three for the rest of the course.
Arithmetic. A progressive course leading up to vulgar fractions, percentages, and the use of abacus. Five hours a week during the first two years, six in the third and fourth, four in the fifth and sixth.
Japanese history. Two hours a week in the fifth and sixth years.
Geography. Two hours a week in the last two years.
Drawing. One hour a week in the fourth year, and two hours for boys and three for girls in the fifth and sixth years.[a]
Singing. One hour a week through the course.
Gymnastics, Drill, and Sports. Varies for boys and for girls, averages about two hours a week throughout the course.

[a] "In the first, second and third years drawing may be taught one hour per week. With regard to practical exercises, they may be given outside the stated number of hours for instruction."

[12] This is taken from *Rules for Teachers* published on January 4, 1916 (as given in the Appendix to A. Ireland's *New Korea*). They are still effective.

[13] The text is taken from *New Korea* by A. Ireland, New York, 1926, pp. 204-205. As far as we know there have been no essential changes since that time.

HEALTH, EDUCATION, AND RELIGION

Sewing. Two hours in the fourth year, and three hours in the fifth and sixth.

Manual Work. In the first, second, and third year manual work may be taught one hour per week, and in the fourth and fifth year two hours."

The author of this summary omits one important point: all education is conducted in the "national" *i.e.* Japanese language, so that this "national language" fills all hours of instruction except three or four school hours a week left for the Korean language. As for "morals," they should not be mistaken for what we understand by the term. For us, morals mean above all the guiding principles in our human relations; official Japanese "morals," on the other hand, mean loyalty to the Emperor and state, and filial piety. Thus selling one's daughter to a brothel, according to this code of morals, is not immoral; but criticism of an official is. The student is also taught something about Korea and more about the center of the world—the Japanese Empire—but nothing about other countries. Lessons in natural sciences take less than ten per cent of the school time given to the Japanese language, and only half as much as drill. Thus the chief purpose of primary school education is to turn Koreans into submissive subjects who can understand the commands of their master.[14] Every year an investigation is made as to the number of Koreans who *understand* the Japanese language. The progress is as follows:

SPREAD OF THE JAPANESE LANGUAGE IN KOREA

Year	Number of Koreans in thousands	Number of Koreans who understand the Japanese language in thousands	Those who understand Japanese language as per cent of the total number of Koreans
1913	15,170	92	0.6
1919	16,697	304	1.8
1923	17,447	712	4.1
1928	18,667	1,290	6.9
1933	20,206	1,578	7.8
1938	21,951	2,718	12.4
1939	22,801	3,069	13.9

Source: *Kokusei Gurafu*, a monthly, October 1940.

This table shows that the percentage of Koreans who understand the Japanese language rose from 0.6 in 1919 to 13.9 in

[14] The authorities recently formulated their aims as follows: "The important points for education in Korea is to acquire a knowledge of the national language, to absorb the spirit of true love for honest toil, to strengthen an inclination for thrift and industry," *Thriving Chosen*, Keijo, 1935, p. 11.

1939.[15] However, if we take only men, almost one quarter of them could understand the Japanese language (2,463,000 men as compared with 606,000 women). This means that Korean women, with few exceptions, do not know Japanese even according to the modest yardstick of official classification; it means that in Korean homes the Korean language is the only one used and the children are brought up under the influence of Korean culture. Nor is this influence effaced by drilling in Japanese schools.

Libraries

Statistics of libraries in Korea are incomplete, because they do not distinguish between Korean and Japanese books and readers. Yet they offer a certain interest when compared with the corresponding figures for Japan.

LIBRARIES, KOREA AND JAPAN, 1936

	Korea, total	Japan, total	Units (not thousands) per 10,000 of population	
			Korea	Japan
Number of libraries[a]	46	4,730	0.021	0.673
Number of books in Oriental script, thousands	520	12,052	236	1,715
In western script, thousands	24	596	11	85
Number of readers, thousands	1,541	24,124	699	3,433
Readers per day, persons	4,222	66,093	1.9	9.4

[a] Public and Private.
Source for absolute figures: *Dainippon Teikoku Nenkan*, 1939.

This table shows that there were only 46 libraries in all Korea in 1936; that the books in these libraries numbered only half a million (of which half were in one library in Keijo), and visitors numbered only one million and a half. When we reduce these figures to ratios (the third column of the table) we see that there was only one library for almost half a million people (0.021 per 10,000 population); only 236 books for each 10,000 of the population; and only 1.9 readers out of each 10,000 visited the libraries in a day. The relative figures for Japan are five, ten, and thirty times as large as in Korea. In view of the fact that most, if not all, of the books in the Oriental script are in Japanese or in Classic Chinese and that the

[15] Persons with a knowledge of English in India form about two per cent of the population.

HEALTH, EDUCATION, AND RELIGION

libraries are concentrated in the places with the largest Japanese population, it seems clear that the existing libraries in Korea serve chiefly the Japanese population.

Theaters, Cinemas, Playgrounds

In 1937 Korea had only seventy-two theaters and fifty-one cinemas. On the average, for each ten thousand of population, only fifteen persons (probably mostly Japanese) visited the cinema each day, as compared with 113.2 in Japan.

STATISTICS OF THEATERS, CINEMAS AND PLAYGROUNDS FOR 1937

	Korea number	Japan number	Per 10,000 of population Korea	Japan
Theaters	72	32,338	0.032	4.5
Cinemas	51	94,853	0.023	13.3
Visitors during the year—1,000	11,960	294,049	14.6[a]	113.2[a]
Playgrounds	536	27,083	0.24	3.81

[a] Persons per day.
Source for absolute data—Dai-ippon Teikoku Nenkan, 1939.

But if theaters and cinemas are practically unknown to Koreans, the Japanese administration is more successful in another direction. Writes W. H. Chisholm, a missionary doctor: "The whole lower part of that section of town was fairly infested with saloons and brothels."[16] Another missionary, E. Wagner, says: "The hellish system of licensed prostitution had been introduced into this country [Korea] from Japan... The inmates of these houses of prostitution are literally slaves, human beings held under the most revolting and hideous of laws... The lives of these women are very short and after an average life of four years, death comes as merciful relief."[17]

[16] Vivid Experiences in Korea, Chicago, 1938, p. 111.
[17] Korea, the Old and the New, New York, 1931, pp. 87-88. On the other hand, it is important to note that such evil customs of old Korea as the selling of little girls were tolerated by the Japanese administration: "It sometimes happens also that quite small girls of poor families are bought by a broker and afterward sold as wives to men in other parts of Korea long before they have reached the marriageable age. The price runs to about sixty or seventy yen and a bill is made out just as in the case of any other merchandise. The Korean out-door servant of one of my acquaintances in Keijo bought a young wife for his son through a woman broker for seventy yen. A girl who is bought in this way belongs to the purchaser absolutely and may be sold again by him." (Sten Bergman, In Korean Wilds and Villages, London, 1938, p. 58.)

Newspapers and Magazines

In 1940, thirty-four newspapers, seven daily news reports (*tsushin*) and sixteen magazines were published in Korea in the Japanese language. In addition, eight newspapers and four magazines were published by Koreans, presumably in the Korean language. Besides these, 419 periodicals of local importance were published in the Japanese language and 19 publications in Korean national script. Though these figures are revealing in themselves, let us examine the Korean publications more carefully.

KOREAN NEWSPAPERS

Title (translated into English)	Term of publication	Year of establishment
Daily Newspaper	Daily	1906
People's Newspaper	Weekly	1930
South Korea Economic News	Daily	1924
Great East News	Weekly	1922
Eastern Asia Economic News	Bi-weekly	1932
Christian News	Weekly	1938
New Cinema News	3 times a month	1938
National Newspaper	Weekly	1938
Korean magazines:		
New People	Monthly	1921
Medical Reports	Monthly	....
Korean Business	Monthly	1932
Medical Review	Monthly	1932

This enumeration shows that in 1939 there were only two dailies published in the Korean language, one of which was an economic newspaper. Most of these publications were for a very limited group of specialists. There is no information as to whether these newspapers are edited by Japanese puppets or not, but we may be sure that they publish nothing displeasing to the Japanese authorities. In 1936, for example, the Japanese made the mistake of putting a Korean, Ki Chung-sou, on the Japanese team sent to the Berlin Olympic games. This Korean was the winner in the Marathon race, and the news that a Korean had taken first place in a world contest aroused the whole Korean nation. Two Korean newspapers, *Dong-A* and *Choong Ang*, the only newspapers which had shown any semblance of independence, published a picture of Ki Chung-sou in which he was not wearing the Japanese emblem. As a result, these two papers were suppressed, and since 1936 no independent newspaper in the native language has been published. It is

HEALTH, EDUCATION, AND RELIGION 273

difficult to find another colony in the world in which control of the native press is so complete.

Religion

Of all the human activities in Korea those of the Christian Churches are probably the best known abroad because they have been described in considerable detail by missionary publications in the United States and Great Britain. In 1940, the number of Christians of all denominations was estimated by authorities at 501,000. In proportion to the population this probably represents the largest number in the Orient, except for Asiatic Russia and the Philippines.

According to official sources three religions are practiced in Korea: ▆▆▆▆▆, Buddhism, and Christianity. There are several religions of native origin, but it is said that "they are not recognized by the state as having the true marks of religion,"[18] and in Korea a religion in order to be a religion must be recognized by the Japanese military man who happens to occupy the post of Governor-General.

NUMBER OF FOLLOWERS OF VARIOUS RELIGIONS IN KOREA IN 1938

	Japanese	Koreans	Total
Shintoism, all sects	74,900	21,000	95,900
Buddhism, Korean	....	194,600	194,600
Buddhism, Japanese, 28 sects	294,400	15,300	309,700
Christianity, all faiths	....	about 500,000	500,700
Tendokyo	....	about 80,000	about 80,000
Jitenkyo	....	about 17,000	about 17,000
Other Native Religions	....	about 20,000	about 20,000
Total	369,300	about 800-900 thousand	about 1,200,000

Source: (1) *Takumu Tokei*, 1939.
(2) *Annual Reports* of the Government-General.

Since Shintoism is a purely Japanese religion, the newly converted 21,000 Koreans, as well as 15,300 Koreans professing Japanese varieties of Buddhism, probably represent those in Government Service who are anxious to prove their complete assimilation.

A comparison of the totals in the above table with the size of the population shows that a large number of Koreans are unaccounted for. It is not clear whether these figures include children as well as adults. In any case, the Japanese population

[18] *Annual Report*, 1936-37, p. 100.

is well represented: there is information concerning 369,300 (and with Christians probably 373-375 thousand) out of 653,000. But information concerning Koreans is very meager: we know only of some eight or nine hundred thousand out of a total of more than twenty-three million. What religions do the remaining twenty-one or twenty-two million profess? Presumably none, or in any case they have no definite affiliations. In this connection a description given by Dr. L. G. Paik[19] is very interesting:

"It has often been said that Korea is a land without religion . . . Yet while the Korean gave few outward indications of being religious, he has never been without deep-rooted conviction of the presence of spiritual beings.

"The religious life of the Korean people manifests itself in three faiths. There is, first of all, Shamanism, a form of animistic nature worship consisting of a universal worship and fear of spirits; secondly, there is Buddhism; and thirdly, the practice of the teachings of Confucianism. . . .

"An adequate description of this belief [Shamanism] is almost an impossible task, for it is formless, documentless, and without system. . . .

"With exception of the few strict orthodox devotees of these religions, no one adheres to any one in such a manner as to lead him to look upon the cults as mutually incompatible. As a result, the average Korean takes his religious ceremonies from ancestor worship, seeks the efficacy of Buddhist prayers, devoutly bows his head at the shrine of mountain demons, and recites Confucian classics."

It may be argued that such a state of affairs results from indifference to religion on the part of the Korean people; or that it is due to the prevalence of superstitions—the more divinities, the more blessings one may receive from all of them. Dr. Paik believes that this state of affairs in Korea actually shows a religious hunger, a demand for a universal religion which combines "the high ethical and moral standard of Confucianism, the religious inspiration of Buddhism, and the mysteries of life and death of the spiritual world of Shamanism."

Whatever the answer may be, it is clear from these passages that the missionaries found a fertile field for their work in Korea. On the one hand, there was no organized established religion—such as Mohammedanism in Turkey, Buddhism in Burma, the Orthodox Eastern Church in Russia—which could

[19] *The History of Protestant Missions in Korea,* 1892-1910, Union Christian College Press, Pyeng Yang, Korea, 1929, pp. 16-23.

organize resistance to their activities. On the other hand, they found a people who could be interested not only in the outward forms of the Church services, but also in its teachings. In 1920[20] the number of Christians was estimated by the Churches at 360,000, not including 3,000 preachers. A rise from 360,000 to 501,000 in about eighteen years (1.8 per cent annually) means that Christianity had just succeeded in holding its own with the growth of the population. Why it could not achieve much greater success is a question which can be answered only by a person with intimate knowledge of Korean conditions and the work of the missions. One circumstance however, would clearly seem to have been a contributing factor to this relative inactivity of the Churches, namely their timid and at times even subservient policy toward the Japanese administration, especially after 1919. Of course, it is understandable that the missionaries wanted to avoid conflicts with the administration and because of this were ready to avoid any activities or semblance of activities that might compromise them with the Japanese authorities. But in applying this principle some of them went so far as to preach acceptance of Japanese rule. However, Christianity is not merely a set of dogmas; it is also a way of life. Korean youth flocked to the missions not only in search of religious truths but also because these missions represented American democracy in a land of serfdom. There is no contradiction between these two aims of Korean youth. In the early thirties the missionaries complained that the younger generation was full of socialist or even communist ideas. This was unavoidable: they could not reconcile themselves to the realities of Korean life, and were attracted by those who continued the struggle against Japanese imperialism.

All this is said not in order to belittle the outstanding work of the missions. Their churches, schools, hospitals, and leper-homes have often offered the only ray of light to many Koreans in these dark thirty-two years of Korean history.

[20] Or perhaps 1921; the year in the *Annual Report*, 1923-24, p. 105, is not specifically given.

CHAPTER XVI

PROBLEMS OF KOREAN INDEPENDENCE

The thirty-third year since the annexation of Korea by Japan brings new hopes to the Korean people. Japan is at war with a powerful democratic coalition. The United States and Great Britain have proclaimed in the Atlantic Charter that "they wish to see sovereign rights and self-government restored to those who have been forcibly deprived of them." Furthermore, the Cairo Declaration of December 1, 1943, stated that the United States, Great Britain, and China, "mindful of the enslavement of the people of Korea, are determined that in due course Korea shall become free and independent."

There is no question that Korea was forcibly deprived of her sovereign rights and on numerous occasions during the last thirty-three years, the Koreans have demonstrated that they do not accept Japanese rule but cling to their own nationality. When the iron lid of the incredibly severe Japanese censorship in Korea is lifted, we shall know much more than we do now about this struggle, and we shall certainly see that it has been far more intense than the Japanese rulers have ever allowed us to realize. The question may be raised, however, as to whether Korea has all the elements necessary for an independent state.

Material and Human Prerequisites

The area of Korea is only four per cent less than that of the United Kingdom;[1] her population is equal to that of Spain and is greater than that of Rumania, Turkey, Czechoslovakia, Yugoslavia, Mexico, Argentina, or Canada. She is self-sufficient in cereals, in fish, and, as has been shown in the chapter on industry, has all the resources needed for industrialization such as iron, coal, abundant water power, and many minerals. The actual development of industry is not great, yet even today it is larger than in such countries as Mexico, French Indo-China,

[1] Excluding Northern Ireland.

or Turkey. Thus Korea has ample material resources to stand upon her own feet.

But has her population the ability to organize and successfully conduct the business of state? There is no doubt that the record of the autocratic Korean government in the final decades before the annexation was definitely bad. The ability for self-government, however, could not have appeared before 1904 or 1910, because then the country was ruled by an Oriental despot, and the population had no voice in this rule. Thus, the pre-annexation record has no direct bearing on the problem.

It may be argued that thirty-three years of Japanese domination can hardly have improved the ability of the Koreans to manage their own affairs. But, on the other hand, the life of the population during these thirty-three years has altered in many respects. Hundreds of thousands of Koreans are now at school; hundreds of thousands are in factories and mines; tens of thousands have visited foreign countries as workers and some thousands as students; many thousands are fighting Japanese troops in guerilla detachments; and tens of thousands have passed through the rigorous school of Japanese courts, police detention and prisons as political offenders. The Korea of 1943 is different in so many ways from the Korea of 1910 that to apply any generalizations which may have been true in 1905-1910 to the present situation is, at the very least, superficial.

Unfortunately, this is what Mr. Hugh Byas does in his recently published book, *Government by Assassination*. In his opinion "to thrust self-government on Korea in its present stage of development would be a cruel gift. Administrators have to be trained, standards built up; an intelligent but wholly inexperienced people has to be protected from native exploitation while it learns how to use the machinery of representative government."[2] On this and other grounds, including the security of Japan, the author proposes that Japan be entrusted with "the mandatory role in respect to Korea."[3] Thus, the power which has deprived Korea of any possibility of self-government, the power which has ruthlessly exploited Korea for its own imperialistic aims; the power which has presented Korea with the police force as the only standard of authority; this power

[2] *Government by Assassination*, New York, Alfred A. Knopf, 1942, p. 359.
[3] *Ibid.*, p. 360.

is now to be entrusted with the mandate "to protect" [Korea] "from native exploitation," to "build up standards," and to teach the Koreans "how to use the machinery of representative government," although, as Mr. Byas himself shows, Japan has not herself mastered this art.

Proofs of Organizing Experience

Such proposals as that of Mr. Byas make it especially important that we evaluate the ability of the Koreans to rule themselves without benefit of guidance from Japan. Fortunately, we have some evidence of this ability.

First, we know that in the Russian Far East Koreans are taking an active part in self-government, and that their countrymen occupy important positions in the administration, the army, and in social life. Secondly, we know from the missionaries working in Korea that the Koreans have shown themselves apt in the organization of Y.M.C.A.'s, churches, schools, and other institutions, in spite of all the obstacles put in their way by the Japanese administration. Thirdly, the development of the credit cooperatives (*kin-yu kumiai*) shows that the Koreans can fend for themselves when the Japanese Government does not interfere too much with their activities. The growth of the cooperatives may be seen from the following:

GROWTH OF CREDIT COOPERATIVES IN KOREA

Year	Number of cooperatives	Number of members	Paid-up capital 1,000 yen	Borrowed capital 1,000 yen	Deposits 1,000 yen	Loans 1,000 yen
1907...	10	6,616	....	100	....	16
1910...	120	39,051	....	1,209	....	779
1915...	240	65,886	178	2,506	198	2,128
1920...	400	244,316	2,556	21,995	16,479	39,719
1926...	521	409,750	5,942	33,935	46,117	66,358
1930...	644	671,844	9,010	65,145	80,128	123,368
1935...	698	1,363,392	11,497	86,299	153,417	179,225
1936...	709	1,561,350	12,462	116,877	162,355	228,464
1937...	719	1,636,788	13,644	118,875	179,515	232,178
1938...	723	1,747,728	14,723	122,917	229,036	257,915
1939...	723	1,934,009	15,139	132,696	283,520	306,471

Sources: 1 (Chosen) *Kinyu Kumiai Nenkan*, 1935.
2 *Chosen Nenkan*, 1941.

From a modest beginning in 1907, the credit cooperatives of Korea have grown to a mass organization united by the *Kinyu Kumiai Rengokai*—Union of Credit Cooperatives—

with a membership of 1,934,000, paid-up capital of 15,139,000 yen, reserves of 28,898,000 yen, deposits of 283,520,000 yen, and loans of 306,471,000 yen, as of December 31, 1939.

Certain facts concerning the cooperatives must be stressed, however, in order to avoid misunderstanding. (1) The credit cooperatives in Korea (and they form by far the largest part of the cooperatives there) do not constitute an independent force in Korea capable of independent action now. They are, admittedly, a part of the Japanese Government-sponsored organization, the purpose of which is to control agricultural production in Korea. The executive officials of each cooperative must be approved by the governors of the provinces, and no persons disapproved by the Japanese Government can be elected as officials of cooperatives. (2) Many of these cooperatives, by the fact that they are permitted to receive deposits from non-members and make loans to non-members, are gradually being transformed into ordinary commercial banks. This is especially true with respect to the urban cooperatives. In 1935, the deposits from non-members were larger than those from members. There is no information available as to what proportion of the total loans go to non-members, but it is known to be high.

These reservations are not, however, important for our present purpose. What is important is the fact that two million persons have been drawn into cooperative organizations and that many thousands have had a chance to manage the affairs of a sizable organization, preside over meetings, and conduct discussions, while the members of the Union of Credit Cooperatives have had such experience on an all-Korean scale. Thus there are in Korea people with ability to organize, with education, with some experience in handling public affairs; and there is no reason to think that the new country would be handicapped in that respect any more than Yugoslavia or Lithuania was after 1918.

Korean Nationalists

One may say that before 1942 the Koreans in exile showed a marked inclination to divide and subdivide into small factions and to disagree perpetually among themselves. However, this is inevitable under conditions of exile and harsh oppression at home. Disagreements characterized Russian political emigration; disagreements characterize the present activities of the

French political exiles; but this is not a proof of the inability of the Russians or the French to agree among themselves under changed conditions. Nor should one lose sight of the fact that the Japanese Government has tried its best to keep these disagreements alive and to intensify them. If it was able to bribe some American journalists to spread its propaganda in the United States,[4] how much more easily was it able to promote dissent among the Koreans.

The Nub of the Case

Therefore, there appears to be no reason why Korea should not be given a right to organize herself as an independent state. There are few more just causes in this world than the restoration of Korean independence. In Chapter I we quoted the solemn promises of the Japanese Emperor and Japanese Government to the people of Korea. The annexation was made, they said, in order "to advance the happiness and well-being of the people" of Korea and the promise was made that *"all*[5] Koreans . . . will enjoy prosperity and welfare," and that "the new order of things . . . will serve as a fresh guarantee of enduring peace in the Orient." All these guarantees have been flouted by the Imperial Government of Japan. No one can say that a period of thirty-three years was not enough to carry out at least *some* of the promises made.

But what about the danger that the peninsula may become a field for foreign intrigues and a threat to Japan as a springboard for possible future aggressors against that nation? On this question Mr. Byas writes: "Korea is separated from Japan by only one hundred miles of sea, and Japan cannot disinterest itself in Korea's future since Korea, either helpless, as she was before, or dominated by a hostile power, is a mortal danger to Japan . . . Korea might shrink from the prospect of becoming a Far Eastern Alsace-Lorraine."[6]

Mr. Byas should show some concern, however, not only for Japan, but also for the neighbors of Japan. He himself says that one of the three major causes of this war was "the possession (by Japan) of jumping-off places for aggression."[7] We

---
[4] This has become known in the case of *The Living Age*, for example.
[5] Author's italics.
[6] *Op. cit.*, pp. 359-360.
[7] *Ibid.*, p. 361.

know that Korea was one of these places. We also know that in the last fifty years Japan has used Korea as a springboard to attack China at least four times (not counting minor cases of aggression) and four times to attack Russia (again not counting numerous encroachments on the border). In the light of this experience, to give Korea to Japan would amount to giving her one more chance of attacking her neighbors.

As for the dangers to Japan, it would seem that the sea would be a better protection against China than the hundreds of miles of the Korean land frontier. As for Russia, she already has a land frontier with Japan on Sakhalin and thus is not in need of a special springboard for an attack on Japan.

This line of reasoning incidentally presupposes a belief in the impossibility of peaceful neighborly relations. France is separated from Great Britain by a channel narrower than the Straits of Korea and Tsushima. Should Great Britain be given a mandate over France? Or Germany a mandate over Sweden? It is high time that the world abandoned such nineteenth-century slogans as that of a dagger pointed at someone's heart—a slogan so often used to justify aggression. Canada's Great Lakes' peninsula might be conceived of as "a dagger pointed at the industrial heart of the United States," yet hardly anyone thinks of it in such terms.

Korea should be an independent state irrespective of the fears or doubts which some Japanese or some Americans may entertain in respect to her geographical position. Denial of such a status to Korea would be the most flagrant of any pledges made in this war by the United Nations.

Form of Government

As to the political form of the new state, there is every reason to believe that it should be a republic. The former reigning House of Li accepted a Japanese pension; its princes and princesses married Japanese, were educated in Japan, and thus lost all connections with Korea except the fact that they continue to receive 1,800,000 yen annually from the Government-General of Korea, and have property there. There is no reason why the House of Li or any other House should be placed upon Korea's throne. The spirit of the time and the Koreans' tradition of democracy in all local matters over which they had control demand that Korea should be a democratic republic.

Korea will be organized on the ruins of the Japanese empire, and it is our duty to do everything in our power to make of Korea a country which will be our ally. This means that no pro-Japanese or pro-imperial elements in Korea should be recognized at the time the new state is organized.

Furthermore, in view of the size of the country and its homogeneity of culture and language, Korea should be made a centralized democratic republic with no property qualifications as a requirement for voting, because such a qualification in a poverty-stricken country would give the power to the landlords who, in Korea, are an almost purely parasitic group of the population.

The Danger of Class Government

But our sympathy with the Korean people and their sufferings under the heavy hand of Japanese imperialism should not close our eyes to the reality of their diversity—which may be as great as that of any other people. We have seen that there are about one hundred thousand landlords in Korea, of whom thirty thousand—and by now probably forty or fifty thousand —are absentee landlords whose "work" consists of supervising their agents who exact exorbitant rents from the tenants. With the members of their families, this group is probably half a million strong. We also know that in 1938 there were in Korea 2,504 Korean factories, 2,307 of which employed less than fifty workers each; and that the conditions in these factories with respect to wages, hours, sanitation, and safety were worse than in the big Japanese enterprises. Furthermore, there is a small group of Koreans who are closely connected with the Japanese in government and business, who visit Shinto shrines or the temples of Japanese Buddhist sects, who have changed their Korean names into Japanese names, and who send their children to Japanese schools. We know that there are some Korean volunteers fighting with Japanese troops against the Chinese, [one of them was even awarded a high Japanese decoration] and that thousands of Koreans have been camp-followers of the Japanese army during the conquest of China, that they have opened gambling houses, opium dens, and brothels—competing in these enterprises with their Japanese masters. All these facts should be clearly recognized, in order to avoid unnecessary mistakes in our estimates of the Korean situation. Stating these facts means no disparagement of the Korean people. France has its Laval and Norway its Quisling; it is only natural that Korea should have its Marquis Boku or Viscount Bin, the more so because Korea has for thirty-three years been in Japanese hands, while the Lavals and Quislings are the product of a recent defeat. These men and these facts should not be used to belittle Korea, because the Korean nation, exploited, abused, and in chains, is not responsible for their appearance; it is Japanese imperialism that has produced them.

And yet, we cannot close our eyes to these facts. Through their subservience to their Japanese over-lords, through cooperation with them, these men were able to preserve their households and lands, and amass new fortunes, while the masses of the Korean people sank lower and lower in their poverty. If nothing is done to restrain these parasites they will seize power in the New Korea and will continue much the same type of regime that has existed there during the Japanese occupation—or an even worse one. They have money, they have connections, they have experience. Their children have studied in Japan; some of them have graduated from leading American universities. They have been advisors to Japanese companies and corporations, vice-presidents of Japanese banks, councillors of the Japanese Government, Lord-Stewards to his Imperial Highness, or second secretaries in some government departments. Let us take two examples. (1) Da-shoku Bin is a director of the Chosen Trust Company and of the Chosen Beer Brewery Company, auditor of the Keijo Electric Company, director of the Chosen Land Improvement Company, president of the Teichi Bank, and a Privy Councillor. He was formerly an instructor in the military school. When the Japanese took over his country, he did not commit suicide; he did not take part in rebellions; he did not retire into private life; he began to serve his new masters. (2) So-ryu Kan, graduate of the Tokyo School of Foreign Languages, is a member of the Advisory Council of Korea and advisor of the famous Oriental Development Company—the purpose of which is Japanese colonization and the economic penetration of Korea and adjacent regions; he is also chairman of the Board of Directors of Chosen Trust Company; president of the Chosen Life Insurance Company, and president of the Kanjo Bank.

Even if such persons were deprived of the right to occupy

official positions for a certain number of years, their influence would be as strong as if this limitation did not exist, because in an impoverished Korea a possessor of tens of thousands of *koku* of rice would still wield power behind the scenes. How then is the nascent democracy of Korea to be saved from these aristocrats who for centuries have exploited the Korean people?

Form of Social Organization

In this connection another problem of tremendous importance for the future of Korea should be considered. We have seen in the preceding chapters that perhaps as much as one quarter of the cultivated area and more than half of the total area of Korea is in Japanese hands; railways, telegraphs, telephones, shipping companies, electric power stations, coal mines, most of the gold mines, and almost all large industrial enterprises are Japanese-owned. There is general agreement among students of foreign affairs in the United States and Great Britain that in the event of an Allied victory the Japanese should relinquish their investments in China, Korea, and Formosa. It is quite probable that the consequences of defeat will be such that these investments will be relinquished even before the final peace is signed. Now, the question which should be raised, discussed, and somehow solved beforehand, is: what should be done with these investments, or, practically considered, what is to become of all modern industry and communications in Korea?

One may reply: that is not our business, let the Koreans decide this question. But such an approach would be fatal. First of all, it *is* our business. When Korea becomes free, it will be largely at the expense of blood and labor on the part of the Allied nations; and these nations are and should be interested in the future organization of Japan, Korea, or any other country in the Pacific, in order to avoid bloodshed every ten or twenty or forty years. Of course, we are told that the Koreans are the most peaceful people in the world, just as we have so often been told that the Chinese are pacifists by nature. All this may be true, but it has no relation to the problem. The Japanese are very peaceful people at home and are probably in this respect no worse than the Korean or Chinese people. But any peaceful people dominated by a militaristic group can become what the Japanese and Germans have demon-

PROBLEMS OF KOREAN INDEPENDENCE 285

strated to us during the last few years. It is the system, the social organization, which molds them as they now appear to the world. In order to undermine this lust for conquest, expansion, and domination over other countries, we should remove the organization that creates such a state of affairs and prevent its appearance in a newly formed state. The kind of social organization that will be established in independent Korea is not a matter of indifference to the Allied nations because on it, as well as on the form of government, depends in what direction the influence of Korea will be exerted in the post-war world.

Saying, "let the Koreans decide this question for themselves" may actually predetermine the answer to the question: "Who will be the Koreans to decide this question?" Twenty-four million people cannot decide this question directly, and even in the case of a plebiscite much depends upon the control of the press and radio, and of government organization *at that particular moment*. The decision of the Koreans on this question is not something already in existence which we can simply uncover and put into practice. If the United Nations work out some scheme and agree upon it, the very existence of such a scheme can become a powerful factor in the decisive struggle ahead.

Must the large enterprises wrested from the Japanese be entrusted to Koreans? On what basis? Should they be sold? It is clear that the Koreans have no capital to buy such enterprises. Should they be sold on an installment basis? But it is quite clear that the persons who could make the first installment payment would be precisely those who have worked for the Japanese against their own people. Should such enterprises be given to persons who have no capital now, but are ready to become entrepreneurs? What will then be the basis of selection —for, certainly, there will be many willing to get millions for nothing? Will it be party affiliation or blood relation to the ministers of the Provincial Government? Or the number of years spent in some Japanese prison?

The moment of Japan's final defeat will be the most momentous in Korean history, a moment which may not return for hundreds of years, when so much public good can be achieved without bloodshed, without decades or centuries of strife and conflict. The fall of the Japanese regime will permit the complete eradication of the social wrongs of the old Korean regime which have been so eloquently described by G. Kennan and so many of which are still alive today in Japanese Korea.

Nationalization of Japanese Enterprises in Korea

A possible solution for the central problem of Korean reconstruction is nationalization of industry and land, and a marked progress in cooperation. Nationalization of the Japanese enterprises which rightfully belong to the Koreans could be a painless process. It is a task that would involve only a few individuals because the number of Korean enterprises with fifty or more workers is only about two hundred (we assume that smaller enterprises should be left in private hands), and most of these individuals have "earned" their capital through collaboration with the Japanese.

The land should be taken from the landowners and given to those who have worked it through the centuries. It should be taken without recompense because payment for this land would put the same burden on the farmers that they have borne before, only in a different form. Some help should be given those families of landlords which as a result of this nationalization would be placed in an exceptionally difficult position. If houses and movable property were not nationalized, cases in which such help would be needed would not be numerous. Moreover, there will be a tremendous demand for labor in general and for skilled labor in particular. As a rule, the landlords were able to give their children the best education which one could obtain in Korea or in Japan. Those physicians, teachers, engineers, and jurists, who have had little if any chance to obtain employment under the Japanese, would be needed and welcomed under the new conditions.

The state need not run the industries: it could lend the enterprises to the cooperative organizations in return for payment of an annual royalty. We believe that this separation of state and private enterprise would make the state less powerful and would thus contribute to greater democratization and freedom in Korea. Korea should become a cooperative state.

A Cooperative Commonwealth

What are the advantages of such a scheme, and what possible objections are there? The present poverty will exist even under changed conditions unless a rapid improvement takes place. Capitalism in its present form is unable to perform this task quickly. A policy designed to turn all farmers into owners of their land and to safeguard their position would be a mistaken one because, as we have shown, the productivity of labor in Korean agriculture is very low, and industrialization is an absolute necessity. Such a policy could succeed only if the number of those occupied in agriculture diminished and that of persons engaged in industry, transportation, and to a lesser degree in commerce, grew rapidly. But to dispossess millions of farmers, to transfer them to industry, to give them an opportunity to develop their best talents—this has been a slow and painful process even in countries much more favorably situated. In densely populated, poverty-stricken Korea it would take even more time and would be more painful.

On the other hand, a cooperative system of national economy would permit rapid development. Consider, for example, life in the villages. Mechanization of agriculture, which is the result of industrial development, would free tremendous numbers of workers. These workers need not leave the villages and swell the number of unemployed in the cities: the village cooperatives would find the means to build the necessary establishments in rural localities. One may ask where the capital will come from? Now the villages pay in rent hundreds of millions of yen (in kind and money). Under a plan for complete cooperative organization of the country this capital would be easily available for new construction without endangering the new standards and without making the future development of the country depend on foreign loans. Much discussion is now going on concerning the future rehabilitation of China, Poland, and other countries ravaged by war, with schemes based on the necessity of "subsidizing" such countries for a long period of time with loans from the United States. Though in the first few months after the war, relief in various forms will be necessary in such countries—and in Korea too—yet the Koreans could rapidly be helped to stand on their own feet.

Other advantages of this scheme are: (1) it easily fits into the existing pattern of economy in Korea. The existing cooperative organizations, with a sprinkling of new political figures and with foreign advisors, could quickly take over Japanese establishments as "going concerns" and continue the work without interruption.

(2) Under this arrangement it would be possible to keep in service many Japanese experts, engineers, physicians, teachers, managers. Under the system of private enterprise, such employment of Japanese might be undesirable and even dangerous because such men would still perhaps serve Japanese enterprise and become agents for competing Japanese corporations. With this kind of competition eliminated, Japanese specialists can be very useful, especially during the first ten or twenty years when Korea would launch an ambitious program of building up its own reserves of specialists. The Japanese specialists should be given assurances that there will always be a place for them under the new conditions—they would not become persons only temporarily tolerated.

(3) It is unlikely that capitalism of the British or American type will exist after the war in either Japan or China. Among Korea's neighbors, the Soviet Union is a socialist state; China may become a nation in which state control of industry will considerably increase. Under these conditions, a Korean cooperative economy would be more suited for cooperation with those of her neighbors; and we should expect considerably more than half of Korea's foreign trade to be with these three countries: Japan, China (including Manchuria), and Russia.

(4) When the entire life of a country has to be rebuilt, and rebuilt quickly, ordinary motives of profit are not sufficient. We know that no country in time of war, or in any period of extreme national danger, relies upon such motives. One cannot be expected to go to battle and meet death for the sake of profit. Great spiritual sources will have to be tapped for such a campaign of national regeneration as Korea will have to face. We believe that such forces do exist in Korea and can be released for this tremendous task if reconstruction proceeds on the basis of cooperation—work in common. We believe that all the missionary organizations, with tens of thousands of persons educated by them, with all their enthusiasm, experience, and spirit of sacrifice, can be involved in this Korean rebirth.

Among the objections which may be raised against this project are the following:

(1) Fear of a dictatorial regime which would deprive the

population of its rights and restore the situation now existing under the Japanese, so that it would be only a change of masters. We believe that such fears are exaggerated. There will exist in Korea at least four independent organizations: (a) political, with several political parties struggling for the right to represent the interests of the Korean people; (b) economic-cooperatives, the members of which are elected and are independent of the government organization; (c) religion—Christian, Buddhist, and native churches must be given complete freedom in the propagation of their faith and in practicing their religion; (d) trade unions.

Though rigid separation of executive and legislative powers may be undesirable under Korean conditions, yet all efforts should be made to make judicial power really independent of the executive, and as accessible to the masses of the population as possible.

(2) Fear that an individual having no capital of his own will be left completely at the mercy of political organizations. However, individuals will be permitted to own houses, small plots of land, personal belongings of all kinds, deposits in the bank; they may even open small businesses (limited, let us say, as to the number of workers and/or the amount of capital to be employed); and they will be completely free in the disposal of their property.

(3) Fear that individual initiative would be suppressed and in this way the development of Korea stunted. These fears are to a considerable degree groundless. Initiative may be encouraged through the numerous organizations mentioned above. On the other hand, if some individuals should find fewer possibilities than, say under the American or British system, the permanency of the economic system and careful economic planning for years to come would permit a smoother, more constant growth.

One important problem should be mentioned here: the problem of defense. The question which naturally arises in all such cases is this: "Defense against whom?" The United States and Great Britain can hardly threaten Korean independence. Three possible countries remain: Japan, China, and Russia. Each of them is endangered if any one of the others keeps Korea; and they should all be interested in Korea's independence. It would seem that under these conditions the best thing would be a joint guarantee by China, Great Britain, Japan, Russia, and the United States of Korea's independence and territorial integrity. This guarantee would permit Korea to reduce her army and navy to forces sufficient to police the frontiers and surrounding waters, and thus make ample revenues available for peaceful construction. In recent centuries the Hermit Kingdom has shown no martial inclinations; there is no necessity to create them anew. The best insurance for Korea's safety is not to create a powerful army against her more powerful neighbors, but to win their goodwill by a peaceful friendly policy toward all.

APPENDIX I

AGRICULTURAL STATISTICS OF KOREA

TABLE 1. AGRICULTURAL POPULATION
(in thousands of families)

Year	Total	Japanese	Korean	Chinese	Owners	Owner-Tenants	Tenants	Laborers	Kaden-min
1929	2,815.3	10.4	2,801.8	2.0	611.9	885.6	1,283.5	....	34.3
1930	2,870.0	10.5	2,856.1	3.3	608.0	890.3	1,334.1	....	37.5
1931	2,881.7	10.8	2,868.6	2.3	593.3	853.8	1,393.4	....	41.2
1932	2,931.1	11.4	2,917.4	2.2	581.2	743.0	1,546.5	....	60.5
1933	3,009.6	9.0	2,998.2	2.3	545.5	724.7	1,563.1	94.0	82.3
1934	3,013.1	8.7	3,001.8	2.6	542.6	721.7	1,564.3	103.2	81.3
1935	3,066.5	8.4	3,055.4	2.6	547.9	738.9	1,591.4	111.8	76.5
1936	3,059.5	8.0	3,048.6	2.9	546.3	737.8	1,583.6	117.0	74.7
1937	3,058.8	7.6	3,049.0	2.1	549.6	737.8	1,581.4	117.0	72.9
1938	3,052.4	7.3	3,042.8	2.3	552.4	729.3	1,583.4	116.0	71.2

Source: *Takumu Tokei*, 1938.

TABLE 2. CULTIVATED AREA
(in 1,000 *cho*)

Year	Total Cultivated Area	Total Paddy	One Crop	Two Crops	Dry Fields
1929	5,566.5	1,625.5	1,280.1	345.4	2,830.0
1930	4,466.1	1,643.8	1,286.6	347.1	2,822.4
1931	4,455.3	1,653.1	1,286.0	367.1	2,802.2
1932	4,460.4	1,669.6	1,285.4	384.2	2,790.8
1933	4,489.2	1,681.8	1,285.5	396.3	2,807.4
1934	4,505.5	1,692.7	1,277.5	415.2	2,812.7
1935	4,500.2	1,703.3	1,267.8	435.5	2,796.9
1936	4,503.9	1,718.5	1,266.2	452.3	2,785.4
1937	4,506.2	1,736.4	1,271.3	465.1	2,769.9
1938	4,515.7	1,750.8	1,290.5	460.3	2,764.8

	Owner-Cultivated		Rented Land		Area per family (*cho*)			Kaden
	Paddy	Dry Field	Paddy	Dry Field	Total	Paddy	Dry Field	(fire-fields)
1929	551.9	1,452.2	1,073.5	1,377.8	1.60	0.58	1.02	176.8
1930	549.8	1,435.8	1,093.9	1,386.6	1.58	0.58	1.00	180.7
1931	540.6	1,413.3	1,112.5	1,388.9	1.57	0.58	0.99	201.2
1932	544.9	1,400.0	1,124.7	1,390.4	1.55	0.58	0.97	202.2
1933	546.4	1,415.7	1,135.4	1,391.7	1.53	0.57	0.96	366.6
1934	540.0	1,387.9	1,152.7	1,424.8	1.59	0.60	0.99	422.6
1935	547.5	1,382.3	1,155.7	1,414.6	1.56	0.59	0.97	417.8
1936	548.0	1,370.7	1,170.5	1,414.6	1.47	0.56	0.91	437.7
1937	556.6	1,359.4	1,179.8	1,410.5	1.57	0.61	0.96	437.1
1938	563.9	1,344.0	1,186.9	1,420.8	1.48	0.57	0.91	442.0

Source: *Takumu Tokei*, 1938.

TABLE 3. AMOUNT OF RENT
(per 100 *tsubo*)

	From Paddy Fields, in koku					From Dry Fields, in yen				
	South	Central	West	North	Average	South	Central	West	North	Average
1929	0.42	0.39	0.36	0.38	0.39	1.97	1.88	1.33	1.94	1.80
1930	0.41	0.38	0.36	0.33	0.36	1.84	1.66	1.29	1.48	1.62
1931	0.44	0.39	0.34	0.33	0.39	1.20	1.08	1.00	1.03	1.10
1932	0.44	0.39	0.33	0.32	0.38	1.38	1.21	0.96	1.00	1.19
1933	0.42	0.38	0.35	0.32	0.38	1.39	1.32	1.03	1.10	1.25
1934	0.45	0.41	0.37	0.32	0.40	1.51	1.46	1.09	1.18	1.35
1935	0.43	0.41	0.38	0.34	0.40	1.86	1.77	1.37	1.41	1.65
1936	0.44	0.42	0.38	0.37	0.41	2.15	2.12	1.60	1.70	1.95
1937	0.45	0.43	0.40	0.38	0.42	2.24	2.16	1.67	1.77	2.01
1938	0.46	0.45	0.43	0.40	0.44	2.45	2.27	1.79	1.89	2.16
1939	0.46	0.46	0.45	0.40	0.45	2.62	2.60	2.05	2.23	2.42

Source: *Kokusei Gurafu*, Tokyo, July, 1940.

TABLE 4. INDEX OF COMMODITY PRICES IN KEIJO
(July 1910 = 100)

1910	103	1921	230	1932	144
1911	112	1922	229	1933	160
1912	119	1923	228	1934	162
1913	120	1924	246	1935	180
1914	110	1925	259	1936	191
1915	109	1926	234	1937	206
1916	129	1927	219	1938	237
1917	173	1928	214	1939	274
1918	235	1929	207	April, 1939	259
1919	296	1930	180	April, 1940	312
1920	305	1931	145		

Source: *Chosen Keizai Nempo*, 1939, 1940.

TABLE 5. PRICE OF AGRICULTURAL LAND
(*yen* per 100 *tsubo*)

	Paddy Fields					Dry Fields				
	South	Central	West	North	Average	South	Central	West	North	Average
1929	51	45	41	35	45	17	17	14	18	16
1930	41	40	35	30	38	16	14	12	14	14
1931	31	26	26	22	27	11	9	10	8	10
1932	33	28	25	21	28	11	10	9	9	10
1933	35	31	27	23	30	12	11	10	10	11
1934	39	37	31	26	35	13	13	12	11	12
1935	47	47	40	33	43	15	16	14	13	15
1936	57	59	48	42	53	19	20	17	17	18
1937	62	46	51	46	58	21	22	18	18	20
1938	66	67	58	50	62	23	23	19	19	21
1939	75	79	67	62	72	26	27	23	23	25

Source: *Kokusei Gurafu*, July 1940.

TABLE 6. COMPARISON OF RICE PRICES IN JAPAN AND KOREA
(yen per *koku*)[a]

	Japan	Korea
1922	36.85	30.48
1923	31.57	27.31
1924	37.64	33.14
1925	41.95	37.27
1926	38.44	33.67
1927	35.93	30.45
1928	31.38	26.74
1929	29.19	26.67
1930	27.34	23.00
1931	13.46	16.23
1932	20.69	20.27
1933	21.42	20.56

Source: Hishimoto, *Chosen bei no Kenkyu*, Tokyo, 1938.
[a] Prices for Japan are those of the Fukagawa market, Tokyo, for Japanese *chubei*; prices for Korea are averages for Fusan market and Jinsen market, for third grade unhulled rice.

TABLE 7. INDEX OF WHOLESALE PRICES IN KEIJO BY GROUPS OF COMMODITIES
(1936 = 100)

	Cereals	Food-stuffs	Textile Materials	Textiles	Bldg. Materials	Metals	Fuel	Fertilizer	Drugs	Miscellaneous	Average
1938											
Jan.	104.8	110.6	101.6	103.9	128.4	217.9	122.4	122.6	159.7	140.2	121.2
April	107.6	117.0	112.9	120.4	133.2	217.7	126.9	123.5	192.2	157.8	131.0
July	113.0	115.8	130.3	144.0	148.3	267.4	132.2	124.1	192.8	202.9	143.2
1939											
Jan.	120.2	119.9	133.2	151.1	152.3	255.9	148.2	128.8	210.2	197.5	148.5
April	126.1	127.6	152.2	171.8	157.4	252.8	145.6	132.8	213.8	199.7	156.4
July	143.1	133.0	155.9	180.6	165.6	246.7	144.9	132.2	216.3	202.9	162.5
1940											
Jan.	169.0	147.4	182.0	182.0	177.2	240.0	157.7	154.1	230.9	203.2	175.2
April	168.7	159.7	172.7	190.8	177.5	240.0	159.2	154.1	235.6	210.0	180.3

Source: *Chosen Keizai Nempo*, 1940.

TABLE 8. DISTRIBUTION OF FARMS IN KOREA BY SIZE IN 1938
(in 1,000)

		Owners	Part-owners Chiefly Owners	Part-owners Chiefly Tenants	Total	Tenants	Total
Size							
Less than	3 *tan*	71.7	48.2	67.6	115.8	300.9	488.3
" "	5 *tan*[a]	91.7	74.1	94.3	168.4	353.3	613.4
" "	1 *cho*	114.4	92.9	115.9	208.8	390.0	713.2
" "	2 *cho*	114.9	82.8	96.1	178.9	271.7	565.6
" "	3 *cho*	86.9	47.5	46.8	94.3	131.6	312.8
" "	5 *cho*	47.2	20.0	18.3	38.3	50.7	136.1
" "	10 *cho*	14.2	4.5	4.2	8.7	11.1	34.0
" "	20 *cho*	2.2	0.5	0.5	1.1	2.1	5.3
20 *cho* and more		0.3	0	0	0.1	0	0.5
Total		543.5	370.5	443.7	814.3	1,511.4	2,869.2

Percentages

Less than	3 *tan*	13.2	13.0	15.3	14.2	19.9	17.0
" "	5 *tan*	16.9	20.0	21.3	20.7	23.4	21.4
" "	1 *cho*	21.1	25.1	26.2	25.6	26.8	24.9
" "	2 *cho*	21.2	22.4	21.7	22.0	18.0	19.7
" "	3 *cho*	16.0	12.8	10.6	11.6	8.7	10.9
" "	5 *cho*	8.7	5.4	4.1	4.7	3.4	4.7
" "	10 *cho*	2.6	1.2	1.0	1.1	0.7	1.2
" "	20 *cho*	0.4	0.1	0.1	0.1	0.1	0.2
20 *cho* and more		...	...	...	...	...	...
Total		100.0	100.0	100.0	100.0	100.0	100.0

Source: *Kokusei Gurafu*, Tokyo, July, 1940.
[a] Though the Japanese statistics say "less than — *tan*" they clearly mean "3 to 4.9 *tan*," "5 to 9.9 *tan*," "1 to 1.99 *cho*" and so on.—A.J.G.

TABLE 9. PRODUCTION OF MOST IMPORTANT CROPS IN KOREA[a]
(Area in 1,000 *cho*; crop in 1,000 *koku*; value in million yen)

Part One	Rice			Wheat and Barley		
	Area	Crop	Value	Area	Crop	Value
1910	1,353	10,406	92.9	858	6,208	23.7
1914	1,484	14,131	168.3	1,034	8,100	38.6
1919	1,538	12,708	516.3	1,204	9,302	129.7
1925	1,585	14,773	474.3	1,245	10,420	128.5
1929	1,632	13,702	322.4	1,293	9,388	89.8
1930	1,662	19,181	251.6	1,318	9,964	80.0
1931	1,675	15,873	268.8	1,317	10,208	50.4
1932	1,643	16,346	308.9	1,322	10,619	64.4
1933	1,697	18,193	341.6	1,336	10,371	76.1
1934	1,712	16,717	415.5	1,354	11,117	88.7
1935	1,695	17,885	489.6	1,366	12,311	119.0
1936	1,601	19,411[b]	540.5	1,406	10,405	117.2
1937	1,639	26,797[b]	777.0	1,450	14,680	166.0
1938	1,660	24,139[b]	762.3	1,476	11,760	150.3

Source: *Chosen Keizai Nempo*, 1939, 1940.

[a] Data before the year 1919 are hardly reliable because the land survey was finished only in 1918.—A.J.G.

[b] In 1936 the method of calculation of rice crops was changed, and this resulted in figures for the following years 1.26 greater than what the crop would have been if the old method were used.— A.J.G.

Part Two	Beans			Other Cereals			Total Including Others
	Area	Crop	Value	Area	Crop	Value	
1910	708	3,636	18.2	839	5,296	22.4	200.6
1914	951	4,892	42.7	1,088	7,087	33.9	370.3
1919	1,077	3,891	72.1	1,293	6,334	83.4	1,080.7
1925	1,116	5,803	94.5	1,323	8,124	92.6	1,020.1
1929	1,098	5,013	78.3	1,320	8,995	82.7	753.0
1930	1,096	5,628	41.4	1,313	9,069	53.0	558.9
1931	1,092	5,212	42.3	1,317	7,851	46.3	546.6
1932	1,104	5,525	59.5	1,339	9,008	64.2	655.7
1933	1,095	5,707	58.1	1,312	8,076	59.6	704.7
1934	1,087	4,930	59.2	1,322	6,188	62.6	803.8
1935	1,086	5,576	78.2	1,327	7,709	84.9	926.1
1936	1,075	4,769	81.5	1,306	8,116	91.1	976.6
1937	1,069	5,412	89.8	1,284	9,144	101.3	1,303.5
1938	1,049	4,918	88.3	1,245	8,097	103.5	1,295.9

APPENDIX II

RELIABILITY OF KOREAN AGRICULTURAL STATISTICS

Dr. Elizabeth Boody Schumpeter, of the Bureau of International Research, Harvard University, has used official Japanese statistics to demonstrate that the conditions of the Korean people are improving, and has expressed her belief that the failure of crops in 1939 only "temporarily reversed . . . the general trend toward greater production, exports and consumption."[1] Before accepting this conclusion, however, a more critical appraisal of the data is in order. This is attempted below.

CULTIVATED AREA IN KOREA[2]

Year	Paddy Fields	Dry Fields	Total
1910	841.0	1,321.4	2,162.4
1919	1,546.6	2,834.9	4,381.5
1938	1,750.8	2,764.8	4,515.7

Increase (+) or decrease (−) in percentages of the preceding data.

	Per Cent	Per Cent	Per Cent
1919	+84	+114	+103
1938	+13	−2.11	+3

Average *annual* change, in 1,000 *cho*

1910-19	+78.4	+168.0	+246.4
1919-38	+10.7	−3.7	+7.0

Source for cultivated area: *Chosen Keizai Nempo*, 1939, and *Takumu Tokei*, 1938.

This table shows that during the first nine years after annexation, if we trust the statistics, there was a remarkable increase in the cultivated area: the area of paddy increased by 84 per cent; that of dry fields by 114 per cent (*i.e.*, it more than doubled), and the total area by 103 per cent; but during the following nineteen years the area of paddy increased by only 13 per cent, and that of dry fields *decreased* by 2 per cent, so that the total area increased by only 3 per cent. How could this be? During the first few years the Administration had neither the money nor the desire to undertake large reclamation works,

---

[1] *The Industrialization of Japan and Manchukuo*, New York, 1940, p. 292.
[2] *Kaden*, "fire-fields," are excluded for reasons explained below.
One *cho* is equal to 2.45 acres.

and the addition of 246,400 *cho* every year for a period of nine consecutive years in an agriculturally *old* country would represent a really remarkable achievement. But after 1919, when all the efforts of the Japanese Government in Korea were bent on increasing the production of rice to supply Japan Proper, the only change that occurred was an annual increase of paddy at the rate of 10,700 *cho*—and this partly at the expense of dry fields.

The secret of this paradox is very simple: between 1910 and 1919 a cadastral survey of agricultural land was undertaken for taxation and other purposes, and it revealed that the actual cultivated area was larger than the area for which farmers had been paying taxes. Statistical increases of cultivated area between 1910 and 1919 thus represented only paper increases, resulting in greater taxation for the Korean population. Land statistics in Korea are more or less reliable only after 1919.

Let us now turn to the crop statistics. The following table gives the size of crops in 1910, 1919-1921 (average), 1934-1936 (average), 1937, 1938, and 1939 figures that have been used by Dr. Schumpeter and others without examining their reliability.

PRODUCTION OF CEREALS AND BEANS IN KOREA
(in 1,000 *koku*)[a]

	1910	1919-21 (average)	1934-36 (average)	1937	1938	1939
Rice	10,406	13,971	18,004	26,797	24,139	14,355
Barley, wheat, rye	6,208	9,781	11,278	14,680	12,263	....
Other cereals	5,296	8,853	7,338	9,144	7,594	....
Beans	3,636	5,376	5,092	5,412	4,918	....
Total	25,546	37,981	41,712	56,033	48,914	....
Increase, per cent of preceding period	....	48.7	9.8	34.3	−12.7	....
Average annual increase or decrease (in thousand *koku*)	....	1,244	249	14,321	−7,119	....

[a] One *koku* is 5.12 U.S. bushels, or 4.96 imperial bushels.
Sources: *Chosen Keizai Nenkan* and *Chosen Nenkan*.

This table, like the preceding one, shows a rapid rise of production in the first ten years, then a slow growth. But there is one difference. The cultivated area in 1937, 1938, and 1939 did not show any substantial change; but the production of crops in 1937 suddenly rose by 34.3 per cent, as compared with that in the preceding three-year average. It is this remarkable increase which accounts for the sudden rise in Dr. Schumpeter's upward trend. But if the growth of crops obtained between 1910 and 1919 can be explained by the improvement in statistical reporting and coverage, and if the increase between 1919 and 1935 can be explained by normal growth because of the growth of population, investments in irrigation, etc., how can the remarkable rise in 1937 and 1938 be explained? Fortunately, we have an authoritative explanation: in *Chosen Keizai Nempo*, 1940,[3] it is stated that in 1936 the authorities changed their method of calculating rice production. Fortunately, they also supplied us with "recalculated" figures of rice production from 1929 on, so we can easily see how this method would work:

RESULTS OF CHANGES IN METHOD OF RICE CROP CULTIVATION

	Old Method (1,000 koku)	New Method (1,000 koku)	Ratio
1928	13,512	16,998	126
1929	13,702	17,237	126
1930	19,181	24,129	126
1931	15,873	19,968	126
1932	16,346	20,563	126
1933	18,193	28,886[a]	159
1934	16,717	21,030	126
1935	17,885	22,500	126
1936	unavailable	19,411	...
1937	"	26,797	...
1938	"	24,139	...
1939	"	14,355	...

[a] Probably a misprint. It should be 25,886.

From the comparison of the two sets of figures it is clear that the new method consists of increasing the yield by approximately 26 per cent. This new method may be good or bad—without knowledge of the reasons why it was adopted we cannot say which is the better method. But every statistician is under an obligation to use the figures calculated by the same method, and not to jump from one set to another and then to project non-existing trends. If we use the old method, then the data for 1936-39 would appear as follows:

	New Method (1,000 koku)	Old Method (1,000 koku)
1936	19,411[a]	15,400
1937	26,797	21,200
1938	24,139	19,200
1939	14,335	11,400

[a] We can establish the date when the method of calculation was changed. We read in the *Annual Report* for 1936-37, p. 63: "During 1936 *agriculture* suffered from catastrophes caused by storms and floods in the south and drought in the west, in addition to disease in the rice fields in the central districts. The forecast of the rice crop therefore was only 16 million *koku*, the lowest since 1931. The crops of soya beans, red beans, barley, wheat, millet, and cotton, the principal other agricultural products were also very bad." Thus a "very bad crop" was turned into an excellent one after the forecasts already were made: i.e., in September, 1936.

[3] p. 52. Published by Zenkoku Keizai Chosa Kikan Rengokai, Tokyo.

APPENDIX II

In the description of Korean agriculture in this book figures calculated by the "old method" for 1936-39 were used; not because they are better or worse, but because they give us comparable quantities.

APPENDIX III

SOME INDUSTRIAL STATISTICS

TABLE I. NUMBER OF INDUSTRIAL ESTABLISHMENTS IN KOREA
(with five workers and more)

	1929	1931	1935	1936	1937
Textile	241	270	377	402	426
Metals	237	244	239	259	264
Machinery	221	235	324	344	417
Ceramics	318	321	336	336	346
Chemical	393	677	1,161	1,425	1,588
Lumber	153	181	240	271	311
Printing, etc.	208	237	285	286	306
Food	1,958	2,173	2,326	2,258	2,273
Gas, Electricity	75	52	51	50	40
Others	221	223	296	296	327
Total	4,025	4,613	5,635	5,927	6,298

Source: *Takumu Tokei.*

TABLE II. NUMBER OF EMPLOYEES IN THESE ESTABLISHMENTS
(in thousands)

	1929	1931	1935	1936	1937
Textile	17.5	18.2	29.1	33.8	35.6
Metals	4.7	4.5	6.3	6.8	6.8
Machinery	3.4	2.9	6.5	7.9	9.5
Ceramics	5.8	4.8	8.0	8.3	9.7
Chemical	9.4	17.9	34.4	42.0	50.9
Lumber	3.2	2.6	4.5	4.9	5.6
Printing, etc.	4.1	4.2	5.9	6.3	6.6
Food	24.8	27.6	35.0	32.6	35.0
Gas, Electricity	0.8	0.6	0.7	0.8	0.8
Others	4.4	3.1	5.4	5.4	6.6
Total	78.2	86.4	135.8	148.8	166.7

Source: *Takumu Tokei.*

TABLE III. GROSS VALUE OF INDUSTRIAL PRODUCTION
(in thousand yen)

	1929	1931	1935	1936	1937	1938
Textile	38,211	24,439	82,328	99,477	141,154	164,821
Metals	20,383	16,106	26,989	33,735	50,766	91,966
Machinery	4,543	2,308	11,525	13,503	16,565	26,799
Ceramics	9,116	7,291	17,563	21,876	25,072	35,877
Chemical	17,413	31,913	147,834	195,431	304,948	352,819
Lumber	7,721	6,381	8,243	9,936	11,737	15,054
Printing	9,954	8,381	12,744	13,133	1o,304	16,948
Gas, Electricity	16,389	16,129	39,804	39,989	40,076	24,502
Food	223,412	156,480	169,420	199,883	238,033	277,208
Others	4,309	4,221	91,027	103,842	114,653	134,124
Total	351,451	273,649	607,497	730,807	959,303	1,140,118

Source: *Takumu Tokei* and *Chosen Nenkan.*

APPENDIX III

TABLE IV. COMPOSITION OF INDUSTRY
By branches (per cent of total)

	1929	1933	1936	1938
Textile	10.9	10.5	12.7	14.4
Metal	5.7	7.9	4.0	8.1
Machine	1.3	0.8	1.1	2.3
Ceramics	2.6	2.4	2.7	3.1
Lumber	2.2	2.7	2.7	1.3
Printing	2.8	2.6	1.8	1.5
Food	63.5	54.6	45.1	24.3
Gas and Electricity	4.7	3.0	5.6	2.2
Chemical	5.0	14.1	22.9	30.9
Others	1.3	1.4	1.4	11.9[a]
Total	100.0	100.0	100.0	100.0

Source: Calculated from data in *Chosen Keizai Nempo*, 1939-1940.
[a] The rise of "Others" in 1938 is caused by inclusion of public enterprises, such as the tobacco monopoly.

TABLE V. GEOGRAPHICAL DISTRIBUTION OF INDUSTRY IN KOREA, 1937

A. Absolute data (in million yen)

Provinces	Textiles	Metal	Machine	Ceramics	Chemicals	Lumber	Printing	Food	Gas & Elect.	Others	Total
Chusei North	1.7	0.1	0.0	0.2	1.1	0.0	0.0	5.7	0.0	2.0	10.8
Chusei South	3.5	0.2	0.2	0.3	0.8	0.3	0.2	7.2	0.8	3.1	16.6
Zenra North	3.1	0.4	0.5	0.3	3.6	0.3	0.3	13.7	0.5	9.9	32.6
Zenra South	22.6	0.6	0.6	0.7	4.5	0.8	0.2	20.4	0.9	6.7	58.0
Keisho North	9.8	0.7	0.5	0.4	4.8	0.7	0.6	22.1	0.1	17.5	57.2
Keisho South	27.6	1.2	2.5	4.5	11.6	2.0	0.9	39.6	1.9	10.1	101.9
Keiki	53.8	5.3	7.4	3.1	18.0	3.8	12.4	44.2	2.1	37.8	187.9
Kokai	2.6	31.4	0.4	2.2	17.2	0.4	0.1	12.5	2.6	3.2	72.6
Kogen	2.5	0.2	0.2	0.1	11.5	0.1	0.1	8.9	1.3	2.5	27.4
Heian South	7.7	1.9	1.7	4.5	6.8	0.9	0.5	37.3	0.0	11.3	72.6
Heian North	3.1	1.4	0.8	0.3	10.5	0.6	0.3	9.8	0.3	6.4	33.5
Kankyo South	2.7	7.0	0.7	5.5	165.9	1.0	0.4	11.2	29.3	2.0	225.7
Kankyo North	0.5	0.4	1.1	3.0	48.6	0.8	0.3	5.4	0.3	2.1	62.5
Total	141.2	50.8	16.6	25.1	304.9	11.7	16.3	238.0	40.1	114.6	959.3

Source: *Chosen Nenkan*, 1940.

B. The same as percentages of the total for each industry:

	Per Cent of the pop.										
Chusei North	3.9	1	0	0	1	0	0	0	2	0	2	1
Chusei South	6.8	3	0	1	1	0	3	1	3	2	3	2
Zenra North	7.0	2	1	3	1	1	3	2	6	1	9	3
Zenra South	10.9	16	1	4	3	1	7	1	9	2	6	6
Keisho North	10.9	7	1	3	2	2	6	4	9	0	15	6
Keisho South	9.8	20	2	15	18	4	17	6	17	5	8	10
Keiki	11.2	38	10	45	12	6	32	76	19	5	33	19
Kokai	7.5	2	63	2	9	6	3	1	5	7	3	8
Kogen	6.9	2	0	1	0	4	1	1	4	3	2	3
Heian South	6.7	5	4	10	18	2	8	3	15	0	10	8
Heian North	7.3	2	3	5	1	4	5	2	4	1	5	3
Kankyo South	7.3	2	14	4	22	54	8	3	5	73	2	24
Kankyo North	3.8	0	1	7	12	16	7	2	2	1	2	7
Total		100	100	100	100	100	100	100	100	100	100	100

These two tables show that the distribution of industries by provinces is, as one would expect, very uneven. We see, first of all, that two provinces are more advanced than others in their development—Keiki, the seat of the Japanese Government, and South Kankyo—a rapidly developing area. The tempo of development of South Kankyo is greater than that in any other province. The reasons are shown below. Next in importance come South Keisho, with the important industrial city Fusan, and South Heian, the place of the ancient capital, and the important new industrial center, Heijo. North Heian and North Kankyo, though not now very prominent in industrial growth, are growing rapidly and with further general expansion may in their development overtake Keisho and South Heian.

Turning now to branches of industry, we see that the textile industry is concentrated mainly in Keiki, South Keisho and South Zenra—in other words, in Keijo, the capital; in Fusan, the first port of entry from Japan and the oldest Japanese settlement in Korea; in Moppo and Koshu, the main silk and cotton producing regions.

The metal industry is concentrated chiefly in Kokai where Kenjiho is the most important center in this respect. But there can be little doubt that by now its importance has diminished, and the center of this industry has moved to South Kankyo and to both South and North Heian.

The machine and tool building industry, modest as it is, is concentrated in Keiki and South Keisho, that is, in and around the capital Keijo and Fusan.

Ceramics—in the Japanese classification—may be divided into two types—new, such as cement, isolators, etc. with centers in both Kankyo and South Keisho, and old—pottery, earthenware—in South Heian (in and around Heijo) and Keiki.

As to the chemical industry, its concentration is largely conditioned by the distribution of waterpower resources; the two Kankyo provinces are responsible for 70 per cent of total production, while in all other provinces it comprises chiefly household industry. With the start of the Yalu electric station, Shingishu and other cities in North Heian may increase their share.

The lumber industry is well represented in the old centers—Keijo, Fusan, and Heijo leading. Printing is concentrated in Keiki, or, more exactly, in Keijo—with three fourths of the total gross value of production; this illustrates the centralized control of the country by the Japanese government from Keijo.

The food industry, as might be expected, is more evenly distributed than any other—first, because many of its branches should be near the consumer, and secondly because, as we have seen, so large a part of its output is produced by household industry.

As to electricity, it is concentrated in Southern Kankyo, though with the completion of new works, especially the Yalu Power Station, a wider distribution is inevitable.

As to the "other" industries, the large share of Keiki (province of Keijo, the capital) is explained by inclusion in this group of the government tobacco monopoly which is in Keiki.

TABLE VI. CORPORATIONS OCCUPIED IN SPINNING AND WEAVING, 1938

Corporation in operation:	Number of spindles	Number of looms	Locality
Korea Spinning & Weaving	39,376	1,210	Fusan
Keijo Spinning & Weaving	25,600	896	Eitoho (Keijo)
Toyo Spinning & Weaving	31,488	1,292	Jinsen
Toyo Spinning & Weaving	45,328	1,440	Eitoho (Keijo)
Kanegafuchi Spinning & Weaving	31,800	1,440	Koshu (S. Zenra)
Kanegafuchi Spinning & Weaving	39,520	1,525	Eitoho (Keijo)
Planned:			
Kanegafuchi Spinning & Weaving	30,000	1,000	Taikyu (N. Keisho)
Dainippon Spinning & Weaving	42,000	1,000	Eitoho (Keijo)
Chosen Cotton (Weaving only)		1,200	Moppo
Chosen Rayon (Mixed goods)		97	Keijo
Asahi Rayon		378	Fusan
Kaito Weaving (Mixed goods)		108	Keijo
Chosen Weaving (Rayon)		1,084	An-yo
Taisho Weaving (Rayon)		300	Keijo
Chosen Beseki (Rayon)		319	Fusan
Fusan Weaving (Rayon)		149	Fusan
Empire Hemp		150	Fusan
Keiki Corporation		860	Keijo

In addition, in Keijo, Jinsen and Fusan there are some enterprises which specialize only in the dyeing of textiles.

TABLE VII. A LIST OF MACHINE BUILDING CORPORATIONS IN KOREA IN 1938

(in operation)

1. Chosen Shoko Corporation, in Chinnampo, mentioned before; it added mining equipment to the list of its products.
2. Chosen Keiki Corporation, in Keijo, mentioned above.
3. Tekkosho in Jinsen, mining equipment.
4. Ryuzan Corporation, making rolling stock; mentioned before.
5. Chosen Kikai Seisakusho, in Jinsen, est. in 1937, produces mining equipment, was established by Mori and Nezu interests. Its capital was rapidly increased; and it included among its products machinery needed for the cement industry.
6. Chosen Seikosho, in Jinsen, established in 1937, produces mining equipment.
7. Chosen Jukogyo, in Fusan, est. in 1937, making ships and general machinery. This corporation was organized by Mitsubishi and Totaku interests. It began the construction of vessels of 800 tons and in 1935 of 5,000 tons. At the start the capital was 1.5 million yen, but this was later considerably increased.
8. Chosen Sakuganki Seisakusho, in Keijo, established in 1938, produces drills and pneumatic machinery.
9. Nippon Sharyo Corporation, in Jinsen, est. in 1937, rolling stock.
10. Hironaka Shoko Corporation, in Keijo and Fuhei (between Keijo and Jinsen), est. in 1939, produces all kinds of machinery.
11. Kanto Kikai Seishakusho, in Keijo, est. in 1938, mining equipment.
12. Nippon Seiko Corporation, in Keijo, drilling equipment.
13. Nikkosha Chosen Kojo in Sosha, drilling equipment.
14. Toyo Tokushuimono Corporation, in Shingishu, produces bores.
15. Hokusen Seikosho, in Sennairi (north of Genzan), est. in 1938, mining machinery.
16. Seisen (i.e., Western Korea) Jukogyo Corporation in Kaishu (south of Kokai), est. in 1938, expanded in 1939, mining equipment, ships.

Under construction in 1939 and 1940:

1. Shitaura Seishakusho in Jinsen, electric dynamos and equipment.
2. Chosen Chuo Denki Corporation, in Jinsen, electric machinery and equipment.
3. Chosen Kinzoku Kogyo Corporation in Kunsan (a port of Northern Zenra), vessels and mining equipment.
4. Chosen Kako Corporation, in Taiden (southern Chusei), electric and Autogenous welding equipment.
5. Chosen Riken Kinzoku Corporation, in Taiden, piston rings.
6. Tokyo Jidosha Kogyo Corporation, in Fuhei (near Jinsen), assembling and repairs of motor cars according to Kojima (*Sen-man-shi Shinko Keizai*, pp. 120-121) it was also planned to manufacture cars. Planning was done with the help of the Army; the capital to be invested was 5-10 million yen.
7. Showa Heikoki Corporation, in Heijo, to manufacture airplanes.
8. Chosen Chuzo Corporation in Goryodo, to make forging equipment.
9. Fuzan Diesel Engines Corporation, in Fusan, to make Diesel engines for vessels.
10. Chosen Zosen Zotetsu Corporation, in Jinsen, vessels.
11. Chosen Kyodo Kaiun Corporation, in Jinsen, small vessels.

APPENDIX IV

EXTERNAL TRADE OF KOREA
[including trade with Japan]

EXPORTS FROM KOREA, VALUES
(in thousand yen)

	1929	1936	1937	1938	1939
Cows	3,549	4,328	4,830	8,131	13,446
Others	....	330	418	535	3,693
I. Total living plants, animals	3,549	4,658	5,248	8,666	17,139
Rice	148,816	250,395	231,330	313,069	174,638
Wheat	657	616	860	535	532
Beans	23,269	24,447	24,178	23,926	22,970
Starch	38	2,699	4,139	4,050	4,479
Wheat flour	61	415	1,020	4,283	4,245
Others	701	1,973	5,381	6,167	4,247
II. Total cereals, flours	173,542	280,545	266,908	352,030	211,111
Fresh fish	6,217	5,123	6,818	8,742	12,418
Dry fish	6,472	3,929	4,461	6,283	8,803
Salted fish	1,054	1,511	2,077	2,578	6,686
Laver	4,320	4,076	4,188	6,558	9,144
Sugar	5,604	4,019	4,480	3,873	2,846
Sake	....	184	496	3,810	2,060
Apples	1,644	765	470	1,778	4,413
Fruits, nuts	....	4,959	5,301	3,024	7,115
Canned fish	1,323	1,515	1,436	2,076	3,576
Tobacco	224	605	1,154	1,770	3,297
Others	6,718	11,763	12,263	17,711	35,504
III. Foods, drinks, tobacco	33,576	37,684	42,674	56,425	91,449
Cow hides	2,762	2,199	3,448	5,671	917
Other hides, furs	1,566	2,509	3,455	7,464	7,105
IV. Total hides, furs, etc	4,328	4,708	6,903	13,207	8,047
Cotton oil	594	1,849	1,495	835	2,047
Fish oils	5,892	8,261	10,029	7,864	12,343
Mineral oil	....	1,045	3,409	8,052	15,059
Other oils, fats	1,985	10,373	19,533	5,963	2,505
V. Total oils, fats, wax	11,067	31,996	50,099	22,714	31,954
Hard oils	....	3,549	6,634	3,951	6,153
Fatty acids	....	3,219	4,193	2,516	4,579
Glycerine	....	2,284	3,897	3,979	3,139
Ginseng	2,596	1,416	909	711	1,764
Others	includes into "others," group V			11,557	16,319
VI. Total chemicals, drugs	included into group V			22,714	31,954
VII. Dyes, paints, etc	included into group V			1,159	1,535
Ginned cotton	6,809	11,469	8,271	7,994	11,872
Raw silk	20,143	15,421	18,962	15,832	24,169
Wild silk	9,397	4,431	....	6,647	7,945
Silk cocoons	4,381	1,401	1,440	984	....
Threads	....	654	....	668	0
Other yarns, etc	11,800	17,921	29,069	9,545	16,492
VIII. Total yarns, raw materials	55,425	62,186	90,588	41,670	60,478
Cotton tissues	2,895	7,541	23,102	32,186	16,579
Rayon	....	3,348	9,744	5,293	12,129
Other tissues	included into "others," group VIII			9,403	32,162
IX. Tissues, total	included into group VIII			46,882	60,870
X. Clothing, total	included into group VIII			13,852	23,232
Pulp for paper	478	45	5,594	9,236	8,943
Europ. paper	2,341	4,401	4,887	7,094	6,783
Others	see misc.	1,073	1,223	2,334	13,147

305

MODERN KOREA

	1929	1936	1937	1938	1939
XI. Total pulp, paper, mfrs......	see misc.	5,519	11,704	18,664	22,29⬛
Gold ores................	1,944	6,498	6,217	6,973	6,68⬛
Iron ores................	1,676	1,106	4,921	2,562	3,03⬛
Tungsten ore.............	20	1,543	5,738	9,978	16,37⬛
Gold, silver, copper......	209	20,499	25,220	26,526	51,69⬛
Gold, silver, lead ores.....	117	2,946	6,409	7,856	7,607
Iron....................	7,088	18,145	....	....	....
Others..................	3,689	15,956	50,742	62,439	96,232
XII. Total ores and metals.......	21,814	81,501	111,814	116,334	181,626
XIII. Metal mfrs................	included into group XII			8,639	20,931
XIV. Machinery, Vehicles.........	included into group XII			22,842	43,954
Cement.................	1,997	5,915	3,229	3,282	4,497
Coal....................	2,840	6,628	7,305	11,792	14,258
Graphite................	1,234	2,265	2,303	3,393	5,837
Others..................	included into "others," group XII			10,241	11,813
XV. Minerals and mfrs...........	included into group XII			28,708	37,579
XVI. Pottery and Glass..........	included into miscellaneous			1,717	3,492
Lumber.................	4,137	7,448	9,390	5,323	11,741
Sea weeds...............	1,351	1,755	....	1,408	3,808
Fish meal (flour).........	....	1,903	3,637	8,387	14,013
Fertilizers...............	9,977	40,427	37,906	40,328	53,229
Straw bags..............	....	....	....	1,085	3,184
Others..................	16,798	21,763	30,820	22,231	33,428
XVII. Total miscellaneous.........	28,714	73,296	81,753	78,762	119,403
XVIII. Parcels sent by post.........	10,729	9,138	12,150	11,272	14,717
Total....................	342,745	591,258	679,842	877,394	1,003,455
Re-export...............	2,919	2,055	5,701	2,213	3,339
Grand Total..............	345,664	593,313	685,543	879,607	1,006,794

QUANTITIES

Cows, 1,000 heads................	48.9	62.0	59.4	81.8	100.5
Rice, 1,000 *koku*...................	5,541	8,423	7,336	9,521	4,930
Wheat, 1,000 *koku*.................	46	36	47	32	20
Beans, 1,000 *koku*.................	1,434	1,304	1,196	1,149	839
Maize, 1,000 *koku*.................	10	1	7	36	40
Wheat flour, 1,000 tons.............	0.4	2.6	5.2	18.7	16.5
Fresh fish, 1,000 tons...............	39.4	38.0	48.0	59.5	62.7
Dry fish, 1,000 tons.................	11.8	6.8	9.6	12.2	13.6
Salted fish, 1,000 tons..............	8.4	11.2	15.1	17.0	33.5
Laver, 1,000 tons...................	0.82	1.73	1.36	1.70	2.00
Sugar, 1,000 tons...................	30.0	33.0	32.5	22.1	12.5
Sake, 1,000 *sho*....................	145	545	417	620	391
Apples, 1,000 tons..................	8.4	5.6	3.3	7.7	16.1
Fish, canned thousand dozen........	477[1]	617	572	924	1,298
Cow hides, 1,000 tons...............	2.84	2.53	2.76	3.00	0.59
Cotton oil, 1,000 tons...............	1.49	3.76	3.04	2.15	3.24
Fish oil, 1,000 tons.................	36.3	37.4	42.5	41.5	119.5
Hard oils, 1,000 tons................	....	9.2	19.4	12.7	15.4
Fatty acids, 1,000 tons..............	....	12.2	14.4	10.5	12.9
Glycerine, 1,000 tons................	....	1.52	1.65	1.61	13.8
Ginned cotton, 1,000 tons...........	7.3	12.1	8.2	8.3	9.9
Raw silk, tons......................	940	1,180	1,390	1,287	1,030
Wild silk, tons......................	990	705	1,140	1,140	890
Cotton tissues, mill. sq. yds..........	8.58	35.67	103.57	104.81	41.27
Rayon, million sq. yds...............	....	11.78	39.25	23.86	26.07
Gold ore, 1,000 tons................	13.5	64.5	51.4	66.5	76.5
Iron ore, 1,000 tons.................	313	242	302	367	400
Tungsten ore, tons..................	2,530	915	1,420	1,855	2,360
Gold, silver, copper ore.............	1.02	2.17	2.78	4.10	7.05
Gold, silver, lead ore...............	0.36	2.43	5.17	5.80	5.80
Graphite, 1,000 tons................	24.6	39.7	43.5	5.02	78.3
Coal, 1,000 tons....................	286	672	653	943	900
Cement, 1,000 tons.................	67	294	148	151	165
Paper pulp, 1,000 tons..............	2.4	0.3	25.5	32.4	22.9
Foreign paper, 1,000 tons...........	11.6	12.6	13.3	16.3	15.8
Fertilizers, 1,000 tons...............	149	511	445	561	479

APPENDIX IV

IMPORTS INTO KOREA, VALUES
(thousand yen)

	1929	1936	1937	1938	1939
I. Living plants and animals	777	1,496	2,143	2,485	5,881
Rice	14,203	5,017	4,916	2,112	13,493
Barley	762	8,880	4,664	311	3,782
Kaoliang	278	98	68	47	3,103
Corn	95	2,192	721	52	2,672
Millet (*awa*)	20,866	22,702	14,953	13,534	19,655
Wheat	423	3,305	431	2,087	7,801
Buckwheat	759	1,449	1,022	1,100	2,301
Millet (*kibi*)	1,112	1,522	1,001	1,150	3,048
Beans	4,821	7,752	14,748	6,820	15,791
Wheat flour	6,911	7,832	5,939	5,983	7,903
Starch	150	1,307	2,409	3,295	5,006
Sesame seed	782	1,623	1,562	1,355	1,585
Others	3,970	4,082	3,937	3,303	5,702
II. Total grains, seeds, flours	53,261	67,761	56,011	41,149	91,842
Sugar	9,285	9,046	9,895	10,502	12,085
Confect., etc.	4,430	8,645	10,267	14,015	15,474
Total sugar and confect	13,715	17,691	20,162	24,517	27,559
Sake	1,578	1,975	1,983	2,670	3,429
Beer	2,386	803	946	971	924
Other beverages	982	882	832	914	1,145
Total beverages	4,946	3,660	3,761	4,555	5,498
Salt	1,465	2,247	2,488	3,205	2,984
Foodstuffs, other	14,170	27,995	32,814	40,174	57,823
Tobacco	2,713	5,831	4,841	1,718	77
III. Beverages, foodstuffs, tobacco	37,010	57,421	64,065	74,168	93,941
IV. Hides, skins, leather	1,869	4,203	5,868	10,968	6,197
V. Oils, fats, manufactures	17,968	38,215	44,510	42,384	44,926
VI. Chemicals, drugs, explosives	12,834	25,646	28,500	44,425	51,717
VII. Dyes, paints	3,045	5,870	6,733	8,645	11,793
Ginned cotton and wadding	7,222	25,331	34,982	22,266	10,852
Threads, yarns	9,853	5,738	3,828	1,775	305
Rayon	....	2,325	2,487	6,302	3,635
Staple fibre	....	....	....	10,409	8,263
Wild silk	9,278	4,463	6,619	5,722	5,775
Others	4,913	11,477	12,224	16,315	24,218
VIII. Total Yarn and Textile raw material	31,166	49,334	60,140	62,789	53,408
Cotton tissues	37,430	32,148	32,397	25,634	10,144
Woolen tissues	5,989	13,248	12,535	15,060	22,317
Hemp tissues	5,783	2,601	3,708	3,259	2,026
Silk (nat. art.) tissues	13,894	36,545	40,827	75,103	125,863
Fishing nets	2,480	2,789	3,541	4,749	3,874
Other tissues	5,555	10,986	12,072	17,795	19,940
IX. Total tissues	71,150	98,337	105,081	141,599	194,164
Underwear	5,035	13,766	14,281	18,141	22,340
Rubber shoes	2,891	5,494	4,415	4,339	5,881
Other clothing	15,509	26,952	27,286	40,878	52,341
X. Clothing	23,435	46,212	45,982	63,358	80,562
XI. Pulp, paper, books, paper mfr.	13,747	24,959	30,966	40,979	47,103
Coal	10,237	17,231	20,336	31,247	40,185
Cement	3,234	7,400	4,917	2,524	5,827
Others	8,924	22,312	26,102	30,389	48,424
XII. Total minerals, mfrs. pottery	22,395	46,943	51,355	64,160	94,436
XIII. Ores, metals	23,805	54,907	89,035	116,781	148,940
XIV. Metal manufactures	16,305	45,598	55,870	74,521	102,698
XV. Machines, vehicles	31,294	84,182	105,432	132,278	206,447
Timber	8,871	15,572	18,045	25,063	40,968
Bean cakes	7,818	9,173	3,567	3,072	2,517
Other fertilizers	16,110	32,218	24,763	35,584	23,931
Others	16,826	38,317	44,872	50,104	72,580
XVI. Total miscellaneous	49,625	95,280	91,247	113,823	139,996
XVII. Post parcels	12,000	13,726	16,140	18,074	19,523
XVIII. Passenger luggage	243	235	242	330	354
Total	421,930	760,324	859,328	1,052,917	1,383,924
Re-import	1,163	2,093	4,225	3,012	4,524
Grand Total	423,094	762,417	863,553	1,055,929	1,388,448

IMPORTS, QUANTITIES
(1,000 tons; unless stated otherwise)

	1929	1936	1937	1938	1939
Rice	99	26	25	8	49
Barley	6.9	76.0	35.2	2.1	18.9
Wheat	3.8	22.4	2.6	12.4	38.2
Awa	225	184	115	109	112
Kaoliang	4.1	1.2	0.8	0.5	18.0
Corn	1.3	28.0	8.9	0.7	2.4
Kibi	11.4	11.9	7.4	8.0	15.3
Beans	59	66	67	56	57
Wheat flour	38.5	41.1	26.6	25.2	30.2
Starch	0.7	0.7	1.3	1.8	1.9
Sugar	52.8	66.4	66.5	55.5	57.4
Sake, 1,000 *sho*	1,380	1,845	1,785	2,203	2,628
Beer, 1,000 lt.	5,844	2,556	1,983	2,670	1,403
Tobacco leaf	3.5	7.4	4.9	0.9	0.0
Salt	136	159	153	166	111
Soap	1.5	6.7	8.3	11.5	12.4
Cotton ginned, wadding	8.3	29.6	34.8	29.3	15.8
Wild silk	1.08	0.72	1.14	0.96	0.48
Cotton yarn	6.36	4.44	2.40	1.14	0.12
Artificial silk yarn	....	3.60	1.38	3.54	1.86
Cotton tissues, mill. sq. yd.	147.6[2]	163.6	135.1	93.0	18.0
Hemp tissues, mill. sq. yd.	13.3	8.4	8.9	5.9	2.3
Woolen tissues	4.2	10.0	7.7	8.5	8.5
Silk (pure) tissues	15.8	10.1	8.8	15.7	30.8
Artificial silk tissues	11.8	94.4	113.7	179.8	64.7
Staple fibre tissues	....	....	4.2	30.4	58.1
Fishing nets tons	1.06	1.63	1.99	2.36	1.54
"Foreign" paper	14.3	32.0	36.1	42.0	37.6
Coal	894.3	1,544	1,649	1,903	1,975
Cement	106	353	227	113	218
Window glass, million sq. ft.	5.9	13.6	14.4	13.2	12.9
Raw rubber, tons	1.68	4.06	4.34	2.65	0.62
Fertilizers	257	515	376	434	301
of which bean cakes	108	128	43	37	24
sulph. of amm.	....	104	80	116	....

Notes: [1] Year 1930.
[2] In 1928—174.2 million square yards and in 1930—168.6 million square yards.
Sources: (1) *Keizai Nenkan*, 1929-1940
(2) *Chosen Keizai Nempo*, 1940
(3) *Takumu Tokei*, 1938.
(4) *Nippon Boeki Seiran*, 1935.

EXTERNAL TRADE OF KOREA BY CATEGORIES
(as percentages of total)

	Exports					Imports				
	1929	1936	1937	1938	1939	1929	1936	1937	1938	1939
Living plants and anim.	1.0	0.8	0.8	1.0	1.7	0.2	0.2	0.2	0.2	0.4
Cereals, flours, seeds...	50.6	47.5	39.3	40.2	21.0	12.6	8.9	6.5	3.9	6.6
Foodst., bever., tobacco	9.8	6.4	6.3	6.4	9.1	8.8	7.5	7.5	7.1	6.8
Hides, skins, mfrs.....	1.3	0.8	1.0	1.5	0.8	0.4	0.6	0.7	1.0	0.4
Oils, fats............	included into chem.			3.7	5.3	4.3	5.0	5.2	4.0	3.2
Chemicals...........	3.2	5.4	7.4	2.6	3.2	3.0	3.4	3.3	4.2	3.7
Dyes, paints.........	included into chem.			0.1	0.2	0.7	0.8	0.8	0.8	0.9
Yarn, thread........	included into tissues			4.8	6.0	7.4	6.5	7.0	6.0	3.9
Cotton tissues.......						8.9	4.2	3.8	2.5	0.7
Woolen tissues.......						1.4	1.7	1.4	1.4	1.6
Hemp tissues........						1.4	0.3	0.4	0.3	0.1
Silk tissues..........						3.3	4.8	4.8	7.1	9.1
Other tissues........						1.9	1.8	1.8	2.1	1.8
Tissues, all..........	16.2	10.5	13.3	5.3	6.1	16.9	12.8	12.2	13.4	13.3
Clothing............	included into tissues			1.6	2.3	5.6	6.1	5.3	6.0	5.8
Pulp, paper, mfrs.....	incl. misc.	0.9	1.7	2.1	2.2	3.3	3.3	3.6	3.9	3.4
Minerals, mfrs.......	included into ores			3.3	3.7	5.3	6.2	6.0	6.1	6.8
Ores, metals.........	6.4	13.8	16.4	13.3	18.1	5.6	7.2	10.4	11.1	10.8
Metal mfrs..........	included into ores			1.0	2.1	3.9	6.0	6.5	7.1	7.4
Machinery, vehicles...	included into ores			2.6	4.4	7.4	11.1	12.3	12.6	14.9
Pottery, glass........	included into misc.			0.2	0.4	included probably into minerals				
Miscellaneous........	8.4	12.4	12.0	9.0	11.9	11.8	12.6	10.6	10.9	10.3
Parcel post..........	3.1	1.5	1.8	1.3	1.5	2.8	1.8	1.9	1.7	1.4
Total...............	100.0	100.0	100.0	100.0	100.0	100.0	100.0	100.0	100.0	100.0

APPENDIX V

LIST OF EQUIVALENTS OF GEOGRAPHICAL NAMES IN KOREA IN JAPANESE AND KOREAN LANGUAGES

Japanese	*Korean*
Agochi	Aoji
Ampen	Anbyon
Angaku	Anak
Batsudo	Poltong
Chinkai	Chinhae
Chinkai Wan	Chinhae Man
Chinnampo	Chinnamp'o
Chirei	Chirye
Chohakusan	Changpaiksan
Chosen	Choson
Choshinco	Changjingang [River]
Chosui	Changsu
Chumanko	Ch'ungmangang [River]
Chusan Wan	Ch'uksan Man [Bay]
Chusei Hokudo	Ch'ungch'ong Pukto [Province]
Chusei Nando	Ch'ungch'ong Namdo [Province]
Chushu	Ch'ungju
Daidoko	Taedonggang [River]
Dokushin	Tokchin
Eian	Yongan
Eido	Yongdong
Eiju	Yongun P'yong Wan [Plain]
Eiko	Yongnung
Eisen	Yongch'on
Eitoho	Yongdungp'o
Eitoku	Yongdok
Fusan	Pusan
Fusenko	Pujon Gang [River]
Gensan	Wonsan
Gensh'u	Wonju

APPENDIX V

Japanese	Korean
Gishu	Uiju
Gunzan	Kunsan
Hakuto	Paektusan [Mountain]
Hanhen	Panbyonchon [River]
Heian Hakudo	P'yongan Pukto [Province]
Heian Nando	P'yongan Namdo [Province]
Heijo	P'yongyang
Hojoko	Posonggang [River]
Hokusei	Pukch'ong
Jijoko	Chasonggang [River]
Jinsen	Inch'on [also Chemulpo]
Josenko	Songch'ongang [River]
Joshin	Songjin
Junten	Soonchun
Kaijo	Kaesong [also Songdo]
Kainan	Haenam
Kainei	Hoi-lyong
Kaishu	Haeju
Kakuzan	Kwaksan
Kampei	Hamp'yong
Kanjo	Kansong
Kanko	Hangang [River]
Kanko	Hamheung [City]
Kankyo Hokudo	Hamgyong Pukto [Province]
Kankyo Nando	Hamgyong Namdo [Province]
Kansho	Hamch'ang
Keikido	Kyonggido [Province]
Keisho Hokudo	Kyongsang Pukto [Province]
Keisho Nando	Kyongsang Namdo [Province]
Keishu	Kyongju
Kenjiho	Kyomipo
Keishu	Kyongju
Kinko	Keumgang [River]
Kogendo	Kangwondo [Province]
Kokaido	Hwanghaedo [Province]
Kokei	Kanggyong
Komosan	Komusan
Konan	Hungnam
Kongo	Kumgang san [Diamond Mountains]

Japanese	Korean
Koshu	Kwangju
Koshu	Kongju
Keijo	Kyongsong [also Seoul]
Kinko	Kumgang
Kunsan	Kunsan
Kunsen	Kunson
Koryo	Kwangnyang [Bay]
Kyosai	Kojyei [Island]
Mampochin	Manp'ojin
Moppo	Mokpo
Mosan	Musan
Naijo	Naesonch'on [River]
Oryokko	Amnokkang [River, also the Yalu]
Rakusan Wan	Naksan Man [Bay]
Rakutoko	Naktonggang [River]
Ranan	Nanam
Rashin	Najin
Rashin Wan	Najin Man [Bay]
Reisan	Yongsan
Reiseiko	Yesonggang [River]
Reisen	Yech'on
Riri	Iri
Ryuzan	Yongsan
Sainei	Chairyung
Saishu	Chejudo [also Quelpart Island]
Sanchoku	Samch'ok
Sanroshin	Samnangjin
Seisenko	Ch'ongch'ongang [River]
Seishin	Ch'ongjin
Seishu	Chyongju
Sensen	Syonchyong
Senshinco	Somjingang [River]
Sh'ariin	Sariwon
Shinanshu	Sinanju
Shingishu	Sinuiju
Shinshu	Chinju
Shohakusan	Syopaiksan [Mountains]
Shojo	Changsong
Shunsen	Chyungchyon

APPENDIX V 313

Japanese	*Korean*
Suian	Syuan
Suigen	Suwon
Taiden	Taejon
Taihakusan	Taipaiksan [Mountains]
Taikyu	Taegu
Tashito	Tasado [Island]
Tetsugen	Ch'orwon
Tetsuzan	Ch'olsan
Toei	Tongyeng
Tomanko	Tumangang [also Tumen River]
Torai	Tongnai
Unzan	Unsan
Urusan	Ulsan
Utsuryoto	Ullungdo [also Dagelet Island]
Yujo	Susong
Yuki	Unggi
Zenra Hakudo	Cholla Pukto [Province]
Zenra Nando	Cholla Namdo [Province]
Zenshu	Chonju

Korean names	*Japanese equivalents*
Amnokkang	Oryokko [the Yalu River]
Anak	Angaku
Anbyon	Ampen
Aoji	Agochi
Chairyung	Sainei
Ch'anghungni	Shokori
Changjingang	Choshinko [River]
Changpaiksan	Chohakusan
Changsong	Shojo
Changsu	Chosui
Chasonggang	Jijoko [River]
Chejudo	Saishu [also Quelpart island]
Chemulpo [also Inch'on]	Jinsen
Chinhae	Chinkai
Chinhae Man	Chinkai Wan
Chinju	Shinshu
Chinnamp'o	Chinnampo
Chirye	Chirei

Korean names	Japanese equivalents
Ch'olsan	Tetsuzan
Cholla Namdo	Zenra Nando [Province]
Cholla Pukto	Zenra Hakudo [Province]
Ch'ongch'ongang	Seisenko [River]
Ch'ongjin	Seishin
Chonju	Zenshu
Ch'orwon	Tetsugen
Choson	Chosen
Ch'ungch'ong Namdo	Chusei Nando [Province]
Ch'ungch'ong Pukto	Chusei Hokudo [Province]
Ch'ungju	Chushu
Ch'ungmangang	Chumanko [River]
Chyongju	Seishu
Chyungchyon	Shunsen
Haeju	Kaishu
Haenam	Kainan
Hamch'ang	Kansho
Hamheung	Kanco [City]
Hamgyong Namdo	Kankyo Nando [Province]
Hamgyong Pukto	Kamkyo Kokudo [Province]
Hamp'yong	Kampei
Hangang	Kanko [River]
Hoi-lyong	Kainei
Hungnam	Konan
Hwanghaedo	Kokaido [Province]
Inch'on [also Chemulpo]	Jinsen
Iri	Riri
Kaesong [also Songdo]	Kaijo
Kanggyong	Kokei
Kangwondo	Kogendo [Province]
Kansong	Kanjo
Keumgang	Kinko
Kojyei	Kyosai [Island]
Komusan	Komosan
Kongju	Koshu
Kumgang	Kinko
Kumgang san	Kongo [Diamond Mountains]
Kunsan	Gunzan
Kunsan	Kunsan
Kunson	Kunsen

Korean names	Japanese equivalents
Kwaksan	Kakuzan
Kwangnyang	Koryo [Bay]
Kwanju	Koshu
Kyomipo	Kenjiho
Kyonggido	Keikido [Province]
Kyongju	Keishu
Kyongsang Namdo	Keisho Nando [Province]
Kyongsang Pukto	Keisho Hokudo [Province]
Kyongsong [also Seoul]	Keijo
Manp'ojin	Mampochin
Mokpo	Moppo
Musan	Mosan
Naesong ch'on	Naijo [River]
Naksan Man	Rakusan Wan [Bay]
Naktonggang	Rakutoko [River]
Najin	Rashin
Najin Man	Rashin Wan [Bay]
Nanam	Ranan
Paektusan	Hakuto [Mountain]
Panbyonchon	Hanhen [River]
Poltong	Batsudo
Posonggang	Hojoko [River]
Pujon Gang	Fusenko [River]
Pukcho'ng	Hokusei
Pusan	Fusan
P'yongan Namdo	Heian Nando [Province]
P'yongan Pukto	Heian Hakudo [Province]
P'yongyang	Heijo
Samch'ok	Sanchoku
Samnangjin	Sanroshin
Sariwon	Shariin
Seoul [also Kyongsong]	Keijo
Sinanju	Shinanshu
Sinuiju	Shingishu
Somjingang	Senshinko [River]
Songch'ongang	Josenko [River]
Songdo [also Kaesong]	Kaijo
Songjin	Joshin
Soonchun	Junten
Susong	Yujo

Korean names	Japanese equivalents
Suwon	Suigen
Syonchyong	Sensen
Syopaiksan	Shohakusan
Syuan	Suian
Taedonggang	Daidoko [River]
Taegu	Taikyu
Taejon	Taiden
Taipaiksan	Taihakusan
Tasado	Tashito [Island]
Tokchin	Dokushin
Tongnai	Torai
Tongyeng	Toei
Tumangang	Tomanko [the Tumen River]
Uiju	Gishu
Ullungdo	Utsuryoto
Ulsan	Urusan
Unggi	Yuki
Unsan	Unzan
Wonju	Genshu
Wonsan	Gensan
Yech'on	Reisen
Yesonggang	Reiseiko [River]
Yongan	Eian
Yongch'on	Eisen
Yongdok	Eitoku
Yongdong	Eido
Yongdungp'o	Eitoho
Yongnung	Eiko
Yongsan	Reisan
Yongsan	Ryuzan
Yongun P'yongwan	Eiju [Heigen]

BIBLIOGRAPHY

Akagi, R. H., *Japan's Foreign Relations,* published by Hokyseido Press, Tokyo, 1936, xiv—560 pp.

Akiyama, Kenzo, *The History of Nippon,* translated by Toshiro Shima nouchi, published by Kokusai Bunka Shinkokai (the Society for International Cultural Relations) Tokyo, 1941, viii—279 pp.

Allen, H. N., *Things Korean,* published by Revell Co., New York, 1908, 256 pp.

Allen, G., Gordon M., Penrose, E., Schumpeter, E., *The Industrialization of Japan and Manchukuo, 1939-40.* Edited by E. Schumpeter. The Macmillan Company, 1940, 944 pp.

Azbelev, I. P., *Yaponiya i Koreya* [Japan and Korea, in Russian] published by A. Levenson, Moscow, 1895, 276 pp.

Bain, H. B., *Ores and Industry in the Far East,* published by the Council on Foreign Relations, New York, 1933, 288 pp.

Bank of Chosen, *Economic History of Chosen,* Seoul, 1920, 266 pp.

Bank of Chosen, *Pictorial Chosen and Manchuria,* Seoul, Oct. 1919, 316 pp.

Bergman, Sten, *In Korean Wilds and Villages,* translated from Swedish by Frederic Whyte, published by J. Gifford Ltd., London, 1938, 232 pp.

Bishop, Isabella Lucy, *Korea and Her Neighbors,* two volumes, published by J. Murray, London, 1898.

Bland, J. O. P., *China, Japan, and Korea,* published by Heinemann, London, 1921, x—327 pp.

Brown, Arthur J., *The Mastery of the Far East,* published by C. Scribner's Sons, New York, 1919, ix—3-671 pp.

Brunner de, Schweinitz, E., Professor, *Rural Korea,* published by the International Missionary Council, New York, 1928, 120 pp.

Byas, Hugh, *Government by Assassination,* published by Alfred A. Knopf, New York, 1942, 369 pp.

Carnegie Endowment for International Peace, *Korea: Treaties and Agreements,* Washington, 1921, viii—68 pp.

Carpenter, F. G., *Japan and Korea,* published by Doubleday Page and Co., Garden City, New York, 1926, xiv—306 pp.

Chamberlin, W. H., *Japan Over Asia,* published by Little, Brown and Co., Boston, 1937, viii—395 pp.

Chisholm, W. H., *Vivid Experiences in Korea by a Missionary Doctor,* published by the Bible Institute Colportage Association, Chicago, 1938, 136 pp.

Chosen Keizai Nempo, [Korea's Economic Annual, in Japanese], 1939, published by Kaizosha, Tokyo, March 1939, pp. 454-66-45.

Chosen Keizai Nempo, [Korea's Economic Annual, in Japanese]. 1940, published by Kaizosha, Tokyo, Sept. 1940, pp. 575-52-47.

Chosen Kinyu Kumiai Rengokai, Chosa ka [Research Division of the Korean Credit Cooperatives' League] *Chosen Kinyu Kumiai Nenkan, 1935*, [the Yearbook of the Korean Credit Cooperatives for 1935, in Japanese] published by the Chosen Kinyu Kumiai Rengokai in Keijo (Seoul), March 1935, 420 pp.

Chosen Nenkan, 1941, [Korea Yearbook], published by Keijo Nipponsha, Keijo (Seoul), October 1940, 734 pp.

Chung, Henry, Dr., *The Case of Korea*, published by F. H. Revell Co., New York, 1921, 365 pp.

Chung, Henry, Dr., *Korean Treaties*, published by H. S. Nichols Inc., New York, 1919, 3-xii—226 pp.

Clement, Ernest W., *Handbook of Modern Japan*, published by A. C. McClurg and Co., Chicago, sixth ed., 1905, 423 pp.

Clyde, P. H. Professor, *A History of the Modern and Contemporary Far East*, published by Prentice Hall Inc., New York, 1937, xix—858 pp.

Commissioner of Customs, *Korea, Returns of Trade and Trade Reports*, Annual, published in Seoul.

Dainippon Teikoku Tokei Nenkan, [The Statistical Yearbook of the Japanese Empire in Japanese language], 1935-1939 issues.

Drake, H. B., *Korea of the Japanese*, published by John Lane, London, 1930, 225 pp.

Financial and Economic Annual of Japan, 1920-1935.

Fischer, E. C., *Beobachtungen auf Reisen in Korea und der Mandschurei* [Observations on Travel in Korea and Manchuria, in German], Abdruecke aus den Mitteilungen der Geographischen Gesellschaft in Wien, 1931, 20 pp.

Gale, J. S., *Korea in Transition*, published by Eaton and Mains, New York, 1909, 270 pp.

Goldschmidt, Richard, Professor, *Neu Japan* [New Japan, in German], published by J. Springer, Berlin, 1927, vi—303 pp.

Government-General of Chosen (before annexation—Resident-General, Seoul, Korea,) *Annual Reports on Administration of Chosen*, 1907-1936-37.

Government-General of Chosen, *Chosen in Pictures*, 58 plates, 1921.

Government-General of Chosen, *Chosen Today*, 1930, 60 pp.

Government-General of Chosen, *The New Administration of Chosen*, July 1921, 76 pp., no place of publication is given.

Government-General of Chosen, *Results of Three Years' Administration of Chosen since Annexation*, January 1914, 66-95 pp.

BIBLIOGRAPHY

Government-General of Chosen, *Revised Educational Regulations*, Keijo (Seoul), 1923, 105 pp.

Government-General of Chosen, *Thriving Chosen*, Keijo (Seoul), 1935, 94 pp.

Gowen, H. H., Professor, *Asia, a Short History*, published by Little, Brown and Co., Boston, 1938, 463 pp.

Graves, J. W., *The Renaissance of Korea*, published by P. J. Jaison and Co., Philadelphia, 1920, 74 pp.

Griffis, W. E., *Corea, the Hermit Nation*, published by C. Scribner's Sons, New York, last 8th edition, 1907, 512 pp.

Hamilton, Angus, *Korea* [with Terauchi], published by J. B. Millet Co., Boston and Tokyo, 1910, xvi—328 pp.

Hishida, Seiji, *Japan among the Great Powers*, published by Longman, Green and Co., London, 1940, 400 pp.

Hishimoto, *Chosenbei no Kenkyu* [Inquiry into Korean Rice, in Japanese], published by Chigura Co., Tokyo, September 1938, 819 pp.

Hulbert, H. B., *The Passing of Korea*, published by Doubleday, Page and Co., New York, 1906, xii—473 pp.

International Institute of Agriculture, *International Yearbook of Agricultural Statistics, 1938-1939*, Rome, 1939, xxxvi—1,033.

Ireland, Alleyne, *The New Korea*, published by E. Dutton and Co., New York, 1936, 352 pp.

Ito, S., *Chosen ni okeru Katei Kogyo Chosa* [Investigation of Korean Household Industry, in Japanese], published by Keijo Shokokai, Keijo (Seoul), March 1937, 217 pp.

Japan Chronicle, *The Korean Conspiracy Trial*, published by Japan Chronicle, Kobe, Japan, 1912, 136 pp.

Japan Economic Federation, the Research Division, *An Inquiry into National Income of Japan*, published by the Japan Economic Federation, Tokyo, 1939, 116 pp.

Keijo (Seoul) Chamber of Commerce and Industry, *Tokei Nempo* [The Annual Statistical Report, in Japanese], Keijo, September 1937, 173 pp.

Kendall, C. W. *The Truth about Korea*, published by the Korean National Association, San Francisco, 2nd edition, 1919, 104 pp.

Kennan, G., Three articles published in the *Outlook*, a magazine published in New York. "The Japanese in Korea," "Korea: a degenerated state," "The Korean People: the product of a decayed civilization."

Kim, Helen, *Rural Education for the Regeneration of Korea* [Columbia thesis], New York, 1931, 124 pp.

King, F. K., *Farmers of Forty Centuries*, published by Mrs. F. H. King, Madison, Wisconsin, 1911, 441 pp.

Kojima, Seiichi, *Sen-man-shi Shinko Keizai* [Rising Economy of

Korea, Manchuria and China, in Japanese], published by Shun shusha, Tokyo, February, 1938, 4—400 pp.

Kokusei Gurafu [The State of the Nation in Diagrams], a monthly publication in Tokyo in Japanese, 1936-1941.

Korean Commission to America and Europe, *Korea Must Be Free*, New York, 1930, 32 pp.

Korean Student Federation of North America: *Korean Student Bulletin*, a magazine, 1926-1939.

Korf, N. A., *Voennyi Obzor Severnoi Korei* [Military Survey of Northern Korea, in Russian], St. Petersburg, 1904, 256 pp.

Ladd, G. Trumbull, "The Annexation of Korea, an essay in benevolent assimilation," an article in Yale Review [a magazine published at New Haven], July 1912, pp. 639-656.

Ladd, G. Trumbull, *In Korea with Marquis Ito*, published by C. Scribner's Sons, New York, 1908, 477 pp.

Lee, H. K., *Land Utilization and Rural Economy in Korea*, published by Kelly and Walsh Ltd., Shanghai, 1936, xii—289 pp.

Longford, J. H., *The Story of Korea*, published by Fisher Unwinn, London, 1911, 400 pp.

McCune, Shannon, *Climate of Korea: Climatic Elements*, 1941, 33 pp.

McCune, Shannon, "Climatic Regions of Korea and Their Economy," an article in the *Geographical Review*, Jan. 1941, pp. 45-99.

McKenzie, F. A., *The Tragedy of Korea*, published by Hodder and Stoughton, London, 1908, xii—312 pp.

McKenzie, F. A., *Korea's Fight for Freedom*, published by Simpkin, Marshall and Co., London, 1920, 320 pp.

Ministerstvo Finanstvo [Ministry of Finance, Russia], *Opisanie Korea* [Description of Korea, in Russian], St. Petersburg, 1900, three volumes in two.

Miyake, Seiki, *Shinko Kontsuerun Tokuhon* [Rising Concerns Reader, in Japanese], published by Shunshusha, Tokyo, May 1937, pp. 8—364.

Moriya, S., Director of General Affairs Department, Government-General of Chosen, *Development of Chosen and Necessity of Spiritual Enlightment*, 1924, pp. 41.

Moulton, Harold G., Professor, *Japan, an Economic and Financial Appraisal*, published by the Brookings Institution, Washington, D. C., 1931, xix—645 pp.

Nasu, Shiroshi, Dr., *Land Utilization in Japan*, Tokyo, 1939, pp. 4-262—6.

Nippon Gakujutsu Shinkokai [Japanese Society for the Advancement of Science], *Chosen Beikoku Keizairon* [Economics of Korean Rice, in Japanese], published by Iwanami Co., Tokyo, April 1937, 147 pp.

Nippon Gakujutsu Shinkokai [Japanese Society for the Advancement of Science] *Chosen bei Seisampi ni okeru Chosa* [Investigation Concerning Cost of Production of Korean Rice, in Japanese], published by Iwanami Co., Tokyo, June, 1936, 51 pp.

Nippon Shimbun Nenkan [Japan Newspapers Yearbook, in Japanese], 1939, 1940.

Okurasho [Ministry of Finance], *Teikoku Yosan Teiyo* [A Summary of the Budget of the Empire, in Japanese], Tokyo, August 1940, 540 pp.

Paik, L. G., Dr., *The History of Protestant Missions in Korea, 1902-1910*, published by the Union Christian College Press, Pyeng Yang, Korea, 1929.

Percival, Lowel, *Chosen, the Land of the Morning Calm*, published by Ticknar and Co., Boston, 1886, x—412 pp.

Popov, K., *Ekonomika Yaponii* [Japan's Economy, in Russian], published by the Sots.-Ek. Izdatel'stvo, Moscow, 1936, 550 pp.

Resident-General, Seoul, Korea, *The Material Progress of Korea for the Last Five Years, 1905-1910*, Seoul, 1910, iv-iii—52 pp.

Robinson, A. H. and McCune, Shannon, "Notes on a Physiographic Diagram of Tyosen," an article in the *Geographical Review*, Oct. 1941, pp. 653-658.

Sands, W. F., *Undiplomatic Memories*, published by Whittelesey House, McGraw Hill Book Co., New York, 1930, 5—328 pp.

Seka i Nenkan, 1939, [World Yearbook, in Japanese], published by Nippon Kokusai Mondai Chosakai, Tokyo, May 1939, 1476 pp.

Shirushi, Sadanaoo, *Chosen no Nogyo Chitai* [Korea's Agricultural Regions, in Japanese], published by Seikatsusha, Tokyo, November 1940, 212 pp.

Sieroszewski, W. L., *Korea, Land und Volk* [Korea, Land and People, translated from Polish into German by Stefani Goldenring] published by Verlag Continent [T. Gutman], Berlin, 1905, vii—302 pp.

Smith, E. H., *The Other Side of the Korean Question* [re-published from the Japan Advertiser], Seoul, 1920, 266 pp.

Steiger, G. Nye, *A History of the Far East*, published by Ginn and Co., Boston, 1936, 928 pp.

Takahashi, K., *Gendai Chosen Keizairon* [Contemporary Korean Economy, in Japanese], published by Chigura Co., Tokyo, April, 1935, 12—593 pp.

Takeuchi, Tatsuji, *War and Diplomacy in the Japanese Empire*, published by Doubleday, Doran and Co., Garden City, New York, 1935, 505 pp.

Takumu Daijin Kambo, [Office of the Overseas Minister], *Takumu Tokei* [Statistics of Colonies, in Japanese], 1938, Tokyo, July 1940, 207 pp.

Takumu Daijin Kambo [Office of the Overseas Minister], *Takumu Yoran* [A survey of Colonies, in Japanese] 1939, Tokyo, September, 1940 pp. 720—13.

Teikoku Nokai [Imperial Agricultural Society], *Nogyo Nenkan, 1941* [Yearbook of Agriculture, in Japanese], published by Teikoku Nokai, Tokyo, January 1941, 812 pp.

Tisdale, Alice, "A Korean Highroad," an article in *Asia*, Sept. 1920.

Togawa, Kantaro, *Chosen Shin Nogyo Tokuhon* [Korean New Agricultural Reader, in Japanese], published by Chosen Komin Kyoikukai, Keijo, [Seoul], June, 1938, 249 pp.

Toyo Keizai [Oriental Economist], a weekly, published in Japanese in Tokyo, 1936-1941.

Toyo Keizai Shimposha [The Oriental Economist Co.], *Keizai Nenkan* [Economic Yearbook, in Japanese], 1936-1941, Tokyo.

Toyo Keizai Shimposha [Oriental Economist Co.], *Nippon Boeki Seiran* [Survey of Japan's Trade, in Japanese and English], Tokyo, November, 1935, pp. 48-43—708.

Trautz, F. M., *Japan, Korea and Formosa*, published by Westerman, New York, 1931, 256 pp.

Treat, Payson J., Professor, *The Far East, a Political and Diplomatic History*, published by Harper and Brothers, New York and London, 1928, x—549 pp.

Underwood (Horton), L., *Fifteen Years among the Top-knots*, published by the American Tract Society, Boston, 2nd edition, 1908, xviii—271 pp.

Urquart, E. J., *Glimpses of Korea*, published by the Pacific Press Publishing Association, Mount View, California, 1923, 103 pp.

Van Buskirk, James Dale, *Korea, Land of the Dawn*, published by the Missionary Education Movement of the U. S. and Canada, New York, 1931, xiii—200 pp.

Vantier, Claire, and Frandin, H., *En Coree* [In Korea, in French], published by C. Delagrave, Paris, 1904, 188 pp.

Vinacke, H. M., Professor, *A History of the Far East in Modern Times*, published by Alfred A. Knopf, New York, 1928, xx—479 pp.

Wagner, El C., *Korea, the Old and the New*, published by F. H. Reve and Co., New York, 1931, 160 pp.

Watana be, Kijiro, *Nissei Nichiro Senso Shiwa*, [History of Sino-Japanese and Russo-Japanese Wars, in Japanese], published by Chigura Co., Tokyo, August 1937, pp. 5-9—410.

INDEX

Afforestation, 13, 50, 51-52, 217-218
Agochi, 133, 165
Agricultural capital, 173-175; education, 262-263; legislation, 116; machinery, 102-103, 151-158; population, 74, 77-79, 291; production, 84-88, 93-94, 287, 295, 297-298; products, 188, 204, 229; system, 5, 18 *footnote*
Agriculture, 14, 50, 84-122, 291-299; Japanese policy, 61, 92-94, 213, 217-218, 221, 240, 243, 279; *see also* Dry fields and Paddy fields; Farm and Farmers
Air transport, 121, 217, 221, 235
Alcohol, 119 *footnote*, 152, 164, 167-168, 181, 214
Aluminum, 140, 143-144
Americans, 32, 34-40, 48-49, 57, 70, 114-115; capital of, 144, 146-147, 201
Amusements, 271
Anti-aircraft defense, 258
Anto, 190
Antung, 170, 188
Apples, 21, 305-306
Area, 8, 276
Armament works, 149
Army, 29, 37, 42, 211, 217-219, 290
Assembly, freedom of, 48, 61
Awa, see Millet

Bamboo, 22; ware, 69, 152
Bank of Chosen, 201, 203, 204, 206
Banking, 38 *footnote*, 173, 174, 175, 201-209
Barley, 21-22, 87, 118-119, 295, 297, 307
Barytes, 144
Bean cakes, 307-308; oil, 164
Beans, 87, 119, 229, 295, 297, 305-308
Beer, 167-168, 230, 307
Benzine, 214
Beverages, 167-168, 181, 214, 215, 230, 234, 305, 307-309
Bicycles, 192-193, 235
Bin, Da-shoku, 283
Black market, 204
Boats, 151, 158
Books, 176, 270, 307

Bread, 152, 167
Brewing, 173, 174, 176
Bricks, 151, 159
Briquettes, 160
Buckwheat, 307
Buddhism, 23, 24, 273, 289
Bumpei, 143
Business enterprises, 172-177, 222-224, 226 *footnote*, 227; restrictions on, 52, 173-174; taxes on, 154, 155, 214, 223

Candy, 152, 167, 169, 230, 307
Canned goods, 167, 169, 230, 305-306
Capital, foreign, 144, 146-147, 201, 236; industrial, 152-153; Korean, 171-177; *see also* Japanese holdings and Landownership
Carbide, 163
Carts, 151, 192-193
Casks, 152
Cattle, *see* Livestock
Cement, 144, 235, 303, 306-308
Censorship, 258
Central Council, 46-47, 243-245
Ceramics, 151, 158-159, 173, 174, 183, 300-301, 303
Cereals, 21-22, 87, 89, 118, 119 *and footnote*, 203, 229, 234, 276, 295, 297, 305-309; *see also* Barley, Beans, Rice, etc.
Chemicals, 150, 151, 159-163, 173, 175, 176, 183, 188, 234, 300-301, 305, 307, 309
Chemulpo, *see* Jinsen
Chi-ho, Yun, 53-54
Children, 155, 182-184, 261, 264-270, 271 *footnote*
China, 23, 25, 26, 27, 81, 82, 227-228, 289
Chinese, 23, 82, 291
Chinkai, 189, 194
Chinnampo, 80, 143, 144, 163, 169, 189, 194-195
Chiri Zan, 14
Choko, 143
Chokusan Ginko, 204, 207

323

324 INDEX

Chosen-Manchurian Colonization Corporation, 82
Chosinko, 136-137
Chotin, 190
Christianity, 53, 266, 273, 275, 289
Chuchu, 190
Chusei, 74, 145, 190, 302
Chusuin, see Central Council
Cinemas, 271
Cities, 61, 80, 217-220, 222, 225, 248, 255
Civil liberties, 61-62, 246
Civil Service, *see* Public Service
Climate, 5, 9, 14-22
Clothing, 305, 307, 309
Coal, 5, 131-133, 134, 159, 170, 276, 284
Coke, 160, 165
Colleges, 243, 261, 263
Commerce, 77, 78, 79, 173, 174, 175, 287
Commodity prices, 292-293
Communications, 4, 6, 77, 78, 79, 178, 193-200, 212, 214, 217-218, 221, 284
Communism, 62, 64-65, 67, 257
Confectionary, 152, 167, 169, 230, 307
Confucianism, 23, 47, 274
Conscription, 121
Construction, 178, 217-219, 221
Conveyances, 173, 183, 192-193, 223, 235, 306-307
Cooperatives, 286-287, 289; credit, 174, 204, 207, 278
Copper, 144, 145, 306
Corn, 169, 307
Corporations, 172-177; *see also* Business enterprises
Cotton, 5, 21-22, 93, 152 *footnote*, 154, 156, 164, 181, 232-233, 235, 303, 305-309
Counties, 248, 255
Courts, 217-219, 251-253, 255
Cows, 305-306
Crime and punishment, 47, 243, 246, 252-256
Crop failures, 59, 70, 119, 230
Crops, *see* Agriculture
Culture and Customs, 61, 250, 271 *footnote*
Currency, 37, 39, 50-51, 121, 140, 201-203, 206, 210
Customs duties, 214

Dagelet, 14
Daido River, 10
Daidoko, 188
Dentists, 260
Diamond Mountains, 13, 190

Diseases, 259, 261
Domestic service, 77
Donkeys, 103-104
Drainage, 19
Drugs, *see* Medicines
Dry fields, 74, 92 *footnote*, 106, 111, 291, 296-297
Dyes, 235, 307, 309

Earthenware, 303; *see also* Ceramics
Education, 4, 37, 63, 68, 217-220, 223, 248, 261-270
Eian, 133, 165
Eisen, 186, 188, 189
Eitoho, 154, 159, 168
Electricity, 38 *footnote*, 134-139, 165, 173, 174, 175, 176, 181, 183, 235, 300-301
Employment, 68, 223, 264 *footnote*
Enamelware, 159, 235
Engineering works, 223-224
European capital, 146-147
Eusan, 10
Experimental stations, 217-218, 221, 262
Explosives, *see* Gunpowder
Exports, 5-6, 92, 102, 129, 155, 159, 164, 166, 226-233, 305-306, 309

Farmers, 50, 68-69, 79, 96, 98, 102, 105, 107-121, 151, 181-182, 204, 208, 243, 291, 294
Farms, number of, 86; size of, 113, 291, 294
Fats, 151, 160, 305-307, 309
Fertilizers, 5, 100-102, 119 *and footnote*, 121, 128, 151, 160-163, 203, 235, 236, 306-308
Fiber, staple, 155-156, 307-308
Fir forests, 21
Firecracker, 69
Firefields, *see* Kaden
Fish, 5, 127-128, 181, 230, 276, 305-306; products, 128-130, 151, 152, 164, 169, 175, 188, 230, 305-306
Fishing, 13, 77, 79, 84, 127, 173-175, 178, 214, 223; nets, 235, 308
Flax, 155
Flogging, 47
Floods, 18, 217-218
Flour, 152, 167, 169, 176, 229, 305-307
Fluorspar, 144
Food, 94, 117-119, 129, 150-152, 166-169, 173, 176, 180-181, 183, 203, 229-231, 236, 300-301, 307-309
Footwear, 121, 152, 160, 204

INDEX

Foreign capital, 53, 144, 146-147, 201, 236; trade, 26, 37, 38 *and footnote*, 164, 227-237, 288, 305-309
Forest products, 13, 84, 123-127, 188, 236, 300-301; *see also* Lumber and Paper
Forests and forestry, 13, 21, 29, 50-52, 77, 84, 106 *footnote*, 116, 123-127, 134, 173-175, 212-213, 216-218, 243; tax on, 223
Formalin, 165
Formosa, 4, 6, 102
Fowl, 103-104
Franchise, 61, 247-248, 282
Freight, 186-188, 191
Fruit, 230, 305
Fu, see Cities
Funei, 137
Furniture, 152
Fusan, 5, 6, 80, 81, 153, 155, 164-166, 170, 186, 188-189, 190 *footnote*, 191, 303
Fusenko, 136

Gas, 170-171, 183, 300-301
Gasoline, 165
Gendarmes, 47, 63
Genshu, 137, 186
Genzan, 9, 16-19, 80, 81, 158, 186, 189, 190, 194, 196, 198
Geography, 6, 8-21
Germany, 227-228
Ginseng, 215, 305
Girls, 155; selling of, 271 *footnote*
Glass, 144, 145, 159, 235, 306
Glycerine, 235, 305-306
Goats, 103-104
Gold, 5, 140, 142, 145, 156, 157, 174, 217-218, 236-237, 284, 306
Gota, 152
Government, *see* Japanese Administration and Korean Government
Government loans, 216
Governor-General, 46, 59, 238-239
Grain Grading Stations, 217-218, 221
Graphite, 144, 306
Grass ware, 152
Great Britain, 32, 227-228, 289-290
Gunny bags, 235
Gunpowder, 163-164, 235, 236, 307
Gunsen, 194
Gunzan, 80, 81, 155, 165, 189

Han River, 8
Harbors, 38 *footnote*

Hasegawa, Marshal, 54, 56, 62, 245
Hayashi, Gonsuke, 31
Health services, 4, 54, 63, 217, 218, 223-224, 258-261
Heian, 74, 132, 145, 302, 303
Heijo, 10, 14-19, 80, 81, 132, 155, 158, 164, 165, 170, 171, 189, 190 *footnote*, 254, 303
Hemp, 151, 154, 155, 181, 232-233, 309
Hides, 305-307, 309
Hideyoshi, Toyotomi, 24
History, 3, 6, 23-71
Horses, 103-104
Hosan, 158
Hospitals, 4, 54, 63, 212, 220, 259-260, 266
House of Li, 27-28, 33, 44, 45, 217-219, 281
Household industry, 69, 105, 149-152, 156, 157, 158, 166, 167, 172

Imperial University, 217-218, 220, 243, 263-264, 266
Imports, 129, 226-237
Income tax, 214-215, 223
Independence, 6-7, 25, 28, 29-33, 39, 246, 276-290; movement for, 38, 54-58, 62, 64-65, 67, 279-280
India, 227
Industrial Bank, 204, 207
Industrial schools, 261
Industry, 38 *footnote*, 52, 63, 69, 77, 78, 79, 80. 84, 85, 120 *footnote*, 148-184, 185, 193, 276, 282, 287, 300-304
Inflation, 203-204, 206
Inheritance tax, 214, 215
Insurance, 173, 174, 175
Insurrections, *see* Resistance to Japan
Interest rates, 97, 121 *footnote*, 207-208
Iron, 140-141, 144-145, 156-157, 190, 235, 276, 306
Irrigation, 13, 19, 61, 94, 95-100, 174; associations, 96-98
Islands, 248, 255
Ito, Hirobumi, 26, 32-34, 39 *and footnote*, 40, 42, 81
Iwashi, 127, 128, 129, 160

Jams and jellies, 230
Japan, history of relations with Korea, 24-71; Koreans in, 81, 237; Korean importance to, 5-6 24, 92-93, 125, 135, 140, 146, 164, 186, 220, 222,

227, 235-236, 280-281; trade with Korea, 5-6, 92, 102, 129, 227-229, 233
Japan Nitrogen Corporation, 133, 161
Japanese Administration, agricultural policy, 61, 92-94, 213, 217-218, 221, 240, 243; budget, 54, 59, 99 *and footnote*, 210-224; effect of, 4-5, 36-38, 50-71, 78, 92, 105, 120-122, 142-143, 171-177, 211-225, 235-236, 243, 253-254; governmental organization, 46, 238-249
Japanese holdings, 75; agricultural, 79, 105, 106 *and footnote*, 110, 115, 126, 284-286; industrial, 130, 138, 146-147, 152-153, 161-162, 171-172, 174-177, 197, 201-204, 222, 237, 284-287
Japanese in Korea, 37, 47, 83, 170-171, 184, 199-200, 220-221, 227-228, 230-231, 237, 248, 288; education, 261-267; occupations, 79-80, 105-106, 130, 178-179; population figures, 75-77, 178-179, 231, 291; role in government, 46-47, 60, 63, 243-244, 246-247, 251, 257
Jijo, 141
Jinsen, 80, 81, 142, 154, 155, 157, 158, 163, 164, 166, 169, 170, 188, 193-195
Jitenkyo, 273
Jonai, 189
Joshin, 165, 196
Joyo, 189
Judges, 251
Junsen, 190
Junten, 189
Jusan, 158
Justice, *see* Courts, and Crime and Punishment

Kaden, 21, 95, 107, 291
Kadenmin, 107, 108 *footnote*, 109, 111, 112, 124, 177, 182, 291
Kaijo, 80
Kainel, 190
Kaisen, 132, 141, 190
Kaishu, 80, 143, 158
Kakugan, 190
Kakuzen, 189
Kan River, 10, 13
Kan, So-ryu, 283
Kanan, 145
Kanegafuchi, 155
Kanko, 80, 81, 155, 198, 254
Kankyo, 74, 128, 132, 141, 144-145, 189-190, 192, 196, 209, 302, 303

Kaoliang, 307-308
Kasen, 137
Katakura, 155
Keian, 141
Keijo, 10, 14-19, 62, 80-81, 171, 179-180, 186, 195, 197 *and footnote*, 198, 254, 259, 292-293, 303; industries in, 137, 154-155, 158, 164, 166, 169, 170; railways in, 188-190, 190 *footnote*, 302
Keiki, 14, 190, 302, 303
Keisho, 10, 74, 128, 132, 145, 146, 189, 190, 302, 303
Keizanchin, 190
Kenjiho, 136, 141, 142, 159, 303
Kerosene, 181
Kibi, see Millet
Kin River, 10, 13
Kinro Hokoku Undo, 182
Kinsen, 134, 190
Kin-yu kumai, *see* Credit Cooperatives
Kinyu Kumiai Rengokai, 278-279
Kisshu, 144, 166, 190
Knitted goods, 154
Kogen, 74, 132-133, 144, 163, 165, 189, 190, 302
Kogendo, 141, 145
Koiso, General, 60, 245
Kokai, 74, 132, 137, 141, 302, 303
Kokaido, 144, 190
Komosan, 158
Konan, 143, 144, 152, 157, 162, 163, 164, 165, 189
Kongo Zan Mountains, 13
Korea, history of relations with Japan, 24-71; importance to Japan, 5-6, 24, 92-93, 125, 135, 140, 146, 164, 186, 220, 222, 227, 235-236, 280-281
Korea Nitrogen Fertilizer Corporation, 133, 136, 152-153, 161, 164, 175, 190
Korean Government, corruption of, 34-35, 37-38
Korean Government-General, *see* Japanese Administration
Korean Imperial House, *see* House of Li
Koreans, appraisal of, 24 *and footnote*, 33-35, 38, 41, 48-49, 53, 68, 70-71, 97, 99, 120 *footnote*, 151 *and footnote*, 255-256, 264 *footnote*, 277-279, 282-284; capital of, 171-177; emigrants, 65-66, 67-68, 69-70, 81-83, 217-218, 221, 237, 278, 279; role in government, 46-47, 60, 63, 243-249, 251, 256-257; treatment by Japanese, 5,

INDEX

36-37, 207, 248, 251, 254, 260, 262-264, 267-270; well-to-do, 230, 231, 249
Koshu, 80, 155, 189, 198, 254, 303
Kunsan, 10, 163, 186, 195

Labor, 51, 120, 151, 286; agricultural, 81-82, 108-109, 110 *footnote*, 111-112, 120, 177, 287, 291; conditions, 120, 147, 149, 154, 172 *footnote*, 177-184, 282; distribution, 77-80, 177-178, 183; female and child, 182-184; industrial, 69, 81-82, 120 *footnote*, 121, 147-149, 156-159, 166-167, 178-179, 300-301; legislation, 154, 179; unions, 182
Labor Patriotic Front, 182
Lacquer ware, 69
Land prices, 292; tax, 54, 114, 214-215, 223
Landownership, 41, 51, 54, 78, 82, 96-97, 105-117, 282
Language, Japanese, 251, 263, 268-269; Korean, 23, 176, 217-218, 221, 251, 268-269, 272
Larch forests, 21, 166
Lathework, 152
Laver, 305-306
Laws, 250, 252
Lead, 145, 306
League of Nations, 42, 70
Leather, 164
Leper homes, 275
Libraries, 217, 270-271
Lime nitrogen, 163
Lithium, 145
Livestock, 88, 93, 103-105, 229, 234, 305
Living conditions, *see* Social conditions
Lumber, 10, 123-125, 127, 151-152, 166, 173, 176, 183, 235, 300-301, 306

Machinery and tools, 147, 151, 157-158, 173, 176, 183, 228, 234, 235, 300-301, 303-304, 306-307, 309
Magazines, 272
Magnesium, 140, 144
Maize, 87, 306
Mampo, 190
Mampotin, 189
Manchukuo, *see* Manchuria
Manchuria, 8, 10, 13, 65-66, 69-70, 134, 141, 186, 188, 189, 227, 228; Koreans in, 69-70, 81-82, 237, 257
Maritime Provinces, 8, 25
Masan, 80, 155, 186, 194

Matches, 164
Mats, 69
Meat, 119 *footnote*, 181
Medicines, 151, 160, 173, 174, 176, 305, 307
Men, 224, 225
Mercury, 145
Metals, 140, 150, 151, 156-157, 173, 174, 176, 183, 203, 234, 235, 300-301, 303, 306-307, 309
Metanol, 165
Mica, 145
Midwives, 260
Militarism, 245
Milk, 230
Millet, 21, 118, 119, 181, 307-308
Minami, General, 60, 94, 245
Minerals, 234, 276, 306-307
Mining, 29, 77-79, 81, 84, 121, 139-147, 153, 158, 173-175, 178, 182, 188, 193, 276; experiments, 221; subsidies, 217-218; tax, 214, 223
Miso, 152, 167, 180
Missions, 3, 33-34, 265-266, 275, 278
Molybdenum, 145
Money, *see* Currency
Monopolies, 213, 214, 215-216
Moppo, 14-19, 80, 155, 164, 186, 189, 194, 195-196
Morphine, 213 *and footnote*, 215-216
Motorcars, 192-193
Motorcycles, 192-193
Motor transport, 173, 192-193
Mountains, 8-9, 13-14
Movies, 271
Municipalities, *see* Cities

Nagamori's land scheme, 41 *and footnote*
Naktong River, 10
Nationalism, 38, 54-58, 62, 64-65, 67, 279-280
Native culture and customs, 61, 250, 271 *footnote*
Needlework, 152
Neietwi, 137
Netherlands Indies, 227
Newspapers, 61-62, 176, 264, 272
Nickel, 145
Nochirei, 115-116
Nurses, 260

Oats, 21
Occupational distribution, 77-80, 130, 177-178, 183

INDEX

Oils, 121, 128-129, 131, 133, 151, 160, 164, 165, 235, 236, 305-307, 309
Opium, 38, 41, 63, 213 *and footnote*, 215, 216, 282
Oriental Development Corporation, 204

Paddy fields, 74, 92 *footnote*, 96, 100, 106, 111, 291, 296-297
Paint, 235, 307, 309
Paitoushan Mountains, 8, 9
Paper, 151, 160, 165-166, 305-309; products, 152, 165-166
Paraffin, 133, 165
Parcel Post, 306-309
Pensions, 217-219
Pharmacists, 260
Physicians, 260
Pigs, 103-104
Pinson, Dr. W. W., 53
Plants, 234, 305, 307
Playgrounds, 271
Police, 47, 61, 63, 217-219, 242
Political organizations, 43, 47-48, 62, 64-68, 289; prisoners, 47, 243, 254
Population, 3, 72-83, 178, 185, 231, 233-234, 276, 291
Ports, 193-197, 217, 235
Post office, 4, 198-200, 213
Potatoes, 21, 87, 164
Pottery, 303, 306-307; *see also* Ceramics
Poverty, 49, 68, 85, 86, 119, 121, 193, 199, 209, 213, 252, 254, 256, 260
Power, 131-139, 276, 284; water, 13, 131, 276
Press, 61-62, 176, 264, 272
Prices, 50-51, 133, 138, 140, 150, 179-180, 202-204, 206, 233, 292
Printing, 166, 173, 176, 183, 300-301
Prisons, 212, 217-219, 254
Production, agricultural, 84-88, 93-94, 287, 295, 297-298; industrial, 148-151, 154, 157, 159, 167, 172, 236, 300
Professions, 77, 78, 79, 261-267, 286
Prostitution, 38, 269, 271, 282
Provincial government, 46, 60, 217-220, 222, 225, 246-248, 255
Public finances, 37, 210-225, 240, 247; service, 77, 78, 79; works, 239
Publishing, 173
Pulp, *see* Paper
Punishment, *see* Crime and Punishment
Pyengyang, 10

Quelpart, 14, 22, 164

Radio, 198
Railways, 4, 14, 37, 38 *footnote*, 50, 51, 133, 173, 185-191, 212, 213, 215, 216, 217, 235, 284
Rakuto River, 10, 13, 14
Ranan, 165, 170
Rashin, 80, 170, 191, 194, 196
Rattan ware, 152
Raw materials, 152 *and footnote*, 156, 236
Rayon, 151, 154, 155, 232-233, 305-307
Real estate, 173, 223
Reed ware, 152
Reisei River, 10
Reisui, 186, 195
Reisuiko, 189
Religion, 23, 53, 266, 273-275, 289
Rent, 113-114, 292
Resin, 165
Resistance to Japan, 27-28, 36, 40 *footnote*, 41, 43-45, 48, 51, 55 *and footnote*, 56 *and footnote*, 65-67, 257-258, 276
Resources, *see* Agriculture, Fishing, Forests, etc.
Rice, 5, 13, 21, 61, 87, 90-94, 110, 117, 221, 229, 235, 295, 297, 299, 305-309; cleaning, 169, 173, 174, 176; consumption, 117-119; prices, 98, 293
Rickshaws, 192
Riri, 189, 198
Rivers, 9-10
Roads, 4, 38 *footnote*, 50, 51, 59, 121, 191-193, 217, 235
Roosevelt, Theodore, 32-33, 43
Roots, 89
Rope, 155
Rubber, 166, 175, 307, 308
Rural indebtedness, 97, 208-209
Rush ware, 152
Russia, 25, 28-30, 32, 38, 227-228, 289
Russian Far East, 81, 82, 201, 278
Rye, 297
Ryogampo, 143
Ryoken, 165
Ryuzen, 190

Saiho, 189
Saishu, *see* Quelpart
Saito, Makota, 56-59, 60, 65, 66, 245
Sake, 152, 167-168, 230, 305-308
Saloons, 271
Salt, 116, 167, 213, 215, 217-218, 307-308
Sanchoku, 165

INDEX

Sanitation, 37, 38 footnote, 39, 50, 282
Sanroshin, 189
Savings banks, 204
Schools, 4, 54, 217, 248, 261-270
Seaweeds, 128, 167, 306
Second International Conference, The Hague, 42
Seed, 100
Seihei, 137
Seisen River, 10
Seishin, 80, 81, 142, 144, 157, 164, 165, 170, 189, 190, 193, 194, 196, 198, 254
Seishu, 155, 190
Self-sufficiency, 276-277
Sen-Man Takushoku Kabushiki Kaisha, 82
Senshin River, 10
Seoul, see Keijo
Sericulture, 61, 88, 116
Sesame seed, 307
Shamanism, 274
Shariin, 155
Sheep, 93, 103-104
Shinanshu, 10, 190
Shingishu, 16-19, 80, 164, 165, 166, 170, 188, 194, 195, 197, 254
Shinshu, 80, 189
Shintoism, 273
Shipping, 37, 173, 174, 191, 193-197, 217, 284
Ships, 151, 158
Shochu, 167
Shoes, 121, 152, 204, 307
Shogen, 189
Shohaku Zan, 13-14
Shokori, 188
Shoteiri, 189
Shrines, Japanese, 217-219, 242
Silk, 24, 151, 152 footnote, 154, 232-233, 303, 305-309
Silver, 145, 156, 306
Smuggling, 237
Soap, 166, 181, 308
Social conditions, 49, 68, 85, 86, 102-103, 105, 107-122, 139, 147, 151 footnote, 170, 180-181, 186, 192, 199-200, 226, 252, 282-283
Social services, 217-220, 222-223, 239, 243
Socialism, 62, 65
Soft drinks, 167, 169
Sonnairi, 158
Soy, 152, 167, 230
Soy beans, 21, 164
Speech, freedom of, 61-62, 257-258

Spinning, see Textiles
Spruce forests, 21
Squeeze, 34, 38
Staple fiber, 155-156, 232, 307-308
Starch, 167, 169, 305, 307-308
Steel, 140-142, 157
Straw ware, 69, 152
Student movement, 65
Subsidies, 59, 126, 142, 146, 217-218, 222, 224, 236, 247
Suffrage, 61, 247-248, 282
Sugar, 167, 169, 181, 214, 215, 230, 305, 307
Suigen, 164, 186
Sulphate of ammonia, 101-102, 152, 160, 162-163, 235, 308
Sulphuric acid, 145
Superphosphate of lime, 101, 163
Superphosphates of acid, 163

Taiden, 80, 81, 155, 164, 189
Taidong River, 10
Taikyu, 16-19, 80, 81, 155, 166, 170, 188, 189, 197, 254
Tansen, 141, 144, 145
Tanyo, 189
Tar, 133
Taxation, 210, 212, 213, 217-218, 223-224, 247, 254, 297
Tea, 181
Teachers, 261, 264, 266-267
Telegraph and Telephone, 198-199, 213, 217, 284
Tenancy, 105, 107 and footnote, 108-117, 177, 182, 208-209, 291, 294
Tendokyo, 273
Tenkai, 155
Terauchi, Masakata, 54, 60, 62, 245
Tetsugen, 155
Textiles, 105, 121, 150-151, 152 footnote, 153-156, 173-174, 176, 180, 183, 203, 214-215, 231-234, 300-301, 303, 305-309
Theatres, 271
Tiger, 141
Tiles, 151
Timber, see Lumber
Tissues, 232-233, 305-309
Tobacco, 181, 213, 214, 215, 230, 234, 305, 307
Tokusen, 137
Tong Hak, 26
Towns and townships, 224, 248
Transportation, 121, 173, 174, 175, 185-198, 217, 221, 235, 287

Trusts, 204
Tsinnanpo, 10, 141
Tsushina Straits, 6, 8
Tubs, 152
Tumen Kan River, 10, 13, 29, 134, 191
Tungsten, 146, 306
Twine, 155
Tyosen Minzoku Kakumeito, 67
Typhoons, 19

Ugaki, General, 59, 60, 68, 93, 94, 120-121, 142
United States, 32-33, 140-141, 227-229, 289-290; *see also* Americans
University, *see* Imperial University
Urothropin, 165
Urusan, 197
Usury, 121 *and footnote*, 122, 130, 208
Utensils, *see* Machinery and tools
Uturyo, 14, 22

Vegetables, 89, 230
Vehicles, 173, 183, 192-193, 223, 306-307
Villages, 61, 96

Wages, 112, 147, 151 *footnote*, 154, 156, 177, 178-182, 267, 282
Warehouses, 173, 174
Waterpower, 13, 133-139, 224

Water transport, *see* Shipping
Weaving, *see* Textiles
Weights and measures, 158, 212, 216
Wheat, 21, 87, 90, 118, 167, 169, 229, 295, 297, 305-308
White Head Mountains, 8
Willow ware, 69, 152
Wine, 168
Women, 120 *footnote*, 182-184
Wood, 131
Wool, 93, 232, 309
Workers, *see* Labor

Yalu River, 8, 10, 13, 29, 134, 137, 191, 195
Yamanashi, General, 60, 245
Yokei, 189
Yokuho, 164
Yotoku, 189
Yu, 224, 225
Yuho, 189
Yuhodo, 190
Yujo, 189, 190
Yuki, 170, 190, 194, 196

Zenra, 10, 74, 132, 189, 190 *footnote*, 195, 302, 303
Zenshu, 15-19, 80, 155
Zinc, 146